THE GUARDIAN
YEAR, 2001

THE GUARDIAN YEAR, 2001

Edited by Ian Katz

Introduction by Ian Jack

Atlantic Books
London

First published in 2001 by Atlantic Books, on behalf of Guardian Newspapers Ltd.
Atlantic Books is an imprint of Grove Atlantic Ltd.

10 9 8 7 6 5 4 3 2 1

A CIP catalogue record for this book is available from the British Library

ISBN 1 903809 22 3

Printed in Great Britain by CPD, Ebbw Vale, Wales
Design by Helen Ewing

Grove Atlantic Ltd
29 Adam & Eve Mews
London W8 6UG

CONTENTS

Political animals

Home front

Foreign parts

Blood, milk and honey

On the move

Small world

State of the art

Sporting life

Not forgetting...

Passing through

INTRODUCTION

Ian Jack

For a few days last September I was in Blackburn, Lancashire, looking through the private memorabilia of the singer, Kathleen Ferrier, which are packed in boxes in the town's museum. Ferrier grew up in Blackburn and I was trying to write a piece about her. At lunchtime on September 11, I left off reading and went out to the market, bought a meat pie and sat on a bench in the street to eat it. It was a calm and indeterminate kind of day, the heat of summer over but the chill of autumn yet to come. As I ate, I listened to the sound of a *muezzin* calling the faithful to prayer – Blackburn has a large Muslim population and the minarets have microphones. The sound floated over the town hall and down the street that has Debenhams on one side and Marks & Spencer on the other. It struck me then that, over two days in Blackburn, this was the first time that I'd heard a form of the music which the conductor, Bruno Walter, said that Ferrier was best at singing; music that men had written 'in moments of solemnity and devotion'. Of course, by that Walter meant Handel, Bach and Brahms, and Christian devotion rather than Islamic. Still, this amplified male voice intoning Arabic words over a Lancashire town was closer in feeling to the music of those long-dead European composers than anything I'd heard since I stepped from the train. Out of the pubs in Blackburn, out of the cars in Blackburn (male youths of various races at the wheel, windows down, sound up, round and round the one-way system) came the same monotonous percussion, the call to... what? Perhaps sex, or a more violent physical appetite, or perhaps just violent sex. God, love, grief: these things did not figure in it.

Thinking about this, but attaching no conclusions, I went back to the museum to carry on reading. It would be about nine a.m. on the east coast of the United States. An hour later I came out for a cigarette and found a message on my mobile phone. Could I ring an editor at the *Guardian* urgently 'for the obvious reasons'. As I'm not employed by the *Guardian*, was then half-way through the 1949 Ferrier letters and was running short of time, I resisted the temptation to discover what the obvious reasons were and returned to the archives. When I went back to my digs in the early evening, by now informed about the World Trade Center and the Pentagon, a fellow lodger said on the stairs: 'I don't know what you think, but I think all these Moslems should be sent back to where they came from.' And then I watched it on television, for the first of several dozen times, from a large armchair in the lounge. And of course I thought about the coincidence of timing: that when I was listening to the call to prayer, and being taken by its melodious gravity, other people at the controls of aircraft were deploying their religious instincts in a different and less passive way. A solipsistic thought, entirely useless and trivial and shaming, of the kind used by people (and especially people who write) to gain some personal purchase on terrible events that, luckily for the thinker, are very far away.

That was my September 11, 2001. You will have your own. The question is, did that day cut a line through history? Were the days that came before it, as Blake Morrison writes in this anthology, 'the last week of the world as it was'? In other words, will it be a day like September 3, 1939, or August 4, 1914: all change, and no going back. Or a day like June 28, 1914, when a Serbian nationalist knocked off Franz Ferdinand, the heir to the Austro-Hungarian throne, and for a month Vienna and Berlin debated what to do? (Retrospective memo to the Austrian government: do not invade Serbia, because out of it will come the Somme). Or was it merely a day like April 12, 1912, when the Titanic went down, 1500 dead? Many people, especially writers and other preachers, chose to see the last as a massive symbol of hubris, God or fate teaching over-confident 'Western civilisation' a lesson, rather than as a marine accident that changed nothing other than safety regulations for ships and the career of Leonardo DiCaprio. (Contemporary memo to self and others: 'hubris' comes too easily to mind for the collapsing towers of the World Trade Center, but what needs always to be remembered, as with the Titanic, is that thousands of non-hubristic people died in them.)

Reading this anthology, I wondered if I would find that the pieces originally published in the *Guardian* before September 11 would substantiate this idea of a world changed utterly – that they would now seem to belong to a different era, as though I were a subaltern sitting in a trench in 1916 and reading a guidebook to the church architecture of Ypres, or an account in an old *Morning Post* of the Henley Regatta two years before. They don't. Life has gone on. I cannot write, and hope never to be able to, the sentence that Orwell used in 1941 to introduce his essay, the Lion and the Unicorn: 'As I write, highly civilised human beings are flying overhead, trying to kill me.' In fact, I can write an opposite kind of sentence, though not nearly as well as he would have done: 'As I write, I can see the *New Yorker* for October 15 on my desk, which is filled cover-to-cover with pieces about "The Culture Business"'. So even in New York life goes on (although Kabul is a different question).

In this collection, the pertinent is no less pertinent, the irrelevant still enjoyable, the witty pieces still as witty. Lord Archer and William Hague have gone to their different destinations, but they will receive no more fitting monuments than the reports by Simon Hoggart and James Fenton. Hoggart at Archer's trial: 'For decades now Jeffrey Archer has been dancing on the rim of a volcano; now he has fallen in.' Fenton on the election trail with Hague: '...it's as if Hague keeps jumping up on stage and saying: "Look at me, I'm normal." And the audience responds with one voice: "Oh no you're not!" And he says: "Oh yes I am!" And this goes on for some time, and can on a good day be quite entertaining, but nobody's mind is changed at the end of it.'

In Britain, many things happened in the twelve months covered by this book. Ronnie Biggs came home; Peter Mandelson got the sack again; the railways went to hell; foot and mouth disease brought British farming closer than ever to the edge of collapse; a general election fell into a swamp of public apathy; and the *Guardian* decided that it favoured a republic – eventually. To many observers outside Britain, as well as many Britons, the country seemed to be cursed: Polly Toynbee has in this collection a piece that describes the phenomenon brilliantly. The real omens of change, however, were mainly happening elsewhere: in Israel, on the West Bank, in poorer countries everywhere. It might be wrong to say that September 11 was a product of these omens. We don't precisely know the motivation of the terrorists, or the social and religious forces that shaped them. But it is hard, after September 11, to read the pieces here on the Palestinian question and on the disparities and desperation that lie behind global migration, and not see these things in a starker light. The great paradox of the Titanic, after all, is that the ship *only became unsinkable after it sank*. Its owners had only briefly, when it was still on the stocks and in very small print, ever advertised it as such, and similar claims ('virtually unsinkable') were made at the same time for other ships. Unsinkabillity became the leading feature of the Titanic's short life only after it hit the bottom, and the fabulists and symbolists took over. And perhaps that's what September 11 has really done; not so much changed our lives as altered our perception of previous things – in this case warnings rather than boasts – and given them the worrying, large size of print they have always deserved.

What do I mean by this? A good example is Suzanne Goldenberg's report of August 17 from Jenin, a town on the West Bank. It tells the story of a young Palestinian policeman who became a suicide bomber and blew himself up, blessedly too incompetent to kill others with him. By the standards of the intifada and the behaviour of the state of Israel, a small enough event, but given the many square feet of newspaper space which have been devoted to how the suicidal terrorists of September 11 managed to steel themselves to do it, might it not have been a wise idea for us to have asked similar questions earlier, more seriously and more often?

There are many fine pieces in this book by writers with a capital W. It would be hard to better Ian McEwan's compassionate reflection on the World Trade Center and the place in its tragedy of the mobile phone and the words 'I love you'. There are also many thoughtful and well-expressed commentaries by columnists, among them Martin Woollacott, Hugo Young, and Polly Toynbee. For me, however, this collection is distinguished above all else by the quality of the reporting. As a skill, it is often overlooked these days in favour of the mug shot at the head of a column ('What *will* she say today?'). What this collection proves is that the day-by-day transmission of information, often done quickly – scenes observed, words taken down – has a life beyond this morning. Engel, Williams, Brockes, Carroll, O'Kane, McAskill and many more: the *Guardian* and its readers are lucky to have them. A first draft of history, maybe, but this year (if no other) has taught us that we need to pay more attention.

EDITOR'S NOTE

Ian Katz

As the events of September 11 unfolded on our TV screens, many of us who work in newspapers, I'm sure, entertained a similar thought: what could we possibly add? By the time our efforts hit the newsstands most of our readers would have watched the second plane sail into the south tower of the World Trade Center countless times. They would have seen the skyscrapers capitulating like mortally wounded giants and heard goggle-eyed eyewitnesses describe how the desperate hurled themselves to their deaths. Could printed words and still pictures tell people any more about an event most of the world had witnessed live?

The answer, I think, was an emphatic yes. Gulnara Samoilova's extraordinary photograph of dust-covered and dazed survivors making their way from the ruins of the World Trade Center (see plate section) was every bit as powerful as the most horrific video footage shot that day. Ian McEwan's account of the first plane 'disappearing into the side of the tower as cleanly as a posted letter' was as vivid as any image burned onto the collective retina. And as the dust began to settle in Manhattan and Washington, only newspapers were asking the difficult questions about the spiral of hatred that spawned the attacks, and what should be done next.

That's the good news. The bad news is that this collection of pieces scarcely did justice to a year of *Guardian* writing and reporting, even before the apocalyptic events of September 11. After the brutal re-edit that necessarily followed the attacks, it feels an even less adequate reflection of the paper's riches. Every year, the arrival of the first copies of *The Guardian Year* in our Farringdon offices triggers a bout of *sotto voce* grumbling: 'Why are so many of the year's "best pieces" missing?'; 'Why are so many of the paper's finest writers not represented?'; 'Why are some of the year's biggest stories missing?' Now I understand.

The biggest problem derives from the sheer size of the modern *Guardian*. When the first *Bedside Guardian* was published fifty years ago, an average edition of the paper contained around 50,000 words. Today the average weekday paper contains around 250,000 words (a little over twice the number in this volume) and the Saturday edition regularly runs to 400,000 words (40,000 more than you'll find in *David Copperfield*). At the same time the paper has been producing more and more special issues and investigations that could fill short books on their own: our two-day focus on public sector workers featured the work of 200 journalists and ran to 115,000 words; G2's week long series on asylum featured more than 30,000 words of reporting and commentary. Editing this collection has frequently felt like packing for a very long holiday with a very small suitcase.

The second factor that prevents *The Guardian Year* from being a straightforward collection of 'greatest hits' is that it is necessarily a compromise – an attempt to reflect the year's biggest events *and* the paper's finest writing. Frequently, happily, the two criteria overlap. But not always. A final problem conspiring against any editor of the *Guardian Year* is that not all great writing bears re-publication. The most elegantly turned pieces of court reporting, the most illuminating investigative reports, rarely invite re-reading after their subjects have slipped from the headlines. Editing *The Guardian Year* is a frequently harsh way of discovering quite how much of what we do is ephemeral.

These pressures, amplified by my own inadequacy, mean that many parts of the paper are grossly under-represented here. A loose ban on any piece over 3,000 words discriminated unforgivably against the Weekend magazine and Saturday Review, which tend to feature longer articles. The Guide and many of our specialist feature sections have been similarly hard done by. Our special report on public servants, arguably one of our most important journalistic statements of recent years, is not represented here, simply because it defied anthologising.

So much for the weaknesses. There is plenty to celebrate too. An election so unedifying that fully 40 per cent of voters declined to exercise their right called for inspired writing, and got it. There are gems here from familiar names like Simon Hoggart, Matthew Engel and Gary Younge, as well as virtuoso turns from 'short run' signings such as Joe Klein and James Fenton. Klein's search for the 'ineffable something missing' about Tony Blair, shone an unforgiving torch on aspects of the prime ministerial persona which had become boringly familiar to more seasoned observers of the British political scene. Younge's observations on the way people react to a blind politician (David Blunkett) were as revealing as the most erudite political analysis.

Guardian writers rose to what were the other biggest stories of the year, until September 11, too. In Israel Suzanne Goldenburg found a way to convey the horror of every fresh atrocity, even as the calculus of the long-running conflict diminished the news-worthiness of each new victim. Closer to home, Angelique Chrisafis and John Vidal witnessed the carnage engulfing Britain's farms with just the right mixture of detachment and compassion. And retracing the footsteps of one Afghan refugee to Britain, Maggie O'Kane revealed the human truth behind the asylum statistics that rippled through the news pages – and public debate – for much of the year.

One of the most striking aspects of this collection is the versatility demonstrated by several writers. Science correspondent James Meek reports on the Paris haute couture shows as compellingly as he describes the rush to patent newly discovered human genes. The knowledge of Eminen lyrics displayed by our deputy literary editor Giles Foden is so extensive that even now no-one is quite sure whether his encomium to the controversial rapper was satirical, or deadly serious. The peerless Matthew Engel captures the drama of America's anthrax panic as crisply as he assesses the career of the late Donald Bradman.

One of the least conspicuous, but most significant, strengths of the *Guardian* is its tradition of continuity. It is embodied in Emma Brockes's interview with David McKie – the current Young Journalist of the Year, paying tribute to a retiring colleague who arrived at the *Guardian* almost a decade before she arrived in the world. With luck, it will be embodied, too, in the connection between the

'Best of Bedsides' volume that comes with this fiftieth Guardian Year and the writing that follows.

Finally I'd like to thank Sarah X. Hall, Esther Addley, Laura Barton, Andy Bodle, Danny John, Elizabeth Roberts, Helen Healey and the *Guardian's* Research and Information department for their help assembling the material for this volume and Mathew Clayton and Alice Hunt for their guidance, patience and good humour.

Enjoy!

London
17 October, 2001

SEPTEMBER 11
AND AFTER

Steve Bell, 12 September 2001

13 September 2001

MICHAEL ELLISON

He was up to his neck in rubble

Twenty-four hours earlier Bill Coscarelli was an anonymous motorcycle mechanic from Long Island, a member of the benign vigilante group that patrols public places, the Guardian Angels.

But yesterday he was transformed into that rare thing, a man who really deserved the description of hero, trudging away from the enormous breaker's yard that was once the World Trade Center.

Mr Coscarelli, his scarlet Angels beret dulled by a film of silt, a grappling iron over his shoulder, had his reward for spending all day and all night crawling through the wreckage: he had helped to save the life of one of the seven people rescued where perhaps thousands died simply going about their work.

'He was a police officer from the New York Port Authority,' said Mr Coscarelli, thirty-six, standing against the backdrop of the stump that was all that remained of one Trade Center tower, burst open like a Christmas cracker, a horrifying, inadvertent piece of public art. Most of the other six people prised alive from the devastation so far were reported to be firemen.

'Apparently he was from the 64th floor and he was up to his neck in debris that they had to take away piece by piece. They said they were going to amputate his leg but they didn't do it. They were trying to see if they could identify him by the serial number on his gun. He was moving his head. He was talking a bit and saying "yes" because everybody was talking to him.'

Rescue workers fear that they may never be able to identify some of the victims, many fire-fighters and policemen among them, a fact that made the task more poignant in a scene that gave new mileage to the cliché of the war zone.

Hundreds of National Guardsmen in camouflage gear and helmets, firemen, police and medics milled around in the trade centre complex, the dust of the previous day turned to sludge by the hoses that continued to play yesterday on the compacted rubble and gnarled metal beams. Face masks were easily the most popular protective item and, where those were not available, people improvised with handkerchiefs and tissues.

A large piece of aluminium, possibly part of an airplane, lay on the ground, banal office documents fluttering nearby: reports on meetings ('FMM stated to WJP: Didn't you ever cheat on your income taxes?'); updates on work in progress ('Seems project is done in five phases'); a business card for Christine J. Schneider, vice-president of Hartford Financial Products, with a World Trade Center address.

The rescue operation caused a traffic jam of compassion in the area, where cranes, trucks, buses, police and fire vehicles wheeled around each other. Fire-fighters, working twenty-four hours on, twenty-four hours off, were arriving by bus and often leaving with eyes streaming from the effects of gypsum dust.

Policemen were being bussed in too, each one greeted with a handshake by the officer there to receive them.

Medical workers came in by bicycle, the only reliable form of transport in the lower part of the island of Manhattan, where security became more difficult to breach in a series of increments below 14th Street, where Downtown starts.

Rest areas had been set up and the Salvation Army was operating emergency food trucks, providing free pasta and salad for the people of the emergency services.

A truck towed from the scene a Ford Taunus with 'help us' etched in the grime covering its bodywork. 'What's so important about that?' a fire-protection man asked a colleague. Maybe it was just something to do, with victims harder to find than might have been expected and fire-fighters talking about steel they just could not cut through.

'Where do the volunteers go?' asked a man in a green T-shirt pulling hard on a cigarette. Mr Coscarelli, the Guardian Angel, could have told him.

The immigrant from Argentina talked about how he helped to save a life in the dark: 'The police officer was right on top of the debris. I'm sure I walked over him maybe thirty times before we realised he was a guy. I went up to the parking lots and looked for people in the elevators. People are dead in the basements. We found two bodies, covered in dust and metal, but you've got to remember it's been twenty-four hours now and we've only found a few people alive.

'I found a lot of stuff to use, police and fire equipment lying around. There were big aluminium pieces of the planes. It's hard to find people. We found some people and they were squished. There's not much of them. They were squished so hard that basically there's nothing. We were asking for small body bags because otherwise they were going to get lost.

'We were marking the bags and saying "that's a body". We found two half-guys. It's really bad in there, a lot of confusion. There wasn't too much emotion, the police and fire-fighters were looking for their guys.

'I thought: "I can't just watch this on television." If I didn't do it, I would just feel…I drove to Brooklyn and then walked about an hour to get here. Probably I'll come back tonight.'

A fire truck with most of its windows out came out from under the plume of muck marking the point of the kamikaze attacks on the Trade Center towers, the vehicle trawling behind it old audiotape snagged on its rear.

'It's nasty, it's devastating. It's something you never want to see,' said Corporal Andy Marcus from US army battalion 258 of Brooklyn.

Fire-fighters are by far the most admired public servants in New York City and when, say, three die at a job the grieving is long and lasting. The police are known as the Finest, fire-fighters as the Bravest. In this disaster, hundreds of firemen have died.

Dominic DeRuebio, forty-seven, a battalion commander from Staten Island wearing shades, was about to return to work on the complex. Reluctantly, and without any apparent emotion, he said: 'I was just on to my old company. They want to come down here and they want to work.'

Then his tone changed: 'My younger brother's in there in the wreckage somewhere. A lot of my friends are there too. What else can you do? It's the job.

You've got to do it.'

Three fire-fighters from Brooklyn had just done twenty-four hours of it and now they were sitting dog-tired among the trash and weeds on the central reservation of the cordoned-off West Side Highway.

So had Brian Gavin just put in his twenty-four hours. His crew, too, dug out someone alive, and may have saved him. The 33-year-old, stationed in Harlem, ran his hand through his hair, his face blackened and stubbly.

'We're used to tragedies, but these are our guys. In the bigger picture, I know…but this is what we're looking at here, that's what's on everybody's mind. I would hope the president will blow these people, the ones that did this, off the face of the earth. That's what they deserve. Oh, yeah.'

Trash and slivers of what had been something useful continued to dance in the air while the fireman who has served for eight years transferred his jacket to the other shoulder.

'It's absolutely terrible. I've seen some tragic things on the fire department. There were eight dead on 125th Street in a fire started by an arsonist, eight young people and I thought that was the worst.

'But here I've seen pieces of victims. Crushed, yes. That's all I can say. Legs, arms, body parts. Torsos, feet, hands. Thank God I never seen any children, only perhaps some baby feet.

'People had their clothes ripped off, yeah, but it's hard to tell. We were still working last night on a guy who was still alive. He was busted up pretty good. We were digging and digging and digging. It was very tough. We handed him down through a line from guy to guy.

'This is going to take weeks. We can't just go in and start digging around. There's so much rubble and steel. It hurts deeply. So far, from what I've heard, eight or nine guys I know are in there and it's only going to go up. A bunch of them have families.'

As Mr Gavin left, Alexi Nizza, a Greek Orthodox priest from the Bronx, arrived, his black cloak trailing in the muck, the smutty badge of all those who have been to the disaster area. 'I'm just here to give any assistance I can,' he said.

Mayor Rudy Giuliani, part of whose legend rests on his facility with crisis-management, indicated the level of assistance that would be required.

'The numbers we're working with are in the thousands,' said the mayor. 'The best estimate we can make is that there will be a few thousand left in each building.'

It is thought that between 10,000 and 20,000 people were in the 110-storey towers when the aircraft crashed into them.

The number of confirmed dead in the World Trade Center is forty-one, with 260 police officers and fire-fighters missing.

The mayor urged people in the city and its suburbs to stay out of Manhattan yesterday unless their jobs were essential.

Stock exchanges, Wall Street businesses and city schools were closed. The region's three major airports, like the rest of the country's airports, were closed at least until noon local time by the Federal Aviation Administration.

New Yorkers trying to track down friends and family members were trekking from hospital to hospital – there are twenty-one in the region treating the wounded – checking the names of those who had been admitted. Daphne Bowers of Brooklyn, adopting the same approach as many others, arrived at Bellevue hospital carrying a picture of her 28-year-old daughter Veronique who was working at the World Trade Center on Tuesday.

'She called me, when the building was on fire,' said Mrs Bowers.' She called me and said: "Mommie the building is on fire. There's smoke coming through the walls. I can't breathe." The last thing she said was: "I love you Mommie. Goodbye."'

Another woman whose missing husband worked on one of the upper floors said: 'I wish I could go and dig myself. He could be dying and I am not there to hold his hand. He could be in pain and I can't help him.'

Medics at the scene saw images that will stay with them for ever. 'I saw a human hand on the street,' said Benjamin Fogelm twenty-eight, medical technician. 'We had to try not to step on body parts.'

Only about seven storeys of the north tower were still in place, the girders splayed. The south tower was just a two-storey heap of rubble. National Guardsmen patrolled the ruins.

The reek of natural gas and the sound of portable generators pervaded the site. Grit from pulverised concrete, insulation and paper filled the air, hence the ubiquitous masks. It covered the streets with a grey blanket a few inches thick.

An elevated walkway that once ran between the World Trade Center and the World Financial Centre had plunged to the ground, blocking one street. Huge steel beams and aluminium panels littered the streets.

A few blocks away, corner markets still had fruit neatly stacked in pyramids out front. The produce was covered with soot. Search dogs and about a dozen mini-robots with rubber treads were being readied for use in the search-and-rescue efforts. Fire-fighters in a crane lorry hosed down the ruins of Building Seven, the smaller, forty-seven-storey structure that collapsed after the twin towers.

Other buildings around the centre sustained varying degrees of damage. Some, like the Embassy Suites Hotel, had only soot covering their windows. But a building to the north-west was completely caved in. Only its corners and part of its outer walls remained.

Joe Meyers, a nurse from Rockaway, New Jersey, said he had treated more than thirty rescue workers, mostly for eye injuries from the dirt and grit. Medical workers set up a post where they rinsed rescuers' eyes with saline solution. 'You have to drag them out because they just want to continue the retrieval,' Mr Meyers said of the injured rescue workers.

Paralegal Thomas Warren said he found a man dazed and stumbling out of the area wearing shoes that did not match. He had lost his in the blast and grabbed any that were handy.

Robert James, manager of a sporting goods store near the complex, was in the basement when he heard the explosion. He said he came above ground to see at least five bodies fall from the skyscraper. 'They looked like rag dolls,' he said. 'It was like the kind of thing you see in movies.'

All over the city, hospital workers yelled on the streets: 'Blood donations! Blood donations!' Hundreds lined up to donate.

Everywhere there was anodyne material strewn around the streets among the grit: coffee cups, empty water bottles, half-eaten fruit and newspapers from the day before the day before yesterday, their contents after this utterly irrelevant. An old copy of a *New York Times* was open at a page with the lead headline: 'Emphasis on sportsmanship.'

13 September 2001

IAN BURUMA

The walls don't work

In many third-world cities – Manila, say – the rich like to live in heavily guarded villa parks. Inside the walls of these 'villages', as they are called in Manila, you could be in a plush part of California: neatly polished cars, dark-skinned servants busying about, the discreet sound of sprinklers on well-tended lawns. You might almost forget, in these urban oases, protected by armed guards from the angry poor, that the violent, teeming, crazy world around them even exists.

The United States is not quite like this. The slums and the craziness are difficult to ignore, especially in a place like Manhattan. And yet, to many Americans, outside the few truly cosmopolitan centres, it must often feel as though the outside world doesn't exist. Local newspapers and television stations pay little attention to foreign affairs. Life is good in the richest and freest nation on earth. There is the odd mad bomber to hit the evening news, and you might possibly get mugged if you stray into the wrong street, but, by and large, the United States seemed like a well-guarded refuge from the world's bad neighbourhoods.

No wonder, then, that the politics of isolationism and retreat have always had a strong appeal for Americans. The much-vaunted missile shield is a bit like those high fences around Manila's 'villages'. Most people arrived in America to escape from the mad and the bad, and many would love nothing more than to wash their hands of the lot of them. Involuntary migrants, such as African slaves, would have doubtless taken a different view, but even their descendants, as more and more move into middle-class American comfort, are often grateful to be insulated from the outside world's ills.

This feeling of contented insulation breeds a peculiar complacency. I have noticed, for example, a certain exasperation among comfortable, secular, assimilated American Jews with the problems of fellow Jews, who were foolish enough to choose Israel as their preferred place to live. Why the hell didn't they come to the United States, where they would be safe from all the crazies who would do them harm? If they want to live in the Middle East, amidst the meshuggenehs, well then, they almost deserve what's coming to them.

Complacency takes different forms, to be sure, often depending on political inclinations. But both right and left varieties of American isolationism feed off a deep distrust of government. Rightists fetishise the citizen's right to bear arms, and see the State as an arch-enemy of their God-given liberties. Leftists tend to see government conspiracies everywhere, out to control American citizens by conjuring up imaginary threats. The curled lip with which some commentators on the left spoke about 'the war against terrorism' suggested that terrorism was a mere fiction of the American empire. The cold war, too, has been described by people of this persuasion as a kind of hoax, concocted simply to beef up the 'industrial-military complex'. As with all forms of paranoia, this one contained a kernel of truth. But retreat from the world's problems was never a sensible option, morally or indeed practically.

If Americans have felt the tug of splendid isolation, however, they have been pulled in the opposite direction too. US foreign policy has been equally marked by a crusading zeal to spread the blessings of American freedom among others less favoured. This has often been a noble enterprise. Many Europeans owe their lives to American generosity. But it has got the United States into an awful lot of trouble too. If it was always hard to strike the proper balance between crusading and retreat, the attack on New York and Washington will make it harder still.

One temptation will be to hide behind higher, more formidable fences. Another will be to lash out wildly in the cause of freedom. Before Black Tuesday, it was still possible to do both, by dropping bombs from great heights, killing bad foreigners without risking American lives. But to track down terrorists in hostile terrain will be a different proposition. Americans will almost certainly die. This is one lesson of war to get used to. The other is that the United States can no longer afford the luxury of retreat, for the mad, bad world has scaled the walls and come home. Active engagement in the Middle East, North Korea and other lethal spots is not a matter of crusading any more, but of simple self-defence.

14 September 2001

SIMON SCHAMA

New York rises

It came, literally, out of a clear blue sky, one of those eye-poppingly beautiful mornings when you forgive autumn for polishing off summer. All around New York, the last rituals of America's innocence were being enacted: huddles of mums and dads at the roadside reassuring their seven-year-olds that there was nothing frightening about the big old yellow school bus lumbering towards them. A grey heron was dabbling in the mill pond in our Hudson valley suburb, oblivious like the rest of us to the fact that American history, in the shape of its most irrepressibly ebullient city, and American power, in the shape of its fortress Pentagon, was about to take the hit of its life...

Two nights before, millions had watched the Spielberg-Tom Hanks second world war TV epic, *Band of Brothers*, based on Steven Ambrose's history of a paratroop company in the Normandy invasion. Like *Saving Private Ryan*, its selling point was supposed to be the unsparing realism of its combat scenes, its willingness to concede pain and terror. Up to a point. The tobacco tint of the images told you this was history, inspirational, consoling. And a history in which everything worked out just fine. Some, at least, of the good guys would make it. And whole nations of bad guys would bite the dust.

The media, reaching for one of their war-horse clichés (the other being sports) were quick to chorus that what happened was beyond the imaginings of the most feverish disaster movie. But the truth is that if the script of Bloody Tuesday had been offered to a studio, it would have been turned down not for the scale of the horror but for its failure to supply identifiable villains. America's only usable analogy, Pearl Harbor, 7 December 1941, is on everyone's lips, on the streets and in the news studios. But there was no rising sun – nor for that matter a crescent moon – painted on the fuselage of the airplanes which slammed into the World Trade Center on Tuesday. Their markings belonged instead to United Airlines, whose corporate logo welcomes passengers to 'The Friendly Skies'.

Franklin Roosevelt (where are you now FDR, when we need you?) bunched up American anguish and fury in his big meaty fist and smacked it out again as a war launched against an identifiable foe. The high-voltage energy on which American culture runs could be harnessed right away on concrete, practical work. Enlistment lines stretched round the block. Rubber and aluminium drives got under way. Trepidation surrendered to resolution. It was all very clear cut – the way America likes it.

But this time the go-and-get-'em American responses are scrambled by the terrifying diffuseness of the threat and the inconvenience of the enemy not being any sort of discernible nation state. 'Should the president and congress make a formal declaration of war?' asked one CNN correspondent last night to another. 'Against whom, exactly?' he reasonably replied. She wasn't listening. 'But shouldn't we declare war?' she repeated, pointlessly. 'How about carpet bombing everything between Jordan and Nepal?' one of my downtown friends who had seen the towers collapse in front of his eyes sardonically asked a belligerent comrade-in-suffering. 'Well yes, that might take care of it,' was his reply. America, as Alexis de Tocqueville noticed in the mid-nineteenth century, was founded, and runs, on impatience.

Allied to impatience and impetuousness, De Tocqueville thought, was an uncompromising individualism, the American religion of self-sufficiency before which any sense of community would always have to yield. And you would suppose that if self-interest is a national cult on this side of the Atlantic, New York, the 'look-at-me' metropolis would be its cathedral. But you'd be wrong. Foreigners – especially perhaps Britons who, on the basis of very little first-hand experience, still think of America as some sort of petulant child liable to throw a thermonuclear tantrum when denied its ice-cream, always get New York, not to say the rest of the republic over which they used to fly en route to a ski-lodge in Colorado or the Golden Gate Bridge, wrong. This is a loud city all right, but decibels have nothing to do with decency, or the lack of it, and in the ten years I've been here, I've seen countless acts of spontaneous humanity that belie New York's reputation for callous narcissism.

In our first winter here, we managed to blow a tyre in the midst of a snow-storm, right under the George Washington Bridge, the neighbourhood which at that time richly merited its reputation as the crack capital of the western world, and with the burned out hulks of what once had been cars ominously decorating the roadside. But the cops who came to our rescue not only asked what they could do but went ahead and changed the tyre (perhaps instantly sizing me up as someone seriously challenged in the jack-and-lugnut department). Since then I've seen ordinary New Yorkers go out of their way to help out people who were ill, lost or distressed in street subway and park.

Don't get me wrong. It's not that this is the real city of angels. It's just that it's a city where people want to be doing, and if good is what has to be done, it gets done. So if there was any doubt that New York wouldn't be able to 'take it' on the chin like blitzed London, or that its citizens were too pampered a bunch to respond to catastrophe with anything but a panicky stampede to save their designer-label jogging shoes, it ought to have been laid to rest, first by the grieving calm which characterised the city, and then by the outpouring of mass volunteerism which followed hard on the heels of the inferno. So many lined up quietly to volunteer for anything they could be called on that they had to be turned away. Lines formed round the block waiting for hours to give blood even when, to everyone's sorrow, there seemed to be precious few to give blood to.

We already have our local heroes and 300 of them are dead – the firemen, police and paramedics who were on the scene, attempting to get people out of the World Trade Center when the towers fell on them. Their graves are the twisted remains of fire engines, shrouded, like everything else below 14th Street, in a thick pall of grey ash, much of it dense with asbestos. Entire ladder companies disappeared in that holocaust.

Even to card-carrying liberals like me who have sometimes had misgivings about his red-hot temper, Mayor Giuliani changed overnight from Mussolini to Mother Teresa, appearing everywhere, often putting himself in harm's way, to comfort the distraught, encourage the exhausted and, perhaps most important of all (especially at his press conferences), to tell the truth. A more inspiring example of common decency and instinctively practical humanity in public life, you could not possibly imagine.

In glaring contrast, George Bush has yet to show his face on the island of Manhattan, lest a sooty cinder or two land on the smoothly shaved presidential chin. New Yorkers, who don't take kindly to being stood up, especially at times like this, are beginning to sound as though they might want to land something else, for all their initial basic instinct to rally round the flag and the man who is supposed to embody it.

Nor has the presidential performance on television been exactly Churchillian. Instead of bringing a traumatised country together as a family, united in shared grief and fortitude, instead of evoking the spirit of American trials past and how the republic has endured them, Bush (or his speechwriters, who need to get out of the East Wing and into the back yards of the bereft) have depended on warmed-up platitudes inherited, like much of the National Security cabinet, from the administration of Poppy and Reagan.

With every repetition of the fighting cliché, 'make no mistake', the deeper the sinking feeling that neither he, nor his administration, has a clue about how to reboot their systems away from the comic-book obsession with 'missile defence' to actually protect America from men with razor-blades, box-cutters and Arabic flight-training manuals, much less an elementary degree in anthrax 101.

So instead of listening to cowboy pieties, or endlessly respooling video horror, or seeing in our mind's eye those twin towers as phantom, 110-storey tombstones, we turn to those who do, miraculously, know what they're supposed to say, feel and do: to Jeremy Glick who phoned his wife from the hijacked plane over Pennsylvania to tell her there had been a vote of all the men aboard to try to overpower the hijackers, even though they knew it would cost them all their lives, and who saved who knows how many other lives by doing just that; to the son and daughter of one of the dead passengers letting themselves be interviewed on morning TV so they could appeal to the airlines to get their sister, marooned in London, back to the States for their father's funeral; to the handful of politicians who know when to speak and when to shut up; to all those in this suddenly, shockingly loving town who understand, especially when they hear the word 'revenge' thundered out by talk-show warriors, that the best, the only revenge, when you're fighting a cult that fetishises death, is life.

14 September 2001

BLAKE MORRISON

This time we saw Rome burn

For all of us, there is some banal detail, beyond the vast horror, that brings it home. In my case it came from reading about Seth Morris, a broker at the World Trade Center, who was calling his wife from the office when the plane loomed up outside his window. He had time to describe it before the phone went dead. My elder son is called Seth and almost shares the surname. That's how this tragedy gets you. Even if you're lucky and have lost no one, it feels like family.

Familiar, too. That plane sailing into a skyscraper is the routine stuff of dreams and childhood fantasies. 'Unimaginable,' we tell each other, but the scenes are ones we've imagined already. The hijacking. The last 'I love you' into the cellphone. The office block crashing earthwards like a lift down a lift shaft. Which of us hasn't been there in our heads? It is as though we were always waiting for this to come.

Perhaps that is the answer to those accusing voices – some of them inner voices – that say we are glutting on horror. How much longer are we going to sit waiting for new footage, watching New Yorkers cheer on the rescue teams, listening to grave spokesmen prophesying war, channel-hopping to another rerun of Tuesday morning as if in hope that this time the planes will miss? What more can be learned now? Isn't it time for us to move on?

And it's true. Most of us are fixated: by that skyline, the backdrop to a thousand movies and a billion holiday snaps, now shorn of its twin towers by the thought of those passengers calling home on their mobiles; by the varieties of fire we saw – orange flames, oily black plumes, then those grey-white clouds rolling down the street, easing themselves round buildings, feeling their way through the concrete canyons, people running from them like characters in a movie fleeing from a dragon or dinosaur. Or by the dust.

Why the dust should be so emotive I don't know, but it is. Thick as snow, it hoods the survivors and rescue workers in all the footage, overlaying them like an extra skin and making a desert of the place, so that the cars abandoned in the streets look like marooned buggies in the Sahara. These shots intercut with Osama Bin Laden's training camp in the Afghan hills – all sand and dust and craggy outcrops there as well – so that the two are now connected in our eyes and minds: the scene of the crime, and the possible criminals. Within the dust are the ashes of many who died, burned alive in their offices. And also a cliché, now revivified: 'When the dust settles.' When the dust settles, we'll know not only the death toll but the vengeance the Bush administration has in store.

With so much to haunt and horrify, is it any wonder we can't prise ourselves from the screen? Even if we switch channels, there's no escape. David Attenborough's *The Blue Planet*, a nature documentary, should have provided an interlude, but those finned sharks angling through the blue, those long-necked gannets hurtling down at impossible speeds, were Tuesday morning all over again. Pick up a book, for light relief, and that's doomed too. Opening a poetry anthology, I found 'Musée des Beaux Arts' staring up, W. H. Auden's famous meditation on how great events always catch us unawares, when we're opening a window or just walking dully along. It was while walking dully along on Tuesday that I first heard the news breaking, from a radio that a passing cyclist had on. Even then I knew I'd always remember that moment.

But haven't there been other tragedies on this scale, the accusing voices say. Do you remember where you were then? What of America's carpet-bombing of Cambodia? And what about Bhuj? Bhuj is the capital of the state of Gujarat, in India, and on 26 January this year it was hit by an earthquake measuring 7.9 on the Richter scale. At least 30,000 people died when the quake hit – perhaps three times as many as those who died in New York and Washington. Admit it, you can't even remember Bhuj. Why hasn't it lodged in the same way? Where was your compassion then? Aren't you guilty of supposing that black people matter less than white?

There are various answers here. Of course, Indian earthquake victims are equally worthy of our pity. But natural disasters aren't the same as war raids or terrorist attacks. With acts of God, the events are beyond human control. With events like this week's – though there never have been events like this week's, and that's part of it – we're haunted by a sense of the avoidable: had the timing been different, had security been tighter, had the US not made so many enemies, innocent people might have been spared.

The might-have-beens preoccupy us as a random natural disaster never can. And whereas an earthquake is a single event (whatever the aftershocks), the assault on New York and Washington was a series of events, spread out over hours, and each a vast drama in itself.

Then there is the history and symbolism. America has just been violated as never before. We've seen the heart of the world's greatest empire – its military brain and financial nerve centre – going up in smoke. None of us was there to see the siege of Troy, the fall of Constantinople, the burning of Rome, the Great Fire of London, but we've often wondered what they were like. This time there were cameras present.

That's another answer – and an uncomfortable one. We might fancy ourselves to be a global village, tuned into lives remote from ours and, thanks to technology, able to leap vast distances and bridge cultural divides. But it's the west that owns most of the cameras. Even if it were minded to (and we'd be right to suspect the will of Rupert Murdoch, etc to provide extensive coverage of third-world catastrophes), the media can't so easily bring us Bhuj.

And there's the final answer. The global village doesn't exist yet, but London to New York has become a short hop. Vast numbers of Britons have holidayed and weekended there in recent years. Many work there. Some commute. There are people in the southern half of this country who know Manhattan far better than they do Glasgow or Manchester. In the designer discount stores by the World Trade Center, half the shoppers speak estuary English. They feel proprietorial, as though the Big Apple were theirs to consume. An older generation might feel more kinship with France, say, but to anyone born after 1945, America is where we are or where we're headed. It's no longer a story of two nations divided by a common language. And it's more than the special relationship. The soaps and game-shows have made Uncle Sam part of the family. So it's natural to feel haunted and moved. The eerie hush in offices and on trains here. The washed-out faces of almost everyone you meet (they've not been sleeping much – but then nor have you). The knowledge when you get up each day that the news will be as bad or worse. The indifference to stuff that seemed important only days ago: a football match, an exhibition, that new haircut you were going to have. The incredulity, thinking further back, at all the trivia through the last decade we got ourselves worked up over. Monica Lewinsky, *Big Brother*, Posh and Becks – who cares? What were we thinking of? Time to get real. All this is part of the shock. Why feel puzzled by it, or guilty? The puzzling thing would be having the capacity to rise above it.

Such feelings will pass soon enough. But in the meantime, better to acknowledge than deny them. There's nothing sick about watching the box obsessively or grieving for people we've never met. Nor does sympathy for what Americans are going through make us capitalist lackeys, stooges of Bush and Blair, or enemies of the Arab world. The liberal conscience has a habit of getting muddled in these matters. But pity knows no bounds. It doesn't mete itself out in meagre allowances. It isn't mealy-mouthed. It won't turn A away because B has suffered too. It's not a pot that runs out if you draw on it. And it can't help feeling what it does.

Dismay at US foreign policy, distrust of George W Bush's temperament, fear of the hawks, understanding of the Palestinians who cheered at the news, sympathy for other Arabs whose cities have been bombed and children starved, indignation at the huge imbalance in wealth between the third world and the west. None of this should inhibit our sense of tragedy and outrage.

The Pentagon had blood on its hands. The World Trade Center was a pillar of mammon. But no one deserved to die in that way. Glutting? Overimmersion? Voyeurism? No. Something momentous has just happened that demands our full attention. If we're going to moderate (the *mot juste*) when Bush and his cohorts plot their vengeance in the coming days, we have to hear what the American people are saying.

Let's not minimise what's gone on and what's at stake here. We're in a new age now. When the dust clears, the scary new order will appear. This is the last week of the world as it was.

15 September 2001

IAN McEWAN

Only love, and then oblivion

Emotions have their narrative; after the shock we move inevitably to the grief, and the sense that we are doing it more or less together is one tiny scrap of consolation. Initially, the visual impact of the scenes – those towers collapsing with malign majesty – extended our state of fevered astonishment.

Even on Wednesday, fresh video footage froze us in this stupefied condition, and denied us our profounder feelings: the first plane disappearing into the side of the tower as cleanly as a posted letter; the couple jumping into the void, hand in hand; a solitary figure falling with a strangely extended arm (was it an umbrella serving as a hopeful parachute?); the rescue workers crawling about at the foot of a vast mountain of rubble.

In our delirium, most of us wanted to talk. We babbled, by email, on the phone, around kitchen tables. We knew there was a greater reckoning ahead, but we could not quite feel it yet. Sheer amazement kept getting in the way.

The reckoning, of course, was with the personal. By Thursday I noticed among friends, and in TV and radio commentaries, a new mood of exhaustion and despair. People spoke of being depressed. No other public event had cut so deeply. The spectacle was over. Now we were hearing from the bereaved. Each individual death is an explosion in itself, wrecking the lives of those nearest. We were beginning to grasp the human cost. This was what it was always really about.

The silent relatives grouped around the entrances to hospitals or wandering the streets with their photographs was a terrible sight. It reminded us of other tragedies, of wars and natural disasters around the world. But Manhattan is one of the most sophisticated cities in the world, and there were some uniquely modern elements to this nightmare that bound us closer to it.

The mobile phone has inserted itself into every crevice of our daily lives. Now, in catastrophe, if there's time enough, it is there in our dying moments. All through Thursday we heard from the bereaved how they took those last calls. Whatever the immediate circumstances, what was striking was what they had in common. A new technology has shown us an ancient, human, universal.

A San Francisco husband slept through his wife's call from the WTC. The tower was burning around her, and she was speaking on her mobile phone. She left her last message to him on the answering machine. A TV station played it to us, while it showed the husband standing there listening. Somehow, he was able to bear hearing it again. We heard her tell him through her sobbing that there was no escape for her. The building was on fire and there was no way down the stairs. She was calling to say goodbye. There was really only one thing for her to say, those three words that all the terrible art, the worst pop songs and movies, the most seductive lies, can somehow never cheapen: I love you. She said it over and again before the line went dead.

And that is what they were all saying down their phones, from the hijacked planes and the burning towers. There's only love, and then oblivion. Love was all they had to set against the hatred of their murderers.

Last words placed in the public domain were once the prerogative of the mighty and venerable – Henry James, Nelson, Goethe – recorded, and perhaps sometimes edited for posterity, by relatives at the bedside. The effect was often consolatory, showing acceptance, or even transcendence in the face of death. They set us an example. But these last words spoken down mobile phones, reported to us by the bereaved, are both more haunting and true. They compel us to imagine ourselves into that moment. What would we say? Now we know.

Most of us have had no active role to play in these terrible events. We simply watch the television, read the papers, turn on the radio again. Listening to the analysts and pundits is soothing to some extent. Expertise is reassuring. And the derided profession of journalism can rise quite nobly, and with immense resource, to public tragedy. However, I suspect that in between times, when we are not consuming news, the majority of us are not meditating on recent foreign policy failures, or geopolitical strategy, or the operational range of helicopter gunships. Instead, we remember what we have seen, and we daydream helplessly.

Lately, most of us have inhabited the space between the terrible actuality and these daydreams. Waking before dawn, going about our business during the day, we fantasise ourselves into the events. What if it was me? This is the nature of empathy, to think oneself into the minds of others. These are the mechanics of compassion: you are under the bedclothes, unable to sleep, and you are crouching in the brushed-steel lavatory at the rear of the plane, whispering a final message to your loved one. There is only that one thing to say, and you say it. All else is pointless. You have very little time before some holy fool, who believes in his place in eternity, kicks in the door, slaps your head and orders you back to your seat. 23C. Here is your seat belt. There is the magazine you were reading before it all began. The banality of these details might overwhelm you. If you're not already panicking, you're clinging to a shred of hope that the captain, who spoke with such authority as the plane pushed back from the stand, will rise from the floor, his throat uncut, to take the controls...

If the hijackers had been able to imagine themselves into the thoughts and feelings of the passengers, they would have been unable to proceed. It is hard to be cruel once you permit yourself to enter the mind of your victim. Imagining what it is like to be someone other than yourself is at the core of our humanity. It is the essence of compassion, and it is the beginning of morality. The hijackers used fanatical certainty, misplaced religious faith and dehumanising hatred to purge themselves of the human instinct for empathy. Among their crimes was a failure of the imagination. As for their victims in the planes and in the towers, in their terror they would not have felt it at the time, but those snatched and anguished assertions of love was their defiance.

17 September 2001

MARTIN WOOLLACOTT

Old quarrels no longer apply

This is a dangerous moment in history. It would be foolish to allow differences about the best way to respond to a terrorist threat to degenerate into an ideological contest that can only make wise choices more difficult, and perhaps fragment popular support for the decisions our governments make.

Unhappily, there are some signs of old reflexes jerking in Britain and in other countries. There is the right's familiar attack on a left that supposedly sees the problem only in terms of western, and particularly American, responsibility for everything that goes wrong in the world. There is the left's familiar attack on a right that supposedly admits no responsibility at all, and thinks only of imposing solutions by force of arms.

This is cardboard stuff. If we in Britain let ourselves talk this up, we could recreate the polarisation of the Suez crisis, but without the genuinely principled differences that accompanied it. That would not be of much use to us, or to the United States.

Suez illustrates the danger of letting discussion be drawn into the vortex of the appeasement row, whether the appeasement is of Nazi Germany, the Soviet Union or, now, of terrorists. The truth is that both right and left have actions in the historical record of which they should be ashamed. Unfortunately, nobody has a monopoly on appeasement. And it is also true that, for a long time, there has been a divide in western societies between those who see opponents mainly as enemies and those who tend to see, and even sometimes endorse, their opponent's point of view. The debate over what the Australians call the 'black armband view' of history, a debate over power, oppression and guilt, is old, continuing and important.

And it has expanded in recent years to encompass the question of whether those now rebelling against what is still largely a western ordering of global affairs are justified in their ends, and even perhaps sometimes in their means. What this debate reveals is that the coarser and simpler the approach – whether it comes from the right or the left – the more it misses reality.

Michael Gove of *The Times* has singled out the *Guardian* for special censure in an article professing to identify a dominant radical chic tendency on the left, a tendency that he feels has always romanticised rebel violence, that is persistently anti-American and anti-Zionist, and that is now, he implies, almost pro-terrorist.

If this were a normal time, it would be a normal knockabout, but this is not a normal time. Of course, there is a silly, and sometimes morally irresponsible, element on the left. This element has been opposed most effectively, and usually by others on the same political side. But to pretend that this element is the whole picture, as Gove does, is itself irresponsible. In a more thoughtful piece in the *Sunday Telegraph* yesterday, Anne Applebaum explored what she sees as a worrying potential axis between the British anti-American left, an anti-American section of the isolationist British right, and British Muslims.

She rightly detects a shift from the phase of pure sympathy after the attacks. In this second phase, the question of whether the United States had contributed in some way to what happened began to be raised, and fears emerged that retaliation would be ill-judged or excessive. But surely these are legitimate concerns, and they do not diminish the genuine grief that people all over the world, wherever they stand politically, feel about America's loss.

Nor are these concerns absent from American minds. They are properly seen as questions needing answers, because those answers will help us make sure that something like this does not happen again. The pathological human zone that exists today in Afghanistan and parts of Pakistan was created by war, social breakdown and the degeneration of religious tradition. Many contributed towards it, including the Afghans, as did the occupying Russians.

But when the United States, Pakistan, and Saudi Arabia, with help from the British and others, joined together twenty-five years ago to make life difficult for the Soviets, funding and arming the Afghan rebels and the international Muslim army that fought alongside the rebels, they thought little of the trouble they were storing up for themselves. After the Russians pulled out, the US and other western countries turned their backs on the mess that was post-Soviet Afghanistan. 'What was more important in the world-view of history ? The Taliban or the fall of the Soviet Empire ? A few stirred-up Muslims or the liberation of Central Europe and the end of the cold war ?' wrote Zbigniew Brzezinski. In retrospect that seems amazingly insouciant.

At least in principle, the need for careful judgment on a military response surely ought not to be subject to dispute across the left–right divide. This is a matter of prudence, and of measuring the situation in the Muslim world. Ahmed Rashid, in his book on the Taliban, entitles his chapter on the Taliban's religious approach 'Challenging Islam'. The Taliban, culturally stripped bare by a generation of war and displacement, have completely lost touch with the diverse and tolerant Islamic heritage of pre-war Afghanistan. They have given shelter to dissidents from some Arab societies who, for other reasons, also follow a distorted form of Islam. It is possible, but very far from proven, that Saddam Hussein may have funded or used them.

In the light of this, the question is whether, as Anne Applebaum thinks, the Muslim world is rotten with terrorism, the extirpation of which may take years. Or whether there is a major problem area, recognised by Muslim as well as western societies, with which they and we have to deal. Or is the truth somewhere in between? That there is a major problem area – Afghanistan and Pakistan – to which we must add many Muslim societies in an uneasy balance (not helped by the Palestinian situation), in which new forms of Islam compete for allegiance, but in which religious and political leadership mostly manage to maintain a complex and relatively humane tradition.

What needs to be considered is how particular military actions will affect, not only those under immediate attack, but those societies in that more general balance. This is not being soft on terrorism, nor is it ruling out the use of military force. It is certainly not being anti-American. It is simply expressing the hope that this time we – Americans and all the rest of us on this complicated planet – will get it right. Getting things right involves discussion, criticism, and consultation. Even then there is no guarantee. But we have a better chance of success if we maintain a calmness of temper and try not to let old quarrels dominate a new situation.

25 September 2001

IAN TRAYNOR

10,000 a day flee press gangs in Kabul

The Taliban press gang arrived in their Datsun pickups in the small hours of Sunday morning, striking terror into every family in a block of flats in north Kabul.

On the fifth floor Wahidullah, a thirty-year-old ethnic Tajik, comforted his two young children and looked on fearfully as the building was shaken by the howling and shrieking of mothers and sisters.

The gunmen moved through the first few floors of the block, seizing all males aged between eighteen and thirty and dragging them away, the hostages were told, to fight America.

'That was when I decided to leave. I thought they were going to take me too,' said Wahidullah yesterday, after a twelve-hour trek with his family out of Kabul to the other side of the lines in Afghanistan's civil war.

Caked in dust, his eighteen-month-old sobbing in the open back of the jeep carrying fourteen people, Wahidullah recounted how the Taliban fighters turned up in fifty vehicles and started hauling men from their beds. One was bound and gagged.

For the past several days, according to scores of refugees who came up the Old Kabul Road yesterday seeking a safe haven in territory held by the opposition Northern Alliance, mayhem has been visited on the Tajik quarter of the Afghan capital.

Taliban militias have been staging night-time raids on the district's homes, dragging the menfolk away to fight for them on the frontline, to get ready to defend the city against US attacks, to be thrown into jail, or to be held as hostages and perhaps human shields.

'Four days ago they began to hold people hostage,' explained Mohamad

Hossain, thirty, who arrived in the village of Denau yesterday with his wife, five children and niece. 'They jail people, then keep them as hostages, because they have many soldiers captive and want to exchange them.'

The traumatised refugees all told similar tales of panic in the streets of Kabul, about how the marauders grabbed the men and looted the flats.

Around 100 of the fugitives came through yesterday, braving brigands and bombs, and carrying babies on foot for hours across no-man's land before being fleeced by 'taxi drivers' waiting on the other side to pack them into estate cars and ferry them to relatives in the Panjsheer valley opposition stronghold.

The Taliban defence minister in Kabul announced yesterday that he was mobilising 300,000 men to defend Afghanistan against feared attacks. 'In view of the current conditions 300,000 well-experienced and equipped men have been stationed in the centre [of the country], and at other significant areas, in addition to its former detachments,' Mullah Obaidullah said. 'Hundreds of thousands of others have showed their readiness to participate in a jihad against foreign invaders. Enrolment is going on.'

The fugitives' harrowing accounts yesterday offered an insight into how the Taliban has already begun a campaign of enforced enrolment. It was clear from their stories that the round-ups started late last week and mark a new stage in the reign of terror in Kabul.

'My name is Dina,' said an eleven-year-old girl with black pigtails perched on a Jeep. She was born in Kabul and has never lived anywhere else. But at 4 a.m. yesterday, her father, Abdulhamid, forty-five, a quiet man who tans leather and trades in sheepskins, rushed the family of eleven into exodus.

'I felt danger, I was afraid. It's getting worse,' said Dina. 'Many people are leaving. They are running for their cars,' said her father. 'I'd say 10,000 people are leaving Kabul every day. The Taliban are taking all the young men during the night.'

Mohamad Karim, a 56-year-old lorry driver and father of twelve, also on the run, said he knew sixteen young men in his neighbourhood who had been abducted.

It is not only the ethnic Tajiks who are fleeing. Refugees said the Taliban were sending their families out of the city in expectation of US air strikes, to the southern Taliban heartland or to Pakistan. But the Tajiks are fleeing because the ethnic issue is also a major factor in the civil war, with the Taliban almost completely Pashtu, while the Northern Alliance opposition is Tajik-dominated.

With 38 per cent, the Pashtus are the biggest nationality in Afghanistan, while the Tajiks are the second biggest at 25 per cent. For the first time in seven years of harsh Taliban rule, the Tajiks are being dragooned into the Pashtu army and many are opting to flee if they can. One man coming out of Kabul yesterday said the Taliban had just rounded up 300 males of the Hazara minority.

The route the refugees use entails leaping out of the frying pan into the fire. The Old Kabul Road from the capital up to Gulbakhar at the Panjsheer gorge runs through Gioava, the last Taliban-held village, and on to Doornama, a bandit-infested black market centre, to which contraband oil and petrol is smuggled from out of the capital by horse and donkey.

All yesterday's refugees passed through fighting at Gioava, where they had to abandon taxis or cars and walk for three hours across the harsh terrain separating the two sides. Around lunchtime the sky above Doornama was broken by one of the Taliban's Soviet-built aircraft and two bombs fell on the town.

Shafiqullah, a 22-year-old worker in a Kabul shoe factory, leapt from his car, laden with packages of ghee, and scrambled to the ground as the jet screamed overhead.

Further up the road, he was fleeced by the brigands who control this stretch and kill without compunction after robbing their victims of everything down to the shoes on their feet.

'You can't go down that road. It's very dangerous. If the thieves stop you, they will kill you,' advised Nabi, thirty-eight, who earns a fortune, by local standards, by picking up the refugees and charging them around £40 for use of his Toyota land-cruiser.

His warnings were confirmed by another man named Nabi, regional administrator for the International Red Cross, who said the Old Kabul Road was a notorious bandit trap. There are said to be three gangs of robbers on the road, often at war with each other. All the refugees said they had to pay a form of road tax to the bandits to complete their escape from the Taliban terror.

'I don't have any money left now,' said Wahidullah after being stopped three times yesterday by the gangs.

'The robbers have always been there,' explained Mohamad Agho, thirty-five, a local fighter who has been in the hills for as long as he can remember.

'There were also Pakistanis and Arabs in Gioava and we didn't know what they were going to do,' said Shafiqullah, who said he was held for a week in Kabul before fleeing.

'They ordered me to take a gun and fight against the Americans. They beat me with a cable. They're very bad people, but now the Taliban people are fleeing Kabul as well.'

All of the Tajik refugees were terrified not only of the Taliban, but also of the prospect of US bombs raining down on the city. And all of them wanted to return to the capital after the Americans had bombed the Taliban out of Kabul.

'I've lived in Kabul for twenty years. My business is there,' said Abdulhamid, the sheepskin trader. Clearly once a wealthy man, he arrived in Denau with next to nothing.

Shafiqullah said he thought Kabul was now half empty. 'We're afraid of being there when the Americans come and capture the city. And we're afraid of the Taliban. But we will be happy if the Americans take Kabul and we can go back.'

9 October 2001

MAGGIE O'KANE

Fear and goading on the frontline

It is the first light after the first night of bombing and the men of the Northern Alliance are back on their walkie-talkies, speaking across a distance not much longer than a village high street. They have some questions from foreigners to put to the Taliban. At first they begin with the usual teasing.

'Hey Turban-Talibs are you out there? That bombing seems to have shut you lot up.'

The voice that responds across the airwaves is cold, a voice of authority. An educated man, our translator says, 'Why will you not hand over Bin Laden?'

'Why should we give him over? He is Muslim,' says the chilly voice.

'What kind of Muslim kills 6,500 innocent people?'

'He did a good thing. Those people were Kafirs (non-Muslims) and they are our enemies.'

'What about the bombing – did you have casualties?'

'What about the bombing? It was nothing. We lost nobody. Nobody was injured.'

'Why are the Taliban fleeing the cities? Are you afraid of the Afghan people?'

'Those that are left can go. It is up to them. If they want to stay and fight they can. Otherwise it is up to them.'

'We have nothing to say to him, or to the Russians, to any non-Muslims – we are the free people.'

'How long do you think you can survive without Pakistan now that Pakistan has stopped supporting you and is backing the Americans?'

'Fuck you and fuck the Pakistanis.'

At the same time, Commander Baba Jan strolls to his command post, built from mud, straw and sticks, as though he might be returning from a light lunch.

The men in the commander's frontline army bring sugared green tea and toffee sweets and move the rough wooden bench into the early morning sunlight. The commander is here.

The commander, who once controlled the security of the capital, Kabul, and now runs the most important frontline with the Taliban – Bagram airport, just 25 miles from Kabul – arrives wearing dark green Castro khakis. In this warren of dusty tunnels, dirt, near drought, no electricity, no running water, no toilets, he has the distinction of perfectly clean and filed nails, his black leather loafers somehow escaping the coating of dust that covers all lesser beings.

'At this rate we won't be going to Kabul in a hurry,' he says of Sunday night's bombing. 'It will take a lot more pressure on the Taliban lines before we will go to Kabul. It is not going to be easy.'

Along the road to Bagram the only traffic heading towards the Taliban line is a horse and trap. The commander's tanks are still in their dust covers. The march to victory could be a long time coming.

At 42, and after 20 years of fighting, he talks with the voices of machine guns in the background, wallpaper music that he doesn't seem to notice.

'The Americans are not talking to us,' he says. 'Even to commanders like me. Maybe they are talking to our defence chiefs but not to us. But if the US wants to get results they must be in contact with us. They should understand that without us and our experience of fighting the Taliban they cannot defeat them.' Above his head is a black and white banner with the words: 'There is no God except one – Mohammed is the prophet.' Another tray of tea arrives.

'We are not in a hurry. We need arms, we need food and action would be a lot better than words.'

Behind him stretch the fields of parched grapevines that have just survived the drought. Their leaves are also covered in a film of toffee-coloured dust. His airport, built in 1951, could have been used as a set for the opening scenes of a Mad Max movie. An angry cactus has seeded in the water tank. Under a hot sky, where a single hawk circles, the debris of 30 years of war stretches out beyond the runway. The Taliban lines are 200 metres away. So close that the dust kicked from the back wheels of their Datsun pick-up trucks leaves a track of smoke along the mountain road.

Less than a mile from the frontline, the fact that the might of a coalition of the world's most powerful armies unleashed their first salvo against the Taliban has not interrupted the preparation for the circumcision of six-year-old Hassan. The men of his village are gathering to pray. First they must recite the entire Koran to prepare for the ceremony. The boy sits between the legs of his father, Rahman Allah, in a crisp white shirt, his big green eyes bewildered by the attention.

'We will read the Holy Koran and then the doctor will come to perform the ceremony in another room with his father.'

Did they consider postponing the event because of the bombing?

'Why should we? We have been listening to bombing for six years. This is a good time for us. We are happy to hit the Taliban and finish the Taliban if America brings enough pressure on them.'

In the corner a 16-year-old boy, his eyes painted with black coal, begins reciting by heart from the Koran, and older men begin to shake and moan. The modulating voice of the boy, Kuri Hamad, fills the room and the younger men bend their head in devout and reverential prayer. Watching them from the wall is another hero, a fighter killed 20 years earlier in the war against the Soviets.

On Sunday night as the bombing began, Commander Baba Jan watched the car lights of hundreds of Datsun pick-ups arrive at a new second front the Taliban have set up a mile behind the airport.

'After six years of watching them we know their movement. They were taking their equipment back from the frontline and leaving the fighters there.'

The ground war for control of Afghanistan will begin here at Bagram airport, if and when the commander and his fellow chiefs decide that the Taliban have been sufficiently pounded by the bombing. Across a runway which has not seen a normal commercial flight since 1979, a small group of soldiers live in what was once the military hospital 10 days on, 10 days off and then back to their farms. Bagram airport has been taken and wrested from the Taliban twice in the past five years. Clattering up the metal stairs to the control tower, the soldiers point out the Taliban positions like weary tour guides.

'Over there behind that house are where the Chechen fighters have their position. The Arabs are at the back of the runway. They've been very quiet these days.'

The control tower, its windows gone for decades, has lost part of its roof to a Taliban rocket. A Russian machine gun, the length of a car, with bullets as long as a pencil sits silent and waiting.

9 October 2001

HUGO YOUNG

Sorry, but this war is about Islam and America

The two myths about this war are that it is not about America and not about Islam. Political correctness allows no other analysis. And the war, it's true, is about more than those totemic powers. America is not the only society threatened by world terrorism. Muslims are not inevitable enemies of the world America dominates. So we must take care not to generalise crudely. But we also need to face squarely the fact that traits embodied by America and Islam are what have brought the world to its gravest crisis since Moscow put missiles into Cuba 40 years ago. Otherwise, the bleak future will become darker still.

Tony Blair has taken the lead in insisting on both of these negative assertions. Four weeks ago he declared that the assaults on New York and Washington attacked not America but all democracies. It's been his mantra, and that of others, ever since. On Sunday, after our own attacks began, he expressed much impatience with the regular usage that ascribes the New York atrocity to 'Islamic terrorists'. It's understandable that he and President Bush should do this. They want to define the nature of the struggle: broadening it to enlist the whole civilised world, narrowing it against a terroristic fraction that merely happens to be Islamic. If people can believe this, it will assist the task, as elementary as it is difficult, of reassuring other Muslim countries, reinforcing their assistance, preventing them being blackened by Osama Bin Laden, and stiffening their stomachs against many domestic enemies.

It's a necessary expedient, but an insufficient argument. It obscures the truth behind useful fictions of the moment. It is not helpful, if we're interested in picking up the pieces, doing better than before, taming the enmities that threaten to tear apart the world with a ferocity and ignorance that may be more pervasive than we have ever seen.

In a sense, Islam is at the heart of what is happening. When commentators muse about the evils of religious fundamentalism, in the modern context there's only one religion they can be talking about. That doesn't mean, in any way, that all Muslims are to blame. But the September terrorists who left messages and testaments described their actions as being in the name of Allah. They made this their explicit appeal and defence. Bin Laden himself, no longer disclaiming culpability for their actions, clothes their murders and their suicides in religious glory. A version of Islam – not typical, a minority fragment, but undeniably Islamic – endorses the foaming hatred for America that uniquely emanates, with supplementary texts, from a variety of mullahs.

'Many Muslims seem to be in deep denial about what has happened,' Imam Hamza Yusuf, the noted Islamic teacher, told the *Guardian* yesterday. 'Islam has been hijacked by a discourse of anger and a rhetoric of rage.'

It has bred terrorists with a cause endorsed by misbegotten theology, quite different, for example, from the Irish or the Basques. To pretend that this is mere criminality is deception on a grand scale. It denies the need for self-examination. The ambiguities and contending loyalties of Muslim leaders in the west, even the most decent and reasonable of them, take cover under the pretence that Islam is not at the heart of what has happened.

Nothing justifies what happened. It had no defence. It was a holocaustic obscenity. But in any analysis seeking for what better might happen in the future, the deformity of Islam has its counterpart. The atrocity was not a random flailing. It challenged the US as the largest, most powerful country in the world. The US may be leader of a collective system, the system of democracy, in which many countries have the good fortune to be numbered. But the US is first among unequals, and is being asked a question about how it has handled that power and privilege for many years.

The challenge may be prompted by American domination. That is unalterable. The more telling Muslim claim is against American insensitivity, Washington's disposal of its assets and blind indifference to the disposition of its power. Sensitivity to the meaning of power ought to be the key to America's global identity. But such an impulse has tended to be lacking. America would like to be benign, and Americans see themselves that way. But, deprived of the matrix of cold war thinking, America has not troubled to learn enough about the shape of the world. A slash-and-burn diplomatic mentality left Afghanistan to the tender mercies of the Taliban after the Soviets had been kicked out. Sectarian bias cossets Israel's refusal to make a reasonable settlement with Palestine, no matter what damage this does to the wider world. America's mono-cultural incomprehension has produced a deep unawareness of the case for off-setting her economic power with an ever-vigilant political wisdom.

It now seems to be recognised that this has to change. The planes are delivering not only bombs but food parcels to Afghanistan. It will be the first war where soldiers and saints purport to walk hand in hand. Belatedly, Americans understand they have a desperate need to engage with the Muslim world at all levels. Perhaps they should start some Persian, or even Pashtu, broadcasting for the first time. The world, they dimly apprehend, needs more than missiles to make it love America. At the very minimum, taking copious action against the destitution in which Afghans live would be more than humanitarian generosity. It's the biggest plank available to rebuild a national reputation which, one must painfully admit, has contributed much to the unregenerate hatred directed against it.

How the war will end is not possible to say. Our leaders give us not a single ground for optimism. They say it must go on and on. Their immediate aim, the elimination of Bin Laden, looks as elusive as their ultimate aim, the end of all world terrorism. Both are desirable, both perhaps unreal. The work has to be started. Bush and Blair had no choice. But, more than any other military engagement in the last 20 years, it defies confident explanation. The commentator is accustomed to making rational sense of things, pointing the way towards an outcome, admitting the reader to the mind of political leaders who know what they are doing. This time these leaders can be by no means sure. They know what they want, but have little idea how far or long they, or we, will have to go to get it.

Meanwhile, let's be clear about this one aspect. Though the danger is universal, the failings that provoked it are particular. The unforgivable act against humanity sprang from a version of Islam that only Islam can set about repudiating, so that among people of goodwill there can be no shred of misunderstanding. On the other hand, the context in which it happened, the target it was aimed at, is the residue of a history that America needs to recognise. Such truths are the start of making a better world hereafter – if the hereafter ever comes.

16 October 2001

LUKE HARDING

A far pavilion

In a scruffy cricket ground in the frontier town of Peshawar, a group of young men with beards are playing cricket. Things are not going well in their homeland: there is drought, famine and American bombardment. On the cricket pitch it looks equally bleak for Afghanistan: they are 125 all out.

'They have very good fielders and very good spinners but their batting is not very good,' the Pakistani umpire, Mian Aslam, admitted in the dressing room over tea.

In one of the most surreal episodes so far in the war on terrorism, Afghanistan's national cricket team yesterday took on a Pakistani side from the dusty town of Nowshera. The fixture had been arranged well before the US decided to drop hundreds of tonnes of bombs on Kabul, and other Afghan cities. Since the country has been at war for more than two decades, few of the players saw any reason to cancel.

'Inshallah [God willing] we will win this game,' Afghanistan's captain, Allah Dad Noory, said, an unlikely proposition since Nowshera's swaggering batsmen had by early afternoon already put on 93 for 2.

These days, there are few forms of pleasure in Afghanistan. The Taliban have banned high-heeled shoes, kite flying, television and music. But the ultra-prudish regime has so far discovered nothing immoral in cricket, a game recently imported back into Aghanistan by a generation of young men who grew up in Pakistani refugee camps.

'The Taliban allow us to wear cricket whites,' Javed Ali, 17, said. 'Football is very popular too. The Taliban let footballers wear shorts, as long as they are baggy.'

Ali, an all-rounder, said he had left his home in Jalalabad last week.

'A lot of people are leaving because they are afraid of US attacks,' he said. 'The poor people especially do not know where to go. We have no connection with the Taliban. I'm very sad because a lot of our Muslim brothers have been killed in these attacks.'

Sitting in front of the clubhouse, Ali recounted how worshippers had been killed when a bomb hit a Jalalabad mosque. With bombs falling, and the Nowshera fixture only days away, Ali decided it was time to flee.

'Pakistan had closed its border, so I climbed over the mountains. I stuffed a bag full of clothes, including my cricket whites,' he said. 'I sat in the back of a pick-up truck. My leg was hanging off the end when a second truck bumped into us. That's why I'm not playing now.'

In Jalalabad, Ali had given up studying to concentrate on cricket.

'All the subjects are Muslim subjects,' he complained.

There are 240 cricket associations in Afghanistan, including one in Kandahar, the home of the Taliban's leader, Mullah Mohammad Omar. Banned from the Olympic games, Afghanistan was admitted into the International Cricket Council in June as an associate member, a minor triumph.

During the Taliban's five-year reign in Kabul, sport has improbably flourished. Last summer the Taliban reopened Afghanistan's only swimming pool, in the grounds of the Intercontinental Hotel. In a city starved of entertainment, the pool was an instant hit. But the capital's football stadium is also used on Fridays as the venue for public executions, a grim reminder that even innocent pastimes in Afghanistan can manifest a darker side.

18 October 2001

MATTHEW ENGEL

Testing time in the corridors of power

The great dome of the Capitol still stood reassuringly yesterday, gleaming in the sunshine, just as it did on September 11. But all the legislative power inside has been rendered impotent in the face of the most mysterious and insidious development of the crisis so far.

Tom Daschle, the prime target of the Washington anthrax attack, insisted that the business of the Senate, which he leads, would go on. At the same moment, members of the Republican-controlled House of Representatives, whose offices are several hundred yards from the nearest detected anthrax spores, were scuttling back to their districts.

But though the Senate show goes on, one of its most cherished traditions has gone. Voters, tourists, and, most especially, lobbyists, are normally given open house to look round, see the usually verbose, thinly-attended and tedious sessions, and sample the famous bean soup in the Senate restaurant. Yesterday, those without passes were turned abruptly away. Senate politics suddenly seemed irrelevant to the very people who normally spend their lives worrying about little else: the dozens of staff who work for each of the 100 senators – researching their subjects, writing their speeches, satisfying their whims – and, most relevantly, opening their letters. More than the senators themselves, perhaps, they pride themselves on their influence and their connections. Yesterday they could do nothing except stand and wait.

The staffers were inside one of the Senate office buildings in a queue that stretched hundreds of yards, waiting hours for a one-minute nasal swab that may prove they have not got anthrax. The testers were operating in a room normally used for senatorial hearings. The line to see them snaked along three corridors of the Hart building, where Mr Daschle is based, through the connecting doors to the adjoining Dirksen building. The wait for those at the back of the queue seemed likely to exceed the disease's incubation period, especially after officials decided to give priority to those most at risk: people who work in the south-east corner of the building near Mr Daschle's offices, or anyone who had visited the mail room.

The south-east corner was cordoned off, with yellow police-tape outside the office belonging to senator Craig Thomas of Wyoming. But, bizarrely, the swab line went straight past the infected area. Several people reckoned they were more likely to get anthrax there than sitting in their normal offices.

'Yesterday it was all downplayed, and business as usual,' said one senator's aide. 'Today we've all come down. Actions speak louder than words,' he said, indicating the long, long line. Then he pointed towards the south-east.

'You might want to get tested yourself.'

Outwardly, it was more good-humoured than, say, the average early morning airport check-in line.

'Hey, it's just like a singles bar,' said someone. 'Have you been tested yet?' But several people sneezed and blew their noses, as people do. One could sense their neighbours shifting away from them. I approached one of the queuers.

'Excuse me, I'm from the *Guardian* of London. Can I just ask...'

'No, you can't. Ask someone else.'

'I'm sorry. Do you mind telling me why you won't...'

He started barking.

'Because I'm in a line waiting to be tested for anthrax. Right?'

The women seemed far more level-headed than the men.

'It's just a precaution, designed to make us all feel better,' said Melanie Snider, who works for senator George Voinovich of Ohio.

Debbie Johnson, on the staff of senator Bob Graham of Florida, was moved into the priority line because she had been in the mail room.

'It's a sensible safeguard, just in case,' she said. 'I'm not worried.'

If she is really unworried, she is in a small minority, whether in the Senate or the most remote corners of the country. The anthrax threat might just be routine craziness, the kind of thing we regard as typically American. But in this jumpy country, nothing right now is routine or typical.

CRIME AND PUNISHMENT

Geoff Thompson, 23 July 2001

ERWIN JAMES

A life inside: Cody's long wait for freedom

Good news this week. (Good news travels fast in prison, though not as fast as bad news. That's because, for many inside, bad news is often better received than good news, just so long as it has arrived addressed to somebody else.) As usual with the big scoops it was Ragby, the governor's tea boy, who was first to report. Raggers is no 'boy' mind you (late forties, grey ponytail, pebble-dashed face), but his eyes and ears are no less keen for it – hence his still unchallenged position as 'camp oracle'.

The other day he was in the governor's office serving herbal tea to a group of Ukrainian penologists over here on a fact-finding mission when the governor's fax machine started humming. The memo that appeared in the in-tray was marked 'confidential' but it might as well have been marked 'for the attention of Mr Ragby'. By the time he reached the exercise yard, he was breathless. 'It's Cody,' he wheezed at the two off-duty kitchen workers who were walking in front of me and Big Rinty. Ragby rested his hands on his thighs and gulped down a couple of lungfuls of air before adding: 'He's got his cat D!'

I suppose we should have rejoiced. This was very good news indeed. After twenty-three years of mainstream prison life Cody had finally been given a squeeze. 'Cat D' meant re-categorisation to 'suitable for open conditions'. In a couple of years he could be walking the streets a free man.

Of course we were pleased for him. Everybody was. But there was a lot of sadness too. For ever since Cody began his life sentence in 1978 he has been protesting his innocence. His last appeal was in the early eighties. It failed due to the 'fresh evidence' he believed would clear him not being presented to the court in time.

He never gave up. Year after year he petitioned the authorities. Then, three years ago, a new independent body charged with investigating alleged miscarriages of justice agreed to look into his case. I wasn't acquainted with Cody then, but by all accounts there was no question of 'cautious optimism'. As far as he was concerned, with an independent investigation under way, he was home and dry. All that remained was the calculation of the compensation.

These things are never quite so straightforward. The independent body began looking into Cody's case in late 1998. After countless communications, notifications and clarifications, it looked like a decision was imminent last autumn. But still the weeks passed with no answer.

Everybody who knew Cody was rooting for him. The delay served only to raise hopes even higher. What a Christmas present this was going to be, everybody thought. Yes. What a Christmas present.

I met Cody's family last summer. It was during a special family visit day and I was helping out in the tea hatch. Cody's son and daughter and his daughter's partner were up. His son and daughter are in their late thirties now and his daughter has daughters of her own. He introduced me when I took them over a tray of tea. As I shook hands with his loved ones, Cody nodded towards his daughter and said to me: 'You know what?' Cradled in his arms was his three-month-old granddaughter. She was sound asleep and looked as safe as the Bank of England. 'She was just fourteen when I came away.' I took my eyes off the baby and smiled awkwardly. 'And now,' he continued, 'she's got a fourteen-year-old daughter of her own.' This was obviously the blooming adolescent sitting next to him with her face pressed hard against his shoulder. I smiled awkwardly again. I wanted to say something encouraging, something hopeful. Instead, I said it was nice to meet them all and left.

Back at the tea bar I wanted to kick myself. Why didn't I tell that son and daughter how well their dad was managing this strange life? And how irrepressible he is, and how generous and funny?

Cody received the decision from the independent review body by special letter on December 18. The investigators, it said, were 'not minded' to refer his case back to the court of appeal. That was it. His Christmas present.

It didn't stop him helping Felix the gambler and the other kitchen lads prepare the food for the new year party held in the visits hall each January for the local old folks though. Felix and Cody volunteered as servers on the night, and me and Big Rinty volunteered too. We had to wear hats labelled 'I'm Rinty' and 'I'm Felix'. Cody wanted to make us all laugh and wrote: 'I'm Cody – and I'm innocent!' We couldn't help but oblige him.

Is Cody innocent? Who knows? But one thing is for sure. Now he's got his cat D, he's going to get another chance.

8 May 2001

JAMIE WILSON

After thirty-five years, Biggs is back in jail

The moment Ronnie Biggs has spent most of the last thirty-five years trying to avoid came just after 9 a.m. yesterday. Minutes after the private jet that had flown the last fugitive of the great train robbery from voluntary exile in Brazil touched down at RAF Northolt, Detective Chief Superintendent John Coles boarded the aircraft.

'Are you Ronald Arthur Biggs?' he asked the frail, sunken-eyed figure. The Scotland Yard detective produced a warrant for being unlawfully at large and with the words 'I am now going to formally arrest you' brought to an end the 13,068 days Biggs had spent on the run.

Within hours, the man who was for years Britain's most-wanted criminal was back behind bars more than three decades after he escaped from Wandsworth jail, where he had served fifteen months of a thirty-year sentence for his part in the heist of the century.

From Northolt, Biggs, seventy-one, and debilitated by three strokes, was taken to Chiswick police station, where a doctor declared him fit to appear before a district judge at West London magistrates court. After an eight-minute hearing, the fugitive was sent to the high-security confines of Belmarsh prison in south-east London, to resume his sentence.

The shuffling figure clutching a walking stick who made his way into the silent courtroom under the stare of the massed ranks of the press and court staff appeared a shadow of the man who had thumbed his nose at British justice as he lived out a playboy lifestyle on the beaches of Rio de Janeiro.

The gaunt figure was only able to respond to questions from the clerk of the court with a grunt, and a police doctor repeatedly passed him handkerchiefs so that he could wipe away the saliva dribbling down his chin. Biggs confirmed his name and date of birth before summoning enough energy to puff out his chest when asked if he was the man sentenced at Buckingham assizes on 16 April 1964 to twenty-five years imprisonment for conspiracy to stop mail and to thirty years for robbery with aggravation.

'I'm satisfied that you are the person named in the warrant and have been unlawfully at large,' district judge Tim Workman said. 'The law requires me to return you to prison, which I will now do.'

With that, Biggs, his white hair combed loosely over his head, shuffled from the dock to be led down the stairs and through a back entrance of the court where he was put into a waiting Securicor prison van and driven away.

His legal team immediately announced that he would be seeking a hearing before the court of appeal against his outstanding sentence.

'All he seeks is a fair and balanced hearing at which all relevant issues can be addressed,' said Jane Wearing, of Leftley Mallett solicitors.

'Mr Biggs is not in good health. The authorities responsible for his welfare are aware of this and he will receive proper medical attention as soon as possible.'

Biggs spent the last of his £147,000 share of the 1963 train robbery long ago and it was his failing health that led him to turn to the *Sun* to orchestrate his journey home.

The exercise has been a massive coup for the paper, although the press complaints commission yesterday said that it will conduct an investigation into the affair, which, it claimed, raised a number of issues under the newspaper code of practice relating to payments to convicted criminals. Biggs's son Michael is reported to have received £20,000 in 'expenses' with the mastermind of the great train robbery, Bruce Reynolds, and his son, Nick, getting £12,000 each.

A spokesman for the *Sun* said the PCC code was taken fully into account before it decided to fly Biggs home 'at no cost to the British taxpayer'.

20 July 2001

SIMON HOGGART

The judge's every word dripped with loathing and contempt

In the end it happened with manic suddenness.

After the jury had spent four days trawling through mountains of files, papers and diaries, there was a shout of 'verdict' and it seemed that everyone in the Old Bailey was running into Court No. 8, jamming the door, scrambling for the seats, pushing QCs aside.

Jeffrey Archer was almost the last to arrive. He stood in the dock staring glumly and fixedly ahead, as he had for the previous thirty-five days. Except this time there were two officers to guard him. He was grinding his teeth, a muscle in his cheek flexed rhythmically as he waited. His wife Mary sat below, to his right, legs together, hands upon her knees. She was in black, with a silver crucifix around her neck. For the first time, her eyes were hooded. Her younger son, William, seemed on the brink of tears.

By this time they must have known. Juries aren't told to find a majority verdict, then come back less than an hour later in order to acquit.

The British legal system, like the army, provides hours of tedium interspersed with moments of high drama and terror.

We waited for the judge and then – it seemed like for ever – for the jury to file in. Meanwhile, squads of barristers moved around, smiling and joking. For them this was just another day at the office, and of course they cannot lose; the only fight they face now is to decide who pays their massive fees.

But we were certain of the verdict as soon as the jury arrived. While Archer glowered at them, not one of them even glanced towards him. A basilisk could kill you by looking at you; juries work on the opposite principle.

The foreman, a young black man, was asked by the clerk, a young black woman (Lord Archer can console himself that this has been an ethnically diverse hearing) for a one-word verdict.

A pause, and the word 'guilty' dropped like a boulder into a duck pond. Some young women in the public gallery had time to yell an ecstatic 'Ye...!' before being silenced. Archer didn't flinch.

He did a moment later when the foreman cleared Ted Francis, the man he believes betrayed him. He jerked as if he had been shot, and his lips pushed forward in what looked like unbelieving anger.

Then the other verdicts, including one acquittal out of five. His expression had been recomposed in an instant and it didn't change again. Then the sentence and a speech from the judge which surely smashed into him as hard as the prison term. It must have been like being hosed down with sewage.

Every word dripped with loathing and contempt: 'As serious an offence of perjury as I have experience of, and as serious as I have been able to find in the books'.

The judge spoke of the way he had preyed upon the weak and vulnerable to concoct his alibis; the way he had hurried along the original libel trial in order to tell his lies and spin his fabrications.

It was a short speech, but lethal. Mr Justice Potts was about to take away his liberty, but first he wanted to strip off what shreds were left of his reputation.

He said he took 'no pleasure' in sentencing him, though he certainly took a deep draught of satisfaction.

'Lord Archer, will you now stand down, please,' he said in a somewhat gentler voice – though these things are comparative – and for the first time the convict left the court by the green padded door that leads to the cells. 'Thank you,' he said to the guard who opened the door, and received what might have been a nod of acknowledgement, but which looked like a small bow, of the type only fitting for a man who is still a peer of the realm.

So he is off to jail, to learn if vintage Krug can be smuggled in as easily as drugs. For decades now Jeffrey Archer has been dancing on the rim of the volcano; now he has fallen in.

We wait to see how long it will be before his fingers can be seen desperately scratching their way back up. And of course the two years he is likely to serve are really just another chapter in the long and thrilling *roman-fleuve* that is his life.

It may, however, be a long time before he returns, for there is much about his business affairs which has not yet appeared, and now he has lost the protection of the courts. He has become, in the old sense, an outlaw.

The cliché about Archer is that he believed the truth to be infinitely flexible, that the facts meant whatever you could get away with. But the opposite was really the case. He always dealt in fiction; it was his stock in trade, his equivalent of the pianist's fingers.

When he was bankrupt, he turned to fiction, and it made him rich. When his self-esteem faltered, he invented mini-fictions (such as the time he claimed to be talking to the prime minister on the phone while John Major was actually on live TV).

When his reputation came under a terrible threat, he created more fictions, and it was those that sent him to jail yesterday.

5 September 2001

EMMA BROCKES

Death of a teenager

Bugsy was first through the door, bloodstained and panting. It was a Sunday afternoon in July, when the only thing to do on the Casterbridge estate was to sit out the heat until sunset.

From the 13th floor, north London looked like a canopy of green pierced by steeples. 'St John's Wood,' residents would say, cocking a chin at the view as if at a particularly hard joke enacted on them by higher authorities.

To Ivan Cardona, slumped Buddha-like on the sofa, it looked as if Bugsy, a Staffordshire bull-terrier, had been fighting with another dog. Of the two Cardona brothers, 21-year-old Ivan was widely reckoned to be the troublemaker. Ione was soft, holding open doors for mothers with pushchairs, running errands for shopkeepers, folding his lanky frame into knots when addressed by an adult. The dog, people sniggered, was more likely to get into trouble than Ione was. But when the fifteen-year-old rolled into the flat that afternoon, there was blood on him too.

'I said: "What happened?"' says Ivan. 'He said: "I fell down the stairs." I said:

"Don't give me that. What happened?" He said nothing happened. I said: "Who is it?" He said: "That kid. Devon."' Ivan ran from the flat, plunged thirteen flights down and attached himself to the fringes of a gathering crowd.

Whatever had happened that afternoon, he was confident he could talk his brother's way out of it. Within minutes of reaching the street, however, it became clear the time for diplomacy had passed. 'Someone pointed me out to the police as Ione's brother,' says Ivan. 'I couldn't lie. I took them back to the flat.'

As Ione was taken to Kentish Town police station, Suzan Allen, working at a newsagents in south London, received a phone call informing her that her eighteen-year-old son Devon had been taken to hospital, stabbed twice in the heart. There was a pain in her chest she could not account for. A religious woman, she thought it might be coming from Devon. 'It was GBH at first,' says Ivan. 'Then, late that night, the kid died and the police said: "We're calling in the murder squad."'

Devon Allen died a year ago. It is five months since Ione (pronounced 'Yonny') Cardona was sentenced to six years detention for his manslaughter. In many ways, it was an unremarkable case. Last year in London 170 people were murdered and 6,000 were attacked with an offensive weapon. The Metropolitan police confiscated knives, guns and assorted weapons from a further 5,000, almost a third of them people under eighteen. So when Devon Allen was stabbed to death outside a laundrette in Swiss Cottage, it scarcely rated a mention in the press.

Unlike Damilola Taylor, Devon Allen was of an age when being stabbed to death did not particularly distinguish him.

There was, however, one aspect of the case that stood out. After his arrest, Ione put in a claim of self-defence and said he had been maliciously provoked. It was the manner of this provocation that startled the police. In mitigation, the teenager told them: 'I saw my work had been lined through. I took it as an insult because it dented my pride.' The 'work' he referred to was graffiti.

The first, and possibly biggest, problem this conferred on the authorities was a conceptual one. If Devon had died over graffiti, then graffiti signified a far deeper estrangement in its young practitioners than had previously been thought.

'Two young lives have been ruined over the most trivial of causes,' said Detective Inspector Martin Ford, the investigating officer. He struggled with Ione's line of defence. 'It was a dispute that would usually end with no more than a black eye.'

What had happened, the police wondered, to promote the status of graffiti on the estate from an idle recreation into something more fundamental? To persuade Ione that the boy who obliterated his graffiti – or tag – obliterated more or less everything of value about him?

Residents of the Casterbridge estate had a good idea. Over the last five years, something in the alchemy of the place had changed. It had never been an easy spot to grow up in, one of three deprived estates nestling among some of London's wealthiest neighbourhoods. To the east are the luxury flats of Swiss Cottage, St John's Wood is to the south and Hampstead, where 10 per cent of households have an income of more than £100,000 a year, is to the north. On the Casterbridge estate, more than half the families are on housing benefit. Depending on their ages, their children walk to school past a Ferrari dealership, the Saatchi gallery or a shop selling grand pianos.

This is where Ione was born, the second son of Colombian immigrants. When he was twelve, Devon moved in two blocks away. The boys were similar in temperament, with strict parents and an inclination for quietness. They were nice boys, polite to their elders. Residents of the estate collapsed at the news of what happened to them and said: 'Responsibility lies with all of us.'

Us, in this case, had a large constituency, reaching back to the mid-sixties and the architects of two nineteen-storey tower blocks connected by a footbridge. Of the three estates in Swiss Cottage, the Casterbridge has the meanest accommodation and is designed, the only high rise, on social housing principles now widely discredited. 'The flats only have two bedrooms, so siblings have to share,' says Kristyan Robinson, a member of the management committee. 'It is not ideal for a family with two big, adolescent boys. There is nowhere for their energy to go.'

This did not matter much when Ione was little. His parents worked long hours as cleaners and brought him up to be grateful for what he had. 'We kept ourselves to ourselves,' says Olga Cardona, Ione's mother. 'We are a good family, good manners. We did not interfere with other people. If we had known Ione was carrying a knife, Jesus to God we would have killed him. His father would have killed him.'

When Ione was small, he went on a family holiday to New York. The graffiti there enthralled him. 'When we got back, he'd pester me to bring him pens from school,' says Ivan. 'He loved drawing.' The one GCSE Ione passed was in art.

In court, his defence team characterised him as a boy of 'exceptionally low intelligence', barely conscious of his own actions, but this is not an image his family cares to recognise. Ione, they say, was ambitious. His favourite catchphrase was 'speculate to accumulate', and he would run around repeating it, to his brother's amusement, vowing one day to be rich. One Halloween, Ione dressed up as a ghoul and hit the pubs at closing time, correctly anticipating that the punters would give more generously if they were drunk. He was right: one erroneously gave him a £50 note instead of a fiver.

As he got older, however, the limitations of the Casterbridge estate became harder to ignore. The place was disintegrating. The youth club shut, the basketball nets fell into disrepair and were dismantled, boys ranged about the estates, feared and ignored. In response, the council offered to repaint the stairwells and put up a trellis on some grass behind the tower.

In 1995, as Ione was entering his teens, his brother's headmaster, Philip Lawrence, was stabbed to death outside the gates of his own school, St George's in Maida Vale. The culprits were teenage gang members. A year later Ione started secondary school. Less well built than his brother, he resolved on a policy of unobtrusiveness. 'You wouldn't have noticed him,' says George Benham, headmaster of Cardinal Hinsley high school. 'He rarely led. He was self-effacing. He would tag on and follow. He had a very small personality. He was an underachiever, but he was never in serious trouble at school.'

'Ione was a quiet boy,' says a shop owner on the estate. 'They said in court that he was slow, but he wasn't slow. He was an average kid. Maybe he didn't do so well at school, but there are other kinds of intelligence. If I was on my own on the till, I would send him out to buy me chips and one for himself. He was trustworthy.'

'I thought I'd be the first one to get into serious trouble,' says Ivan, who now works as a security guard. 'Everyone did. When Ione was arrested, the first thing people said was: "Don't you mean Ivan?"' But Ivan had enjoyed certain privileges that his brother had not. When the older boy was a teenager, most of the families on the estate knew each other. There was no shortage of supervision.

'About four years ago, a lot of the old families moved out,' says Ivan. 'The crackheads moved in. Now kids stand in the foyer, urinating on the floor, tagging and spitting. I'll say to them – "fuck off outside, you're making a mess". And they'll say: "Ivan, where is there to go? There's nothing to do."' The less attention they got, the more the boys misbehaved; the more they misbehaved, the less they were tolerated.

'It's like, people see you coming and they cross the street,' says Lee, an eighteen-year-old gang member from the Hilgrove crew, scuffing his trainers and assuming a hurt, bent-headed pose. 'You walk around feeling self-conscious.' But you do trash the place with graffiti? Lee shrugs. 'We don't mean anything by it. It's just something to do with your mates. You tag up a wall and it's like – "here I am".'

Two blocks away, Devon was pursuing a very different life. A tall boy, slim and self-assured, he was born in Trinidad, the fourth of six children to a mother whose chief ambition was to bring her family to Britain. Too late for the older children, Suzan Allen thought if she could get Devon and his brother Akil into the country, they might enjoy a better start in life. In 1997 when he was fifteen, Devon moved to London, to the Hilgrove estate in Swiss Cottage. His mother thought it a more suitable environment for a studious teenager than the £25-a-week room she rented in Brixton on cleaner's wages. Devon was billeted with his Uncle Brian in a ground floor flat.

By the standards of the area, the Hilgrove is a superior estate. It went up in the postwar flush of the fifties, a low-rise complex interspersed with green spaces. 'It was quite lah-di-da,' says Buddy Whitman, housing manager for the Casterbridge estate and a former caretaker at the Hilgrove estate. 'It always had a set-apart feel. There was a selective renting policy – the tenants used to be older, working-class Jewish people, a cut above the Irish on the Camden estates. That feeling of superiority washed over to the younger generation, which is more ethnically mixed. There's a tension between the white, semi-affluent older residents and the younger of mixed lineage. The older people were grounded in work; the younger have been brought up in the context of twenty-five years of unemployment.'

In the late nineties, a half-hearted gang culture grew up around the Casterbridge estate, the Hilgrove and a third local estate, the Rowley Way. 'Gang rather overstates it,' says Lee Dempster, an officer on the investigating team. 'There were only three people in one and four in another. They called themselves the Rowley Way crew and the Hilgrove crew.' Ione was part of the former; he went around with Bugsy, who looked mean but was, say the neighbours, as soppy as hell.

Devon was part of the latter. Their main recreation was graffiti and in 1999, a phoney war broke out, fought via the medium of competitive tagging. Ione and Devon's graffiti pseudonyms were, respectively, Blast and Mr Reach and they surfaced as far afield as Camden, two miles away.

One in particular stands out: in round-handed script, 'Mr Reach', sprayed on a wall on the Rowley Way estate. A line of red paint has been drawn through it and the paint has run, collecting in stalks and baubles down the brickwork. In graffiti parlance, Mr Reach has been lined out and its author insulted.

To most residents of the estate, the graffiti was intimidating – a set of mindless hieroglyphics that made them feel uneasy. But to a few perceptive adults, the tagging looked curiously innocent. It didn't seek to shock. There were no swear words, unless coyly disguised in acronym, like FTS ('Fuck the System'). It had more to do with recognition than rebellion: most of the tags eschewed daredevil placements on trains and the top of tower blocks, to appear at eye level. The point, it seemed, was to get them seen. Ione, cramped at home, invisible at school, amplified his presence by scrawling his name all over north London. 'We don't do it on the posh houses, because they paint over them right away,' says Dean, fourteen, a former member of the Rowley Way crew. 'If you tag on the council, it stays up for months.' When Devon lined-out Ione's tag, the insult remained on show to mock him each time he passed. It is still there now.

More often than not, Devon was not around to be evened with. With his mother living in south London, he cut a marginal figure on the estates. Graffiti was a minor distraction, the one self-indulgence of a life on track. 'In Trinidad, you have opportunities if you have money,' says Suzan Allen. 'It's like that. I had my children, one, two, three. Then I came to Britain so the fourth and fifth could have a chance.' Devon seized it with both hands: within a year of joining Quintin Kynaston secondary school, he was captain of the running team, had higher education in sight and was holding down a part-time job washing dishes in a restaurant in Hampstead.

'My aims for the future are to go on to study A-levels in maths, sciences and computing,' he wrote in a personal statement commissioned by the school. 'After that I hope to go to university to do more maths and business studies and computing course.' At the time of his death, he had half-completed an IT course at South Thames College.

'He was a bright lad,' says John Greaves, Devon's tutor. 'He was always keen to complete his assignments – working quietly but purposefully. He was a committed and enthusiastic student with a promising future ahead of him.'

'He had never used a computer before,' says Mrs Allen proudly. 'He came over here and he just took off.'

On the morning of his death, Devon visited his mother in Brixton to give her £50 saved from his washing-up job. He asked her to send it to his siblings in Trinidad. Returning home, he ran into Ione outside an arcade of shops on the Rowley Way estate. Ione was arguing with another boy. His attention shifted to Devon, with whom he had a dispute over graffiti. The two began arguing and

Devon knocked Ione to the ground. Ione recovered and stabbed him twice with a vegetable knife. It penetrated 8.5cm into Devon's heart. Ione ran to the flat. Devon dragged himself to a phone box and called for help before collapsing.

Both boys' mothers maintain their sons acted in self-defence. Mrs Allen will not countenance that Devon was involved in graffiti. He died, she says, protecting the other boy from attack. Mrs Cardona says: 'God give us strength to get over this. It breaks our hearts.' Of Devon, she says: 'That poor, poor boy. We feel very sorry for the other family. But it was a fight. It could just as easily have been Ione who died.'

Passing sentence, Judge Ann Goddard told Ione: 'Devon Allen lost [his life] because you took a knife out with you. I do not accept it was just to scare him. You wanted to fight.'

Ivan Cardona says: 'You can't take someone's life away and not to be punished. There are consequences. You have to live with that and he knows it.'

'I am strong,' says Suzan Allen, 'because I know Devon was a good boy. I don't hate Ione. I want him to feel the love that Devon had. I love Ione.' She looks for things to be grateful for. 'Devon died the week that little girl Sarah Payne went missing. I thought, at least I knew, at least I didn't have to wait while they found a sock here, a sock there.'

Devon's friends shuffle at the mention of him and look embarrassed. 'That is over, man,' they say angrily. 'Devon is over.' They exude a sense of collective guilt. 'Why didn't you walk away when you saw someone you didn't like?' the police asked Ione. He replied that he did not want the other boys to think he was scared.

To members of the management committee, the onus is now on the local authorities to address the lack of space, physical and cultural, for youth on the estates.

There are bureaucratic problems to resolve. The estates sit on the borders of three councils, Westminster, Camden and Brent. 'There are separate authorities for police, education, health,' says Father Andrew Cain of St Mary's parish church. 'No one ever gets a full picture of what is going on.'

'There's a huge amount of devolved feeling,' says Buddy Whitman. 'It makes it easy for people to defer responsibility. They'll say, it's not our problem, it's the kids on Rowley Way. Unfortunately, while the authorities observe boundaries, the kids don't.' Provision of resources is difficult. A youth club built on the Hilgrove estate would be expected to cater for teenagers two streets away on the Casterbridge. But there is no guarantee they would be welcome.

And so things go on as before. Appalled by the crime, older residents give teenagers an even wider berth than they used to. Youth initiatives fail for want of adult volunteers to run them. The boys retreat further into sullen machismo. 'The reaction of the adults is, get these kids off our estates,' says Father Andrew. 'But they live on the estates. The authorities have to understand that youth provision is no longer about having a tatty room with a table tennis kit. They need to feel they are being invested in, that they have something to feel proud of.'

'They haven't been allowed to grieve or be angry or anything,' says Kristyan Robinson. 'The only way they can express themselves is through these crappy tags.'

There have, however, been small indications of change. After Devon's death, five or six boys went to the church, lit a candle and said a prayer. And in the last six months an anti-vandalism forum has been set up, a well-meaning body that solicits opinions from the boys on how to make the place better.

'A lot of them just want to be listened to,' says Mike Stuart, chairman. Their requests are touchingly modest: some rubbish bins on the estate would be nice, they say, and somewhere to play football. Since the forum's inauguration, the level of graffiti has been marginally reduced.

Suzan Allen gets on with it. She quit her job at the newsagents after the customers, thinking themselves kind, kept reminding her of what a nice boy Devon had been. 'I have to keep living for my other children, although it is sometimes hard. When I have a bad day, I stand in the middle of my room and cry.' She wants to scatter her son's ashes in Trinidad. On returning to Britain, she would like to get out of London for a while and has thought, whimsically, of heading south to Devon. 'It sounds like a good place, doesn't it?'

Meanwhile, the Cardona family, frightened of reprisals, have moved from the estate.

After Devon's death, the gang system broke down and boys from the two sides hang out together now, wreaking petty havoc. 'It's like being dissatisfied with something and making it worse rather than better,' says Buddy Whitman. 'From the perspective of a comfortable background, it's easy to say: "By messing up the estate, it's only yourselves you are hurting." But they are not in a position to understand.'

Stuck for alternatives, they tag and spit and smoke dope. If you stand in the foyer of the Casterbridge estate, you can hear them clambering on the balcony above. 'You monkey brain!' one yells. 'What did you do that for? What did you do that for?' Gobs of spit rain down. The air smells sweet. Someone on the estate is cooking bacon.

NO CONTEST

Steve Bell, 16 May 2001

16 May 2001

EWEN MAcASKILL

To the north, to grease palms

Tony Blair, almost a week into the election campaign, finally made contact with the British public yesterday. It was a brief and messy encounter, lasting four and a quarter minutes.

He walked five shop lengths down Bradford Road, Brighouse, West Yorkshire, shook a few hands, and bought a bag of fish and chips in the Happy Haddock. He had only one conversation, with the owner of the fish and chip shop. A Labour official said the walkabout had been arranged after Mr Blair read criticism that he preferred meetings with Labour supporters to chance encounters in the street.

Labour stress that Mr Blair is only following the advice of security officers, even though predecessors Margaret Thatcher and John Major took to the streets, often with noisy results. The Conservatives found out about the walkabout in advance and party members in Brighouse duly demonstrated outside Labour's campaign headquarters. After calling at the HQ, Mr Blair tried to shake hands with people, but was largely unable to because of the pack around him.

Almost carried by the scrum into the Happy Haddock, he checked the menu: Spam fritters 50p, chip butty £1.10. He went for two haddock and chips from owner Teresa D'Arcy. Mr Blair dug out a £20 note but she refused to take it. Mrs D'Arcy said Mr Blair was 'very nice' but she was not interested in politics: 'I am nothing. I do not vote.'

The PM, who began eating his chips on his way out of the shop, was stopped by someone wanting to shake his hand. He wiped the vinegar and salt onto his trousers and obliged, before making his way back to the bus. He was away from Brighouse but not away from the criticism, which will persist until he goes on proper walkabouts and holds real question-and-answer sessions.

22 May 2001

SIMON HOGGART

This is Planet Vaz, but no sign of the Vaz of Vaz

In the rest of Britain, an election is taking place. But not, apparently, in Leicester East. For this is Planet Vaz. Here we find no election, no campaign, no posters at all, except in Vaz's window. The people who live on Planet Vaz have no need to be told why they should vote for their leader. For he is the Vaz of Vaz. His wisdom is unquestioned, for the simple reason that he is never there to be questioned. Why should he be? His people know his manifold virtues. If, unaccountably, they do not, the world's plenipotentiaries will tell them. In the latest publication hymning the praises of Vaz, Robin Cook writes: 'He has been an astounding success as a minister...he has unparalleled knowledge...'

Other leaflets show pictures of the great one with his humblest citizens, visiting old people's homes, learning about their puny traffic problems. How fortunate they are, for normally the Vaz meets only the world's wealthiest and most celebrated people. 'Keith Vaz met the world entertainer Michael Jackson and presented him with a gift...Keith told Michael he has quite a few of his records.' How fitting that two controversial recluses should have so much in common!

Some colleagues and I tried to meet him. (Keith Vaz, that is: it would probably have been easier to find Michael Jackson.) We started at the Labour party offices. This is Fortress Vaz. Most such places are full of bustle and jollity. This is locked and sealed and silent. I rang the entryphone and a suspicious voice asked my business and phone number. They promised to call back. No young woman freshly seduced by a philandering rake was ever more sceptical about being phoned again.

A Mr Keith Bennett, who turns out to be the agent of Vaz, came out. 'We will make a decision whether you can see him or not,' he told us. The Vaz whereabouts were 'a confidential matter'. He was not, strictly speaking, on the stump – 'but if he comes across a voter he might try to seek his support'. Since we didn't meet a single voter who had set eyes on the great one, this didn't seem likely.

We rang his previous agent, John Thomas, who lost the job a few days ago, for no reason yet satisfactorily explained. Mr Thomas refused to say. No, he wasn't campaigning. 'I'm returfing my lawn.' Ah, the famous electoral returfing officer.

Off to a drop-in centre which he was rumoured to visit. They said he 'might' be in later this week. We called on a Labour councillor who had fallen foul of Vaz. He begged us not to print his name. Bewilderingly, this man – of Asian origin himself – did not share Robin Cook's view of Vaz's greatness. 'We used to have a fantastic constituency Labour party here. You'd get 140, 150 people at meetings. Now it's about half a dozen. People have been hounded, harassed and thrown out of the party.'

Out to the large home owned by the great one's mother. Four cars are parked in the drive but evidently no one is in. Mrs Vaz is disabled herself, but happily has just been able to take on the onerous task of secretary to her son's constituency party, giving her a crucial behind-the-scenes role in vital votes. Back at the constituency office a couple of Tories, including the candidate John Mugglestone, had gathered to protest. No one left and nobody came. Two policemen stopped. 'We want to report a missing person,' we told them. They smiled wanly.

In Melton Road, every business is Asian and so are 99 per cent of the people. None had seen Vaz. We called at his favourite haunts – the Friends Tandoori, the Safari Club, the Belgrave Centre. No sign of him, nor of anyone who had ever met him. The Vaz of Vaz has a majority of 18,000. He will win next month. But as one of his enemies whispered: 'If Martin Bell was standing here, he'd walk in.'

1 June 2001

JAMES FENTON

Whose idea was this?

On a wet Wednesday morning, in a country lane not far from Glasgow, I stood waiting for the taxi that would take me away from the Tory campaign. A few hundred yards behind me, William Hague was entering the phase called: Carry On As If Nothing Has Happened. He was gazing into the pit of history.

A hundred yards or so to my left was the site of an incident that will intrigue historians for ever. For there at Floors Farm, sixty years ago (on 10 May 1941), Hitler's deputy Rudolf Hess parachuted out of a borrowed Messerschmitt and asked, on landing, to be taken to meet his acquaintance the Duke of Hamilton. It was one of those schemes that seemed like a good idea at the time, however much it has puzzled historians since. And that is as far as I shall take the analogy.

Life tosses these analogies in our direction, and we must make of them what we will. Life tosses us these ideas which seem so good at the time, and which we later look back on aghast. Did I really jump out of the Messerschmitt? says Hess. Did we really, says the Conservative party, choose William Hague as our leader?

And Hague, or a bit of Hague – a bit of Hague that is as yet unavailable for interview – asks himself: did I really allow my name to go forward as the fall guy? Did I really agree in 1997, when I had nothing but modest success behind me, nothing but a brief record of overpromotion, did I really agree to lead the wounded Tory party back into the face of the enemy guns? Did nobody warn me?

And the record shows that Hague was indeed warned. His illuminating biographer, Jo-Anne Nadler, tells us as early as page nine of *William Hague in His Own Right* (Politico's Publishing, £17.99) that an Oxford chum, Guy Hands, a 'close friend and political ally', told Hague to forget about the leadership for at least five years, because he had some real living to do first before he could qualify for the role. Hague should enjoy some time with his new fiancée. Or, as the 'blunt but persuasive' message actually put it, Hands advised him: 'Fuck your brains out for the next few years.' As Nadler comments: 'It must have seemed an attractive option...'

Well, yes, indeed it must. He was offered the post of running mate to Michael Howard. He could have spent the last four years in bed (his mother, less bluntly, gave him the same advice), and emerged to view the ensuing debacle. He could have slept this one out. But who, in his position, could have resisted the appeal to his vanity, in whatever terms it was couched? 'There is a tide in the affairs of men,/Which taken at the flood leads on to fortune.' What does it mean, this boating analogy? Few people ask themselves, but few can resist the insinuation of the lines. 'Once to every man and nation/Comes the moment to decide.' Once...and only once. And so Hague stabbed Howard in the back, and in due course received his reward, which was to discover that people didn't think he was quite normal, and therefore couldn't really be pressed into voting for him.

What was meant by 'not quite normal' has never been easy to define. But it's as if Hague keeps jumping up on stage and saying: 'Look at me, I'm normal.' And the audience responds with one voice: 'Oh no you're not!' And he says: 'Oh yes I am!' And this goes on for some time, and can on a good day be quite entertaining, but nobody's mind is changed at the end of it.

This theme of normality is introduced the moment Hague and his wife appear at the venue, because it's a case of 'this is normal me' and 'this is my normal wife' and we're married and not ashamed of it, because we're in favour of marriage even if nobody else is. And one begins to wonder: who are all these people who are against marriage, and why do we need so much reassurance about Hague's own position?

He has a joke, which of course he repeats from place to place, and he sometimes tells it quite well. It's about tax. He says the only people who would have benefited under Labour are those who don't smoke, don't drink, don't have a car and don't want to get married. And the only people he knows like that are in the cabinet.

He doesn't have to push the last line very hard for people to get the point that there are gay ministers, and I ought to add that it is not maliciously done. It is really quite humorous. And it leads to a point about normal people (he calls them real people) which is nothing to do with sexuality – it is to do with normal economic circumstances. But the point is that Hague is the last person to be saying that this or that politician is not normal. It creates a dissonance.

It is exactly the mistake that John Redwood's supporters, during the Tory leadership campaign, made when they mocked Hague's entourage as 'the bachelor boys' – that is, perhaps not entirely conventional in their sexuality, not normal. Redwood may have possessed many virtues at the time, but normality was not considered his strong suit. Hague is one of those people of whom it has become the practice to write: 'He's not queer.' Such people do not escape from this category by pointing out the eccentricities of others.

John Major, in his strange speech in Brighton, tried to explain to the audience that Hague was not a creature of spin, that he told the truth as he saw it and was not some kind of manufactured or synthetic object. In the course of the emphasis on Hague's humanity, Major said something that puzzled me, and will no doubt be the only phrase from the campaign to stick in my mind. 'He' – that is Hague – 'can't weep a tear from either eye, on cue and straight to camera.'

The implication seemed to be that there was somebody else who did indeed possess this gift of weeping from either eye – weeping first with the left, then with the right. Some people thought that perhaps here we had a reference to Hague's inability to come up with an impressive tribute to Princess Diana on her death. But that would seem (and perhaps it was) like reminding people of a reasonable criticism of Hague on the pretext of answering it. The great political weeper was a Conservative: Harold Macmillan. The catch-phrase in *Private Eye* for a politician working up insincere emotion – 'takes out onion' – was devised to describe Macmillan.

The experts who commend Hague's political acumen, a specialised group, are hard put to explain a particular mistake this astucious populist has been making, *vis-à-vis* the populace. This is the central mistake of the campaign. Everybody knows that the people, when consulted, have always been against the euro. If we ask ourselves how Labour is going to achieve a yes vote when the question is eventually put, the answer is far from obvious.

When Charles Kennedy, the Lib Dem leader, has his talks with the prime minister, this is a question that often comes up. Kennedy is given the impression that Tony Blair believes that as soon as he steps out into Downing Street the terms of the equation will somehow have been changed. As soon as the prestigious leader is ready, the people will start to think differently about the single currency.

Maybe this is so. But the people who most want the yes vote to win are very far from convinced that it is so, and for a long time they have been nagging at the government, essentially to get them to start the campaign. Hague, by contrast, has been saying to the people: by the time you get to vote in the referendum, it will be too late. The pound will be lost.

But this at once creates a dissonance. A referendum, after all, is only a formalised opinion poll. Why should the public be unable to vote in a referendum the way they have voted in every opinion poll to date? For the point to have been worth making, there would have to have been some very convincing explanation of the impediment, the trick that would be played.

Hague was going around until Wednesday saying that the government would choose the timing of a referendum. But that is what the government themselves have been saying for years that they will do. Of course they will choose the timing. Then he said that the financing of the campaign would be rigged, and that the question would be slanted or loaded in such a way as to affect the outcome.

Immediately, both allies and opponents began to see a danger that, if Hague insisted that the present election was the referendum, Labour could turn around and say: well, you had the referendum and you lost it. The worse fault seemed to me to be going around the country and saying to the people: although you may be under the illusion that you will vote no in the referendum, you are mistaken. When you emerge from the polling booth, you will find you have been gulled into voting yes.

Only one crucial polling issue has been continually in the Tories' favour: the question of the European currency. And this is the poll that Hague seeks to undermine. Would it not have been better for him to say: whatever the outcome of this election, we have no doubt that a majority of the people of this country will vote to save the pound? If that was what he was saying, then a majority of listeners would believe that what he was saying was true.

By Tuesday, everyone was asking what the form of the question could be that would so mislead the people. Michael Portillo, on the *Today* programme, seemed to be arguing that any form of question that did not mention the pound would be slanted or somehow unsatisfactory. Robin Cook's simple 'Do you want to join the euro? Yes or No' would be, by that criterion, a deceitful question. But if the Tories fear this question, then they fear the referendum itself.

I asked among the Tories in the marketplace at Kingston-upon-Thames, and was told that it was inevitable that Labour would put the question to a focus group. As soon as the question was focus-grouped, you could be sure that the outcome was being massaged. But nothing I heard on the campaign trail explained to me how massage could turn to cheating, how a rigged referendum could be achieved.

And while I was asking these questions, it soon became plain, from interviews conducted elsewhere in the country, that the Tory leadership had crumpled, and that the line could not be held. It was no longer a question of ten, nine, eight days to save the pound. There might well be another chance to do so, and it might well be in the referendum.

So what was the point of hopping around the country, to Blackpool, to Llandudno, Kingston and Brighton, to say something one day and take it back the next? What was the point of going all the way to a fifth-division rugby club in rain-drenched Glasgow, and telling the people (for this was by now the implication of Hague's change of tack) that we were in the Last Chance But One Saloon? What was the point of standing on the promenade at Llandudno and hearing from Hague that the cost of conversion to the euro was to be £36bn, only to get back on the bus and see Francis Maude on television clearly admitting that there might be no basis at all for these figures?

When Hague's disposition was still sunny, I thought that his chief problem lay in the dissonance between that sunniness of disposition and the solemnity of his message: if things were so bad, why did he look so chipper? When he began to look a bit down in the dumps, I thought he began to look a bit more normal, a bit more real. I can't say I felt sorry for him, although I can't say I wish him ill either. But it was his idea, four years ago, to climb into the Messerschmitt. And now he has jumped. Now he is where he wanted to be.

4 June 2001

OLIVER BURKEMAN

Shaun through the looking glass

They have a saying in St Helens, repeated throughout the labyrinthine shopping malls of the town centre with a mixture of resignation and self-mockery: 'You could put my dog up for Labour round here and it would get in.' They didn't get a dog, they got Shaun Woodward – but he has been busy trying to make up for that in the last few weeks, trotting between the tight-packed, redbrick terraces of the St Helens South constituency like an eager-to-please puppy demanding to be loved. Or that's what his campaign aides say: actual sightings have been rare. He has, notoriously, been one of the Invisible Men of the election campaign, so it comes as a surprise when he returns a phone call to say he will briefly be adopting physical form in the bar of his hotel, the Raven Lodge, in five minutes' time.

'No photos of me smoking,' he says, as soon as we arrive. He is looking tired, impatient, cross and sullen. 'I'm really enjoying it,' he says, gloomily. 'I'm really enjoying it – the hard work of going out and meeting people.' Nobody, he insists, is asking him about his domestic servants or his marriage to millionairess Camilla Sainsbury except the 'Tory press', a designation that appears to include the *Guardian*.

'People come here with a story mapped out in their heads. But they didn't look at the work Camilla's family is doing in deprived areas, or that my dad started life as a porter, that my mum started life as a barmaid, that my dad left school at fourteen without qualifications.' The way he tells it, everything about him and his campaign is a mirror image of the way it has been portrayed. For example: Labour activists have not been refusing to campaign for him – he has had '70 to 80 people' volunteering to hit the streets, while the outgoing MP, Gerry Bermingham, could only muster 'about four'.

Rage never seems far beneath the surface but it is the suggestion that some in St Helens may be voting Labour with a heavy heart on Thursday that causes him to explode. That, he says, is another invention of the media, who have portrayed St Helens as a hell-hole inhabited by stupid people programmed to vote Labour. (In 1997, Bermingham won a majority of 23,739 – well over the total votes for all the other parties put together.)

'The national press has come here and painted this place in a way which is grotesque,' says Woodward. 'They've come here with their cynicism in buckets, and people here on the ground don't like it.' He has a point. The town has come in for a battering from parts of the national media, which have portrayed it, in the words of the local weekly the *St Helens Star*, as being 'full of flat caps, whippets, wailing urchins, black pudding, scoffing and shin-kicking contests'. It's not an awful place: at nearly 6 per cent, unemployment is a serious problem, especially following job losses in the glassmaking industry, but it is not one completely without hope of solution.

But the logic of Woodward's position is curious: either there is nothing remotely questionable about his selection for the seat, or you are effectively saying the people of St Helens would vote for a jar of fish-paste if it wore a red rosette. Not many voters seem to accept this dichotomy. Some put the pragmatic argument for voting for Woodward – 'You're virtually guaranteed a minister, aren't you?' – but there is a deep reluctance, too. 'I've voted Labour all my life and I'll still vote Labour, but this man was pushed on them,' says Thomas Kelly, a retired Pilkington worker. 'I see their point – do you want the old Foot-type Labour or the wheeler-dealer Labour? But the thing is, I'd like a bit of both, really.'

Another seven reasons why Shaun Woodward will become the MP for St Helens South on Thursday night are on display that evening in the parish church hall, lined up alongside Woodward for a church-organised candidates' debate. With disarming organisational uselessness, the socialist left is offering three choices: Neil Thompson, a Fire Brigades Union official, for the Socialist Alliance, Mike Perry, for Arthur Scargill's Socialist Labour party and Mick Murphy, a handlebar-moustachioed former TV actor and prop-forward for St Helens RLFC who made a last-minute decision, as his election literature puts it, to 'join the scrum-down for St Helens South'.

The role – compulsory in every high-profile constituency – of Swivel-Eyed Maniac Candidate is being taken in St Helens by David Braid of the Battle of

Britain Christian Independence party. An ex-military type running on an anti-sodomy platform, he announces that he has in his possession a 'horrible magazine' featuring pictures involving 'live gerbils', but he has decided not to share it with us tonight. (The chairwoman seems relieved.)

It is a peaceable, mainly churchgoing audience, although there is a small amount of heckling when Woodward explains that his role model in politics is Robert Kennedy. Afterwards, in the darkness of the fire escape, he lights another cigarette and reflects on the habit of his Tory opponent, an engagingly nerdy researcher called Lee Rotherham, to quote his pre-defection speeches back at him in local debates. 'Look, I've already said those were stupid things to say. I had a year or so of real inner torment, you know.' And as for all this butler business: 'We have a few people to help around the house, that's all. They don't bring drinks in on trays.'

The returning officer for St Helens South isn't looking at a very late bedtime on Thursday. Normally, the count comes in among the earliest. This time, thanks to the extra candidates, a council spokesman warns, we could be talking 11.30 p.m., maybe even midnight. But it probably won't be much later than that. After all, you could put a dog up for Labour in St Helens.

6 June 2001

GARY YOUNGE

Blunkett tenses for the next challenge

David Blunkett keeps slipping tenses. By the end of the week he will be home secretary. He knows it. Everybody knows it. But he won't admit it.

'I won't speculate about what other people might do,' he says unconvincingly. His syntax, however, keeps giving him away. He cannot help referring to his current job as education secretary in the past tense: 'I tried', 'I wanted', 'I thought'.

So while his mouth keeps saying 'class sizes', you feel his mind has moved on to 'crime figures'. But this is more than just a job promotion. In the public imagination, Mr Blunkett is about to ascend from the middle of the premier division to the champions' league. Once the holder of a key cabinet position, he is about to be anointed as a possible successor to the prime minister himself.

Which makes it all the more frustrating that he won't talk about the future. 'Just tell me,' I say. 'And I promise I won't tell anyone else.' He laughs – head back, mouth open, not a camera in sight – and rolls down the car window. 'I'll just whisper it out the window and then it'll be out in the open,' he says, then laughs some more and taps me on the shoulder.

Mr Blunkett is a rare phenomenon in New Labour – someone who manages to keep on message but still write his own script. With most cabinet ministers you could hold your breath and wait for 'boom and bust', 'prosperity and opportunity' or 'sustained economic growth', safe in the knowledge you will never be short of air.

With Blunkett, the two phrases you are most likely to hear are 'In Sheffield city council' – which he led during the eighties – and 'I know in my heart'. Both are significant.

The first because it refers not only to his home town and constituency, but also his political apprenticeship. Unlike most of his peers, he cut his teeth in the municipal Labourism of the eighties. It was a bleak and challenging time for Labour councillors. They were faced with the choice of trying to make Tory cuts as painless as possible or risking rate-capping or abolition.

'I go back to Sheffield every weekend, which keeps me in my place. I'm not a cabinet minister there. I'm David.'

The second is important because it implies an emotional intelligence that has been lacking in political leadership of all persuasions for some time. Mr Blunkett does not have to go off the record to sound like a human being.

Recalling the first time he went to university, he says: 'I kept thinking: "What am I doing here?" You have to build up a very hard shell of confidence. But then you have to get rid of it or you get chippy.' The hard shell may have gone but he has needed a thick skin in the job he is about to leave.

While he boasts of the extra cash he has extracted from Gordon Brown to modernise buildings and get class sizes down, teachers bemoan the culture he has bequeathed of performance-related pay as well as state-set targets for children scarcely out of nappies. Has anything been lost in the drive for standards?

'I've found a similar problem to the one I had as leader of Sheffield city council,' he says. 'In trying to do things as quickly as possible, you don't always take people with you. I regret that I haven't been able to raise teachers' morale.'

Where public services are concerned, his emphasis, he admits, has always been on the needs of the consumer rather than the interests of the producer. One wonders whether he will take on the police with the same tenacity as he has faced down the teaching profession.

Mr Blunkett's arrival provokes complex reactions. On the one hand he is a minister, a man to impress and defer to. On the other he is blind, a man who needs assistance and, literally, guidance. The two are by no means contradictory. But for the many who have met neither a minister nor a blind person, they can present a challenge. How do you behave in the presence of someone who is simultaneously powerful and vulnerable?

The standard response is to overreact. As his guide dog Lucy took him down some stairs at the Albany Road school in Cardiff two teachers rushed to hold him back. 'It's all right,' says Mr Blunkett calmly. It is the patient tone of a man used to putting others at their ease before he can relax himself. In a country still awkward in its dealings with people with disabilities, it will take a while for some to realise Mr Blunkett is the man to look out for, not to look after.

As we drive away he talks about a little boy from the Congo, an asylum seeker, who has just started his first day at the school. 'That must be very difficult,' says Mr Blunkett. 'But it's better that he should start at this stage of the year, when they can give him more help,' he says.

One only hopes he expresses as much care and compassion about the welfare of the little boy and his parents in his next job as he seems to do in this one.

Two seconds to doomsday. The second United Airlines jet just before impact with the south tower of the World Trade Center, Tuesday 11 September. (AP Photo/Carmen Taylor)

A city in shock. Dust-covered survivors evacuate downtown Manhattan after the attack. (AP Photo/Gulnara Samoilova)

A time for heroes. Emergency personnel assess the scale of the task facing them.
(AP Photo/Graham Morrison)

7 June 2001

JOE KLEIN

True colours

Tony Blair is coming straight at me, shaking hands along a gauntlet of cheering supporters after a strong speech in Croydon. It seems unavoidable: he and I are about to have a Moment. Hastily, I prepare a clever greeting, ready my right hand to shake his. But he clocks me out of the corner of his eye – great peripheral vision – and, having grasped the hand of the fellow immediately to my right, the prime minister spins to greet the cheering supporters on the opposite side of the gauntlet. Then he returns to shake the hand of the woman immediately to my left. I have been surgically avoided. Right hand grasping at air, I am as mute as Ffion Hague, stunned by the athletic elegance of the move.

So, what's this? Have I been dissed? I don't think so. Blair means me no offence. His central nervous system has simply registered that my hand doesn't qualify as one that needs shaking...and, furthermore, that he might actually have to stop and pretend to be friendly for a moment. Waste of time. There are, after all, actual voters about, devoted party workers who require care and feeding. It is a remarkable thing, really: a reflexive act of efficiency by a hyper-alert politician. And it is another example of Tony Blair's most impressive quality on the campaign trail: how sleek he is, sleek as a shark – if not nearly so vicious (although that fierce, metallic smile does begin to seem a bit shark-like after a while).

It is, in fact, great sport to watch Blair going through his paces, even when he is not taking his shirt off to reveal his underwear in the presence of journalists. He is alert to everything around him. (Is it conceivable that he took off that shirt on purpose?) Earlier, in Brighton, the prime minister had found himself seated in a circle of young mothers and their toddlers for a photo opportunity. No official words were to be uttered, just snaps. There was a dour little girl in an orange jumper just next to Blair, squirming in her mother's arms – and a crucial decision had to be made: pick up the girl and put her on his lap, or not? Important calculation: can't have photo of squalling child on lap. But orange-jumper girl was reaching out, trying to touch the leader's sleeve. Can't have photo ignoring her, either. Oh, all right then: Blair reached over and popped the kid on his knee, but quickly – perhaps sensing an imminent blub, or moisture below – handed her back to mom. A bit awkward, but squall-photo averted.

Blair stood up to go, making a show of noticing the children's art on the walls and then in another lightning move – great peripheral vision yet again! – he turned away just before his glance reached a cruel Tory placard (Failed! Failed! Failed!) that had been tucked through the window behind him. Whew! Tory placard photo averted as well.

These are little things, obviously. New Labour excels at little things. The anal-compulsive tidiness of the project is often hilarious. In Croydon, just before Blair's arrival, I spotted a campaign aide, whose duty apparently was flag choreography. He snatched a red 'Vote June 7' flag and a plastic Union Jack from an

Asian man, who also was waving a placard, and foisted them upon a young woman, called Hilary Bates, who was flagless. Bates took the red flag and shoved it in her pocket. 'I didn't really want the flag,' she said. 'I'm not even a Labour supporter, but the approach seemed more forceful than optional.'

Another compulsive bit: on the day that the climactic 'Schools and Hospitals First' campaign was launched, the words 'Schools and Hospitals First' suddenly appeared on every mirror in the toilets of the press centre at Millbank. There were also 'Schools and Hospitals First' buttons, placards and, I think, T-shirts. The slogan on the sides of the battle buses was changed to – well, guess what? And there was Blair using the phrase about twelve times in the first ten minutes of the morning press conference. But no more than that. Sensing the assembled hacks on the brink of jeers and, perhaps, widespread retching, Blair deigned to answer a handful of questions without mentioning the dread phrase. He answered them easily, as always, all the while counting the moments until he could safely complete the arc of the press conference by reiterating that oh, by the way, Labour was also interested in schools. And hospitals.

The opportunity came with a question from *Sky News*: 'How do you feel, as a person, when you find yourself in a confrontation with an aggrieved citizen like Sharon Storer and some of the others who have complained about the quality of public services?'

'I feel as I always do,' Blair replied, impatiently. 'These services desperately need improvement.' He went on to speak of the 'good' that he had seen in the NHS along with the bad. 'But the only answer in the long term is a combination of increased investment and reform – and that is why, during this last week of the campaign, we are emphasising...'

But enough of that.

We should, however, linger for a moment on the question from Sky, particularly the 'How do you feel as a person?' formulation. This is the perennial Blair question. Even now, as he approaches a likely second landslide, no one seems to know how Tony Blair feels as a person or, more to the point, who he is. This is both extraordinary and mystifying. He is about as familiar as a public figure can be. His quirks and passions are manifest. We know that he is religious. We know that he was reasonably athletic (captain of the Fettes College basketball squad – hence, the peripheral vision). We know that he was an accomplished schoolboy actor. We know that he plays the guitar or, at least, carries one around. We even know something very private about his marriage – something that was a source of constant, lurid speculation for 275 million Americans during the Clinton years: baby Leo is a living testimony to it. Unlike William and Ffion Hague, who seem to come from Mars and Venus respectively, Tony and Cherie are most definitely from the same planet – they are two clever and ambitious people, pursuing separate careers, who remain extremely married. That should say quite a bit about who they are, who he is.

But there remains an ineffable something missing. There is an antiseptic, impenetrable, stainless-steel brightness to Blair. There are no rough edges – few edges of any sort. Many people seize on the schoolboy drama career as evidence that this is all some sort of act. This turns out to be an ancient theory. In his recent biography of Blair, John Rentoul quotes David Kennedy, who taught Blair at Fettes College: 'He was so affable that you couldn't call him reserved, but you never saw his real self. He didn't like to expose himself in case someone spotted a weakness...He has always been conscious of how he appears to other people; the facade is always there. He is very intelligent and calculating. Don't forget that he was a superb actor.'

Yes, but if he's such a superb actor, why has the current portrayal been so sketchy, so unconvincing? A politician who wanted us to believe he was a regulation human specimen might provide some flashes of legitimate anger, or passion, or inconvenient candour to fill out the portrait. (Within months of his election in 1992, the 'Who is Bill Clinton' stories had disappeared – we knew exactly who he was.) By all accounts, Blair's unscheduled emotions have been few – that sweaty shirt at the Labour party conference, during the fuel crisis, the catch in his voice the day after his son Euan proved himself a teenager. The creative morbidity after Diana's death? Bad acting, I'm afraid.

In search of answers, I asked a handful of Labour stalwarts the following question: 'Suppose I am a visitor from Mars – or merely from America – and I know nothing of your politics. Could you tell me: who is this Tony Blair?'

Gordon Brown, whose sombre, sleepy-eyed mass is a constant reminder of Blair's arrant perkiness, made a magisterial pronouncement: 'He is a man of intellectual depth. He combines an ability to appeal to the public with a deep commitment to society.'

Brown went on to recall the small office that he and Blair shared as infant MPs, the long hours of conversation, the trip to Australia where they spent ten days in close proximity and constant talk, formulating a New Labour 'values' statement. (One imagines Brown doing most of the talking: 'You know, Tony, the problem is that our policies haven't kept up with our values' and so forth.) The chancellor betrayed no hint of the more recent chill with the prime minister but there wasn't much misty nostalgia, or emotion, in the account, either.

On a train to Newcastle, where she was to stump for various Labour hopefuls, Mo Mowlam did a rather funny parody of how one might actually speak to a Martian: 'Tony Blair is the prime minister of the United Kingdom. He is our political leader. He is young, thin, losing his hair. He is a good leader, a good family man, religious, a lawyer. He cares – and he wanted the job. He cannot be stereotyped.' (Blair as lawyer rather than statesman is a frequent theme, by the way: 'He is more of a lawyer than a politician,' one prominent Labourite told me. 'Sometimes he doesn't take politics into account when he makes his judgments. That is not always a good thing.')

On the phone from New Zealand, Bryan Gould – who once fought the sainted John Smith for leadership of the Labour party, and has had a falling out with Blair – ignored my fast-fading Martian conceit and exclaimed: 'I don't think he's a politician at all! He doesn't have any politics. He has principles, courage – but he lacks a serious analysis of what is wrong with society and what must be improved. Let me tell you a story. In 1983, after Michael Foot lost so badly, there was a contest for the leadership of the party. Tony had just been elected for the first time and I was quite pleased to see him attend a small meeting that several of us, supporters of Peter Shore, had arranged in order to organise a campaign. There's a young man who isn't afraid to get involved, I thought. But I later learned that he had attended all of the candidates' organisational meetings. That's Tony...When I see him on television now, he still seems very young to me – just as he was in 1983, refreshingly boyish, wet behind the ears. It's a puzzle to me, why he still seems so young.'

Gould is on to something here: Blair suffers from a generational disease, a perennial callowness that seems to afflict those of us who were born in the years immediately after the second world war, who were raised in the narcotic safety of affluence, who never had to serve or sacrifice for our country. Look across the ocean: George W. Bush, Al Gore, Newt Gingrich and even Bill Clinton – all seem lighter than the politicians of their parents' generation, who fought the war and suffered through the great depression. (Bob Dole, the last of that generation, was not cut out for the presidency but he was almost universally worshipped in the back rooms of the Capitol – a solid, pained man whose ability to find a proper compromise was respected by Democrats and Republicans alike.) Perhaps it is the absence of great issues or great crises, or perhaps it is simply the absence of suffering – but baby-boom politicians, even in middle age, still seem like helium-filled dilettantes.

Even Blair's rather admirable and least fashionable attribute – his faith in God – has an ad hoc, pragmatic feel to it: his religious confirmation, while at Oxford, seems more a philosophical gesture than a full-blown acceptance of a personal saviour, at least as described in Rentoul's biography. Blair is quoted: 'I had always believed in God but I had become slightly detached from it. I couldn't make sense of it. Peter [Thompson, a Christian Socialist mentor] made it relevant, practical rather than theological. Religion became less of a personal relationship with God. I began to see it in a much more social context.'

Was there ever a more secular profession of faith? But Rentoul goes on to limn the headwaters of Blair's politics – and these are more substantial, and considered, than Bryan Gould imagines. Gould's use of the term 'analysis' – as in 'serious analysis of the problems of society' – betrays the problem: analysis implies science, which implies a Marxist determinism. Unlike many of his – my – generation, Blair was never a full-blooded socialist. Indeed, he rejected Marx as morally defective from the start and settled upon a more practicable communitarian caring, which he has maintained, with some vehemence, to the present day. In the Croydon speech, he ginned up a righteous anti-Tory lather, denouncing Lady Thatcher's famously ridiculous nostrum: 'There is no such thing as society.'

'This is not simply about policy. It is also, crucially, about values,' Blair continued. 'We know what their values were. They were narrow, selfish, individualist. People used to say: "Know your place." Do you remember? Well, we have cast all that aside. We believe a person's 'place' is wherever his or her talents take them. The Tories have ignored the fact that without a strong "society" behind them, many people won't have the opportunity to succeed.'

He had uttered these words before, I suspect. But they were delivered with conviction, the crowd was roused and I was impressed. Was I falling for him? My editor thought so. 'I can hear it in your voice,' he said. No, I insisted, he just gave a good speech. No. Well, maybe a little.

On the following day, I watched as Blair almost did an astonishing thing. The situation was surreal: the Bev's Bar set of *Brookside*, at the Merseyside television studios near Liverpool. A group of 'real people' were gathered to ask the prime minister questions. It seemed the ultimate absurdity, the final confusion of politics with entertainment. On the walls, the placards were bogus – 'Feeling lonely? Singles night every Monday from eight' – and slightly less bogus: 'Schools and Hospitals First.' An actor named Dean Sullivan who plays the character Jimmy Corkhill, whose wife and daughter were – I am told – involved in lesbian affairs with the same woman, played the role of David Frost. He assayed solemnity, took questions from the audience and pushed the PM for more specific answers at times.

The crowd may have been culled, but the questions were good. A woman with purple hair said that her teenage son had to wait, in pain, for sixteen months to get a wrist operation. A foster mother, waiting for adoption papers to come through, wondered why she didn't receive the working families tax credit. Another woman complained about the lot of ancillary workers in the public hospitals: 95 per cent of them earned just a bit more than the minimum wage. A man asked why secondary schools couldn't be made more alluring to young people. Blair dived into these with genuine ardour. It was clear that he hadn't just been handed a position on these issues: he knew them, through and through. He asked questions, made suggestions that might meliorate some of the specific problems, and burbled on – in great detail – about his plans for the NHS and the secondary schools. It was an ample demonstration of what we currently lack in the US: a leader who eats, sleeps and breathes public policy.

For a few moments, he transcended the mortal silliness of his surroundings. The crowd was carried along enthusiastically. Even the woman with purple hair, whose son would still have to wait for his wrist operation, was satisfied that: 'At least, I now know, there are plans afoot.'

The mood was so buoyant, in fact, that one gentleman burst in with a suggestion for the prime minister: 'Given the needs, and your enthusiasm to do something about them, why not go with a targeted 1p tax increase for health and education?' The audience cheered. Several actually shouted: 'Hear, hear.' Blair seemed stricken. He stumbled, for once. He started and stopped, then lurched into a mumble about the 'balance' you have to strike between a strong economy and expenditures for public services. He lost the moment, siphoned the glee from the crowd.

'You have to strike a balance between the need for a strong economy and expenditures for public services,' Gordon Brown tells me at Millbank several days later. I am thinking: How awful. Why must these palpably intelligent guys shackle themselves so tightly to the script? But then Brown unleashes a torrent of plans and schemes and statistics – his grasp is every bit as good as Blair's – and he has a point. 'People' – by which he means cynical hacks and nattering pristine, left-intellectual *Guardian* readers who have never had to implement a political plan in their lives – 'underestimate the extent to which we're changing the framework. We have pledged full employment, more than 50 per cent participating in higher education, one-half the child poverty, eliminating pensioner poverty, doubling the rate of productivity. These are ambitious plans.'

But there is still a preternatural caution to it all: Can anyone doubt that

Labour would have been elected if it had proposed a tax increase targeted to schools and hospitals (first)? Why do they so persistently underestimate the willingness of the public to be challenged? 'The fear in the party is too great,' admitted Mo Mowlam. 'We were out in the cold for too long.'

It should also be remembered that Blair's most radical and courageous deeds were acts of revolutionary moderation: he moved Labour from left-frivolity to left-centre plausibility. For Blair, caution – the ability to say no to the left – may seem the purest form of courage.

Politicians claim to love a mandate, but I'm not so sure. A mandate means a clear message from the public: we really want you to do what you have proposed. But the dirty little secret of governance is that nothing ever gets done exactly right for very long. Public life is too complicated for perfection. And that is why we should, perhaps, be a bit more tolerant of those who actually seem willing to give even the mildest form of collective social action a try. For Blair, however, the tolerant days of wait-and-see are over. A hunch: This could be the last 'Who is Tony Blair?' story you will ever see. In the months to come, you will actually learn whether he is overcautious or merely prudent, whether he has the gumption to deliver the goods. Next time around, you will know.

One last word from an appreciative Yank: I interviewed Mo Mowlam, as I said before, on the train to Newcastle. As we pulled into Peterborough, where I was to leave her after a lovely hour of chatter, Mowlam said: 'Here's Peterborough. Give us a kiss and then bugger off.' No American has ever said anything remotely like that to me. So thanks, Mo, for the smooch – any stray moment of humanity shared with a politician is cause for celebration, and that was as sweet as they come.

9 June 2001

MATTHEW ENGEL

Moment of history – greeted with a grimace

Historians will probably describe the opening moments of Tony Blair's second administration as rather downbeat. Actually, they were nothing like as dynamic as that.

Here we had the busy chief executive of a substantial national enterprise, just back from a long, tedious but essential business trip to various branch offices. On his first day back, he was obliged both to make a speech and to pay a formal visit to the company chairperson, an elderly lady who was herself far more interested in getting away to the races. No wonder he looked harassed.

Outside No. 10 he displayed that same look of vague irritation he has worn for much of the past month and which will probably be etched permanently on to his features halfway through the third term. With Alastair Campbell invisible, the only person who looked more cross was Baby Leo, who is cultivating a distinct media scowl reminiscent of the young Princess Anne.

Triumph, what triumph? Landslide, what landslide? William what-did-you-say-his-name-was? In a roundabout way, the Blair family's attitude seemed to mirror the mood of the nation, which is one reason why they can keep their home for the next five years.

Throughout the campaign, the prime minister trailed his two main rivals by miles in the cheerfulness stakes, William Hague's demeanour being testament to the much-observed psychological fact that people always feel much better once they have given up hope.

But Mr Blair was even reported as being subdued on the plane coming down from Sedgefield. True, the turnout was appalling. But this was like being unhappy on your wedding day. It didn't offer much of an omen for the bad days.

As he got into the car to go to the palace, the PM barely even managed a grimace for the cameras. When he came back, he did go walkabout to shake hands with a few of the adoring populace. It lasted approximately forty seconds. This took place outside the gates because the public were not let through them; there were none of the flag-wavers who four years ago were bussed in from Millbank. The fifty or so who cared enough to come were genuine fans. Not having pagers, they had not understood that this was to be a triumph without triumphalism.

There was Paul Bradshaw, a young politics graduate from Liverpool who had voted in the Riverside constituency (where hardly anyone else bothered), then drove through the night with his friend Louise Shevlane to be here at 6.30 a.m. with a red rosette, a placard and a bottle of champagne, which remained unopened.

'The Tories are in freefall. It can't get any better than this, can it?' said Paul. 'We thought there would be loads of people. When we got here, we were alone except for a single drunk.'

Even their devotion was surpassed by Paul Tabone, a retired bank manager from Malta who came over for the week specially to drink in the election atmosphere, as though it were the Rio carnival. In Malta, election turnout is usually around 98 per cent, and passions run high. 'Everybody here just grumbles about the government, then they don't vote,' he said. 'If you don't vote, you have no right to grumble.'

But no one had instructed these people to be there, so the PM was not spending much time with them. He moved on to his speech, a statement of intent with all the campaign trail clichés expunged, which made some of the journalists who have followed him throughout the past month rather wistful. It was not exactly gripping.

This was a suitable follow-up to the day they called an election and nobody came – and the election night when nothing happened. The nation was so enamoured of its politicians that it could hardly be bothered to turf any of them out. Only one seat changed hands in the first three hours of declarations. It was nearly 2 a.m. before a sitting MP was beaten, and then it was a mild, obscure, animal rights-oriented Tory from Cheadle called Day.

Where's the fun in that? Never mind 'Were you still up for Portillo?' Were you even up for Chris Mullin? Or the exit polls?

It is of course important not to ignore the Conservatives' achievement. Overall, they had a net gain of one. As everyone recovering from a terrible self-inflicted damage is aware, it is important to take one step at a time. And if they maintain that progress consistently, they can expect to form a government again (based on four- to five-year parliaments) some time between 2657 and 2821.

Maybe it's the prospect of that happening that makes Mr Blair so depressed. He did agree to the photographers' entreaties to kiss Leo a third time, but he never looked cheerful about it. All the family members who know how to walk then stood in the doorway and half-smiled one last time, with the air of a new manufactured pop group posing for publicity stills, then shut the door behind them with a sigh of relief that might have been audible in Sedgefield.

By then, it was starting to spit with rain. Conservative central office was already almost deserted. One or two party figures were believed to be inside, presumably plotting rather than rethinking. Outside the flag had wrapped itself round the flagpole, as if seeking consolation. In the parking bay there was just one white election minibus belonging to the Tory strategist Danny Finkelstein, crushed by more than 6,000 in once safe Harrow West. His 'Vote Finkelstein' placard had crumpled. All the blue balloons tied to the roof rack had burst, except one. It looked infinitely sad. But then so did the prime minister.

POLITICAL
ANIMALS

Steve Bell, 22 June 2001

PATRICK WINTOUR

Fall of Mandelson

Even Jesus Christ did not earn a second resurrection, and there is no chance of Peter Mandelson ever rising again inside the Labour party he did so much to re-create.

On the verge of a historic second term, Labour's election campaign will not benefit from Mr Mandelson's strategic mind, and it is unlikely that the former Northern Ireland secretary will even stand again in Hartlepool. At forty-seven, he is part of Labour's history, albeit a large part for his role in making Labour electable again.

Any attempt by Tony Blair to restore his friend again, even in five years' time, would be met with an armed phalanx of cabinet members, MPs and party activists blocking his path.

Mr Mandelson once said of himself: 'I was the agent, the publicist and the spin doctor of the modernisers' cause.' But his departure does not mark the end of the Blairites. Instead, it probably signals the final stage in the Labour's transition from a campaigning party of opposition to a party of day-to-day government.

This is very different from his first resignation in December 1998 over the £373,000 loan from the paymaster general, Geoffrey Robinson.

Then the possibility of redemption was explicit. The fact that he spent the tearful night of his first resignation in the company of the Blair family at Chequers showed that the prime minister saw him as a special case. Mr Blair's letter accepting his resignation also promised that he still had much more to contribute to the party.

Mr Mandelson himself took time to recover from the loss of office, admitting to feeling numbed, empty and sometimes maudlin. Although he never forgave the people who had contributed to his demise, or fully accepted the seriousness of his error, he knew he had to reflect.

A lucrative career in business did not attract him then, although it now may be his best option. Last time he ruminated over working overseas. He travelled to South Africa, but even there he advised the ANC on election strategy.

After six months, rumours started to flow that he might be called back to help the Labour European or local election campaigns. He visibly brightened. In an attempt to rehabilitate himself with MPs and the rank and file, he accepted countless speaking engagements in Labour constituencies.

Despite the bile he engenders in much of the party, he was also a prize draw. He was anxious to let it be known that the Labour party, and not Mayfair parties, was his primary love. Within six months, it was clear he would return. It was only a matter of when.

Unlike many Labour politicians, he had had no instinctive dislike of wealth creators – and as he rose in political prominence, the rich and glamorous were drawn to him. They found him amusing company, a little exotic and agreeably indiscreet. He mixed easily and liked dancing a little more than sitting in the Commons tearoom trading the gossip of the day.

The invitations duly poured in from London's social elite – Carla Powell, wife of the former Downing Street private secretary Charles Powell, Elisabeth Murdoch, daughter of the media baron Rupert Murdoch, millionaire Robert Bourne and his theatre impresario wife, Sally Greene, and even from Prince Charles. Peter Mandelson became New Labour's ambassador to the rich and famous. One of his aides – without irony – compared the quantity of publicity his boss received with the acres of newsprint about Princess Diana. But he was as much a manipulator as target of the media.

Back in office as Northern Ireland secretary in October 1999, he tried to mend his ways and show some of the wilder excesses of the period 1997–8 were over. He avoided appointing a special adviser, relying instead on the official Northern Ireland press office. There would be no spin, and no use of the special adviser network, to spread poison about colleagues. Although in private he could be typically droll and imperious about the province's politicians and their self-obsessions, the sheer scale of the task invested him with a new seriousness.

He appeared happier in his private life and less intense. Although for fifteen years he had battled to keep his homosexuality from the public, his relationship with his Brazilian boyfriend Reinaldo Da Silva became a matter for daily reporting.

But even over the water the ability to bury a feud eluded him. For instance, he hardly spoke to Mo Mowlam, his predecessor.

Mr Mandelson would say, by reply, that his Brownite enemies dedicated themselves to his demise, regardless of the damage to the party. The autobiography of Geoffrey Robinson, he believed, had the sanction of the chancellor, Gordon Brown, and his circle.

In reply, the Brownites claim he was far too loquacious in providing destructive detail to furnish Andrew Rawnsley's devastating account of Labour in government.

More worryingly, Downing Street had started to withdraw support. His crime was ill-discipline, and his relationship with Alastair Campbell, the No. 10 press secretary, waned after two unsanctioned speeches on the euro provoked fury in Downing Street and the Treasury. The fiasco of the dome continued through 2000 to raise a big question mark over his judgment.

It may be that one of his greatest strengths – a willingness to take political risks – was also his undoing.

After joining the Labour party in 1985 as a young director of communications, he was immediately more influential than many embittered shadow cabinet members. He came to see himself as someone to whom the normal rules did not apply. The prize, a Labour election victory after so long in opposition, was so great that the ends began to justify the means. It made him perennially careless of the conventions.

His reputation rapidly grew out of control, so much so that Labour politicians began to believe any unfavourable slight in any newspaper must have been planted in one of his waspish asides. He was indeed often ruthless in his private dealings, but left the impression he was reflecting the view of the leadership. More often than not, this was the case. But he also often freelanced and got away with it. He issued briefings on Neil Kinnock's interventions at party meetings designed to portray the party leader in a favourable light, but which were entirely from Mr Mandelson's imagination.

John Smith's unexpected death in 1994, and the rift between Gordon Brown and Tony Blair, created a fissure amongst the modernisers from which Mr Mandelson never extricated himself. It left him even more exposed as the client of the prime minister.

There remains one last curiosity. Mr Mandelson has a sense of strategy, a relentless energy and a premier memory for detail. He was often the first to warn a political colleague of media danger starting to bleep on their radar, yet he seemed inept at handling his own difficulties.

Both in the case of the Robinson loan, and the fateful phone call to the Home Office minister Mike O'Brien, it was his subsequent behaviour that was his downfall. If, as secretary of state for industry, he had informed his permanent secretary of his loan from Mr Robinson, he would have had cover. No conflict of interest would have arisen.

Similarly, if last Saturday lunchtime his special adviser, Patrick Diamond, had been allowed to tell the truth to the *Observer*'s political reporter, Gaby Hinsliff, about Mr Mandelson's personal call to Mr O'Brien, his political career might not be in ruins. There would have been acute questions about the phone call, but no evidence existed of undue pressure by Mr Mandelson. He would probably have survived.

22 February 2001

LARRY ELLIOTT

The £1m question

'Hello, and welcome back to *Who Wants to Be a Millionaire?* Before the break, Gordon Brown had already won £250,000 and for £500,000 he was asked which of the following countries had the poorest public services – Sweden, France, the United Kingdom and Germany. Gordon, you said the United Kingdom. It's the right answer and you've just won £500,000. You couldn't see her, but your girl-friend Prudence is so relieved.

'Now, Gordon, the next question is for £1m. You've got all three lifelines left – ask the audience, phone a friend, 50-50. You might as well have a look at the next question. You don't have to play but it's worth £1m. The UK government is on course for a record budget surplus of £18bn this year. Should it be A: Spent all at once on a nationwide chain of millennium domes, B: Saved for a rainy day, C: Used for tax cuts, or D: Invested long term in rebuilding Britain's decrepit public infrastructure?

'Gordon, you had a smile on your face when that question was coming up. Confident?'

'Well, Chris, I'm the chancellor of the exchequer so it's the sort of question I should get right. But, to be honest, the amount of money rolling into the treasury is becoming embarrassing, so it's not quite so simple as it looks.'

'What are you thinking, Gordon?'

'Well, it's definitely not A. There's definitely going to be a much bigger surplus than I said in my pre-Budget report in November, but that figure of £10bn was always for the birds. It will probably be £17bn or £18bn, although I'll only admit to around £15bn in the Budget, so that it doesn't look too miserly when I only give a couple of billion of it away.

'That said, trying to spend all the money makes no sense. Departments are not even spending the money they've already got. I gave them £7bn to spend on the infrastructure this year and after ten months of the year they've only got through £2.2bn.'

'That's fascinating, Gordon. Why's that, do you think?'

'It's the final revenge of Mrs Thatcher, Chris. The idea that spending public money was bad burrowed its way deep into the Whitehall psyche. Neo-liberalism is stronger than you might imagine. The fact that I froze public spending in my first two years as chancellor merely strengthened the hand of officials for whom spending taxpayers' money is a mortal sin.'

'And what about the other options?'

'I'm certain it's not C. Spending the money on tax cuts would be economic suicide and, in any case, it's not what the country needs. Falling unemployment and rising confidence means that consumer spending is already growing at 4 per cent a year, and it's something of a surprise that, after almost nine years of growth, inflation is as low as it is. Besides, Britain's problem is that we have always spent too much and invested too little. Giving consumers even more to spend would simply open up a big gap between the demand for goods and services and the economy's ability to supply them. The result would be a splurge of inflation and an explosion in the trade deficit; probably both.'

'OK Gordon, your call. What are you going to do?'

'I've got my three lifelines, Chris, so I'll go 50-50.'

'Computer, take away two wrong answers. There we are, Gordon, just as you thought. It's not tax cuts and it's not spend, spend, spend. It's B or D. Not a lot of help really. Do you want to play?'

'Yes, I think I'll go with B, Chris. Yes, definitely B: stash it away for a rainy day.

'Final answer?'

'I think so, Chris. You see, saving the surplus for a rainy day keeps the Bank of England and the City sweet. There's a mortgage war going on, which may lead to another burst of inflation in the property market. At this point, nothing should be done that should frighten the horses. Banking the surplus also cuts interest payments on the national debt, which means the government can spend more on the good things in life, such as schools and hospitals.

'What's more I am investing long term. I've already big plans for the next three years – doubling capital spending, increasing spending on health and education by 6 per cent above the rate of inflation. The surplus is huge now, but we'll be borrowing money again quite soon, and I'm determined not to repeat the mistakes made by Lawson in the late eighties.

'One way of squaring the circle would be to raise taxation to levels seen in most other countries in western Europe, because that would mop up the extra demand. But higher taxation is the love that dare not speak its name, because Britain is now a low-tax nation. That was another of Mrs Thatcher's legacies. So it must be B.'

'Final answer?'

'Final answer. But wait a minute. It could be D. To be honest, the public sector is in a pretty dreadful state. We spent even less in our first two years than the Tories were planning to spend had they been re-elected, and I know, because Ken Clarke told me, that he wouldn't have stuck to his own plans anyway. Discretionary public spending has risen by 2 per cent a year during the past four years, slightly less than John Major's government spent between 1992 and 1997.'

'And that's a problem is it, Gordon?'

'You bet. It's why the schools don't have enough teachers. It's why the health service is increasingly staffed by doctors and nurses from overseas, and it's why the transport system doesn't work. Relative to the state of the economy, the public sector is in an even worse state now than when we took over. Even by 2003–4, we will be spending less as a proportion of the economy than the Conservatives did in their eighteen years in power.

There's certainly a case for using the budget surplus more imaginatively to reinvigorate the public realm. Nationalising the railways, a mass home insulation programme to cut down on energy loss, doubling teachers' pay, pensions – there's no shortage of good, long-term ways of spending the cash.'

'Remember those two lifelines you've got left. You could always phone a friend. Is there anybody who might help you out?'

'Well, there's my next-door neighbour, Tony. But I'm not sure he's going to be a lot of help. He'll say that he was never really one for figures and that one of the joys of being prime minister is that the chancellor of the exchequer has to deal with these sorts of questions. No, I'll ask the audience, Chris.'

'OK, audience, fingers on your keypads please. Let's try to help Gordon be only our second contestant ever to win £1m. Should the government save all its money for a rainy day or should it invest the surplus in rebuilding Britain?

'Well, there we are Gordon. Ninety-nine per cent of the audience believe that it's time to banish the ghost of Mrs Thatcher from Whitehall. They think you should come up with a long-term plan for public spending. But it's your call. The audience may be wrong. They have been in the past. But most of them don't think you should wait for a rainy day. They think the rainy day is already here.'

12 April 2001

HUGO YOUNG

The Westminster sideshow

The first Blair parliament is over. It will meet again after Easter, but only to close itself down prior to the election of another one. There will be time enough to assess the government's record, but I'm already visited by deeper-throated thoughts that suit the confessional season. On the brink of our age-old cere-mony of democratic transition, I find it hard to engage at a fitting level with the awesome political climax that the election is supposed to produce. This has nothing to do with the fallacy that the result makes no difference. The result will matter greatly. My confession concerns parliament itself.

Why do I, for the first time in my life, experience tremors of heretical disbe-lief when I pass that great building in Westminster? Gazing up at Big Ben these past few years, I've begun to see it more as the icon of a theme park than the tower of democracy. It's a huge, magnificent sight, none more elemental in the entire democratic world, especially at night. But what goes on inside? Is that where power in Britain actually resides? How much are the sacred processes – the winding-up and then the rebirth – now symbol, and how much reality?

We know the bottom line. The very presence of these 659 MPs is a massive, immovable guarantee against dictatorship. Because they're there, certain horrors will never happen. Their existence, like the election that will produce the next batch, distinguishes countries such as Britain from great tracts of Africa and Asia, on to which the Mother of Parliaments somehow failed in the last century to graft a permanent culture of functioning democracy. We need elections to be open and uncorrupt, and must hope they engage the maximum number of cit-izens in voting. This is a system worth defending.

But what was once the parliament of an empire is now not the parliament of even a single nation. Perhaps 80 per cent of the government decisions that affect Scotland are no longer made under these ancient rafters. The setting-up of the Scottish parliament means that seventy-two MPs at Westminster are not respon-sible for much of public life as it touches their constituents. Welsh devolution, though less drastic, also drains power away. Thus, two tranches of MPs, 112 in all, will return as impostors – only partially connected to the mandate of legiti-macy, they need to justify the influence they hope to command. The perception of enfeeblement begins.

It homes in from other directions. Against Motorola, or Tesco, or Goldman Sachs, the tribunes of the people can do no more than flap their hands. The power of corporations, and the speed at which trillions of dollars are moved round global markets, sharply confine any big-picture agenda MPs may expect to control.

So does the encroaching writ of the European Union. A decade ago, Jacques Delors famously declared that before long 80 per cent of the social and eco-nomic laws affecting Europe would be decided in Brussels. It never came to that, and now the tendency is to try to move the other way. But Europe is a mighty force for the rearrangement of sovereignty. European verities add to the feeling that the sound and fury we're about to witness is, in part, a charade. Still doing one's best to be impressed by the neo-Gothic palace beside the Thames, all one remembers, unfortunately, is the idleness and lack of tenacity with which Westminster handles its existing right to invigilate what Brussels commands.

Parliament remains, of course, sovereign. It has the power to overturn devolution, cancel the Treaty of Rome, and pass statutes containing solemn words that purport to undo the laws of global economics. It could re-declare itself the potent centre of what it means to be British: a private member, eaten by Euroscepticism, is doubtless at work on a text. The more telling point is that most of the disablement has been at the hands of parliament itself. MPs willingly passed the laws – on Scotland, on Europe – that decimated their own importance. They responded, for very good reason, to imperatives that sent some power down to regions and some up to Europe. They now have to live with the consequences, beside which Big Ben and the Palace of Westminster look more like a protective facade than a fortress of democracy.

Many MPs make the best of this. Invited by the *Guardian* to name what they were proudest of doing in the past four years, a lot of them had answers you could admire. An amendment here, a campaign there, a cause taken up, a constituent rescued from NHS injustice. The accumulation of selfless labour in the Commons rebuts the pervasive and quite false impression of a chamber with its collective hand in other people's pockets, sometimes corrupt, always on the make.

But the sources of pride were mostly small beer: politician as welfare officer, road mender or modest public servant. The members of this place watch the wider world from sidelines more distant than their Victorian forbears could ever have imagined. The theatre to which we will shortly return them is unobserved, to a degree unthinkable thirty years ago.

If there is another Labour landslide, it's hard to imagine backbenchers will be listened to any more by the second Blair government than the first. For the bigger the victory, the less important the MPs. It's one of the paradoxes that corrode our parliament, with its voting system and its deadening discipline: the more emphatic the democratic verdict, the less relevant the individual democrat.

Some of this will change if the next result is narrower. Part of the reason parliament seems otiose is because it is utterly dominated by the government controller. A prime minister who had to worry every week about the 10 p.m. votes might find unwelcome political life breathed back into the theme park.

But not much. The truth is that higher powers have thrust national parliamentarians to the margins. Minor politicians can tinker with small things but not many big ones. A year when the issue that most burned MPs was fox-hunting tells the story. The big stuff is decided by a tiny cabal across the road, in the light of agreements and forces and networks and markets over which this multinational state now has startlingly little control, and never will have again, even if parliament were to exercise its sovereign power to take Britain out of the European Union.

This is no reason not to vote. Pieces of the local agenda are still important. Which side has its hands on executive power will affect the way public money is spent, and determine the British tone of voice. The way in which we fight, or reconcile with, the forces greater than we are could be much affected. But the public, in their apparent distancing from Westminster, may be more realistic than their politicians. Inside the imperial structures of the body politic beats the weakest parliament since universal suffrage.

18 July 2001

MICHAEL WHITE

Hague: my part in his downfall

As I look down from the Commons press gallery this afternoon on William Hague's last question time as leader of the Conservative party, I will not blame myself entirely for his downfall. But there is no doubt in my mind that I – and half a bottle of red burgundy – played a small but significant part.

It is an egotistical claim and it rests on the assumption that Hague was wrong to seek the Tory leadership in June 1997 and wrong to break off his deal to be Michael Howard's running mate in the contest because – I knew, if he didn't – that it would all end in tears. At thirty-six he went on to win the leadership, but he was far too young.

Was Hague the Tories' Neil Kinnock, as many people in 1997 assumed he might prove to be, destined to turn the party's fortunes round for someone else to inherit? Or was he their Michael Foot, as many now claim, as unsuitably young for the task in hand as the Hampstead left-winger had been too old ?

In reality, a bit of both. One of the ironies of Hague's humiliation on 7 June was that he actually did better in terms of his party's share of the vote than anyone cared to notice – up from 30.7 per cent in 1997 to 32.8 per cent. But that amounted to only one extra seat. Shattered, and ignoring all pleas to stay on, he resigned immediately.

The mood was not like that at all when he and I split the fatal second half of red burgundy at Christopher's restaurant in Covent Garden on 20 February 1997. Hague was a coming man, smart enough to have been junior social security minister – Thatcher and Major had both held down that demanding job – and now promoted to secretary of state for Wales.

I had been present in the magnificent Empress Ballroom inside the Winter Gardens at Blackpool in October 1977 when he made that absurdly precocious speech to the Tory conference. There he was, just sixteen with a daft Donny Osmond shoulder-length haircut, lecturing Thatcher on the need to protect his freedom when she won the coming election.

When he won the Richmond by-election, at the age of twenty-seven, in February 1989 I did not know him personally. Since he was clearly going to be more important – shadow chief secretary perhaps – in opposition I thought I should correct the omission.

As I cycled along the Embankment in London and stopped at a traffic light, the back window of a chauffeur-driven car wound down and the soon-to-be familiar head popped out to ask: 'Aren't we meant to be having lunch?' 'Yes, and I shall get there first,' I pointed out. And I did.

Hague has no side to him and was friendly enough. He cautiously accepted a glass of wine – his share of a half bottle of red burgundy, I distinctly recall. We chatted and when he said 'this is very enjoyable', I leapt in with standard hack's tactics. 'Another glass of wine?' 'Why not,' he replied.

I cannot find my notes of our conversation but I recall us talking about the 1992 parliament. The Tories had been reduced to four seats in Wales, and Hague insisted they would win more – possibly as many as thirteen – when John Major called the election. In the event they lost all four. They stayed lost in 2001. A hint here of Hague's misplaced optimism, the quality that allowed him to believe his victory in the 1999 Euro-elections (exaggerated by a new and unpopular form of PR voting plus a feeble 23 per cent turnout) could be repeated in defiance of all polls in June 2001.

After that second half of red burgundy, Hague and I said our farewells at Christopher's and returned to the Commons, where Major had initiated a debate on constitutional reform. A major plank in Tony Blair's modernising agenda for the coming election, it left Major floundering on the back foot as Blair mocked him across the dispatch box.

Then it happened. Suddenly up jumped young Hague and proceeded to intervene. Forcefully, wittily, as we later came to see at PM's question time, and effectively. In Hansard (column 1074) it does not look much but it felt it at the time.

Blair had quoted Hague's views on the hereditary peerage seventeen years earlier (he had been in favour of an elective second chamber) as proof that he had since changed his mind. Hague had no trouble reminding Blair that he had first been elected an MP on Foot's left-wing manifesto as recently as 1983. 'Will he tell us whether he agrees with everything he said seventeen years ago or indeed with anything he said seventeen years ago?' quipped Hague.

It was a style we later came to know well. Hague's belief is that Blair is clever but shallow.

Tory MPs could hardly fail to take note – and be impressed. Was it my second half-bottle of red burgundy, injected into the bloodstream of a 36-year-old at approximately 2.15 p.m., that fired him up? At the time I felt it must have been a factor. I still do. Just as Margaret Thatcher's performance in the finance bill committee in 1975 had shown she had the necessary mettle – just at the right time – so had Hague's pyrotechnics.

The rest is history. After Major's 179-seat defeat on 1 May, the unexpected loss of Heseltine as a possible caretaker leader (heart trouble) and Portillo's fall at Enfield, the leadership contest took an unexpected twist: Clarke, Redwood, Howard, Dorrell, Lilley and then Hague.

Hague had been lined up to support Howard's bid, but after celebrating the deal on champagne, he went home and found his answering machine full of messages urging him to run on his own. He reneged, ran, and beat the hastily constructed Clarke–Redwood 'nightmare ticket' in the final round. This was a double misjudgment. Clearly Labour was set to win the 2001–2 election. If Tory MPs needed a tough guy at the wicket to take the shine off Blair's balls and refused to have Clarke, then they might as well have gone for Howard. He was a brute, unable to spot a belt without punching below it. Blair had faced him twice as shadow employment minister and shadow home secretary. Howard unsettled him. Tory MPs should have known this.

As leader, Hague briefly flirted with the kind of inclusive Toryism that Michael Portillo has been offering. He wore a silly baseball cap and took his bride-to-be to the Notting Hill carnival. It didn't gel with angry and disaffected core Tory voters. Key staff were sacked and Hague began to build the right-wing laager into which his core vote was marshalled on 7 June.

No one who knows him well believes he is a racist or a xenophobe. As he often says, he went to a comprehensive and uses the NHS. He is evidently clever and his jokes are his own. But he is one of Thatcher's Children, an instinctive sectarian, like many of his advisers. They had little sense of history and no sense of irony about their own strategy. Despite the jokes, he duly presided over what became a negative, mean-spirited campaign. How did he get into the mess that seems to have ruined his career at forty?

My own feeling is that, beneath the confident veneer, he was too young, too inexperienced, too easily buffeted. 'The trouble with Hague's campaign,' a senior Liberal Democrat strategist confided at the weekend, 'was that whenever he tried something and it started to work, they dropped it. They were actually gaining ground on Europe and the asylum issue in the last week. We expected to get sixty seats, they pushed us back to fifty-two. He just didn't stick with anything.'

Hague remained admirably calm and cheerful, as Amanda Platell's video diary confirmed on Channel 4 this week. But that interview with *Newsnight*'s Jeremy Paxman remains my abiding memory of Hague's campaign: the errant sixth former being berated by a sneering headmaster prior to getting a thrashing.

You felt very sorry for him, but also that he should not have been there. In a way, that Blackpool speech was a bit like Judy Garland, also sixteen, singing 'Somewhere over the Rainbow' in *The Wizard of Oz*. When the Queen Mother once confided that it always brought tears to her eyes, talented, tragic Judy is said to have replied: 'Ma'am, that song ruined my life.'

19 July 2001

MICHAEL WHITE

Baby Brown to boost family budget

The chancellor, Gordon Brown, put the final detail of his child-friendly budget strategy into place yesterday when it emerged that his wife, Sarah, is expecting the couple's first baby next February.

Wags predicted that, if a girl, it will be called Prudence, though Phoenix may also be appropriate. The child would appear to have been conceived during the weeks when Tony Blair postponed the general election because of the foot-and-mouth crisis.

Delight that the Browns will soon be enjoying £15.50 a week child benefit – up from £11 in 1997 – was drowned out at Westminster by the sound of MPs asking each other where the news fitted into the chancellor's burning ambition to become prime minister.

There was no such cynicism in the joyous statement issued by Mr Brown's office.

'As you would expect, they are absolutely delighted,' said a spokesman for the chancellor. A spokesman for his neighbours, the Blairs, added: 'The prime minister and Cherie are both delighted for the chancellor and Sarah on their news.'

All the same, the development may give the first family even more sleepless nights than the birth of young Leo in May last year. It was Mr Blair's married-with-children status that persuaded some MPs that he, rather than his former mentor, should succeed John Smith as Labour leader in 1994.

Only when Cherie Blair produced her fourth child did the workaholic Mr Brown finally take some extra days off to marry PR consultant Sarah Macaulay in a private ceremony with their families at his home north of Edinburgh.

Mr Brown is fifty and his wife thirty-seven. Until now the chancellor has had to borrow friends' children to illustrate his passionate commitment to eradicate child poverty.

But any Tory attempt to accuse him of undeclared financial interest in introducing the new child tax credit next April is likely to fail. The Browns earn too much to qualify.

14 September 2001

SIMON HOGGART

A coronation with all the pomp of a village fête

You had to feel sorry for Iain Duncan Smith. He has just pulled off the most astonishing coup. A man who was hated and reviled by members of the last Tory government and remains almost unknown outside the House of Commons is now the leader of what is still the second party in British politics and the longest surviving party in the western world. Three months ago his victory would have seemed almost inconceivable.

Yet his coronation yesterday had all the excitement of a village fête forced indoors by the rain.

Outside there was a single media tent, perched like a bivouac on the side of St John's, Smith Square, and a pair of satellite vans – all of it indicating less media interest than when, say, Lady Thatcher goes walkabout.

At the climax of past leadership elections we heard shouting, whoops of joy, cheers of exultant delight. Yesterday there was just a torpid silence, a sense that we were, politicians, officials and journalists, irrelevancies on the fringe of the real and terrible world.

The candidates arrived through the drizzle. Both had had their scrutineers at the count. Both knew the result. Duncan Smith looked correspondingly cheerful, Clarke grimmer with his familiar 'let's get this over with as soon as we can' look, which he no doubt deploys at the dentist.

Politicians love pomp and furbelows and the blare of trumpets. Last night there was nothing.

The returning officer, Sir Michael Spicer, stepped on to the stage and said drily: 'Here is the result of the ballot for leadership of the Conservative Party. The total number of valid votes was...'

Duncan Smith had won with a remarkable 61 per cent of the vote, yet the room hardly stirred, except for one Tory columnist who would have cheered the election of Michael Fabricant as leader.

Clarke came forward and managed a pleased and congratulatory grin as he shook his rival's hand. How do politicians do this? Are there training schools at which they teach the rictus grin, the smile of delight that says 'thank heavens it's you, I could never have coped with the job myself'?

His speech was, perhaps, slightly barbed: 'The party desperately wants to be put back in a winning position,' he said, and since his whole campaign had been based on the notion that IDS could do no such thing, you might see it as a faint but perceptible lip-curl of contempt.

Then he disappeared, as ever like a man who's recalled that he's left a half-drunk pint and a bag of crisps on the bar.

Mr Duncan Smith came forward and thanked everyone: the returning officer, the people who counted the votes, Mr Clarke for 'his few kind words' and the vicar for the use of the hall – not the last of course, but it would have felt appropriate enough.

He said that he would want to concentrate on the issues which 'obsess' people, such as public services, health and education, perhaps implying that he was looking to be an administrator rather than an ideologue.

He echoed Tony Blair, saying he would stand 'shoulder to shoulder' over the killings. Then suddenly he was gone, leaving us with only a vague flap of the hand.

Over at Downing Street you could almost see Blair's grin, Alastair Campbell's amiable sneer. They probably think it's the best result they could have had. But it might be too early to say. The last Tory leader who brought such smug delight to a Labour prime minister was called Margaret Thatcher.

They were very different people, but you can never, ever judge a leader until he has had time to do some leading.

20 September 2001

CATHERINE BENNETT

The latest Tory policy: recycling

Like the face of Lady Thatcher when it looms up from time to time, all powdery and white, there is something unreal, something comically spooky about the cabinet line-up Iain Duncan Smith has resurrected from his party's political past. Here are faces such as Bill Cash's and Michael Howard's that we had no more thought to see again than we expect to go home and find a tub and a mangle sitting where we last saw the washing machine. You have to suppress the thought that he's doing it as a stunt, going back in time for a dare, like those families in the houses from the 1900s and 1940s, for a brand new series: *1980s Cabinet*. Any minute now he'll be laughing over how novel yet instructive it was having to dress up in a striped shirt and red braces and write pamphlets about the renewed fascist threat from Germany in the age before mobile phones. How did people ever do it?

It was, of course, part of the appeal of this preternaturally unappealing man to his deranged supporters that he would secure them a cabinet guaranteed to consign their party to oblivion. The only surprise is that he bothered to go for real people at all. Did he consider how much simpler it might have been to pick a yet more irrelevant and unlikely line-up from the world of fiction, Enid Blyton's Toyland for example? Would not Noddy have had the edge on Tim Yeo, and Big Ears a few advantages over Michael Howard? Wouldn't Tessie Bear as agriculture secretary have presented a more usefully ludicrous sight than Ann Winterton? Maybe not. Neither Noddy nor Big Ears worked through the Tory years of sleaze, nor has either ever been described as having 'something of the night' about him. As for Tessie Bear, she may well be more persuasive in debate than Winterton, who has spent so much of her career fighting abortion, *in vitro* fertilisation, embryo experimentation and divorce. Anyone wishing to get the measure of Winterton's political make-up should remember that, in 1986, she was one of the few Tories to support the retention of caning in schools. Around the same time, Eric Forth (new leader of the commons) was arguing against spending large sums of money on Aids, which he considered 'largely self-inflicted', Michael Howard (chancellor) was pressing ahead with the poll tax, Tim Yeo (culture media and sport) was voting to restore capital punishment, Bernard Jenkin (defence) was declaring 'I used to be a wet but I'm alright now', and David MacLean (chief whip) was supporting bus deregulation, urging that a site of special scientific interest be set aside, and voting against the Anglican ordination of divorced men. Happy days!

Moving on to the nineties, we find Maclean endorsing the use of vigilantes, opposing open access to the countryside, and denying that there are any real beggars in London: 'I always give them something – I give them a piece of my mind!' Meanwhile, David Willetts (work and pensions) is kept busy 'dissembling', then resigning his post as paymaster general, Eric Forth is attending a political meeting at Jonathan Aitken's house, Michael Howard is refusing, fourteen times, to answer a question put by Jeremy Paxman and Cash, the man John Major described as 'a bore', is accepting money from Sir James Goldsmith, the better to prosecute his personal war against Europe. Welcome back, all of you.

From the gaiety of nations point of view, the Duncan Smith combo can hardly be faulted. Most of his favourites – and of course Duncan Smith himself – will only have to open their mouths to have voters shuddering with laughter, and their critics rootling (as I have) through Roth's invaluable *Parliamentary Profiles* for unflattering tales from the past. The Labour party itself could hardly have come up with a finer selection of bigots and deadbeats. Which is why the shadow cabinet is, in fact, a disaster. Faced with a line-up like this, Blair's camp will, and they know it, appear as bright young emissaries for change, as opposed to the clueless second-raters they mostly are. Compared with Howard, Brown will appear a genial, happy-go-lucky genius. Compared with Tim Yeo, Tessa Jowell will sound like the late Isaiah Berlin. Compared with Liam Fox, Milburn will seem cute. Jenkin will make Hoon inspiring, and Letwin will provide a pedestal for Blunkett to stand on. Compared with Maclean – well, compared with Maclean most guinea pigs sound perceptive. Then we come to Duncan Smith and Blair. Compared with Smith, Blair is someone you feel proud to have leading your country. Even when it's obviously going nowhere.

HOME FRONT

Austin, 27 February 2001

6 November 2000

ANDY BECKETT

The man who privatised the railways

During the mid-eighties, some evenings after work in London, two men used to meet for a secret drink near Kings Cross station. One was a manager in British Rail, the other was a bright and slightly nervy young Scotsman called Kenneth Irvine. Their usual rendezvous was convenient but discreet: outside one of the station's side-entrances, beyond the bustle of the taxi-rank, in the half-empty bar of the Great Northern Hotel.

Here, screened by pillars and stranded travellers, with portraits of forgotten locomotives on the dirty cream walls and the worn bulk of the station looming outside the windows, Irvine would lay out a revolutionary but beguiling notion. What if all this, this slowly decaying, state-dominated railway landscape, were to be put in private hands? Profit-making companies were already acquiring and, it seemed, successfully operating the former state-run telephone networks and public utilities in Britain and abroad. Why not trains? After all, compared to British Rail – where Irvine had endured three frustrating years himself – commerce could hardly fail.

Irvine and his contact carried on meeting. They talked to other like-minded British Rail managers. Then Irvine wrote a pamphlet. In March 1987, just in time for the general election campaign, it was published by the Adam Smith Institute, the free-market think tank then most favoured by the Conservative government. By 1988, the secretary of state for transport was dropping heavy hints about rail privatisation at the Conservative party conference.

By 1991, Irvine was giving bold presentations to ministers. By 1993, a bill to privatise the railways had been published, the details of which – such as the commercial separation of trains from track – were precisely, as Irvine puts it now, 'what I was specifying'. Richard Hope of the *Railway Gazette* agrees, with a certain ambivalence in his voice: 'Irvine can reasonably claim to be the author of our present situation.'

Yet in recent years, and particularly in recent weeks, as the railways Irvine sought to reinvigorate have instead almost ground to a halt, he has, intentionally or otherwise, virtually disappeared from public view. He has been hardly mentioned in a newspaper since rail privatisation was completed in the mid-nineties. A call to the Adam Smith Institute elicits a long pause, a muttered conversation in the background, and the following: 'We don't have any contact with him. He has just done the occasional paper for us. He doesn't work here.'

In fact, only eighteen months ago, Irvine hosted a transport privatisation conference for the think tank, as 'Senior Transport Adviser, Adam Smith Institute'. This information, and three of his railway polemics, can still be found in the dustier corners of its website. But downloading the 1987 one, last week at least, proved rather difficult. Perhaps appropriately, the original blueprint for train privatisation appeared only as a blank screen, accompanied by false promises of its imminent arrival. An emergency copy had to be emailed from Didcot.

It all seemed much simpler in the beginning. In 1982, Irvine left university with a business degree and three job offers. Unemployment was high, and British Rail seemed to offer the best management training, so he chose it. His apprenticeship took him all over the ageing railway network. 'At first', he says, 'the industry excited me. I really thought that as a mode of transport it had a lot of potential.' But as he grappled with simplifying the fares and unclogging the old tracks, disillusion with the existing order began to grow. 'You still had four different canteens for the different levels of staff,' he remembers. 'Change was absolutely throttled. There was a tendency to cut things off immediately if they weren't profitable, rather than develop them.'

This bureaucracy and defeatism, as he saw it, was most apparent in British Rail's regional outposts. He particularly disliked York. His girlfriend was in London, as were the few reformers he had encountered. Irvine was stuck in Yorkshire on secondment, at least two hours north. The experience seemed to colour one of his later polemics: 'In the public sector one improves one's lot by empire building...Very few are motivated by a sense of altruistic public duty. Those who are...soon get trampled upon.' In 1985 he resigned from British Rail and took his thoughts about trains with him to London.

Private ownership, he felt, was inevitable. British Rail had already sold off its hotel and hovercraft services in the early eighties, on government instructions to reduce its dependence on the taxpayer. From America to Japan, state railways were being broken up. In Britain, a few academics were recommending partial privatisation.

But Irvine was bolder. Why not sell off the whole lot? 'Each line segment and each train would become its own profit centre,' he promised in his first pamphlet. The entire rail system, instead of being a public burden, would be an 'enterprise zone' – he sensed how to push the right Thatcherite buttons – alive with competing companies seeking clever ways to benefit passengers and balance sheets alike. As for the long-declining stations and track, a private company would be created to improve them, leaving 'the infrastructure burden considerably lightened' for the new train entrepreneurs. Perhaps Richard Branson, he mused, would end up running a 'speeding' express service.

Irvine was twenty-five when he wrote this. He had a new non-railway job at British Gas. But he also had connections. At university, he had met Madsen Pirie, director of the Adam Smith Institute, and they had kept in touch. During the mid-eighties, a friend of Irvine's was hired by the think-tank. With the 1987 election approaching, it decided to put Irvine's pamphlet out as soon as possible – so fast in fact, he says, that 'there was a major production problem'. The original draft, itself done 'very, very quickly', was scrambled and lost. 'They cobbled it back together.' The phrase 'safety standards' was misspelled twice.

Nowadays Irvine says that *The Right Lines*, as he punningly titled it, was intended mainly to provoke debate. 'I honestly thought that the ideas would be kicked around, and slowly disappear into history.' He insists he was 'the front man' for a wider constituency of disgruntled British Rail staff. But the response to his polemic – the interest from the media and politicians was 'unbelievable'

– sharply raised his ambitions and status. In 1988, he produced a second, more confident Adam Smith Institute pamphlet. 'Privatisation is a form of liberation,' he wrote. 'It has always been assumed that railways are expensive to improve. This is because they have been in the hands of the State...Private firms perform better.' Fares would be lower, he said. Journeys would shorten, the government subsidy would shrink, the environment would benefit, and cheap railcards and a'travellers' rights' scheme would smooth away friction between customer and rail operator.

During the late eighties and the early nineties, Irvine's Scots briskness and ideal schemes were much in demand. For a rapidly changing succession of Tory transport ministers, who now seem reluctant to return phone calls about rail privatisation, the exercise was a way to give their administration, as it began to stutter, ideological momentum. Irvine's pamphlets directly referred to this need in 1990. Cecil Parkinson presented the railway sell-off to the Conservative party conference as a test of political machismo: 'It is the most difficult to privatise...But that's no reason why it shouldn't be tackled.'

Those more aware of the practicalities were less enthusiastic. 'Irvine was inclined to make rather absurd promises,' says Hope. Until after the 1992 election, the BBC revealed last year, the civil servants told to plan the privatisation did little, hoping or expecting that the Conservatives would lose power.

But Irvine was looking further ahead. By 1994, he had helped form the first company specifically designed to acquire rail franchises. 'We knew that he had done papers for the Conservative government,' says Giles Fearnley, one of the other four partners in Prism Rail, 'and he was a very clever chap.' Irvine was the only Prism founder with railway experience (the others had all run bus companies). Even more usefully, he knew which bits of the network were likely to be sold off first. The London to Southend service, for example, was bought by Prism on Irvine's recommendation. He had identified it as an ideal candidate for privatisation a decade before.

The ethics of all this were not thought problematic at the company. Close links between people who helped form government policy and people who collected the private profits that resulted were common at the time – indeed they were essential, in the money-dominated logic of the era, for a privatisation to have any takers. By 1996, Prism was the largest operator of privatised trains. In 1997, with Labour's election-year surge suggesting that the good times might shortly be ending, the company put in bids for seventeen of the twenty-five franchises available.

The workload was crushing. 'At one point, I was working on fourteen bids at the same time,' says Irvine. 'I was working almost every waking hour.' And while he, Fearnley admits, 'wasn't given a huge salary', the other partners were receiving many thousands of pounds each in shares with the acquisition of each franchise. Unlike Irvine, the bus entrepreneurs had invested their own money, and had been able to work for Prism without salaries. The Scotsman grew exhausted and a little isolated: 'He's never been an operational guy,' says Fearnley. 'He was very much an academic.' In 1997, Irvine resigned – his appetite for Prism had lasted exactly as long as his appetite for British Rail. He received £250,000 in shares; the firm's other founders, by the time they abandoned their reward system under pressure from investors the same year, had earned £40m.

It is possible to feel sympathy for Irvine. His former colleagues from Prism are not in touch (the firm was swallowed by National Express in the summer – privatisation is a cannibalistic business). He says he works on 'certain things internationally' these days. 'But I've signed a confidentiality agreement.'

Unlike many of those involved in rail privatisation, Irvine is at least prepared to explain it. He even says some sensible-sounding things about the slackness of Railtrack, and the deflating similarity of today's expensive, inefficient railway to the one he worked for in the early eighties.

But his enthusiasm for privatisation remains infuriatingly intact. 'You look at the uniforms,' he will say. 'It is a considerable improvement.' The current chaos 'might just be the catalyst to make everyone work together'. He still advocates commercial control of the London Underground. He wrote a forceful paper on the subject in 1997, for the Adam Smith Institute. The sentiments within it are not a million miles from those of this government.

I read it and all his others on an eight-hour train crawl to Edinburgh. Coming back, as we edged belatedly into Kings Cross at 1 a.m., past the darkened windows of the bar of the Great Northern, it was even more difficult to feel charitable about what had begun in there.

And when we spoke later that morning, Irvine just happened to mention a more recent acquaintance made in the tight world of railways. He calls the current rail regulator, Tom Winsor, by his first name.

6 December 2000

LEADER

Magic or not, let in the daylight

The Queen will today travel by state coach and horses to parliament wearing the Imperial State Crown. She will sit on a throne in the House of Lords, surrounded by a sea of tiaras, red robes and ermine and command the House of Commons to attend upon her. The Lord Chancellor will, on bended knee, hand her a speech setting out the government's programme. The Queen will perch her spectacles upon her nose and begin with the words: 'My government...' Few of her subjects will, one imagines, be watching this piece of ritual, so heavy with dubious symbolism and history. There will doubtless be a short clip of pageantry on tonight's television news, which will rapidly move on to the subsequent debate. The little royal prelude will be thought by most to be charming, but irrelevant.

The 'irrelevant monarchy' is a common theme amongst royalists, agnostics and even republicans. These days (they argue) the royals are decorative. They have no real power or influence. One may hold them in awe or in contempt, but at a time when we are having to import nurses from Spain and a rail journey from London to Nottingham takes nine hours, there are surely more important things to discuss? The opposite case is simultaneously argued by defenders of the Crown. This runs: like it or not, the monarchy is embedded in our constitutional arrangements and is, indeed, the only constant. Lords reform is a mess. Scotland, Wales, Northern Ireland and even England are on a devolutionary journey with no obvious destination. Our institutional relationships with Europe are neurotically fraught and ever fluid. The stability of having the Queen as head of state is – in some views – essential and – in others – a reassuring veil of continuity that allows a government of the left to be more radical than it otherwise could be.

So the question of who should be our head of state is seldom addressed, and never by our elected representatives. MPs are indeed barred from debating 'the conduct of the sovereign, the heir to the throne or other members of the royal family'. An MP who raised the question of whether Britain might be better off as a republic could be sent to the Tower. A silly bit of decorative irrelevance, of course. Like the Treason Felony Act 1848, which should really be now used by the attorney general against this newspaper, since it threatens that anyone imagining or publishing anything which might lead to the Queen's downfall should be deported for life. For we do question how much longer Britain should remain a monarchy. Today and over the next few days a number of writers argue in these pages that the widespread programme of reform undertaken by this government – the most sweeping since the 1830s – cannot be satisfactorily completed unless we also address the position of who should be head of state, together with the means by which they are appointed.

To be clear from the start, nothing we argue is intended to reflect upon the present royal family. As people we may admire them, despise them, pity them or envy them. That is, in a sense, beside the point. The hereditary principle is a lottery. One generation gets a Winston, the next gets a Randolph. One generation gets the Duke of Marlborough, another the Marquess of Blandford. It is fruitless complaining. We have been extraordinarily lucky with the present Queen, who has behaved throughout her reign with considerable dignity and quiet common sense. Who can tell whether Charles has whatever it takes, or William thereafter? Those who support the hereditary principle as a way of selecting our head of state should accept the throw of the dice.

The problem is not one particular royal family or one particular royal. The problem is the office itself. Now that Westminster has been purged of most of its earls, dukes, marquesses and viscounts there is a general acknowledgement that the purge was long overdue. The present arrangements are widely agreed to be flawed, but no one at all argues for the return of the hereditaries. That leaves the beached whale of monarchy as the only remaining part of our unwritten constitution dependent on the accident of birth.

This is, in itself, indefensible. While much of the rest of our society – its aristocracy, its land, its property, its money, its hierarchies and feudal arrangements – was organised upon hereditary lines, the monarchy comfortably fitted into a wider pattern. Our society is no longer arranged upon these lines and the monarchy no longer fits. But our objections to the continuation of the constitutional monarchy go further. As our writers demonstrate in this series, the crown is far from being an abstract. It lies, like the Rosetta stone, at the centre of our national life. It underpins every aspect of our current set-up – and stands behind most of the flaws or excesses of our system of government.

If you think Britain's degree of centralisation is our core problem, blame the Crown prerogative which hoards all executive power at the centre, placing it in the hands of the prime minister. If you hate the way parliament has been eclipsed, blame the Crown prerogative, which allows a prime minister to govern with barely a nod to MPs. If it is secrecy you loathe, and freedom of information you want, look to the Crown – in whose name the executive can act in the dark. If your beef is with Europe, where you believe the council of ministers takes decisions in your name that you never hear about and cannot change, ask with what authority British ministers act: the answer is the crown prerogative.

If you dislike the culture of patronage that still informs our politics, with a second chamber stuffed with cronies and monied benefactors of the main parties, then blame the crown: for it is the 'fount of patronage' from which all honours, titles and largesse flow. Is your local hospital run by people you never voted for and have never seen? That is because Britain is a quango state, with appointees taking crucial decisions over all our lives: they can, thanks to the power of crown prerogative. If you have ever wondered where our judges come from – people who will be making ever more crucial decisions of life and liberty for all of us – then consider the Lord Chancellor, able to fill the judiciary in the name of the crown. If you wonder by what authority a prime minister can send British troops to Sierra Leone without troubling MPs to consider the matter themselves, then blame the crown prerogative.

It is a shared view on both left and right that the constitution needs rebalancing. Parliament must be given more powers. Prime ministers and their coteries must be more accountable to parliament. The House of Lords needs more legitimacy. There needs to be profound and far-reaching rebalancing of local power against central power, of national powers against supranational powers. Is it really imaginable that this debate can take place without a word of argument about the crown prerogative, as well as the historical loose ends, legal flummery and the malign constitutional impact (as well as the merits) of monarchy? Nor is it imaginable that the constitutional monarchy could be retained while dismantling crown prerogative. Those closest to the Queen are adamant that the vast edifice of power that is the crown must remain. They say the same about the residual royal prerogatives exercised by the monarch herself: the power to appoint a prime minister and refuse a dissolution of parliament. Both underpin her ability to serve as head of state and cannot be taken away.

But the influence of the crown is also cultural, and here, too, there is a need for change. Though we speak of 'an accident of birth', in fact, little is left to accident with our royal family. The Act of Settlement says that in order to qualify as our head of state you must be an heir of the body of Princess Sophia, electress of Hanover, a protestant in communion with the Church of England, not marry a Roman Catholic, not be adopted and have parents who were married at the time they conceived you. More silly ritual, of course. But do not shine a torch on it too brightly in case the whole foundations crumble. One hundred and thirty-five years after Bagehot, we are still told that daylight and magic do not mix.

As things stand, the next king will be asked at his coronation – before a worldwide audience of billions – if he is willing to do 'the utmost of your power to maintain...the Protestant reform religion established by law'. The question expects the answer yes. But, of course, the answer should be no. Charles mutters about becoming 'defender of faiths'. The Archbishop of York calls for its reform, along with the Act of Settlement. The Scottish Parliament calls for its repeal. The palace says nothing, and nothing happens.

This paper's contribution to breaking this logjam is to ask the courts to consider whether the Act of Settlement is compatible with the Human Rights Act. While we are about it, we are also doubtful that the Treason Felony Act is compatible with guarantees on free speech enshrined in article ten of the European convention. The legal process should, in itself, provoke a fundamental debate about how precisely the crown wishes to define its future role and whether it is any longer tenable for church and state (not to mention armed forces and the courts) to be united in one person. It will, we predict, be an unalarming and sober debate. When all but a few hereditary peers left the House of Lords, the ravens did not flee the Tower and our rivers did not run uphill. We will learn that we can discuss the monarchy in a similarly level-headed fashion.

Where should that debate go? It seems fruitless to begin by demanding the immediate advent of a republic in Britain: it ain't going to happen. We should begin instead by asking for a referendum about what sort of head of state we should have once the Queen dies. People ought to be able to say whether they would prefer to have an elected head of state or to continue with a monarchy. Do they want to be citizens or subjects? Our poll today shows a predictably confused picture. One in three supports the novel idea of a referendum. Given the choice between Charles and William, there is an even sharper split, with Charles mustering only 49 per cent against 41 per cent for William. People would – by a majority of two to one – much rather think of themselves as citizens than subjects. And there is a clear view – nearly 70 per cent – that the Act of Settlement is objectionable. A referendum – sooner rather than later – should be threatening to no one. If – as seems likely – the royal family were to win public endorsement, it would give them a form of qualified legitimacy they presently struggle to claim. The public should then be asked whether their monarch – even if s/he remains notional head of state – should have any meaningful powers. Our poll suggests that only a small majority – 54 per cent – is in favour of a hereditary monarch keeping any political powers. Stripping them of any formal constitutional links to either church or government would be half the battle won.

The younger royals must be acutely aware how uneasily a hereditary monarchy now fits into a Britain that is markedly more egalitarian and pluralistic than when the Queen was crowned. This misfit would doubtless cause any family doomed to assume the role great unhappiness. It is an impossible role and will become increasingly so. Engage with your subjects (the Queen taking tea in a Glasgow tower block) and you risk ridicule as well as (expressing sorrow over Paddington) empathy. Stir up controversy (the Prince of Wales on organic farming, architecture, GM foods) and you are indulging in an abuse of power. Remain silent and you become an unaccountable sideshow. Split up with your wife and live with another woman and you mirror all current social trends among your fellow citizens. But can you then head a church whose views on divorce and extramarital sex have not yet caught up with the news from the central statistical office? Defenders of the monarchy argue that it retains its appeal and potency by virtue of its ability to reflect a nation to itself. Consider only the official eighteenth birthday pictures of our future head of state dressed in white tie and Eton tails. Which teenager in the country looked at those pictures and truly saw a reflection of themselves? The Act of Settlement may send an odd message to black, brown, Catholic, Jewish, female, unmarried and Muslim Britons, but the excuse supposedly lies in history. What is the excuse for the William picture? How can those so attuned to the power of symbols be simultaneously so blind to them?

We declare our hand: we hope that in time we will move – by democratic consensus – to become a republic. We are gradualists: we accept that it will not happen tomorrow. Let the Queen remain Queen for as long as she lives, or she wishes, or she remains able. But in the meantime there should be a long, vigorous and grown-up debate – both inside and outside parliament – as to who, or what, should succeed her.

27 March 2001

ANGELIQUE CHRISAFIS

In the killing fields of Cumbria

Downwind, there was a smell like diarrhoea and clotted blood. A block of more than a hundred decomposing sheep thumped from a dumper truck into a pit. Limbs flapping, the yellowed carcasses slid fast, because they were turning to liquid slime. They left a trail of blood and clumps of rotting fleece on the metal container.

The death smell, more pungent than manure, is now common around Cumbria. It is known as 'the honk'. People gag on it but are resigned to it. A quarter of a mile from Britain's first foot and mouth burial site yesterday, there was laundry drying on lines. It would have to be washed again.

Great Orton airfield, near Carlisle, is now known as 'the killing fields'. Long abandoned by the RAF, it was already bleak and grey. By the end of this week, there will be 2km of mass graves there. About twenty trenches, four metres deep and 150 metres long, will hold half a million carcasses.

Yesterday 7,500 dead sheep slid into the pits, were drenched in lime, then covered over by mountains of excavated mud. The thud of landing carcasses was barely audible over the beeps of digging machinery churning out more burial pits. At least 10,000 carcasses will be dumped in the trenches tomorrow. After that 20,000 a day will be buried. Tomorrow, they will start to bring healthy animals here. With 240 cases in Cumbria, more than one-third of the national total, half a million carcasses, stand to be buried here.

At the burial pit, Major Guy Richardson, said: 'It is a colossal operation, which involves a huge team effort, and we are moving things forward. People are just getting on with the job. If people sat back and had time to themselves, they would think. But everyone is knuckling down.'

Major Richardson said the trenches were being built as needed, to avoid the risk of empty pits filling with rain. Carcasses were being dumped at one end of a trench while bulldozers worked at the other end.

Today, twenty-five more containers will arrive. The only touch of humanity was the decoration in the truckers' cabs – leopard-skin seats and curtain tassels.

A quarter of a mile down the straw-lined lanes is the village of Great Orton, population 235. It has two dairy farms and three hobby farms. All animals are disease free but due for slaughter.

At the Wellington pub, the landlady, Liz Currie, said disinfectant was ruining the carpet, and foot and mouth had killed trade. 'It has been drastic. The darts matches have been cancelled, plus the old people's activities. I have spent six months learning my lines for the panto, *Cinderella*, and now that has been cancelled.'

While the first carcasses were heaved into the pit, the minister of agriculture, Nick Brown, flew from London to meet farmers and ministry officials in a Carlisle pub. Outside the Auctioneer drinking house, he jumped out of his car to calls of 'murderer' and jumped back in two hours later to calls of 'you bastard'.

After the meeting Mr Brown denied the government had run out of answers. 'Just because it is a difficult situation, that doesn't mean we don't have answers to it,' he said.

But Steve Heaten, a local National Farmers' Union leader, said of the meeting: 'Frustration is the word. If I had any hair to pull out, I would have pulled it out.'

31 March 2001

JOHN VIDAL

Cattle low mightily, then the thuds begin

The three slaughtermen are young, cheerful and clear-eyed. Killing is their business and they have never known trade like this. In the spring morning light, they were on a farm near Wigton, Cumbria, shooting more than 100 cows and 500 sheep. Now the Ministry of Agriculture has told them to go to Jim Hutcheson's Scale End farm near Penrith.

Our mobile death-squad rattles through the lowlands south of Carlisle. We carry, in the back of a sixteen-year-old white van, cartridges, stun guns, decontamination suits, blue overalls, rubber gloves, sprays, wellington boots, forms and all the paraphernalia of modern slaughter.

The landscape is flat and desolate. Most farms here have been condemned and there are no animals in the field. The white smoke of incineration pyres drifts into the van. We pass decomposing sheep carcasses piled high in the corner of fields where they have been waiting days to be picked up. The sickly stench of death hangs over some farms, while in others the cattle and sheep lie sweetly together, their limbs spread-eagled, bellies swelling, tongues rigid and out.

Scale End was condemned on Sunday, but in the watery sunlight it seems normal. At the end of a long closed road is a tangle of ancient and modern buildings. Seven lambs play in a small paddock behind the farm. A bull stalks the yard. The cattle low quietly in the barns and the sheep are penned in a field beyond. This is spring. There are daffodils on the roadside, birds in the hedges, and the Hutcheson family is waiting expectantly, as if for a relative.

But we bring only death. The three slaughtermen change into their overalls and white suits. They smoke a cigarette and share a joke. They don't like this, they say. It is messy and too human. Yesterday a farmer cracked up.

We cross the straw border that separates the clean from the unclean, and dip our feet in disinfectants. There are handshakes and nods. Mr Hutcheson is almost too emotional to speak, but a toothless old cowherd shows them round. 'There are plenty sheep and cattle,' he says.

The slaughtermen reckon several hundred cows and 400 sheep. It will take four hours, they say, and start moving machinery around the barn to prevent the animals trying to bolt. Now the cattle squeal and low and the sheep bleat hard. The legs of a cow give way and it drops to the ground. Five heads strain out of the barn. 'Of course they know,' says one of the men.

Mr Hutcheson paces the yard, distraught, angry and purposeful. 'It's a bloody, bloody mess. Terrible,' he says. 'It's been chaos from start to finish. No one's told us anything. We've been surrounded for weeks. Three of us round here thought we could escape, but we found it on Sunday. That bloody Nick Brown [the agriculture minister]. How dare he stand up and say it's under bloody control. He should be here in this pen with the animals. I'd take a shotgun and give him one...'

The slaughtermen return to the vans, pick up their guns, spray them with disinfectant, have another cigarette and then, like hanging judges, put on black hats. Mr Hutcheson wants it over quickly, they say.

The doors of the green barn close behind them, the cattle low mightily and then the thuds begin. Every few seconds a thud. And another. Thud. Thud. Thud. For hour after hour the thudding goes on. They move to the sheep. The family does not watch. By six it is over. There is a deep and terrible silence and the white van heads off.

Scale End, Laurence Holme, Raughton Head, Willow Spring, New Hope, Green March, Spare Well, Raggie Whate. The list of Cumbrian farms that the white van and other slaughter vehicles have visited this past month reads like a wartime cenotaph. So far almost 300 have been condemned and at least 100 are still waiting for the stun guns or the hauliers to take the animals to be killed near Carlisle.

The mood across the county is desperate and fatalistic. There is now almost no farmer in Cumbria, the borders or on the high Pennines who believes he or she can or will escape. The consensus is growing that, solely because of ministry failure to act promptly, the disease has gone so far and so fast that it is now uncontrollable. Vaccination is seen by some as a futile gesture, too little and too late, but by others as the only option.

'We know it's just a matter of time,' says Richard Mawdsley, on the edge of the northern fells. His flock of 400 fell sheep graze near Bassenthwaite, several miles from the nearest outbreak but close to Skiddaw and the heart of the Lake District.

'We can see it coming closer every day. It's lost. It's coming in now from County Durham, Weardale, Swaledale,' says Colin Swan, who has 300 breeding ewes near Brampton, east of Carlisle.

'They may as well give up on Cumbria now,' said one farmer from the southern fells at a meeting in Carlisle this week. 'They should concentrate on stopping it reaching the regions where it hasn't hit yet. It's start again time in the Lake District, but I doubt that many will want to stay on.'

A look at the map shows how the disease is marching up the valleys, ever further into the fells from every direction. On Thursday, three cases were found right on the edge of the national park, near Caldbeck. So far there has been just one case in the national park itself, but many fear it is already in the fell flocks, or has actually passed through them. It has not been spotted, they say, because the authorities have not had the resources or, perhaps, the will to check.

But in the past few days it has ominously spread deeper into the Scottish borders, with four cases, and, significantly, into the high Pennines to the east of the lakes. This week the ministry took four days to admit that there had been an outbreak on the vast Alston Moor, preferring to say it was at 'Aldestone', the ancient and never-used name for Alston, the highest market town in Britain.

There are mutterings of a cover-up of bad news before a possible election announcement. 'The farmers are screaming for information. They are beside themselves with worry,' says Philip Walton on whose farm the disease was found.

The Alston Moor case could be one of the most devastating yet. 'It means that it's now on the backbone of England for the first time. It is like one great open field with tens of thousands of sheep, and it has a clear run now down south,' says Jane Mayes, who has thirty sheep within a few miles of the outbreak. She has been leading a campaign for emergency vaccination for the sheep on the moor to stop the disease spreading.

'You can't cull them anyway up there. Some will escape. It's got a hold on the moor – at least if you vaccinate, it won't come back.'

'The disease is spreading like a battle group,' says Alston vet Jim Clapp. He, too, has been advocating vaccination on the fells for weeks and banging in requests and warnings to Maff and the chief vet's office in London. This week, he asked for 20,000 vaccinations but he says: 'Maff laughed at me. The farmers could vaccinate everything in a day. They are crying for something to do.'

Yesterday he was called to the Maff offices, expecting the vaccines to have arrived. They had not and yet again he was frustrated. He still does not know if he will be allowed to treat the sheep, as he wants to do, and is astonished at the ministry. 'It's one terrible state of affairs,' he says.

The farming community, along with the thousands of businesses that depend on it and the tourism that it attracts, is in turmoil, with growing social, political and scientific dissent being voiced against the National Farmers' Union and the government. Why, they ask, did it take more than three weeks before anyone from London came to the region? Why has Nick Brown never admitted the disease is out of control here? 'They'll want blood in time but for now straight talk and information would do,' says farmer John Hitchen.

In the past week there have been three impromptu demonstrations and a well- attended meeting organised by Farmers for Action, which grew out of the fuel lobby. The protesters broadly argue that Maff has betrayed everyone, the union is part of the problem and that vaccination should not just be for cows.

'The slaughter policy is failing because it's always working behind the disease. Sheep farmers want vaccination but say they are being sacrificed to the economic interests of the richer dairy farmers,' said Graham Swain who farms thirty acres in the southern lakes. 'The policy is divisive and ill-thought through.'

Farmers for Action have promised direct action, and called for flying squads to defend farmers. Some farmers have threatened to take direct action. 'I've got a motley crew of animals,' said one woman from the Duddon Valley. 'They will not get them. I've got chains, superglue, vicious geese, barricades and I'll lock myself up with them in my kitchen.'

She and others argue vehemently for vaccination without slaughter. Below the political and military reassurances, there is deep disquiet that in fact the situation is still worsening. Despite Tony Blair's intention to get the time from identification of disease to slaughter down to a day, it is taking more than four days for the carcasses to be buried or burned, with further risk of the disease spreading.

Today, the three slaughtermen will be working flat out at the Great Orton centre outside Carlisle, where a massive trench is filling with sheep, and the army plans a pyre to take 15,000 cattle. It would be the biggest bonfire in British history.

'There won't be anything left after this,' predicts one of the three men, stun gun in hand. 'But there won't be any work for us either.'

6 April 2001

POLLY TOYNBEE

Whimpering nation

This is a country on the verge of a nervous breakdown. The stiff upper lip is wobbling; hysteria is in the air. What are the symptoms? A national nervous reflex, an involuntary panic spasm that greets every event. Any minor setback sets off a *crise de nerfs*, a fit of the vapours turning any mishap into a crisis.

So it came to pass that a law was rushed through parliament this week postponing local elections never before cancelled in peacetime. Why? Because 1.8 per cent of the national herd has caught a disease lethal to neither man nor beast, while the whole of agriculture represents just 0.8 per cent of GDP. A neurotic over-reaction caused filthy pyres that closed the countryside down, destroying tourism, which has created a genuine calamity.

So it was with the Hatfield rail crash. A broken rail shattering into 300 fragments of steel came to symbolise the parlous twenty-year decay of public services everywhere. Four people dead was a tragedy, sacrificed to the wanton privatisation of railways. That political disgrace has turned a sad episode into a genuine national disaster. Neurotic response brought national transport to its knees. Grotesque exaggeration of danger closed the railways, forcing commuters to resort to the roads instead. (Some 3,400 are killed a year on roads.) Worse, it immobilised the country. A curious fatalism fell upon the passengers who ought to have rebelled far more vociferously than the fuel protesters.

Diana tears were bizarre, but since then national neurosis has seen twitchy sensation take over from reason and statistic time and again. Unfortunate incidents become omens and signs from the stars, signifying some bigger, scarier malaise. Every piece of bad luck or bad news is rolled up together as certain proof that the elements are against us. Protests by a handful of rogue dairy farmers and hauliers sent the country into paralysis, and now each crisis escalates. When things go wrong, as they do, it now has symbolic meaning. The doctor has no appointment for a week, the roads are gridlocked this morning, the circle line stopped. TB stalks school corridors and now half Beachy Head has fallen into the sea. Each one becomes more than a personal or national event – it is a portent.

Nations, like people, live in their heads and their imaginations as much as in the real world. Ideas and symbols matter. This Margaret Thatcher instinctively understood; it was her greatest political talent. Now Britain's self-image is flagging even as times are better than ever before for almost everyone, far better than in her day. Our clinical depression has no root in real facts and figures, only in a diseased imagination. But the psychosis is infectious, radiating out a message to the rest of the world: we are as sick as our cows.

An email, one among many (some unprintable, catchlined 'Eat shit, euroscum', 'Lady, you are a total moron' and the like), zaps across the Atlantic in response to my article on George Bush this week. Here's how we look to them: 'Your whole infrastructure is decaying around you. Your crime is higher than ours. Your football hooligans are the recognised gold standard, the most loutish yobs this side of the Taliban. The British have lost their collective wits. Your whole country ground to a halt because a bubble-headed ditz of a princess committed involuntary suicide in a careening automobile with a man who was not her husband. Your tree and bunny huggers are out of control and Luddism is running riot. Until foot and mouth your national priority seemed to be banning of fox-hunting You get the idea?' Yes, alas, we do. There were many others in this vein.

From the other end of the political spectrum, add in a session I had in Glasgow this week with Tommy Sheridan MSP for the Scottish Socialist party, who follows in the rhetorical footsteps of many a red Clydesider. His eloquent tongue left no New Labour achievement untrashed, no sign of progress, all doom and calamity in a land of galloping inequality and social disease. Then a

Dutch TV journalist calls to ask if there is any food left in the shops.

But even more unnerving, an email arrives from the London correspondent of the German *Financial Times*: 'It seems to me that it really is five to twelve for Britain and that it will, in all probability, become a second-world country, side-lined in Europe, run down internally, insignificant politically and economically, a slum in which a few very rich people still lead a good life oblivious of the conditions of the rest.' It takes the breath away, leaves gasping paroxysms of panic. Time to take up your children and emigrate?

No, take a deep breath, calm down and realise that this is just what we are saying to ourselves, reverberating and exaggerating itself around the globe in distorting Chinese whispers. This is our own unreasonable neurosis and our worst midnight fears reflected back to us. Jitters and jumpiness combine with deep 'nothing works' cynicism to paint a portrait of a nation in crisis. We are suffering from clinical political depression.

How did we fall into this melancholia? The Tory party may be in unelectable decay, but in its death throes, its inordinately powerful press still has the capacity to poison the national air. If it can't win, it can still spoil, sour and frighten. By any objective measure, things are getting better with more money in almost every pocket, including benefits and pensions. This has been the most golden economic moment in living memory. What's more, at last serious money is there on the table for health, education and transport. But it has all taken too long, big numbers announced with scant change to be seen yet, results slow in coming. In public services, this is a fertile time to believe superstitiously that nothing makes any difference, nothing works. Things fall apart.

But does the centre hold? Up to a point. Tony Blair, the touchy-feely, is a man of these times: his nose to the wind, he feels our hysteria. Whatever his rational cabinet might say, he knows by the pricking of his thumbs that the election must be postponed, not for good reasons but bowing to the national sentiment. And he was quite right, for these mood swings sweep all before them. Resistance is useless. The question is, does he stop to ask himself why we are in this neurotic and irrational state? Or if there is anything he might do to stiffen the sinews, summon up the blood?

His third way is partly to blame for all this drift and wobble, leaving public sentiment to be blown about like dandelion seed. There is too little political rootedness, no clear markers of where we are headed and why. Clinton's woeful lack of legacy shows a golden economy is never enough without strong ideological leadership too. What is needed now is clarity of purpose and message, no more appeasement, but a manifesto of sufficient boldness to fill a political void that has turned us into a nation of hysterics.

1 August 2001

JONATHAN FREEDLAND

Censure, not censor

We've had two in a week, and it's only Wednesday. That's pretty good going. Normally it takes at least a month for one row about censorship, decency and freedom of speech to die and for a second one to take its place. This week we had to wait just twenty-four hours. No sooner had the fury about Chris Morris's *Brass Eye* subsided, than a fresh lather was foaming about the imminent arrival of Louis Farrakhan – the Nation of Islam leader known in journalistic shorthand as the 'minister of hate'.

Already there's a routine. On Monday politicians were haranguing the TV bosses. Yesterday they were scolding the high court, following Mr Justice Turner's lifting of the exclusion order that has kept Farrakhan away from these islands since 1986. Sticking to the drill, it was the same politician pressed into service on both occasions:. the luckless Beverley Hughes. On Monday she slammed *Brass Eye* as 'unspeakably sick', only to admit later that she hadn't seen the programme. Yesterday the junior Home Office minister was in action again, regretting the court's decision to admit a man with a proven record of anti-Semitism whom successive governments have barred as a threat to public order.

As always the debate follows reassuringly fixed lines, with everyone playing their assigned role. One camp, led by the right-wing newspapers, attacks the person or TV programme (or artwork or play or film), usually demanding the offensive material be banned. Instantly, an enemy coalition assembles, made up of liberals and the left ready to cry censorship and rally to the offender's defence. That's how it was with *Brass Eye*, just as it was with the Saatchi Gallery's display of Tierney Gearon's nude pictures of her children back in March – an exhibition raided by police, apparently tipped off by the *News of the World*.

There's something wrong with this pattern and not only its weary familiarity. It's also bad for the liberal left – a severe, habitual error that puts progressives on the wrong side of too many arguments, leaving them defending the indefensible. At its worst, it is a habit that robs liberals of their morality.

The habit in question is more like a set of impulses. The first is social: liberals simply don't like the people on the other side and opposing them is a reflex. *Brass Eye* is a case in point. Appalled by the constellation of forces attacking the programme – New Labour nannies David Blunkett and Tessa Jowell, the *Daily Mail*, Frederick Forsyth and the whole army of professional harrumphers- card-carrying liberals felt an instant duty to flock to Channel 4 and its besieged star, Chris Morris. Where else could liberals be but on the side of the trendy, cutting-edge artist and against the philistine curtain-twitchers of middle England? To condemn Morris would be terminally unhip and desperately middle-aged.

The same default mechanism will probably kick in with Farrakhan, a black man shut out by a series of white home secretaries. Black kids in Brixton want to hear him, white politicians want to ban him: for most liberals that should make yesterday's court decision a no-brainer.

The second impulse is social too and no more noble, for it is rooted in class snobbery. It regards those who cry obscenity or indecency as pawns of 'tabloid hysteria' – code for any view held by the vulgar masses. If something outrages large numbers of regular people, then the elite rapidly condemns the 'mob mentality' of these gross unsophisticates, usually via the handy device of attacking the newspapers they read.

Last summer presented a clear display of this brand of liberal snobbism, when the citizens of the Paulsgrove estate mobilised in admittedly ugly protest against paedophiles living in their area and were drowned in metropolitan derision – a wave of broadsheet hysteria. Their accusers were cognoscenti who could adopt an impeccably liberal stance towards released child molesters, safe in the knowledge that none was about to be housed next door to them.

But these social instincts, probably unconscious, are compounded by a central and repeated error of logic. In their eagerness to oppose censorship and defend the right to free speech, liberals end up defending the speaker's words as well as his freedom to utter them. They conflate the general right and the specific content, as if to condemn the latter would somehow endorse a curb on the former.

So Channel 4's defence was that *Brass Eye* was effective satire – implying that the government would have every right to ban ineffective satire. Meanwhile, Louis Farrakhan's lawyers insist their client is no longer an anti-Semite and that his talk of the 'synagogues of Satan' or his description of Judaism as a 'gutter religion' was either misunderstood or happened a long time ago.

Such apologism is unnecessary and dangerous. It's unnecessary because a sincere liberal need not defend Morris or Farrakhan on their merits: they simply have to cite their right to free expression. I bow to the American constitution's first amendment: the right to absolute free speech, no matter how ugly – a right which ends only when genuine mortal danger might ensue (the famous 'no right to shout "fire" in a crowded theatre'). With that starting point, censorship rows are easy: Channel 4 had the right to broadcast *Brass Eye*, Farrakhan has the right to come to Britain, Tierney Gearon had the right to display her pictures.

But none of that commits the liberal to endorse those people or their works. One can quite easily support someone's right to speak free of government intervention, and still loathe what they say – even going on to use one's own freedom of speech to defeat them.

For those in positions of power that means exercising judgment. Michael Jackson could have refused to broadcast *Brass Eye*. To do so would not have been censorship, merely an editorial decision: no legal edict denying Morris the right to be heard anywhere, just Jackson's own decision not to broadcast his work on Channel 4. The Oxford Union could have made the same call on David Irving. Refusing to give him a platform to explain his anti-Semitic, pro-Nazi views would not have been censorship – gagging him everywhere and forever – but merely a denial of the Oxford Union stage: just another decision like the thousands they make every term. If Irving then sought to write for this newspaper and was refused, would that be a violation of his human rights – or an act of editorial selection, no different to those meted out to would-be contributors every day of the week?

Liberals should not run away from this logic, nor from this responsibility. Their opposition to censorship does not commit them to an 'anything goes' morality that cannot tell right from wrong. Liberals can censure even if they cannot censor. They can declare things repulsive and unacceptable, without resorting to the blunt instrument of the ban.

We can and we should. For if we do not, we risk ceding morality to the right, leaving untrammelled freedom for ourselves. The truth is that progressives can claim both liberty and morality, granting absolute freedom of speech – even as we condemn those who use that right to spread hatred, cruelty and lies.

8 September 2001

MAGGIE O'KANE

Last stand in the ghetto of hate

It's after midnight and Father Aidan Troy is in the parlour of the Holy Cross monastery in north Belfast. Outside, floodlights illuminate a circle of grass with a huge statue of the sacred heart in the centre. Father Troy is tired.

The phone keeps ringing – *Newsnight*, Radio 5 *Live*, CNN, Italian TV – for a man who has spent the past week leading Catholic school children down a rabbit run of hate.

Father Troy, fresh from Rome and his doctorate in ecumenical studies, is talking about what he learned in his thirty-five years serving God. 'If people say they have a grievance, I now unreservedly accept that grievance, because they absolutely believe it.'

The Protestants of this wet Belfast ghetto that surrounds the Holy Cross primary school will go to bed tonight secure in their grievances and their right to keep protesting on the Holy Cross school run. They will be back on Monday morning and perhaps for many Monday mornings to come. For, in their own minds, they are the victims of a Catholic conspiracy to drive them from their dreary poor streets.

They are women like Kate Riley, fifty-three, whose husband was murdered by the IRA in 1974, three bullets in the back of his head while he was sitting on the sofa waiting for a Scotland football match on a new big-screen TV they had ordered in for the game.

'It's fuck all to do with the school. They want our houses. They took my husband's life twenty-odd years ago and I've worked since then for this house. Now they want to take my home away from me.

'If we don't stand up now, where will the Catholics take over next: Glencairn, Highfield, Ballysillan?'

In the last ten years Protestants have gradually abandoned their streets. Their ghetto around the Holy Cross school has shrunk to half its size: 1,500 Protestants surrounded on three sides by the hardline Catholic Ardoyne.

Catholic Belfast is exploding: Father Troy baptised sixteen children last month. 'Why should we be pushed out to take care of their breeding?' asks

Hugh Megarry, Kate's partner.

The old certainties are gone. The traditional, if triumphalist, parades through Catholic areas are mostly banned. The police force that once supplied their side with the names of IRA men to kill are now beating the Protestant protesters back and the IRA haven't even handed in a single gun. Old heroes like the Reverend Ian Paisley are tired and quiet while 'that bastard Gerry Adams' has become a world statesman.

Hugh Megarry sits chain-smoking at the kitchen table. Blinded when he was seventeen by a Catholic bullet, he calls himself a community worker, but says he hasn't walked past the Catholics at the bottom of the road – a distance perhaps the length of a football pitch – for twenty-three years.

Fourteen of Belfast's seventeen grey steel 'peace walls', the 'interfaces' that rise 20ft high between the two peoples, are in north Belfast. For Kate, it is not enough. 'We want a wall built here so we can live without fear,' she says.

They keep an incident book, a child's blue school exercise jotter. It records the grievances: how Catholic boys scream 'Hun' and 'Orange whores' from a distance and then come and break their windows.

Mostly, it's the stuff of thirty years of division. But, because they're frightened and hemmed in, they see every Catholic parent bringing their child to school as an IRA man casing their streets for another hit.

Kate Riley's neighbour, sitting across the table today, lost her husband to Catholic extremists on his thirtieth birthday in 1974 as the couple unpacked their shopping in the back kitchen.

Between them, among the empty cigarette packets, is a bottle of diazepam tranquillisers. 'I was deprived of the right even to have children when they murdered my husband,' says the neighbour. 'So don't talk to me about what we are supposed to be doing to those kids going up to the Holy Cross school. We have to protect our area.'

'No one knew until all this started happening at the school that we couldn't even go past those Catholics to the shop. Now the whole world sees. I don't care what they think of us – we're damned anyway,' says Kate Riley.

'The Catholics have the biggest propaganda machine in the world. We have been tarred like a leopard and we may as well act like one.'

On Thursday, the Holy Cross Protestants did try to regain some of the propaganda ground. At 4 p.m., they produced for the media a disabled Protestant boy in a wheelchair who couldn't get to his day-care centre because the police were blocking the road to escort Catholic children.

His mother told how the police had chucked her into a garden after last week's blast bomb at Holy Cross injured four officers. Another victim dropped his trousers to show a bruised bum. 'How many victims are there?' the press inquired. Nobody seemed to know.

At the Sinn Fein press office on the Falls Road they are much more polished with their sums. A query about loyalist attacks on Catholics immediately produces three neatly typed pages detailing 169 incidents. A young law graduate, one of their team of eight media workers, talks about the Holy Cross school as though it were Alabama.

He is smart enough to know better, but all week the parallels with how white

American racists stopped black children going to school have been too delicious to discard.

Last night, after a brief detour to the funeral of a sixteen-year-old Protestant boy run over by a Catholic woman, now charged with his murder, the world's press were on their way out of Belfast via the city's new £30m airport. New Belfast was left behind with all its old wounds.

On the Protestant Shankill Road, where three weeks ago Catholic extremists beat a nightshift worker to death with a screwdriver, the paper in the local newsagent carries details of how the mother of the sixteen-year-old Protestant boy arrived just in time to cradle his head as he was dying.

The shop window of the hardware shop next door is covered with small plastic Union Jacks.

Father Troy, back up in the Holy Cross monastery is considering a new idea for a way forward: he wants to ask Catholics to take down the flags that stake out their territory. Blessed are the peacemakers for they have far to go.

FOREIGN PARTS

Steve Bell, 15 November 2000

JONATHAN FREEDLAND

Beginning of the end

Today America will begin to say farewell. It will be a long goodbye, one that fits the outsized character of the man. For the United States has three months to let go of a leader who has, by turns, enthralled, appalled and seduced them for eight compelling years. Bill Clinton won't officially become the ex-president till a minute past noon on 20 January 2001, but by late tonight he will be yesterday's man. He will lose his throne, either to his appointed heir or to the son of the king he slayed to get there. One of them will be the president-elect and, in a heartbeat, Clinton will slip from emblem of America's present to holdover from America's past.

His fellow Americans will miss him – more, perhaps, than they realise. They'll miss the two terms of peace and record prosperity, of course, but they might even miss the psychodrama: an eight-year roller-coaster ride so turbulent that those who followed it become queasy at the recollection. They'll miss the daily triumphs and disasters of a character of Shakespearean complexity, a president who stirred in the American people passions of love and hatred unseen since the days of John F. Kennedy and Richard Nixon – and almost never aroused by a single man. Above all, they will miss his signature feature, one that may well have redefined the presidency itself: an almost eerie gift for empathy.

I will miss him, too. For the years of Clinton's American journey matched my own. I first came to live and work in the country in 1992, just as he exploded on to the national scene. I watched him run for president, and stayed to see him do the job. From then on, and for several years, I watched, read or wrote about Clinton nearly every day. Just as future TV documentary-makers keen to evoke the nineties will flash up an image of the president, I suspect that, when I look back on my late twenties or early thirties, I will do the same. And tonight that era will come to a close.

The memories come so fast that it's not easy to separate them. That 1992 election alone was so chock-full of scandal and turnarounds, such a vintage campaign, that it's hard to forget any of it – whether it was Gennifer with a G, the Vietnam draft-dodging letter, written by Clinton while a student at Oxford, or Hillary on *60 Minutes* insisting she had been no Tammy Wynette standing by her man, and that if you didn't like her husband, then, 'heck, don't vote for him'.

It was a crazy year, but it was that Clinton gift for empathy that saw him through. I had heard about it before – Republicans had already ridiculed the Arkansas governor's tendency to begin sentences with 'I feel' rather than 'I think', a habit that reached its apotheosis in the legendary 'I feel your pain'. But there was no substitute for seeing it in action.

Of course, there were the moments widely witnessed, such as those few seconds during one of the televised debates, when the candidates were asked how the recession had affected them personally. Clinton turned the query around, asking the questioner how she had suffered. Meanwhile, his opponent, George Bush Snr, was caught on camera checking his watch.

But there were also the tiny episodes, too small to be reported in their own right, which offered a glimpse of Clinton's sheer talent for people. It's perhaps hard, after this year's lacklustre contest, to imagine the excitement Clinton generated that autumn. 'The failed governor of a small southern state,' the Republicans had called him. But the voters didn't see it that way. I remember two moments from a Clinton–Gore bus tour through the American heartland. It was a swing through southern Georgia and the buzz was palpable. People didn't just attend rallies, they lined the highways in crowds to catch a glimpse of the man who would be president. Some held banners urging the young governor with the gargantuan appetite (he can eat a whole apple in a single bite) to stop awhile and sample the local peaches or peanuts – and he always did.

His aides would get enraged, every stop delaying the tour by a few more crucial minutes. By the end of a campaign day, Clinton would be running four or five hours late, but it didn't matter. In the town square at Valdosta, a crowd that had gathered for a 9 p.m. rally waited till 2 a.m. Under floodlights on that September night, they cheered themselves hoarse.

Earlier that day, we'd been in a small town called Tifton. Clinton had delivered the usual stump speech, his throat sore, when it began to pour with rain. The reporters ran for cover, inside a makeshift press room where there was the usual supply of chicken drumsticks and Diet Coke. Eventually, an Israeli journalist tapped me on the shoulder. 'Come outside,' he said. 'Look at this.'

The candidate was still out there, shaking the hands of fewer than a dozen elderly voters who had stayed out in the rain. He was talking to each one – not just a 'Hi, how are you?' but a proper conversation – as the rain streamed down his face and theirs. His aides were urging him to hurry out, desperate to whisk him on to the bus and into a new shirt. This was not a pose to show how much he cared about ordinary people: there was not a single camera to record it. Besides me and the Israeli, no one saw it. But Clinton did it all the same.

Who knows why? Maybe the legend was right: maybe Clinton believed that so long as he met every single voter in America, they would all vote for him. Maybe his childhood (widowed mother, alcoholic stepfather) had left him with a near-addictive need for human contact, affection and adulation. Maybe he just cared.

Either way, it worked and worked. The crowds got bigger, his voice got hoarser and the empathy gift won that election. I returned to London determined to get work in America that would let me see the next chapter of the story: how Clinton the candidate would become Clinton the president.

The transition was not easy. A dozen books have recounted the political errors of those first months. Day one saw a promise to let gays into the military, a move which only confirmed the brass's worst suspicions about the new, draft-dodging commander-in-chief. Later, Hillary Clinton took control of healthcare reform – a move that would bring the administration's greatest defeat. The first lady presented Congress with an almost comically complicated blueprint for a new system: expressed as a diagram, it looked like a circuit-board for the space shuttle. The fact that the plan had been hatched by a taskforce of wonks meeting with Hillary in secret added to its Soviet-era aura. By 1994 the plan was dead, and the Clinton administration badly wounded.

Things were no easier for the president himself. The Washington establishment was not sure what to make of this brash southern newcomer. They were both excited by and disdainful of him. They sniffed at the Arkansans who piled into town, supporting their beloved Razorbacks football team with the uncouth chant 'Oooo pig soo-eeee!'. For the Washington elite, Clinton and his friends were hicks, plain and simple.

The greybeards also disdained his way of doing business. They heard that the president would have long 'bull sessions' more akin to the college seminar room than the Oval Office. They saw the pizza delivery bikes skidding up to 1600 Pennsylvania Avenue, as the young, novice staff worked through the night. While Bush had been a grown-up, Clinton's White House seemed to lack adult supervision.

The word of the hour back then was 'unpresidential'. The Washington snobs disliked Clinton's habit of answering reporters' questions while still out of breath, pale thighs wobbling. They winced when he answered an MTV inquiry about his taste in underwear: 'Boxers or briefs?'

What the scolds did not realise was that all this 'unpresidential' behaviour was connected to the president's greatest strength: his common touch. He was comfortable with people. So when a little girl, invited to the Oval Office to take part in a candle-lighting ceremony to mark the Jewish festival of Chanukah, yelped as her hair caught fire, guess who put out the flames and calmed her nerves? Not an aide, but the prez himself.

Clinton was like that *Star Trek* character, the empath, who can psychically read the emotions of those before him he had a mind-reader's ability to see into the hearts of any individual or group he faced.

I saw the trick at work in Baltimore, when the president was out selling his healthcare package. He was addressing an outdoor crowd of thousands of hospital staff. I was standing among a group of nurses, who began chatting and whispering. Their minds were wandering. Somehow, from faraway, Clinton sensed it. He suddenly declared that his plan really mattered, that it would affect all of them, nurses especially – and that they all had to listen up. The women around me hushed.

The gift did not save him from the failure of the healthcare programme, a defeat that was endorsed by 1994's mid-term elections, which the Republicans won by a landslide. Overnight Newt Gingrich became the hottest politician in America, cheerily explaining that he would be prime minister to Clinton's now largely ceremonial president. Soon Clinton was forced to tell a press conference why he and his office were still 'relevant'.

But the mood changed. On 19 April 1995 a right-wing extremist detonated a bomb at a government building in Oklahoma City, leaving 168 dead. Suddenly the anti-government bile of Gingrich's revolutionaries left a much harsher taste in the mouth: America had seen where such talk could lead.

Clinton stepped forward as the calmer voice, leading the Oklahoma families in mourning. Perhaps for the first time, he looked presidential – a father of the nation at a moment of crisis. Just then, America needed a leader who would feel their pain.

In fact, though no official would ever say it out loud, mourning worked well for Clinton: he gave good funeral. He knew how to touch just the right nerve. I remember a ceremony at Arlington National Cemetery, dedicating a memorial to those who had died in the Lockerbie bombing. He spoke well, as always, but it was afterwards that he came into his own. A huddle of relatives gathered around him. He spoke to each of them, but then he extended his big hands to reach the ones who had not pressed forward, the ones too shy to approach the president themselves. He encouraged them and beckoned them closer, his eyes finding the hesitant widow or retiring father who was holding back. Again, I looked around: no cameras. The TV crews had already got their pictures. Clinton was not doing it for appearances' sake. He stayed there a full hour over schedule, maddening his handlers and listening to the stories of bereaved loved ones – and not a word was ever written about it.

This talent or knack or psychosis – whatever it was, it secured Clinton's position as president. Groups who had once been suspicious began to like and eventually adore him.

Take black Americans. In 1992 they had big doubts about Clinton. He was a white politician from the deep south, a Democrat who had signalled his 'centrist' credentials by attacking black rapper Sister Souljah and by breaking off from the campaign to return to his home state – to order the execution of a retarded black man convicted of murder.

Yet within a few years Clinton would be hailed by Toni Morrison, the African-American Nobel laureate, as 'our first black president' and by the rapper Ice-T as 'a brother'. What had changed? Clinton had saved affirmative action from the Republican axe, but he'd also signed a welfare reform bill that hit black families hard. No, it wasn't policy that sealed the bond between Clinton and black America. It was a more subtle connection. The president displayed a comfort with black audiences that was unheard of among white politicians. He could deliver an impromptu speech-cum-sermon from the pulpit of a black church that had civil rights activists admitting they had heard nothing so inspiring since the days of Martin Luther King. The result is a white president who enjoys 95 per cent approval ratings among African-Americans to this very day.

Jewish voters tell a similar story. They were wary of a southern Baptist Democrat in 1992: they feared he might be another Jimmy Carter, too sympathetic to the Palestinians. But Clinton reassured them, using his secret weapon: emotional intelligence. It was his instinct and body language that led to that 1993 handshake on the White House lawn between the PLO's Yasser Arafat and Israel's Yitzhak Rabin. And when Rabin was assassinated two years later, it was Clinton who knew how to massage Israel's wounded spirit. He spoke to them, via TV, in their own language, addressing the dead Rabin with the words 'Shalom chaver' – goodbye friend. The phrase had not existed in Hebrew before then; now it's common Israeli parlance. And so, in 1996, Jewish Americans turned out – alongside blacks and women and Hispanics and trade unions and every other group who felt understood by Clinton – to give him four more years.

I took that as my cue to head back to Britain. I reckoned we'd seen the best of Clinton. The second term would be more of the same, only less so. And for the first year, 1997, I seemed to be vindicated: the economy prospered on autopilot and Clinton barely had to break a sweat. But in the first weeks of 1998 the sky fell in. The allegations of a dress-staining affair with a White House intern, Monica Lewinsky, the finger-wagging denial, the talk of perjury and impeachment – it all came so fast. The Washington punditocracy predicted that the Arkansas hick would be sent back to Little Rock by the end of the week. But they forgot who they were dealing with. Clinton was not just the Comeback Kid, the Houdini who had survived a thousand scrapes. He was also the empath-in-chief, and now he got the return on his investment: the American people empathised back.

They had already forgiven or ignored the waves of scandal that had broken with every season of the first term: Whitewater, Travelgate, Filegate and all the other gates never really swung. The American people apparently felt the same way about the president as a former Arkansas state senator I once interviewed. He had worked with the then governor throughout the eighties and had little sympathy for him politically. But he was adamant: 'Bill Clinton doesn't give duck crap about money.' Americans could see that for themselves: they had a president who had never owned his own house (he had lived in the Arkansas governor's mansion since he was thirty-two, moving from there directly to the White House). He may have been a shameless hustler after votes, but few voters believed Clinton was ever in the business of lining his own pockets. That's why all the stuff about Whitewater never stuck.

Zippergate was different: Clinton may not have lusted after cash, but Americans knew he lusted after flesh. They knew, too, that he had an undisciplined, selfish, self-indulgent streak. They knew he could be reckless and self-destructive, taking a risk he must have known could have ended his presidency.

But here's where empathy became a two-way street. Despite a year-long hammering from the Republicans, and a press united in its disgust for the president's actions, the public stood by him. Americans told pollsters they hated what Clinton had done but, from the first revelations in January 1998 to the senate trial a year later, they remained consistent, approving his performance as president and insisting that he should not be removed from office.

They understood him, just as he had understood them. He had always seemed to cut them a little slack, and now they returned the compliment. In the autumn of 1998 they watched the tapes of a beleaguered president assaulted by excruciatingly personal questions from Kenneth Starr's prosecutors – grainy footage with the visual grammar of a hostage video – and they sided with him. Just like Hillary, they stood by their man.

Once, when speaking about his faith, Clinton described the God he believed in as 'the God of second chances' – and he let out a little smile. That was the Clinton of early 1999: a lucky man, blessed with forgiveness.

In the end, he was less Houdini than Rasputin. The Republicans tried and tried to kill him, but they failed, destroying themselves in the attempt. Where are his enemies now? Gingrich was forced out of the Speaker's chair after the impeachment debacle, and so was his successor. The rest of the president's persecutors in the House are in tight congressional races today, desperate just to hold on to their seats.

And as for Clinton, this is his last day in total command. I can look back now on the last eight years and admit that we, those of us who covered him, were spoiled. We saw a president with towering political skills and a serious intellect – a man who could rattle off the fine-print detail of any policy programme anywhere in America and discuss the domestic politics of most countries in the world, a leader who would think nothing of calling up the great academics and writers of the day, often in the small hours, for a late-night, impromptu tête-à-tête.

And there was that gift for people. I admit it, it spoiled me – it even skewed my judgment. I came back from America to cover Britain's 1997 election, and was soon whispering to friends my anxiety that Tony Blair's success was far from assured: he got such little enthusiasm from the crowds. I'd got used to winning candidates getting a Clinton-sized response. Now I can see that I had witnessed a once-in-a-lifetime phenomenon. Like someone who heard Sinatra sing in the fifties or watched John McEnroe play tennis in the eighties, I had seen a maestro at the height of his powers. Clinton was the Pele of politics, and we might wait half a century to see his like again.

Today America is choosing between two half-Clintons. They can have a version of his smarts, in Al Gore, or a version of his warmth, in George W. Bush. Clinton wants the voters to choose Gore, of course, to protect his legacy. But if America picks Bush, that will be a kind of compliment, too. For it will prove that an ability to connect, which Bush has and Gore does not, is now an indispensable part of the job – thanks to Clinton, the king of empathy.

Smarts or warmth, one or the other is on offer today. Voters who want both will just have to wait. Or they can take one last look at the man from Hope – and remember.

26 June 2001

CHRISTOPHER HOPE

This is the Balkans. No one is nice

When I made my first visit to Belgrade, as a guest of the British Council about ten years ago, there was a man in the Kneza Mihaila, that central boulevard where all Belgrade comes to promenade, and to protest. He was still there last week. You step on to his big, pink scale, he slides the bolt beneath your chin and reads off your weight. He's a big man: his belly touches the back of the scale. And this is a relief. Just about every time I've been back to Yugoslavia in recent years there has been less of it to see. It is the incredible shrinking man of Europe.

Could it have been otherwise? Ex-Yugoslavia is a morality play in four wars. It puts an old question with grim relish: can different tribes with different faiths inhabit the same territory in peace? On the evidence so far the answer is no. What had been, like the man with the pink weighing machine, a generous, varied country of twenty-two million people, living in six republics (and two self-governing regions, a place called Vojvodina and a place no one had heard of called Kosovo), held together by a big fat chap called Tito, suddenly blew itself to smithereens.

What lit the fuse? When exactly did Yugoslavia go round the bend? Choose your combustible moment. I'd say it was in the last week of June 1991. That is when Slovenia and Croatia walked out of the federal assembly in Belgrade and declared themselves independent. The wars of secession began almost immediately. Then Bosnia-Herzegovina collapsed into war, Macedonia did a runner, and Kosovo caught fire and is still burning. Ten years on, that leaves just Montenegro, with Serbia, in a federation of two. 'Montenegro, Ecological State', proclaims the fading propaganda in Belgrade bookshop windows. Another sentimental delusion – it has one of the filthiest coastlines on the Adriatic. If Montenegro separates Serbia will be alone in a federation of one.

'Let it go,' said the Belgrade publisher Zoran Hamovic. 'Yugoslavia is like an old sock that must unravel. First we have the divorce, maybe later the remarriage.'

When I first came here, Slobodan Milosevic was recently in power. Now he is in prison. Belgrade has changed since Milosevic fell. Gone are the swaggering certainties. Belgrade is punch-drunk, excoriated by critics, boycotted by much of the world, and bombed by Nato. It doesn't know where it is. That is hardly surprising. 'Zagreb – this way', say the motorway signs – but it's a bad joke. 'Kosovo – that way', say the maps, and it really isn't kind. What you get in Belgrade now is the view from the amputation couch. Like a man who has lost several limbs, Serbia still feels phantom attachments – but when the patient tries to walk, he keeps falling over.

There is also this strange amnesia, as if time has raced Serbs away from the way things were, and they cannot bear to think about grey yesterday, or the wars, or Milosevic. But yesterday won't go away. The graves of victims murdered in Kosovo are turning up on the doorsteps of Belgrade; the ghosts are walking.

I stayed at the Hyatt, then and now. There are two international hotels in new Belgrade, across the Sava river, reached by the bridge Nato didn't bomb because lots of people stood on it every night with targets pasted to their foreheads. It was a short walk to the smashed Chinese embassy, now overrun by weeds. Nato bombed it because the CIA got the 'wrong' address. What they call the 'Sorry, wrong number' bombing. It was a mistake that has had unexpected effects as far away as Sarajevo.

It must have come as a relief to Belgrade high society that Nato did not bomb the foreign hotels. Their public rooms were always much in demand for weddings and assassinations. It was in the Hyatt that the patriot and gangster known as 'Knele', Aleksandar Knezevic, was gunned down in 1992. It was an occasion few will forget. At the Intercontinental across the way, a one-time pastry cook called Zeljko Raznatovic, otherwise known as Arkan – whose death-squads terrified Bosnians, and quite a few Serbs – was murdered.

In Milosevic's Belgrade, criminality and celebrity merged. Politics moved from Marxism to mystic nationalism (usually about blood and soil, flags and fatherland) to mafiadom (usually about oil or cigarettes or guns). It is a pattern that

Kosovo, Montenegro and Macedonia are emulating.

I wanted to begin my Yugoslav travels where I began some ten years ago – in Novi Sad, the Hungarian ghost of central Serbia and to end them in Kosovo, the Albanian enclave. It's easier said than done.

In the early nineties, when the Balkan wars were breaking out, I came to Novi Sad by train from Vienna, and we were warned to sleep with our heads away from the doors because Hungarian highwaymen leaped aboard in the night and stole whatever they could lay their hands on. Heady times. You could be offered hand grenades in Novi Sad market.

In Novi Sad the bridges over the Danube were still down. It was 10 June – two years to the day since the Nato bombs stopped falling. Traffic is blocked on the river and there is not much inclination to fix things. In an odd way it was a good sign. Despite their reputation as fighters, wars are not what Serbs do best, and the last four have been disastrous. So the bargaining has started. If countries upriver want the Danube opened, let them pay for it. If the West wants Milosevic in the Hague, it had better stump up.

There are other signs of a shift. Sremski Karlovci, not far from Novi Sad, blends Orthodox Serbian buildings and the opulent ochre of the Austro-Hungarian empire to which the little town once belonged. Sremski Karlovci is in gentle ruin. The lead sheeting is slipping from the cupola of the wonderful old theology building. There is a stork nesting in the chimney.

Zoran Hamovic has plans for its revival. He wants to take the old town hall and turn it into Translation City, a home from home for interpreters and translators who use and teach the Balkan languages – Serbian, Croatian, Greek, Albanian and Romanian. Before the Balkan wars, Serbs and Croats spoke the same language, though they would deny it now. Since the wars began, they have been inventing new words and compiling new dictionaries to prove that Serbo-Croat was a gigantic plot by the former Tito regime. And anyway, they can't think of what to say to one another. Hamovic holds that it is useful to talk to your neighbours, and desirable for them to talk back. He wants to encourage it. Anywhere else this might seem a pretty modest proposal, but in ex-Yugoslavia, where they haven't spoken in years, it is an idea of almost demented good sense.

I took the Vienna express from Belgrade to Croatia. It is about a six-hour journey to Zagreb, the Croatian capital. In a delightful old custom from Austro-Hungarian times, the stationmaster appears at his front door and stiffens to attention as the express slides by. You learn to make the most of delightful customs in the Balkans. When the domes of the Serbian Orthodox churches give way to the pointy-hat steeples of Catholic Croatia, the fun is over.

The train stops at the Serbian border and sits in no-man's land for about an hour. Serbian police officers come aboard, documents are requested, scrutinised and checked by walkie-talkie. Then the train inches forward to the Croatian border, sighs, stops and it all happens again. Change your money, your head, your religion, your language – and the locomotive.

I first saw Zagreb in the spring of 1992, when Croatians fought Serbs in southern and eastern Croatia. You drove down the motorway and turned left for the frontlines. In a town called Karlovac, Croat forces faced Croatian Serbs in a war at the end of the motorway. Small polite notices stuck on street corners said

'Mine'. The military base had been burnt and abandoned by the Yugoslav national army. Inside a great hangar were lines of blackened tanks. An officer of the Croatian militia protested to me that the Yugoslav national army was using cluster bombs, supplied – or at least built – by Britain.

In Croatia I saw for the first time the blend of domesticity and brutality that marked the Balkan wars. Wars fought in the suburbs, in the meadows. Wars where the sniper would hide in the belfry of the pretty church, where a hospital was raked with fire because it was a hospital, where an old man went on scything a meadow as the shells came in. Wars where tanks were used to blast away the fronts of houses and leave the curtains swinging in the wind, leave untouched the sofa and the children's photos on the wall, leave empty and nameless a place that had been someone's home until a shell sheared off its face.

Backyard wars, neighbourhood wars, wars of no return, where the aim of the victors has been to wipe out every vestige of the neighbour who once lived next door, obliterate his church or mosque and then rip up his grave. Wars where yesterday's loser is tomorrow's ethnic cleanser. For the past ten years, the former republics of ex-Yugoslavia have been playing a deadly game of Balkan poker. Anyone with a gun can play.

One day in 1992 I saw my first Croatian rally. I was in the great space in front of Zagreb station, King Tomislav Square. It was full of boots, badges, flags and bands. The Croatian leader, Franjo Tudjman, was to speak to his followers – which meant just about everybody, because if you weren't a follower, you were an enemy. It was a nationalist fiesta, with songs and symbols and an angry unabashed nostalgia for Croatia's fascist Ustase past, its collaboration with Nazi Germany. There was a swirling baroque intoxication that took me as close as I will ever get to something of the atmosphere that must have prevailed at Mussolini's rallies.

After the rally, I sat in the Zagreb Pen Club and heard the chairman make a grovelling apology for some wretched scribbler who had dared to criticise Tudjman's new regime – and no one turned a hair. The Croats of Zagreb said it was 'democracy'. They said so loudly, and if you didn't agree they shouted and waved their fists. Their distress was understandable. Dubrovnik was under fire from the Serb navy, and large parts of eastern Croatia, in the Krajina, were in the hands of Croatian Serbs. A fellow writer put it this way: 'For us Croats, the old Federation of Yugoslavia is a lost ideal. Unfortunately, for the Serbs, it is lost property.'

It turned out a few years later that the Croats also felt pretty strongly about lost property. In 1995 they assembled their armies, bought lots of weapons from Argentina, attacked the Krajina Serbs and drove them out in their tens of thousands to refugee camps in Serbia, where they live today.

Cleanse or be cleansed? Victor or victim? These are very Balkan questions. Who will be which today?

What a difference ten years make. I was back in Zagreb. No more marching bands, no more of the nationalist tat they used to flog. Everyone is feeling a lot better, they have mobile phones, and all the right brands are in all the shopping centres. Narrow your eyes and you might be – in Europe. A vintage sound truck belting out rap crossed an empty King Tomislav Square, flying the Croat chequered flag. I don't much like Croatian rap, but it beats the Nuremberg melodies they were playing last time round.

The Croats have set out to reinvent themselves. They've traded Tudjman for the Teletubbies, who beam at you from the new shopping centres. They've swapped their Ustase past for a European future. They've rebranded themselves as cuddly creatures, the koala bears of the Balkans. Gone are the fists and the neo-fascist nostalgia with its flags and badges. Gone are the war cries. Gone too are 165,000 Krajina Serbs.

From Zagreb I took the train to Slovenia. Ten years ago the Slovenes fought the Yugoslav national army and won – in under a fortnight. I suspect that the victory was as much to their own surprise as anyone else's, and Vuk Draskovic, the Serb writer and politician who was slung into jail by the Milosevic regime, spoke for many when he said the Yugoslav national army had been humiliated in tiny Slovenia by what he called 'a gang with lime-tree leaves in their hats'.

I got to Slovenia in April 1992, shortly after that lime-tree leaf war, and I remember it as a most vivid example of instant tribalism – just add gunpowder and stir. The bullets had barely stopped flying and Slovenia was hacking out a border with Croatia. The border between Croatia and Slovenia consisted of two men in baseball caps, under a Marlboro umbrella. They called themselves 'customs' and demanded deutschmarks for a 'visa' fee, a request backed by soldiers.

Today the Slovenian border is permanent, its officials wear spanking Slovenian uniforms and you must change your Croatian money for Slovenian money. Slovenia is strawberries and snowy peaks, yoghurt and yodelling. If Croatia these days is in the business of impersonating a democracy, Slovenia makes a living by giving impressions of other countries. It will do you a convincing Switzerland, or a passable Austria. Slovenia expects to be admitted to the EU any time now. After cutting itself off from the ex-Yugoslav federation, it can't wait to attach itself to another large federal body. And that perhaps explains why, for all its prosperity, there is something twitchy about Slovenia. It has all the eerie animation of a severed limb.

The little capital, Ljubljana, was being spruced up for the visits of the US and Russian presidents, George Bush and Vladimir Putin. The T-shirts read: 'I was in Ljubljana for the George and Vladimir Show!' Bush and Putin met in Brdo Castle, once the winter palace of the Serb prince, Karadjordjevic. Whoever writes the script in Yugoslavia has a baleful wit.

I wanted to go on to Sarajevo from Slovenia. Last time I was in Bosnia I travelled by road. This time I had to fly. Bosnia-Herzegovina is less than an hour by air from Slovenia, but it is several lifetimes removed by any other measure. On that first trip by road, in 1992, I went first to Montenegro and stopped at a monastery. Outside, army trucks were rumbling up the road to Sarajevo. In the monastery garden, over coffee and honey and plum brandy, I asked the abbot: 'Do you think it is right for a Christian to live with hate in his heart?' He thought for a moment and then he said: 'No. But the other side is worse.'

Flying into Sarajevo again, I looked for the television tower. I remember the shells landing nearby and the way it trembled like a flower – massive means to produce such eerily delicate effects. I remember that the casualties of these wars had nothing of Hollywood colour; instead, they seemed alarmingly forlorn, weightless, crumpled like so much scrap paper.

The shooting has stopped in Sarajevo but the sadness remains. Svjetlana Nedimovic and Tarik Jusic are two young Bosnians who keep an eye on what the press and radio are saying, who analyse language, who talk witheringly of the non-governmental organisations (NGOs) and their buzzwords – for NGOs drive hard bargains in their steely, gentle way. Those who take their noble shilling are expected to produce evidence that benevolence works, that Bosnians are improving. The NGOs want value for money; they desire concrete signs of 'multiculturalism', 'democratisation', 'civil society' and the big one – 'inter-ethnicity'. But this is Bosnia, and what they get is division, rancour, clannishness and cleansing. And Bosnia, like other places in the incredibly shrinking Balkans, goes on shrinking. There are few Serbs left in Sarajevo, Tarik says: perhaps 80,000 have left since 1991. And it is not just the Serbs. The young, the bright, the desperate are also going.

'Have a look at the Austrian embassy,' said Jusic. I did. The waves of people besieging the embassy give the place the look of some ghastly street party. They haven't come to be multicultural, they do not wish to democratise. They are ready to storm the exits. It isn't the happiest thing, losing your young to the diaspora. And the politicians of Bosnia, it would seem, are not into inter-ethnicity. They prefer power – theirs. No one much cares to step out of line. To question, to disobey, says Nedimovic, is to take a risk. They do not do it in the political parties, intent on retaining power, or in the universities, where those in charge believe that to question is to betray. The poker players of Bosnia are power freaks. They jumped from Tito's communism to nationalism to NGO-dom, and none of it counts – what counts is a gun stuck in your ear. The mood is nicely caught by Angelina Simic, writing in the English paper the *Bosnia Daily*: 'If I do not control, I do not exist.'

Sarajevo, once a city of many sorts of people, of intermarriage and religious richness, is now a tightly constrained, heavily subsidised ghetto. But it's not all purity in Sarajevo, not at all. And this is where that far-away bombing of the Chinese embassy in Belgrade has the most peculiar results. It led to an ever-closer expression of solidarity between Belgrade and the Chinese government, and it led to Milosevic opening his doors to many Chinese visitors wishing to extend their European horizons.

The Chinese connection runs from Belgrade, down through Serbia's unlovely stepchild in Bosnia, the Republika Srpska. And from there, more and more Chinese are showing up in Sarajevo. And they haven't come to open restaurants. In some of the roughest suburbs in Sarajevo, said Nedimovic, where the locals don't scare easily, people who survived the war are suddenly terrified. It's the downside of ethnic cleansing. You've just got rid of a lot of alien Serbs and look who moved in next door...Nedimovic keeps a straight face. The feeling, she says, is that Gypsies are bad enough – now it's the Chinese! 'Any minute they'll take over.'

In the Balkans, the way forward is often backwards. I flew back to Ljubljana in order to fly forward to Skopje, the capital of Macedonia. Rebel Albanian fighters in the hills had shelled bits of the city and were threatening to hit the airport. Thousands of refugees were on the road to Kosovo. The Museum of

Contemporary Art opened a new electronic show about the human genome and gene manipulation. It was an eerie evening. The museum sits on a hill and makes a good target. For this reason, the computerised exhibits and their all-too-human creators were ringed by soldiers. Inside the museum were advanced computing machines. Outside the museum, the gardens were full of soldiers with advanced weapons. And somewhere in the middle were some human beings.

No one knew who the men with the mortars a few miles outside the city really were. Macedonian Albanians? Kosovo Albanians? Albanian Albanians? Terrorists, extremists, patriots, mercenaries or plain criminals? A taxi-driver called Ahmed offered to take me to Tetovo, where there was fighting. 'We could ask who they are,' said Ahmed. Then he said, 'It will cost you forty German marks.'

We drove for a time. There were lots of Macedonian troops, and Ahmed said: 'What happens if I get shot?' I must have looked puzzled. 'I mean, what happens to the forty marks?' said Ahmed. We were turned away by Macedonian troops before we reached Tetovo. They did not know who they were fighting. They asked me to tell them if I found out. I didn't. Nobody knows. But there are two things that everyone in Skopje – Macedonian or Albanian – does know and says repeatedly: 'Our politicians, all of them, are useless' and We don't want a war. Please let someone make sure there is not a war.'

The only 'someone' able to stop a war is Nato. The Macedonians see it this way: there is Sfor in Bosnia, and Kfor in Kosovo – surely the time of Mfor is near? They may be right. If it happens, then a great stretch of southern Europe will be frozen uneasily, not into peace but into a kind of paralysis: a condition sufficient to prevent the patient from murdering his neighbours, but not enough to stop the mafias who feast on the pain of the Balkans from preying on the weak and the frightened.

I drove from Skopje into Kosovo, along the route the refugees take, mostly 'good' Macedonians fleeing the 'bad' Albanian militias. Moral labels are as shifting as Balkan currencies, as shifting as the ground in this earthquake zone, as shifting as the promises of local politicians, and the well-meaning bluster of western friends.

There is a Greek unit of UN troops installed at the crossing point into Kosovo. They park armoured cars in the gardens of the few surviving Serbian Orthodox churches. In the beastly game they play in the Balkans, wrecking your enemies' places of worship, even his graveyards, wins points – and points in the Balkans mean territory. Serbs destroyed many Kosovan mosques, and now Kosovans are doing the same to Serb churches. A great gulf in perception opens between agencies such as the UN, who are here for reconstruction, and local victors, who are here for revenge. One of the splashes of colour on the baking hillsides as you approach the capital, Pristina, is the Kosovo Liberation Army graveyard, rosy with red flags and wreaths.

I was here last in 1992, when sanctions against Serbia were biting. There were electricity cuts. The Grand Hotel had lost the last two letters of its name and the big neon sign on the roof read 'Grand Hot'. It is as gloomy as ever. Big banners over the main road proclaim 'Pristina – European City'. Another word favoured on the banners is 'transparent'. I don't believe it. Nowhere is less transparent than Pristina. Pristina is as opaque as ever.

The monthly wage – when you can talk in such nonsensical terms – is maybe sixty or seventy deutschmarks (£19-22). For they reckon everything in deutschmarks in Pristina, as they do across ex-Yugoslavia. It is the true currency of the Balkans – everything else is paper. And Kosovo takes only cash. Pristina doesn't have a bank worth the name, nor a cash machine. It takes no cheques, it has no credit cards, but it does have a few posters up preparing people in this cash economy for the arrival of the euro early next year. For what talks in Pristina is money and muscle, mixed in a black economy.

Along the dusty sidewalks, young men are hawking cigarettes, CDs and sunglasses. The cash comes from the troops and bureaucrats, the new occupying forces of Nato and the UN, who have Kosovo in their benevolent bear-hug. You see them sitting in places such as John's Kukri bar (its emblem is two crooked knives and the UN laurel leaves – war and peace). It is a couple of doors down from the Princess Di sandwich shop. Tall men, well fed, rich by Kosovo standards, who drive around in fleets of four-wheel drives, sit over a beer watching the nubile flesh perambulating by on platform heels. On the streets, the boys hawking bootleg software and CDs are also selling their sisters.

There was a notion, useful while it lasted, that Serbs were nasty but Albanian Kosovans were nice. But this is the Balkans, and no one is nice. When they occupied Kosovo, the Serbs drove out hundreds of thousand of Albanian Kosovans. When Belgrade capitulated after the Nato bombing, the Kosovan Albanians returned and the Serbs fled. For good measure, the Kosovan Albanians drove out the Gypsies, accusing them of being 'collaborators'. It is thought there were 100,000 in Kosovo before the conflict began; about 8,000 remain.

I flew out of Pristina airport as the other half of the George and Vladimir show flew in. President Putin had come to present medals to the Russian troops who beat Nato to Pristina airport. I left with a group of visiting Americans. Cordial Christians they were, and one of them was wearing a 'Prayer of Jabez' T-shirt.

'And Jabez called on the God of Israel, saying: "O that You would bless me indeed and enlarge my territory..."'

The prayer of Jabez has been heard in Kosovo, and it is heard in Macedonia, where the rebels in the hills find that what it takes to enlarge your territory are some mortars. With a couple of burned-out villages, you can carve out a little bit of the country and make it all your own. And if one day you add it to existing Albania, you could end up with something called 'Greater Albania'. That's a phrase you hear a lot in Macedonia and Kosovo, in much the same way as people used to talk of Greater Serbia when the Serbs were praying the prayer of Jabez.

To get back to Belgrade from Pristina I had to fly via Vienna – more or less the route once preferred by the Ottoman Turks when conquering this part of the Balkans.

What would Tito have made of it all, I wonder? No one mentions Tito's name except to invoke it as the embodiment of some Machiavellian master-spirit, a baleful enigma. He was, they say, an illusionist – Yugoslavia was held together by a dextrous dictator, a brutal dreamer. It was a trick, a sham, an unworkable paradox. Maybe the view of the old magician is shifting: among the banners of the many marches against Milosevic, my favourite read: 'Tito come home – all is forgiven.'

28 August 2001

GARY YOUNGE

Crisis in Zimbabwe

Andy Mhlanga woke up one morning in 1973, on the same plot of land that his family had lived on for generations, to find a fence being erected around it. 'We didn't know where it had come from or what it was there for,' he says. 'Until a white farmer came and told us that now if we wanted to carry on staying there, we would have to pay.'

Two years later he went to war, training in Tanzania and Mozambique, with guns from China and Russia to fight against South African-backed settlers of British descent.

'The war was about land and freedom but nobody was ever going to give us back the land, so in the end we had to take it back. I was very happy when I found that this farm has now been gazetted [listed for occupation],' he says.

Mr Mhlanga aspires to be Hitler's heir. Following the precipitate death of the previous war veterans' leader, Chenjerai 'Hitler' Hunzvi, who led the round of farm occupations last year, Mr Mhlanga has claimed his mantle as the secretary general of the Zimbabwe National War Veterans Association.

Emerging from his office in central Harare is like walking into a scene from *Goodfellas*. Peeling off Z$100 notes (£1.25) from thick bricks of cash, he slaps one of them into the palm of the teenager minding his car, gives a bodyguard money for petrol, and buys bananas for everyone in the van, all in the short distance it takes him to get from the front door to the kerb.

As we pull out, another driver waves in support, while others pull over to give him a wide berth, as though for a police car with its siren on.

We are off to see some occupied farms. It is a trip few thought I would be allowed to make. Mention the possibility of meeting the war veterans and most Zimbabweans – even senior members of the ruling Zanu-PF party who support them – wince and shake their heads.

My race has helped secure an interview. But it is no passport in itself. The majority of those who have been beaten and killed by the war veterans are black, as are the journalists who have been targeted by the State for writing stories critical of the land occupations and government. Some of the land that has been occupied was bought by black commercial farmers.

'If blacks want to support us then we will support them,' says Mr Mhlanga, as we drive south. 'But if they want to represent the interests of the whites, then we will treat them like the whites.

'We don't hate the whites. If they are prepared to share some of the land they have taken and become true Zimbabweans, then we have no problem. But most of them are still the same, like the old Rhodesians. They are sitting pretty in big houses and with many farms while we still have nothing.'

Few here, including the opposition, doubt the need for land reform in a country where around 5 per cent of the population own some 70 per cent of the best land and employ 65 per cent of the nation's workforce. But few believe that the recent occupations are the way to go about it. The strategy has not only brought lawlessness and political violence to the fore, but has plunged the economy into free-fall, starving it of foreign investment, damaging vital agricultural exports and isolating Zimbabwe diplomatically from its neighbouring allies.

It is an issue, say government critics and some war veterans, that has been exploited by the government in its desperate bid to remain in power.

'There is one thing we must thank Tsvangirai [the opposition leader] for,' says Mr Mhlanga. 'Before he started challenging the government, this would never have happened. They were dragging their feet on the land question. It has caused some economic problems. But it is a war and in any war there will be casualties, just as there were casualties in the war of independence. That has to be expected.'

It is clear from television pictures of those who took over the farms that many are far too young to have taken part in the war of independence.

'I am forty and I am one of the youngest war veterans, so I know that many of them could not possibly have fought in the war, and wherever there is chaos and animosity there will be criminals. But on the whole there are war veterans and there are land-hungry people, and all of them deserve a piece of our country.'

The needs and intentions of those who have either taken or have been allocated their plot vary. Some, who live in towns, travel out at the weekend to till their land or, like Mr Mhlanga, are waiting until they have the time to work on it properly.

Only a minority, say even their detractors, are still occupied by groups of young, drunken men idling in the devastation that they have wrought. Many are inhabited by families like the Murapanis, an eleven-strong unit spread over three generations who moved to land near Beatrice, about thirty miles south of the capital, last year.

The Murapanis were landless, scraping together an existence in the bush near Chitungwiza, just south of Harare. Their eldest son fought not in the popular war of independence against white minority rule twenty years ago but in the unpopular war in the Congo, for diamonds and regional supremacy, a war that still rages.

Now they have a plot growing mealie-meal and tomatoes on what was once grazing land a few miles from Beatrice.

In June they built two clay thatched huts, bare inside, save for the pots and pans that rest on the shelves and a small fire in the centre. Ask Mrs Murapani about the loss of foreign currency because of falling tobacco sales and the farm crisis and she looks baffled.

'What foreign currency?' she asks. 'I have never seen a dollar. That money never came to us. Now we can feed ourselves. But we are not quite happy because the white farmers are still occupying some of the land. These people must pack their bags and go. We don't want to see them any more.'

The land commander, who acts as a foreman for all the newly acquired small-holdings, says that the farmer and some of his labourers have tried to force them off the land and threatened them with an axe. Mr Mhlanga takes a mental note.

'We will send some people back to deal with them. They must learn respect,' he says as we are escorted to the van. 'This is when people get hurt and the foreign press come. It is only when they start to resist that we get heavy-handed.'

When we get back into the car, we realise the petrol gauge reads empty. Mr Mhlanga and his bodyguards head up to the small petrol station in Beatrice. There is no petrol – a shortage that existed before the occupations but which has been exacerbated by them in recent times.

Standing at the door of the staff quarters the station manager is dressed in white Zimbabwean rural uniform: boots, woolly socks up to his knees and faded khaki shorts with short-sleeved shirt to match. With his belly slung over his belt, he has known better days – times when black men would have been either brave or foolish to look him in the eye. But those days are long gone.

As Mr Mhlanga questions him on why there is no petrol he does his best to look composed but keeps his head down. War veterans roaming rural areas in a van are like sparks in search of dry tinder.

During our thirty-minute stay, black and white people come and go. White visitors, travelling in couples, keep the car engines running, scuttling to the counter to buy fizzy drinks, trying not to catch anyone's eye. Black people, sometimes eight to a van, move to the store front deliberately, hoping the scenery will swallow them whole and render them invisible. A local war veteran approaches with news of activity on nearby farms.

And then we head off, the gauge still on empty, motoring slowly and unsteadily back to the capital. Occasionally, a churning sound from the car's innards gives a hint that we might not make it. Another casualty in a long and complex war.

BLOOD, MILK
AND HONEY

Steve Bell, 8 February 2001

12 January 2001

EWEN MACASKILL

The punishment of Palestine

Haythem Abdel Aziz looked bewildered as he stood in the early morning sun amid the tangled iron rods and rubble of what just hours earlier had been his home. Aziz, forty-two, a carpenter, had been having breakfast with his wife, four sons and his parents on 2 January in the village of Ein-Yabroud on the West Bank when the Israeli Defence Force (IDF) arrived with a bulldozer. He was not allowed time to take out all his belongings.

He pointed to various spots where he thought his fridge, washing-machine, chairs, bed and sofa might be buried, crushed under concrete. His wife, Jihad, thirty-four, said yesterday: 'I saw the bulldozer coming with soldiers and five Jeeps. I hoped it was to clear the road but it was soon obvious it was coming here.'

Four other homes in the village were bulldozed the same day. The presence in strength of the IDF was because forty-eight hours earlier a Jewish extremist, Binyamin Kahane, and his wife had been killed by Palestinians in a roadside ambush. He lived at the Jewish settlement of Ofra, only a few hundred yards from Ein-Yabroud. The two communities are divided by a road.

Why had the IDF bulldozed the homes? Maybe the IDF had spotted someone firing a shot the previous night from Mr Aziz's roof and turned up in the morning to punish him? Maybe the IDF had intelligence that Mr Aziz, in spite of his air of innocence, was a Palestinian gunman? A request for an explanation from the IDF mentioned neither shots from his roof or any terrorist background. The IDF explanation was more mundane: 'There were five cases of unlawful building in the area of the fatal terrorist attack which were bulldozed.'

It is an inadequate explanation for destroying a family's home and belongings. There are tens of thousands of homes on the West Bank without planning permission because the Israeli government, while permitting Jewish settlers to build, gives the okay only to a small percentage of Palestinians. Mr Aziz had applied for planning permission, failed to get a permit and, like everyone else on the West Bank, had just gone ahead anyway. That was seventeen years ago.

The reason for the bulldozing is that it was a punitive measure because Jewish settlers had been killed. On the same day that the homes were destroyed, the IDF cut off all access roads to Ein-Yabroud, using the bulldozers to build up 6ft-high mounds of earth across the tarmac. A lawyer, farmers, a taxi driver, an American Palestinian over on holiday for a fortnight, a local councillor: all were standing around, unable to leave, facing a long day of inactivity. The lawyer, Haithim al-Sheik, ready for work in suit and tie, sympathised with Mr Aziz and complained about how it was impossible for a Palestinian to lead a normal life. They did not know how many days they would be cut off.

Brothers grim. Blair and Brown talk tough at a press conference days before Labour's crushing election victory in June. (Martin Argles)

Unidentified right-wing object. William Hague presents his Scottish manifesto to the people of Edinburgh in May. (Murdo MacLeod)

It's my party... Duncan Smith and Hague chew the fat at the Tory conference in Blackpool in October. (Martin Argles)

Stop press. A bomb scare in a nearby shop forces Michael Portillo to cancel a press conference in May. (Murdo MacLeod)

The only way to travel. The Queen shares a horse-drawn carriage with Thabo Mbeki, president of South Africa, on his state visit to Britain in June. (Graham Turner)

No, I'm supposed to kiss you... Margaret Thatcher receives the unwelcome attentions of a fan in Northampton in May. (John Robertson)

There are hundreds of Ein-Yabrouds throughout the West Bank and Gaza every day: abuses, small and large, committed by the IDF again and again. The West Bank and Gaza are supposed to be run by the Palestinian Authority, a step on the way, eventually, to complete independence. In reality, it is occupied territory: the IDF is the oppressor and the Palestinians the oppressed. Any time spent on either the West Bank or Gaza shows it is as stark as that.

Gaza is totally cut off. As in the film *Escape from New York*, all the ways in and out are sealed and those inside are left to make do as best they can in a community isolated from the rest of the world. The West Bank, with its long borders, is harder to block off totally.

Every day the Israelis make new enemies. Israeli soldiers on the West Bank and Gaza are predominantly eighteen- and nineteen-year-olds doing national service. They often behave badly out of fear, knowing that a bullet or a rock may not be far away. But their disdainful attitude is often born out of racism, a sense that Palestinians are inferior. It is evident in the remarks they make and in the contempt an Israeli soldier at a checkpoint shows to a Palestinian old enough to be his grandfather.

The Palestinians face lots of indignities, frustrations and anger every day. It is the lorry driver stuck nose down in a ditch, having foolishly attempted to drive across the desert because the roads to his village were blocked. It is the lost days of employment. It is the cessation of economic activity. It is the man raging at the Israeli-Gaza border because he is refused permission to visit his wife. It is the destruction of an olive grove because it is claimed Palestinian snipers could hide there. It is a newborn child dead because an ambulance would not be allowed through.

Members of the Palestinian leadership, from senior officials to representatives of the Fatah youth movement, are assassinated by the IDF. The British government always denied such a policy in Northern Ireland. The Israeli government boasts about it.

Reporters have been writing about the assassinations policy in recent days, prompted by the killing last week of a high-ranking Palestinian. But most of the other human rights abuses in the West Bank and Gaza are poorly covered, and often not at all. Few Israeli journalists now go to the West Bank and Gaza, afraid of being killed. Many American journalists self-censor their copy, knowing that their editors will tend to be pro-Israeli, reflecting the strength of the Jewish lobby in the United States.

The disastrous consequence of the Israeli treatment of the Palestinians is to create hostility where it had not existed before. A new generation has learnt hatred. Israel was never going to stop Islamic Jihad or Hamas but, since the Israeli–Palestinian agreement at Oslo in 1993, there were signs of the two communities at least coexisting, even if uneasily. That is now gone.

The tentative discussions in Washington towards a peace settlement are now irrelevant. A settlement is possible on paper: compromises can be worked out over the Palestinian refugees, the territorial boundaries, the division of Jerusalem and sovereignty over the holy site in the Old City. The problem is how to make it work on the ground. Even if the Palestinian leader, Yasser Arafat, and the Israeli prime minister, Ehud Barak, put their signatures to a deal today, it would not hold for even twenty-four hours, such is the level of distrust and acrimony created since the Palestinian uprising began in September.

Israeli officers and officials defend their behaviour on the West Bank, saying it is a war. Would it not be better, given that they are always going to have Palestinians as neighbours, to treat them in a civilised manner? An officer in the IDF said a soldier at a checkpoint did not know whether the Palestinian in front of him was an innocent or a Hamas bomber. He said the Palestinians had opted for violence: it had not been sparked by the visit of the former Israeli defence minister, Ariel Sharon, near the Muslim holy site, the Dome on the Rock, but had been deliberately sought by the Palestinians to secure more concessions in negotiations. Would it not be better to try to build up the Palestinian economy instead of trying to destroy it: Palestinians with jobs and a good standard of living might be less inclined to fight? The Israeli officer agreed but asked what was the point of giving money to the Palestinian Authority when so much of it was squandered by corrupt leaders.

Why does Israel just not pull out of the West Bank and Gaza and let the Palestinian Authority leader, Yasser Arafat, declare independence? The Israeli answer is that too many questions about the border would remain unanswered, a permanent source of aggravation and conflict.

An Israeli human rights group, B'Tselem, published a report yesterday on abuses on the West Bank and Gaza. It said the restrictions imposed by Israel on movement was 'one of the primary reasons for the increasing destitution and despair in the Occupied Territories and has made the lives of the population unbearable'. It added that the sweeping restrictions on the entire population rather than specific individuals were justified by the Israeli government on security grounds but the organisation disputed the effectiveness of the policy and pointed to the 'blatant discrimination between the two populations living in the Occupied Territories...solely on the basis of nationality. The restrictions are imposed exclusively on the Palestinian population.'

The Israelis have a siege mentality, touchy about any criticism of their behaviour, present or past. They refuse to acknowledge the injustice of what they did in the first place, taking the land from the Palestinians in 1948. That refusal is central to the main Palestinian claim of a right of return for refugees to Israel. When Benny Morris, one of the new generation of Israeli historians, wrote that the Israelis had been less than lily-white in their behaviour in 1948, he was vilified by Israelis.

He opens a history of the Palestinian-Israeli conflict with a quote from W. H. Auden about the second world war. It is as relevant to the present uprising as it was to the last fifty-three years of conflict.

> I and the public know
> What all schoolchildren learn,
> Those to whom evil is done
> Do evil in return.

Yesterday, amid the ruins of what had been her home up until last week, Mrs Aziz said she had asked a soldier why they were planning to bulldoze her house and he had replied 'revenge'. In a sad reply, she told him: 'There is no peace between us and it is getting worse every day.'

8 February 2001

DAVID GROSSMAN

What now?

When Ariel Sharon made his victory speech on Tuesday night, his supporters whistled in contempt and loathing each time their leader mentioned Ehud Barak, the left and the Palestinians. That triad has clearly been punished in the most painful possible way by the Israeli public. As one voter said, in perfect sincerity: 'I'm not sure that Sharon is the best for Israel, but the Palestinians deserve him!'

May I register my suspicion that Sharon himself does not believe what has happened to him? This man, whom many had already written off as a has-been, this power-obsessed, devious extremist of questionable behaviour, who has failed in nearly every public office he has held, who has injured nearly everyone who has been his ally, has now been handed an entire country. He can now try out his views, and his instincts, on it. Unlike in the past, this time there is no one, almost, who can stop him. But perhaps that is precisely the reason that in the final days of his campaign, when his victory was already assured, Sharon's mood suddenly changed.

Sharon, who has a cynical and venomous sense of humour, and an almost compulsive urge to crack jokes, looked melancholy and lifeless during the days leading up to the election. One of his associates said: 'It's as if something in him went out.' At moments, perhaps for the first time in his life, he looked almost frightened.

All his life Sharon has operated from a position of the opposition, even when he was a cabinet minister. He always, always, challenged the authority of his superiors, both in the army and in the government. A large part of what he did in his military and political careers was done while circumventing authority, disobeying orders, inciting against his leader, and even – as in the case of the Lebanon war – deceiving his superiors.

And now, suddenly, at the age of seventy-three, he is himself the superior. He is the authority. He is the man who is responsible for the country. And there is no one to stop him. Now he is prime minister of one of the most complicated countries in the world, deep in the most extremely delicate situation it has seen for decades. Perhaps Sharon knows, deep down in his heart, that if he does indeed mean to ensure his country's future, he will have to abdicate a large number of the opinions and beliefs and symbols that he has valued for the past generation. If he refuses to do so, there can be no doubt that he will lead Israel into a full-frontal collision, not just with the Palestinians, but with the entire Arab world.

Maybe that is why Sharon is worried. Paradoxically, this anxiety, and this initial awareness of his true political responsibility and of the complexity of the dilemmas that only a leader is forced to face, are encouraging signs that we can be comforted by (given that there is no other hope).

In this context it is interesting to note that, when the right has come to power, there has always been a sense that its leaders do not feel really sure of themselves at the wheel. Something in the rhetoric of Israel's right-wing prime ministers, from Begin to Netanyahu, has continued to be the rhetoric of opposition, of dissent against some lawful regime, even when they themselves were the regime. There were periods during Netanyahu's term, for example, when the government itself behaved as if it were a minority group being persecuted by some wraithlike hostile regime, as if it did not really believe in its own legitimacy.

If that turns out to be the situation this time, we will soon witness a dangerous flare-up of Israeli policy. This is liable to be expressed in more aggressive behaviour on the outside, along with contemptuous arrogance towards our neighbours (remember that Sharon instigated the Lebanon war in order to allow the Palestinians to take over Jordan!). This will also inflame the atmosphere within Israel and make its polarisation more severe. Experience of the years when the right ruled tells us to beware of spectacular, extreme acts that are ostensibly full of 'grandeur' – a magic word for the right wing, a one-word slogan coined by Ze'ev Jabotinsky, the revisionist Zionist leader who was Begin's mentor. In reality, they more often than not take place on the boundary between the grotesque and the catastrophic.

The most extreme, fanatical and fundamentalist groups are now returning to the centre of Israel's public stage. The hopes of the moderate, liberal, secular centre to turn Israel into a truly democratic country – less militant in character, more civilian in nature, more egalitarian – have been dealt a resounding blow.

Again there is that old, disheartening sense that because of an unfortunate series of events, and because of a harsh and difficult history, Israelis are doomed to run again and again through a time loop, once again to accelerate settlement in the occupied territories and escalate the conflict between us and the countries around us. The rule that all of us know from our most private lives has come true once more: again and again we trip ourselves up precisely in those places where we are most in need of being saved, most in need of a new beginning.

Immediately after he was elected – as during his entire campaign – Sharon invited the Labour party to join a national unity government. There can be no doubt that in this he expresses the wishes of many Israelis on both the right and the left who yearn to recreate a sense of partnership and brotherhood that is so lacking in Israel today. It is difficult, however, to see what policies the two parties can unite around. Yet if they do succeed in finding a middle ground between them, Israel will find itself the prisoner of that same familiar tragic error that it has been trapped in for years. Once again Israel will present the Arab world with a position that is a respectable compromise between its centre-right and centre-left blocks. But this compromise will have almost no connection with the demands and troubles and hopes of the Palestinians – that is, no connection with reality. Israel will again conduct virtual negotiations between itself and itself, between itself and its fears. Then it will be surprised, and perhaps feel betrayed, when the Palestinians throw its proposals back in its face while setting off a new intifada.

As for the Palestinians, even when they declare that they see no difference between Sharon and Barak, they know very well how big the gap between the two is, and what the consequences will be. For that reason, apparently, they began, in the two weeks leading up to the elections, to gallop towards a compromise with Israel at the Taba talks. Too bad that this zeal was not evident a few weeks, or even months, earlier. It is also unfortunate that Arafat did not succeed in controlling his people and in channelling the authentic energy of the beginning of the intifada into a momentum for reaching an accord while Barak was in power. Dozens of innocent Israeli men, women and children were murdered by Palestinian terrorists during the election campaign. Each funeral, each orphan's tear, 'proved' to the Israeli public that Barak had erred in agreeing to compromises. The public was pushed towards the man who promised them that he would not negotiate under fire. The despair and anxiety that possessed the Israeli public – and the total lack of awareness of Palestinian pain and suffering – are what has put Sharon in power. Paradoxically, the anxiety and despair are liable to bring about their own realisation.

The obvious conclusion from these elections is that the Israeli public is not yet ready for peace. Israelis want peace, of course, but they are not yet able to pay the heavy price that such an agreement requires. On the other side are the Palestinians, and they also, apparently, have not yet internalised the need for the painful compromises that peace requires. It is hard to see how we can get out of this dead end without another round of bloodshed.

Fairness requires that we give Sharon a chance to prove that he is right. There is a heavy feeling in my heart. Just writing this pains me – it is one thing to report on a train running off the tracks from a vantage point to the side. It is another thing entirely to report it from inside the train.

21 May 2001

SUZANNE GOLDENBERG

Loathing thy neighbour in the Gaza Strip

The daily misery of life for Palestinians in the world's most densely populated piece of real estate is encapsulated in a twin set of traffic lights in the middle of Gaza. When the light is green, the mile-long line of Palestinian cars inches another yard or so past the machine-guns jutting out of the army pillbox on to a road denuded of its palm trees, and squeezed to half its width by giant concrete slabs. When the light turns red – as it does when a single car travels between the illegal Jewish settlements that straddle the junction – life comes to a halt.

The light turned red soon after 10 a.m. yesterday morning when a Jewish settler, Anita Tucker, set out in her white Citroen with a trailer of fresh celery from her greenhouses in the Gush Katif settlement block, to deposit the load at the Kfar Darom outpost.

She left behind a long queue of Palestinian vehicles – and Israeli tanks, military jeeps and barbed wire guarding the two settlements, which straddle the main road linking the southern Palestinian towns of Rafah and Khan Yunis to the territory's capital in Gaza City.

As the collective waiting time of Palestinians stranded at this army checkpoint stretches into thousands of hours, an entire landscape is being transformed beyond recognition.

Since the start of the uprising eight months ago, some 11,000 dunams (one dunam is 1,000 square metres) of Palestinian-owned farmland have been razed by Israel's bulldozers, as have at least ninety-four homes, several posts of the Palestinian police, and last week, a £700,000 yoghurt factory and two wells.

The destruction is gathering momentum, with evidence that the Israeli army is carrying out systematic incursions into lands controlled by Yasser Arafat's Palestinian Authority to bulldoze homes and greenhouses, and rip out citrus groves and farmland with the aim of creating a security cordon hundreds of metres deep around the borders of the 140-square mile territory.

'It is very logical – they are trying to clear all the border areas,' Raji Sourani, director of the Palestinian Centre for Human Rights in Gaza City, said. 'Most of the houses on the border have been destroyed. Anyone who goes there, they shoot at him – civilian or soldier. Their tanks hide in the sand dunes and shoot at everyone.'

The destruction started late last year around the roads leading to Kfar Darom and the other Jewish settlements. It has gathered momentum since 17 April, when Israeli tanks rolled up to the edges of Beit Hanoun, on the northern edges of the territory, and occupied a square mile of land for several hours. A rare and sharply worded rebuke from Washington forced Israel's hard-line prime minister, Ariel Sharon, to pull back his tanks. But since then the Israeli army has briefly invaded territory under the control of the Palestinian Authority dozens of times, Mr Sourani said.

A spokesman for the Israeli army said yesterday: 'We don't keep count.' He added: 'It depends on the situation, and the operation.'

Last week, the Israeli army signalled that it had a free hand to initiate incursions into territory that was awarded to Mr Arafat's control in peace accords seven years ago. Previously, it had described such raids as reprisals for shooting and mortar attacks by Palestinian militias on Gaza's illegal Jewish settlement blocks.

For Ms Tucker, who is eager to show visitors the dimple left by one mortar bomb on the lush lawns of the youth centre in her settlement of Netzer Hazani, the tough stance was overdue.

But evidence gathered during a tour of Gaza's border areas support allegations that the territory's northern, eastern and southern perimeters are being transformed into free-fire zones.

The bulldozers arrived at lunchtime last week in the Salame neighbourhood of the southern town of Rafah, which has been a special target for the incursions, accompanied by a tank.

'Suddenly, a tank came right up to our houses,' said Amna al-Sha'ir, whose clan owns several homes in the hard scrabble border area. 'We were so scared. The children ran out of the house barefoot.'

The extended family of ten huddled in a shed at the rear of their house as the bulldozers tore down the greenhouse where they had been growing tomatoes, and the home of a cousin that had taken ten years' savings to build. 'I kept thinking I was going to die – me and the kids,' Ms al-Sha'ir said.

Some forty-six buildings have been destroyed in the Rafah area since the abortive reoccupation of Khan Yunis. The Israeli army insists that the homes and shops were used as havens for the militias firing mortar bombs on Jewish settlements, and kibbutzim inside Israel's borders. The Sha'ir family flatly deny this.

Such destruction has not been lost on the Jewish settlers of the Gaza Strip, whom the Israeli army claims to be protecting with its widespread demolition. Late last year, bulldozers demolished Palestinian homes on the southern fringes of Kfar Darom. Ten mobile homes, built for new arrivals to the illegal settlement, now stand in their stead.

'Of course, people living here felt terrible because they were friends with these people,' Ms Tucker said. 'But it was not our fault this happened to them. The people living there just let the Palestinian Authority take over and shoot non-stop. Yasser Arafat's Palestinian Authority did this to them.'

Ms Tucker's home at the northern end of the Gush Katif block lies on the other side of the junction from Kfar Darom. For an outsider, it is difficult to fathom the attachment claimed by Gaza's 6,500 Jewish settlers to this tract of unlovable land, an expanse of dunes and scrub surrounded by hostile neighbours. But it is home, insists Ms Tucker, who was born in London and raised in New York, and was a founding member of Gush Katif twenty-five years ago.

Here her family, like many of the settlers, have been raising greenhouse crops for the ultra-Orthodox, and organic produce: cherry tomatoes and cucumbers bound for European markets – including Marks & Spencer.

Despite the uprising, Ms Tucker continues to employ four Palestinian workers from Khan Yunis. Her workers take home an average wage of forty shekels a day (£7) – about a third of the cost of the workers she has had to import from Thailand. In her view, maintaining order in her greenhouses is not unlike peacemaking. 'I know from all my years of working with the Arab workers that if you are nice to them, they walk all over you,' she said. 'If I give a worker a pack of cigarettes, they stop working and will not do anything. But I am just tough and pay them – that's all – then I get good work out of them.'

In the same vein, she dates the start of the Jewish settlers' troubles with the Palestinians to 1993 – when Mr Arafat signed a peace agreement with Israel. Ms Tucker is aware that most of the world sees her settlement as illegal and her presence in Gaza as an occupier, but she believes that is the only way of maintaining harmony between two peoples who claim the same piece of land.

'We lived with our neighbours very peacefully. It is true that they did not have the right to vote, but so long as we remained in charge here and got on with our neighbours, eventually we would have sorted something out.' But that would not have involved evacuating any of the Jewish settlements. 'It is crazy to have all the Arabs living here in Gaza when you know tomorrow they are not going to be your best friend.'

21 May 2001

LEADER

Between heaven and hell

When T. S. Eliot wrote about our inability to bear very much reality, he could scarcely have imagined the special truth his words would acquire for subsequent generations. Who can cope with relentless exposure to all that we are able to know so easily about the world today? We ration our exposure to violence, to grief, to war, to disease and to starvation. We come to despair of solutions. We graduate our tolerance.

And so it is that we shut our minds to what is going on today within and around the borders of Israel. Of course, we cannot isolate ourselves completely. Some murders are so horrible they sneak in beneath radar. We still – at least – notice the violent deaths of children. The use of warplanes on civilian areas still has the capacity to shock. But, by and large, we cannot deal with the enormity of the unfolding tragedy. A fortnight of murder, bombs, bulldozers, maiming, rockets and torture – never mind the ever-present poverty and systematic infringement of human rights – all this passes with a despairing shrug. The abnormal becomes normal. The extraordinary becomes not only expected but accepted.

This tragedy affects all who live within the borders of Israel and the Palestinian Authority (PA). It is a tragedy for beleaguered Palestinian refugees – overwhelmingly innocent of any violence – whose daily lives are little more than a soul-sapping test of endurance. It is a tragedy for those families on either side of the divide directly marked by the continual violence. But it is also a tragedy for Israel itself. The men and women who created Israel wanted it to be a country based on freedom, justice and peace: in May 1948 they promised to ensure 'complete equality of social and political rights to all its inhabitants irrespective of religion, race or sex'. Those intentions were noble, the realisation fraught. But more than fifty years later, we are forced to confront some uncomfortable truths about how the dream of a sanctuary for the Jewish people, in the very land in which their spiritual, religious and political identity was shaped, has come to be poisoned. The establishment of this sanctuary has been bought at a very high cost in human rights and human lives. It must be apparent that the international community cannot support this cost indefinitely.

Israeli Jews are, for easily understood reasons, least able to bear these realities. Professor Stanley Cohen – an eminent sociologist who has a perspective gained from having lived in South Africa, England and Israel – writes in his recent book: 'Denial of the injustices and injuries inflicted upon the Palestinians is built into the social fabric...There are, of course, good historical reasons why Israeli Jews should have a defensive self-image and a character armour of insecurity and permanent victimhood. The result is a xenophobia that would be called "racism" anywhere else, an exclusion of Palestinians from a shared moral universe and an obsessional self-absorption: what we do to them is less important than what this does to us.' The 'what this does to us' was nicely summarised by one Israeli novelist recently in the sentence: 'What should have been heaven has become a form of hell.'

A visitor to Israel today who takes the trouble to visit both the cosmopolitan and historic centres of Tel Aviv and Jerusalem, as well as the captive degradation of the Gaza Strip, cannot but think of the rottenest days of South Africa. The analogy soon falters – South Africa was always one society with a single future while this is the story of two societies sharing the same space and seeking separate (though one day entwined) futures. But the parallels between the two states should be troubling enough for any Jew with a sense of the historical necessity for the creation of the State of Israel.

The Israeli novelist, Amos Oz, used to use the fable of the plank and the drowning man to explain the justness of Zionism. A drowning man (he wrote) is allowed, under all rules of natural justice, to cling to any piece of driftwood even if in doing so he is obliged to push others aside a little. He may even use force. But he has no right to push the others into the sea. The Palestinians have not quite been pushed into the sea, but Israel's share of the plank – and the methods it uses to keep it – are harder and harder to justify.

Few can feel comfortable about the disparity in land, living conditions and power between the two peoples whom the international community intended should coexist as independent states. Israel controls 20,700 square kilometres and six million people against the 1,500 kilometres and 2.9 million people under the control of the Palestinians. The average personal income of an Israeli is $17,000: for a Palestinian, $1,350. Israel's GNP is $100bn, the Palestinians' $4bn (half of which comes from outside the Palestinian areas, including Israel). The regular Israeli army is 195,000-strong against Palestinian forces of 35,000. One army can summon up American-built F-16s, the other has rifles. In the current uprising the number of Palestinian dead and injured outnumbers the Israeli casualties by five to one. Seventeen Palestinian children have died for every Israeli child.

It is true that the Arab states have never used their vast wealth to improve the lot of refugees in Gaza, but the conditions in which a vast number of Palestinians live today should nevertheless be unthinkable in any civilised and humane society. More than a million Palestinians – including 818,000 refugees – are penned into a small strip of land with population densities and conditions that match anything in the apartheid townships of South Africa. Without Israel there is no sustainable life or economy. The borders have been subject to closure for much of the last ten years: at the moment few Palestinians can leave, even to work. The current unemployment rate is as high as 45 per cent. No goods can leave or enter except via Israeli customs. Though the area of land is nominally under the control of the PA, internal movement within Gaza is effectively controlled by Israel, which regularly rations water, bulldozes houses and destroys arable land. The reality is that Israel controls the time and space of every Palestinian living within the area.

And then there are the settlements that defiantly squat within this huddled space the size of the Isle of Wight. At most, 6,500 Jewish settlers occupy as much as 20 per cent of this land – nearly 35 per cent if you include the security installations protecting them. There may be nuanced arguments about the legality or necessity of some of the 150-odd settlements in the West Bank and around Jerusalem. It is difficult to see the settlements within Gaza as anything other than an obscene stain on Israel's honour. It is further difficult to see the treatment of the Palestinian population as a whole as anything other than an indefensible form of collective punishment for the deeds of the few.

Israel argues, of course, that it could afford to build far more positive bridges without these few and without their deeds – and if there were no corruption within the PA and a more engaged and constructive Palestinian leadership. All this is true. Israel also has perfectly justifiable fears about its geography. DJ Schneeweiss of the Israeli Embassy in London wrote to this paper last week: 'The Arab world is rampant with vicious anti-Semitic and anti-Zionist incitement, coupled with the absence of liberal traditions and religious tolerance.' There is much truth in this, too. No peace will be possible unless Israel's neighbours can unequivocally acknowledge the moral necessity of Israel's existence. It is a measure of the desperation of the current situation that this should even need articulation.

But amidst this unremitting bleakness there are some faint rays of hope. Here are some:

• A gradual recognition among the Israeli population that the 73-year-old soldier they voted into power only three months months ago is bankrupt of any ideas about settling this problem beyond the bulldozer, the tank, the sniper and now the rocket. A coruscating editorial in Israel's biggest-selling, politically mainstream Hebrew daily, *Yediot Aharonot*, said last week: 'Only a revenge-seeking fool could believe that eliminations and missile fire, the demolition of neighbourhoods, the killing of soldiers and civilians and the destruction of homes could restore personal calm and security. Many politicians on both the left and the right already know that the use of ruthless force has no purpose, and that we are galloping toward disaster.'

• A growing appreciation that – though the discussions at Camp David and Taba imploded amid much mutual recrimination – the two sides were not a million miles apart. There had been much agreement on the issue of territory and over the division and/or control of Jerusalem. If all else were equal, the Palestinian demand for a Right of Return might be settled as a question of modalities. No one is pretending that there is any immediate prospect of returning to the state of negotiations so delicately poised before their violent collapse. But there is a mature recognition that the talks failed for a number of complex reasons – many of them procedural – and not simply from the impossibility of agreement.

• The involvement of Senator George Mitchell, whose calming influence is as reassuring as it was in Ireland. His proposal for an immediate freezing of settlements in exchange for a cessation of Palestinian violence is such basic common sense it is baffling why anyone should argue with it. But a freeze is a freeze is a freeze. No 'natural growth' of settlements to reflect the 2.3 per cent increase in the population of Israel. No filling up of existing settlements. Just a freeze.

- The recent work of the 'new' historians such as Benny Morris and Avi Shlaim, who have dug deep into the Israeli archives in order to write fiercely honest accounts of Israel's behaviour towards the Palestinians from the forties onwards. This has yet to be mirrored by a similar openness by Palestinian historians, but it has helped begin a process by which ordinary Israelis can come to terms with the injustices done in the process of their country's just creation. It has helped kick-start the movement to acknowledge that there are two different historical narratives, both of which need mutual recognition before any resolution can be achieved.

- Signs that the EU may take a more active part in bringing its influence to bear on the region. America has historically played this role, but the $3bn-plus annual contribution it makes to Israel means that its interventions will always be problematical. Europe has a double historical obligation towards the region: it was on European soil that six million Jews were murdered within living memory and it was the British who were the first architects of partition. But beyond this – and in the absence of any clear indication as to President Bush's intentions, or lack of them – there is an obvious opportunity for Europe to play a role of the sort that is impossible for the two peoples locked in miserable mutual hatred. Some of this pressure will be – and should be – uncomfortable for Israel. One immediate measure would be to suspend Israel's association agreement with the union. Another is to look at the vexed question of 'rules of origin', which Israel has long abused by exporting to the EU goods produced in occupied Arab territories, including those in illegal Jewish settlements, to gain duty-free access. Europe is also well placed to apply pressure on the Palestinians. As it demands a freeze on settlements, the EU should demand of Arafat that he use all his authority to enforce a ceasefire, to prevent incitement towards violence and to control his own security services.

These hopeful strands are, each of them, fragile. They are easily obliterated from the mind at a time – such as the past three days – when disgustingly random attacks by both sides kill and maim the innocent. But Israel – which has by far the greater power and which takes pride in its democratic society – has a great responsibility to take the lead in breaking the unutterably vicious cycle in which it is so fruitlessly locked. One suicide bomber in a shopping centre in Netanya demonstrated the futility of imagining that there is a security solution to this awful mess. There isn't. There is only a political solution and one day – whether it is one month, one year or ten years away – Israeli and Palestinian leaders will once more have to sit around the same table and continue where they left off in Taba last January. Between now and that day there will be much horrible reality that most of us will find hard to bear. Meanwhile, Jews the world over should think deeply about the terrible cost of securing their necessary sanctuary. Israel has accumulated massive power over the past two generations: it is not clear that it yet knows how to use it humanely.

17 August 2001

SUZANNE GOLDENBERG

Why jailer of Jenin turned suicide bomber

Abdel Halim Azideen knew the young policeman who blew himself up in a cafe north of Haifa better than most. Mohammed Nasr was his jailer.

In his living room in Jenin, a place described by Israel's army chief as the 'city of bombs', Mr Azideen, a leader of the militant Islamic Jihad, recalls Nasr as 'a real gentleman'.

'When he first started to guard us, he wasn't even praying,' said Mr Azideen, who was jailed two years ago, in the days when Yasser Arafat's Palestinian Authority (PA) worked with Israeli security services to lock up the bombers of Islamic Jihad and its more powerful rival, Hamas. 'But we were always very tender with him any time he met me he used to shake my hand very warmly. I felt he had a special love and feeling for us.'

Nasr proved that love on Sunday in a cafe in Kiryat Motzkin when he lit the fuse of a bomb strapped to his waist.

His transformation from jailer to bomber was completed last month when he quit Palestinian intelligence. It began in April when another of his Islamic Jihad charges – Iyad Harden – was assassinated by Israel when he made a call from a rigged telephone box in Jenin. Nasr was beside himself.

For Israeli security officials, Sunday's bombing and the far deadlier suicide attack on a Jerusalem pizza restaurant which killed fifteen people last week – also carried out by a Jenin militant – sealed the reputation of this city at the northern limits of the West Bank as a haven of suicide bombers.

Since last March, such attacks within the Jewish State have killed more than fifty Israelis. Nine of the bombers came from villages and refugee camps in the Jenin area. Four were from Islamic Jihad.

Israel has thwarted several other attempted bombings – especially those by Islamic Jihad, which lacks the bomb-making expertise or training of Hamas. Mr Azideen admits that four Islamic Jihad operations from Jenin were thwarted by technical failures or because the bombers were arrested.

Several other attacks – such as Nasr's – resulted in the death of only the bomber. 'Sometimes the attacks have been ordered quickly, and so the martyrs do not get enough training,' Mr Azideen said.

Hamas attacks have proved far deadlier. 'Hamas is a bigger operation, so [its] number of operations are higher, and [its] successes are higher.'

By all accounts, Nasr's was a panic-stricken final journey. After getting lost so badly that he abandoned his target, he tried to master his emotions by showing a horrified waitress his explosives belt. That last moment of bravado sabotaged his operation, and he was shoved outside, minimising the blast.

Israeli security officials describe Islamic Jihad's bombs as crude and dangerous to handle – which accounts for the frequent reports of 'work accidents' in which bomb-makers blow themselves up.

The relatively small bombs – Nasr's weighed 2kg (4.5lb) – are made in home factories from fertilisers and other chemicals, studded with nails and other bits of metal to increase their killing capacity. Several, such as Nasr's, are so crude that the detonators are lit by hand.

With Israel's blockade on the West Bank, it can take a week to plan an operation, and the bomber is usually not brought into the picture until members of the Islamic Jihad or Hamas military wing have finished.

Some militants assemble the explosives and nails, while others define targets; still others must get the bomber through Israeli security to the target. None of the cells are in direct contact, and the bomber, who is brought in at the last moment, must keep his mission secret, even from his family.

At a recent meeting in Ramallah, another Islamic Jihad leader described a lengthy period of indoctrination and vetting before recruits become suicide bombers.

After adopting a regime of regular prayer and the viewing of past suicide attacks on video, bombers are investigated for links with Israeli intelligence, and for money or family problems, which might compromise the motives for an attack.

'By the end of it all, we can read him like a book,' said the activist, who gave only his first name, Ali. 'He must have full commitment and conviction that earthly life does not mean anything anymore. He has to lose all attachments for property, money and family.'

Ali insisted that the bombers are not coerced. And in Jenin there is no lack of volunteers.

'We are proud to be at the centre of the struggle,' said the city's police chief, General Musa Jadallah, who says that sixty people from Jenin have been killed since the intifada erupted eleven months ago.

Local people are hungry for revenge, and there is growing popular sanction for suicide attacks inside Israel's borders.

The radicalisation of Palestinians – the rapid rise in the popularity of Hamas and Islamic Jihad now threatens support for Yasser Arafat's mainstream Fatah movement – leaves the local authorities in no mood to do Israel's bidding by putting men such as Mr Azideen back in prison.

Mr Azideen walked out of prison in April, the day Iyad Harden was assassinated.

'I haven't been released officially, but I told the jail that I would not be coming back,' he said. 'The current situation is not in favour of Arafat. He is no longer the king controlling his kingdom and it is very easy for a man like me to avoid arrest.'

ON THE MOVE

Austin, 21 May 2001

1 March 2001

RORY CARROLL

Willing sex slaves

I was looking for a victim and I found Tanya. Perched on a traffic barrier on Via Salaria, a busy motorway north of Rome, she was reading a crime thriller by the light of a lamppost. I pulled into the hard shoulder and she closed the book. Tottering over on black stilettos, she leaned into the window and in an eastern European accent said it would be £15 for oral sex. We drove to a deserted layby she knew well.

Two carloads of Albanian pimps cruised Via Salaria that night, as they do every night, keeping tabs on their property. To be gone more than fifteen minutes would invite trouble. I turned off the engine and explained that I had lied, that I was a journalist researching an article about human trafficking and wanted only a story. About a slave trade that lures unsuspecting young women into a world of industrialised brutality and rape. The pimps would never know of our interview. 'Tell them whatever you like,' shrugged Tanya. 'I don't work for them. Go ahead, what do you want to know?'

What she told me I believed – reluctantly, for it was not the story I wanted. She was twenty-eight, from Kursk, divorced, had an engineering degree and a two-year-old son. She had assessed her options and decided prostitution, for now, offered the only viable income. During the past two years she had come to Italy four times, each visit lasting around three months. She rented a studio apartment and allowed herself one night off a week. Even a bad week netted more than £500, enough to pay costs and save.

The work was unpleasant and sometimes dangerous. At home a catastrophic economy offered few reasonable alternatives. But nobody owned her and nobody forced her. On this point Tanya was adamant. It was her choice. She pays a gang of human traffickers about £1,100 to get from Moscow to Rome and the same amount to return. Travelling in the back of trucks is unpleasant, sometimes dangerous, but she has weighed the risks and potential gains.

Tanya is the side of human trafficking that newspapers and governments tend to ignore. The satisfied client. There are hundreds of thousands like her, though you would never guess it from the rhetoric about asylum seekers and illegal immigrants. They are labelled victims of evil schemers whose odiousness ranks not far behind paedophiles. Listen to Tony Blair and Giuliano Amato, Italy's prime minister, in a recent joint statement: 'Every day we hear of the horrors illegal immigrants endure at the hands of the people traffickers...[they] have thrown women and children, many of whom cannot swim, into the Adriatic to avoid detection by police patrol boats.'

Thomas Bodstroem, Sweden's justice minister, painted a lurid picture at a European Union summit on trafficking: 'As we speak, poor girls in European brothels are hoping for a break before the next customer comes in. The term 'slave trade' is not a provocative one, it is reality.'

On it goes. The traffickers dupe, kidnap, exploit, rape, enslave. Herding their victims into brothels, throwing them overboard, suffocating them in containers. Industrialised evil. With the rhetoric comes a battery of initiatives: stiffer penalties, standardised laws across the EU, closer cooperation between police forces, joint undercover operations.

Blair, Bodstroem and Amato are right. Traffickers truly are criminal gangs who torture, murder and betray when it suits. They plough enormous profits back into corrupting officials and opening new routes. Some clients, especially young women, start out as customers and end up as chattels, to be routinely brutalised. But before cheering the crackdown, consider Tanya. For her, traffickers offer the only route out of poverty. They have provided a reliable, albeit expensive, service. She hired them, and they did a good job.

About 400,000 asylum seekers and 500,000 migrants illegally entered the EU last year. Although the EU needs labour to replace greying workforces, it keeps the door to legal migration mostly shut. The only way in is to hire a trafficker. How many illegals are enslaved? A few, a lot, all? Such statistics do not exist, but it is likely Tanya's experience is far more common than Bodstroem's slaves. Most of Britain's asylum seekers last year, for example, came from Iraq, Sri Lanka, Afghanistan and Iran. Doubtless each has his or her own horror story about the journey – uncertainty, exhaustion, fear, danger – but these nationalities rarely end up in brothels or sweatshops.

The truth about human trafficking is that for desperate people it is usually a good bet. They are at the mercy of ruthless smugglers, but atrocities are rare because they are bad for business. Official claims to be combating the trade on behalf of clients are a self-serving fiction. Restrictive immigration policies put officials squarely on the side of traffickers. For politicians to pose as defenders of the clients is breathtaking hypocrisy.

The crackdown is likely to have some effect in disrupting the trade. Persuading Bosnia to put controls at Sarajevo airport, for instance, may force more people to travel overland from Istanbul rather than fly – a lengthier, arduous route for which the trafficker will charge more. Demand might be choked.

Blair and Amato again: 'In all that we do, we will honour our obligation to provide protection to those fleeing persecution.' That made them giggle in the immigration service. Asylum seekers and migrants rely equally on traffickers and a crackdown impedes those fleeing persecution just as much as those fleeing poverty. Blair and co conceal this behind the fig leaf of combating slavery.

It tends to go unquestioned because those who report and comment on the issue cannot resist slavery. What a story! A bygone wickedness reborn in twenty-first-century Europe. Odysseys of hope and drama ending in tragedy. Demonic traffickers and helpless victims, sex and violence. No wonder we cannot get enough.

The stories are (usually) real and need to be told, but not in such a way that they distort a complex phenomenon. After Tanya, I interviewed another four prostitutes that night. Three told similar tales: late twenties or older, Russian or Ukrainian, in Italy out of their own volition, they worked only for themselves. Victims of collapsed economies, not traffickers.

The fourth was different. Angela was nineteen, Albanian and clearly terrified. She stammered in staccato and slowly it emerged: a devious boyfriend, sold with other girls at an auction for pimps in Tirana, raped, bundled into Italy and left to stand on Via Salaria from 6 p.m. every night while her pimp trafficker cruised up and down.

Angela was too intimidated to seek help or flag passing patrol cars and hoped merely that within two years she could pay off her 'debt'. She trembled because that night's takings were well under £100. Tanya and Angela. Guess which story I was most interested in.

6 April 2001

PAUL KELSO

Perry Wacker trial

The third weekend of June was the hottest of last year. In the UK and across northern Europe temperatures climbed into the high thirties, and in Rotterdam, Holland, the sun beat down on football fans attending Euro 2000. The harbour city was in party mood and on Sunday the fine weather was a convenient excuse for chilled beer. For sixty Chinese illegal immigrants, however, huddled in the back of a sealed container lorry in a warehouse in the city's docks, the heat was to prove devastating.

Ke Su Di, twenty, was among them. A delivery boy from Fujian, he had left his family home eleven days previously. His parents had paid a snakehead smuggling gang £4,000, the first instalment of a £20,000 fee equivalent to ten years' wages, to get him to the UK. When he left, his head was full of dreams of western prosperity, both for himself and his parents. Now, dressed in three layers of clothing to avoid carrying luggage, he squatted in the decrepit container and waited for the last leg of the journey to get under way. He can have had no idea that he would be one of only two to leave the lorry alive.

The group had gathered at around 2.30 p.m., travelling in two groups from safe houses to the warehouse in Waalhaven, a section of Rotterdam's 35-mile-long harbour. It had been rented by a man claiming to be in the alcohol export trade. Inside was a white 1995 Mercedes truck hooked up to an 18-metre container, its refrigeration unit long broken.

As well as the sixty Chinese, half a dozen other men were present, including a tall, broad-shouldered lorry driver and petty criminal called Perry Wacker, who chain-smoked as he helped the Chinese board the lorry. For Wacker this was to be more than just another driving job. It marked his graduation from the ranks of the gang's petty criminals. In eight years he had travelled across Europe delivering fruit and vegetables, hi-fis and vacuum cleaners, and occasionally he helped himself to a little of his loads. In 1996 he was convicted of stealing TVs. The following year he was found guilty of insurance and benefit fraud, to go with juvenile convictions for vandalism and burglary.

Once all sixty were aboard, four containers of water were passed up along with plastic bags for excrement, and a stack of tomato boxes were loaded by Wacker and others into a specially built frame at the rear of the container. Using sign language, Wacker pointed out a small vent on the left-hand side of the trailer that was to be their only source of light and air. When this was open, he indicated, they should talk only quietly. When it was closed, as it would be at some point, they should remain silent. Then the doors closed.

Shortly before 3 p.m. Wacker climbed into the cab and set out for Zeebrugge with his human freight. Travelling via Antwerp, he arrived at the ferry terminal around 6 p.m., ninety minutes before the ferry was due to depart.

At 7 p.m. he was waved forwards to board the European Pathway, a P&O freight-only ferry bound for Dover. The time had come for total secrecy. Wacker climbed up on to the front wheel arch of the truck, untied the rope with which the air vent had been held open, forced the small door closed, and climbed above deck in search of his dinner. With this act he sealed his cargo's fate. Inside, Ke Su Di saw Wacker's hand reach up, then blackness.

While Wacker dined on roast lamb and watched two videos, *The Mummy* and *Austin Powers*, inside the container the fifty-six men and four women baked. They discarded layers of clothes, finished the water and desperately sucked at the tomatoes for moisture. Within two hours many of them were near collapse. The stagnant, fetid air inside the lorry was slowly turning to carbon dioxide; every breath added poison to the atmosphere. As panic set in, oxygen levels plummeted. Those with any strength remaining began to pound the side of the lorry with their shoes and shout for help, more interested now in survival than secrecy.

'People began to panic because the window was shut and there was no air,' Ke Su Di told Maidstone crown court, describing the last moments before he passed out. 'Some people removed tomatoes and wanted to kick open the doors. There was a lot of shouting and screaming but no one came to help.'

Resigned to their fate, the sixty settled down, held hands and ate some of the tomatoes. In China it is believed you should not leave a hungry ghost. By the time the European Pathway docked at Dover at 11.30 p.m. everyone but Ke Su Di and Ke Shi Guang, twenty-two, were dead.

At Dover, customs officers were waiting. They had already decided to stop Wacker's lorry but had no idea what they might find. The vehicle was registered to an unfamiliar company, Van der Speck Transport, and had attracted the attention of P&O staff in Zeebrugge when Wacker paid the fare of £412.50 in cash. The bulk of freight traffic is paid by account and staff automatically forward details of any vehicle paying in cash to the destination port. The vehicle manifest was faxed ahead, citing the cargo as tomatoes bound for Bristol.

The first thing the search team noticed as they swung open the rear doors of the container was the heat. 'I expected a blast of cold air but this was really warm,' said one officer. Sensing something was not right, a senior officer climbed a ladder to look over the tomatoes and shouted, 'Hello, hello'. He heard a small noise, then silence. 'Illegals, I think they might be in trouble,' he called to colleagues.

Two dock workers were summoned to help clear the tomatoes and they were the first into the container. One of them, Barry Betts, saw what he thought was a pile of pallets. In fact, it was 'a sea of bodies'. As his eyes adjusted to the darkness and took in the horror of what lay before him, he heard moaning and watched as Di and Guang struggled to free themselves from under the dead. Outside, Wacker stood expressionless, stroking the head of a customs sniffer dog.

For the fifty-eight Chinese who met their stifling demise in the back of Wacker's lorry, Dover was the end of a journey that began in the rural Chinese province of Fujian. Ke Su Di wanted to escape, to leave behind his constant feuds with neighbours and to help secure his family's future. He earned around £50 a month delivering food, the same as his father who had a wife and three children to support. 'In China, life was not too good. I didn't have a good life at home and the snakehead told me there would be no risk...we want to come to Britain because you can earn good money. Life is good there,' he said.

The leader of the local snakehead gang was Chen Xiakong, arrested earlier this year in a discotheque in Fujian on charges of people smuggling. He was responsible for a former shipment that resulted in more than a hundred people being returned by the Canadian authorities. Xiakong charged Ke Su Di £20,000 for transport to Dover, accepting a deposit of around £4,000, with balance payable on arrival in the West. Once he had made his initial payment he and the rest of the Dover sixty were locked on a course that would take them through nine countries, guided by a criminal organisation whose sophisticated network stretches from Beijing to Britain and beyond.

Ke Su Di and Ke Shi Guang were cheated. Both men thought they would be flying to the UK, travelling on their own legitimate passports. For at least part of the journey this was the case. They flew from Beijing to Belgrade, the gateway for illegal immigration into the EU. Close ties between Beijing and an increasingly isolated Milosevic regime made access easy for Chinese citizens, and tens of thousands of Chinese took advantage. At any one time around 50,000 of the 200,000 Chinese in Yugoslavia are preparing to leave Belgrade for the West, a senior immigration intelligence source told the *Guardian*.

Wearing their 'uniform' of grey T-shirts and black trousers and armed with codewords issued by the snakeheads to prevent rival gangs picking them up in error, the pair, by now part of a larger group of around fifteen immigrants, moved by road and on foot towards Hungary. Here the journey met its first hitch. Hungarian border police kicked open the doors of the van in which they were travelling, discovered the immigrants and turned them back towards Yugoslavia.

No matter. Within days they tried again and this time succeeded. At this point both men had their Chinese passports confiscated by their snakehead minder, and were given fake Korean documents. With these they passed quickly through Hungary before crossing into Austria in a van with darkened windows, crouching in silence as torches probed the cab.

Here the group had their first brush with disaster. They were left in the back of the van for more than three hours, during which time it became harder to breathe and three people fell unconscious. The others, realising the danger they were in, kicked out the windows and revived their colleagues.

This was the group's last attempt at concealment until the fatal journey to Dover. They proceeded to Vienna, where, on their forged Korean passports, they caught a plane to Charles de Gaulle airport in Paris. From here they took a train to Belgium and then on to Rotterdam, arriving on 15 June to find the station platform a sea of Dutch football fans.

As the Dover sixty were making their way north in small groups, preparations were being made in Rotterdam and London for the final leg. In Rotterdam a local Turkish mafia gang, under the leadership of Gurbel Ozcan, thirty-six, had been sub-contracted to take responsibility for the snakeheads' assets. Ozcan, who cruised Rotterdam in a black Mercedes with darkened windows, was a hardened people smuggler. In 1998 he served six months for people trafficking offences and in the months preceding the fatal June shipment he sent two other lorries laden with Chinese immigrants across the Channel.

Ozcan and his co-conspirators met to discuss the operation in the bar of the New York hotel, Rotterdam, on Monday 12 June, six days before the transport. Unknown to Ozcan, however, his car had been bugged by Dutch police, and his every move was monitored. Inexplicably, the police lifted their surveillance of the gang leader just before the weekend on which the Dover transport was made, convinced that Ozcan had no imminent operations planned.

The opposite was the case. Leo Nijveen, an old friend of Perry Wacker's and a sometime driver for Ozcan's lorries, told police a backlog of migrants was building up in Rotterdam and Ozcan was concerned at the cost of housing and feeding them. He ordered the overloading of lorries heading for England.

On 5 April Nijveen himself had been in charge of one of these lorries with fifty Chinese on board along with the token pallet of legitimate cargo, in this case yoghurt. Halfway through the 3.30 a.m. Zeebrugge-Dover crossing Nijveen heard screaming and banging from the lorry as its human cargo began to run out of oxygen. Nijveen, unlike Wacker, threw open the doors and let the Chinese out. They were processed at the Dover immigration centre, and Nijveen was fined £2,000 per head, then allowed to return to Holland. Police later said there was insufficient evidence to show he knew they were on board.

Despite the 5 April incident, Ozcan was determined to clear the backlog. A number of petty crooks were hired to do the dirty work, thus shielding Ozcan from any investigation. Hubertus van Keulen, fifty, was paid £1,200 to rent the warehouse at Waalhaven, while Willem Jansen, forty-nine, was paid £2,000 to buy the tomatoes, the dummy cargo, which Nijveen and Wacker later collected. The pair also bought the tractor unit of the truck from a garage near Wacker's home, and later purchased the trailer.

Nijveen had been retained as an advisor and it was he who recruited Wacker, a lorry driver from Rotterdam's eastern suburbs. The pair had worked together as drivers for a transport firm run by Ronald Wacker, Perry's uncle, and Nijveen knew his friend was desperate for cash. Wacker was due to be married in Rotterdam on 17 July, a month after the transport, to a Moroccan girl called Nora he had met in Spain the previous year.

Wacker was desperate for money. His fiancée was not an EU national and he had to satisfy Dutch authorities that he could support both of them. Nijveen was keen to offload the driving work to someone else and introduced Wacker to the conspiracy, telling him he stood to make at least £30,000 at £500 per person. Wacker agreed.

With a driver engaged, the final stage in the preparations was to set up a cover company to protect Ozcan and the snakeheads in the event that the consignment was discovered by customs. For this they needed a front man, a *katvanger*, someone paid to provide a cover identity for criminal operations. For the ill-fated transport the gang engaged Arien van der Speck, a punchy petty criminal from the eastern suburb of Terbregge.

Days before the transport, Van der Speck visited the Rotterdam chamber of commerce and founded a haulage firm, Van Der Speck Transport. He took his money and left, hearing nothing more until the Rotterdam police knocked on his door on 19 June. He has since been charged with false certification.

The final stage in the journey was organised by snakeheads living among London's 60,000-strong Chinatown community. To them fell the task of organising asylum applications, and more importantly making arrangements for final fees to be paid. The Dover sixty's first point of contact in the UK was to be a young Chinese interpreter, Ying Guo, twenty-nine, known to many who worked with her as Jenny. Twenty-seven of those that died had her mobile phone number on them, either on a scrap of paper or stitched into their clothing.

A Mandarin speaker from north-eastern China, Guo arrived in England in late August 1996, travelling legally on a student visa to study English, accounting and computing at Edgware College, north London. She had worked in a car factory in China, earning around £500 a month but hoped to qualify as an accountant during her time in the UK.

Within three years, however, Jenny Guo had built herself a successful and relatively lucrative career on the margins of the legal profession, thanks to a chance encounter with a friend who needed an interpreter to help him at a meeting at the Home Office immigration centre in Croydon, south London. Guo went along, and soon she was spending around forty hours a week interpreting for asylum applicants at Home Office screenings and interviews with solicitors. More importantly, she began introducing clients to a network of solicitors across London, clients for whom she then acted. In eighteen months, from January 1999, she had dealings with more than 366 asylum applicants, mostly Chinese, 7 per cent of all Chinese applicants dealt with by the Home Office during that period.

One solicitor spoke of paying her £10,000 in legal aid claimed for translation work for around eighty clients, another of £5,000 for forty. At the going rate Perry Wacker 's lorry was worth £7,500 to Jenny.

Four years after entering the country she was able to afford an £83,000 mortgage on a flat in South Woodford, Essex. Between 3 March 2000 and 20 June she also sent £37,000 back to China, using the account of her boyfriend, You Yi. Guo was the first point of contact in the UK for the Dover sixty and on the morning of their expected arrival she was busy finalising arrangements.

On the morning of Monday 19 June, seven hours after the bodies had been discovered, Guo telephoned Chandika Wolpita. She had referred around eighty clients to him between December 1999 and February 2000, and now asked if he could deal with some asylum matters on behalf of sixty Chinese people. According to his evidence in court, Mr Wolpita called his supervisor, who advised him they could take on about thirty. Wolpita took the request to mean they had already arrived.

Shortly afterwards Gou called again and said she had not heard from the Chinese, and that she would call again later. Around midnight she finally called and said the police had been and removed her computer. In the intervening period Guo had learned of the deaths and panicked, destroying her mobile and deleting files. Many of them were recovered, including draft letters of application for asylum, and a number of invoices to solicitors.

The next day, Guo and her boyfriend You Yi, a chef, turned themselves in to Kent police at Canterbury police station. Yi was released without charge and is working in Chinatown. For her part, Guo, who protested her innocence throughout the trial, was last night beginning a six-year sentence for her part in the deaths of fifty-eight Chinese innocents in search of a better life.

21 May 2001

MAGGIE O'KANE

Sadiq's story

The wallpaper in Sadiq Hanafi's bedsit in north London's Kensal Green has the grubby gleam of paint that is layered on, year after year, burying the embossed leaves of the wallpaper. Outside, Hanover Road's once-respectable semis have the scent of slippage: crooked 'To Let' signs and greying net curtains. This is human cargo land – people nobody wants, trying to get somewhere. They have come a long way. Afghans, Kurds, Iranians, Rwandans and Sri Lankans all squashed in behind the window frames blackened by winter damp.

Sadiq Hanafi, twenty-six, is from Afghanistan. His journey to Kensal Green began five years ago when the Muslim fundamentalists, the Taliban, took away his army officer father, who died in prison two years later. The family fled to neighbouring Pakistan to massive refugee camps where, like two million other Afghans, they waited for things to get better before returning home. Now the waiting is over: nobody is going back. War is scheduled again for the summer and Afghans are selling up their homes to stay alive in exile and fund their great hope – getting a son to Europe to provide for the family.

Sadiq Hanafi's journey to London took seven months and almost killed him twice. In Kabul, he had plans to work as a paediatrician. Now he's lined up for a job in an all-night Pakistani grocers in the Elephant and Castle.

In Afghanistan it is spring, a time when even Kabul, trashed by war, parched by drought and suffocated by fundamentalists, can be beautiful. Boys in bare feet are playing cricket in the grounds of the university.

In the marketplace, women who have never dared to speak to foreigners tug on my shirt. 'Shut up, let me speak,' one shouts at my government-authorised minder. 'I am hungry, there are no jobs, no factories, no education for women, just for the men. Where are you from? England? How do you get a visa to London?'

The only road out of Afghanistan to Pakistan is so bad that the bus rocks like a boat on a rough sea. A lizard as long as a wheelbarrow scuttles across. His prehistoric face fits in this country, trapped in a bizarre and brutal time warp.

Next stop for Sadiq was Pakistan – Peshawar, a border town where drugs, antiquities and people are filtered through a giant switchboard of middlemen and smugglers. The main cargo in Peshawar now is the Afghan sons of the refugee camps.

'Eighty per cent of them want to go to London. They can work illegally there easily,' a smuggler tells me. 'The English money is worth a lot these days and they can send money home. After London the places they want to go to most are Denmark, Sweden and then Germany. The benefits are good in Denmark but if they need fast money to send back, London is the place. The English pound is the best currency.'

The smuggler is watching a *National Geographic* programme on Amazonian monkeys. His office is on the first floor of a shopping arcade. He offers Cokes, is thirty-four and was once a fighter pilot in the Afghan military. 'London is $16,000 [£11,000] by air, $9,000–10,000 [£7,000] by land. Denmark costs around the same. Germany is $14,000 [£9,700] by air. The air route varies depending on where my contacts can pay for things to be fixed. The way it works is that we let our people in the airport know a few days in advance that a group of, say, three people will be coming, and to get them through with fake documents we get made up. Dubai used to be a very good transit point but now the British customs seem to have got some women there who are on the ball when it comes to spotting false documents, so we've had to vary things a bit.

'At the moment the main routes we're using for flying are through Africa. Pakistan to Nairobi, then Nairobi to Germany or London. It's like a computer password. When one route gets cracked, we use another one. The richer you are, the safer the route. The ones with money fly. The ones who don't have money go by land.'

The Afghans who have no money have started dying this summer in exile in Pakistan. In Jalozai camp, the Afghan dead are buried on a windy wasteland above the camp that lies about 40km from Sadiq's road to the west – and London. On Wednesday 9 May there were eleven fresh graves there, mostly children, parched by the lack of water and dehydrated with diarrhoea. The international aid agencies are not allowed to bring enough water or food to keep all of them alive: Pakistan's way of getting tough with their 'spongers'.

In the morning sun, the temperature is already in the eighties. It's seven o'clock and the water tanker has been and gone. The children are fighting under the tank, fiercely concentrating to catch drips like diamonds in their small grubby hands.

Sadiq Hanifi's mother sold the family's land in Afghanistan to buy her son's passage to London for $9,000 (£6,500). He left Pakistan by land, going south through Quetta and then turning west into Iran.

'We got through Iran without too much trouble,' he tells me, back in Kensal Rise. 'The smuggler told us to get off the bus at certain points. We had no papers to go into Iran. We had to sneak over the mountain. It took a couple of weeks to get through Iran to Tabriz near the Turkish border and then we had to wait around for the next smuggler to take us on.'

The wolves of the Ararat mountain range that divides western Iran and eastern Turkey have a special hunting technique for farm dogs in the winter when the snow makes them hungry. One wolf lures the farm dog away from the farm and then the pack pounces, ripping at the throat. 'We began climbing mid-afternoon. We had been in Tabriz for fifteen days waiting for the smugglers to pass us on to the next person who would take us over the mountains into Turkey. We took water and some dates. It was snowing and very, very cold. After about five hours, the wolves attacked. We saw them in the distance coming across a plateau. There were five of them. The shepherds with us had sticks and they started to beat them and they ran off.'

On the Turkish side of the mountain, men with mean faces and hungry children combine smuggling with sheep farming. In the villages they fight for a slice of human cargo by shopping each other to the Turkish army. Their damp village huts are made of mud and outside each is a crooked satellite dish bringing them western and Turkish shopping channels.

I meet a new smuggler who has the face of a rat. 'Everybody is doing it,' he says. 'Some of the smugglers have mobiles but I get a message from Dogubeyazit that my Iranian contact wants to meet me. He lets me know the time and the place and I go up to meet them at a special time. The authorities have marked the border with rocks, so he will say to me, for example, between rocks sixty-one and sixty-three, and I'll know that the mines have been lifted.'

At nights the only sound in the mountains is the barking of dogs, the only sight a string of white lights that marks the border stones. Underneath the shepherd's feet, the soil crumbles away underfoot. 'We only go across when the conditions are too bad for the soldiers to stay on the mountain. People have injured themselves jumping down the hill on the Iranian side. There's a steep bit, with lots of ice and rocks there that they have to cross. The main danger is the soldiers shooting at us.'

'We had been walking all night and were crossing when the soldiers started firing at us,' Sadiq remembers. 'The two smugglers who were with us ran away. We were freezing and had no food so we tried to make our way down. Two shepherds found us and sold us on to another smuggler who put us in a truck that was going to Istanbul.'

Istanbul is 1,400km (840 miles) west of the Iranian border. Sadiq went in a truck. More recently, the smugglers have used oil-tankers secretly refitted with seats. He passed through Istanbul quicker than most of the city's human cargo. Afghans, Kurds, Saudis and Iraqis can spend years in the garment districts of Zeytinburno, which has become a slave colony.

In a basement sweatshop, two men in their early twenties are sewing sheepskin waistcoats for the bazaar. They work from 8 a.m. to 3 a.m. Their boss bought two of them from the police for $500 (£347). It will take the fur slaves six months to pay him back the money, another two years to pay for a boat to take them out of this basement to London, Munich or Rome, where they can begin to help their families.

Jassim is silently trimming fur lapels. 'I can't stand it. I've no idea what happened to my family. It is three years since I left Afghanistan and I promised my father that I would help them. The rain didn't come and everything is finished for them. My father sold the cows and sheep we had to try and get me to Europe so I could send them money. But I can't help them because I can't even help myself. Can you help me get to London? They are waiting for me. I will send everything back to them – 95 per cent and just keep 5 per cent for myself. At home they are saying 'Jassim will help us' and I can't. I can't help myself. I feel so bad I burnt my arms with hot coins. I heat them up and then press them on my flesh. The pain makes me forget about them.'

Sadiq left Istanbul's slave colony after waiting almost two months for his boat. He took a large fishing boat down the Aegean Sea towards Italy. The boat never made it. 'We left Istanbul in the early morning. The sea was rough and there were 300 people on board. We were below and I remember the water rising up and up, past the porthole. The people started praying and crying, opening their Korans. It was dark. Then the captain came down to us and he got up on a chair in the middle of all the people and he was shouting and crying at us: "You want me to try and save you. I am trying to save us but stop screaming."' I really thought that night I was dead, but then a Greek military boat rescued us.'

Many Afghans, like Sadiq, go directly from Istanbul to Italy on illegal fishing boats or sand-dredgers. They have no passports so avoid boats, planes or trains that require customs. Those with the least money take the most dangerous route of all and hand themselves over to the Albanian *scafisti* who have drowned countless refugees, dumping them in the sea when they are chased by the Italian police to lighten the boats for their getaway. 'In Bari, Foggia and Brindisi the morgues are full of their unclaimed bodies,' says Marianna Gocola, twenty-eight, who has worked with the Italian police on the coastline for eight years.

'You don't have to go to a special school to learn how to dump them out of the boat,' says Chichio, a nineteen-year-old *scafisto* with cold, dead eyes. 'It's like taking a sharp bend in the car – you flick the wheel and over they go. There are three of us in the boat, me driving, someone for the diesel and someone watching the cargo. Doesn't matter whether they are women and children on board – they are cargo like guns or women. The most important thing is the boat. If I lose my boat, I lose my job and I have to pay for that boat 50m lire.'

Most nights, Chichio takes his human cargo across the sea from Valona in Albania to Bari in Italy. In Valona, the *scafisti* are more powerful than the police. Sometimes they are the police. From behind his executioner's mask (a Balaclava borrowed from the police for our interview), Chichio speaks for an hour and never shows any emotion.

His boat is a monster dinghy the length of a London bus. With two 500hp engines he can make the 70km (42 miles) crossing to Italy in one and a half hours. His boss can make $60,000 (£41,700) with a single boat load, charging $1,500 (£1,000) per person for a single run. 'We charge more for Afghans because they are the most desperate.'

Chichio has no worries: 'If we get caught by the Italians we get a twenty-five-year sentence but we buy ourselves out in four days. If we get twenty-five years it can cost about 100m lire (£41,000) to buy yourself out. But the most impor-

tant thing is not to get caught and lose the boats. That's why we have to dump
the people sometimes. Don't blame us for what happens – blame the governments who won't let the people in.'

'I have taken the boat with the *scafisti* twice,' says Milenja, a sixteen-year-old
prostitute from Moldavia trying to work in Italy. 'Both times the *scafisti* dumped
all the people on board into the sea. There were about forty of us in the boat yesterday. Only half got picked up.'

Sadiq avoided the dreaded *scafisti*. He was dropped by his military boat on a
Greek island whose name he doesn't remember, or maybe never knew. From Bari
he took a train to Rome, where the Afghan community steered him towards
another smuggler who showed him how to sneak into a wholesale depot where
trucks were leaving for the UK.

'I was under the washing-powder boxes – no one searched us or anything. But
the agents had told us: "Don't move, don't shake, don't talk – otherwise you will
be found." At Dover, when we jumped out, I asked the driver in English where
we were and he replied: "We're in fucking England." He looked really cross and
was walking up and down on the tarmac talking on the phone.'

Sadiq is a very private and proud man. He wants to work. After seven months
on the road, he arrived exhilarated in London. Now he is frustrated and
depressed. His mission to earn money to send back has so far failed. He's still
waiting for his first interview with the Home Office. The process of accepting or
rejecting his asylum hasn't even begun. In the meantime, he is bewildered by
the hatred he sees around him. At a Sainsbury's check-out a few months after he
arrived, he was buying food with his £26 worth of grocery vouchers when a
voice behind him rasped into his ear: 'Look at you, eating our taxes.'

'I felt so embarrassed at the way she spoke to me but how could I explain?'

For a brief second, this man who has been attacked by wolves in the moun-
tains of Iran and made his peace with Allah on a sinking ship on the Adriatic
Sea, came close to tears for the first and only time. And it happened in
Sainsbury's.

18 July 2001

ESTHER ADDLEY AND RORY MCCARTHY

The man who fell to earth

The police didn't know how long the body had been there, but it was clear the
man was dead. Tucked under a tree, just inside the railings of Homebase car
park, the prone figure was spotted by one of the store's staff as she arrived just
before 7 a.m. She assumed he was a drunk who had tumbled over the railings
and fallen asleep while staggering home along Manor Road. It was only as she
edged over for a closer look that she noticed that his limbs were grotesquely mis-
shapen, and the pool of lumpy liquid in which he was lying was not vomit, but
the man's spilt brains.

The area was hastily screened off and police launched an immediate murder investigation. But it soon emerged that a witness had seen the dead man a few minutes before his body was found. A workman at nearby Heathrow airport had glanced upwards to see him plummeting from the sky like a stone, his black jeans and T-shirt picked out against the washed blue early morning sky.

A month after he died, police have finally managed to piece together the skeletal details of Mohammed Ayaz's long journey from a remote village in north-west Pakistan to his final, sorry end in the car park of a DIY superstore in Richmond, west London. It is a story of breathtaking courage fired by a fierce hope that a decent life might lie in a distant country where he knew no one. It seems all the more tragic that this heroic odyssey should have ended in desperate bathos on a sunny Thursday morning, in the sort of quiet, affluent suburb in which the young man probably hoped he would one day raise a family.

At Bahrain airport the night before, at about 1 a.m. local time, the 21-year-old Ayaz somehow broke through a security cordon and sprinted through the dark towards a British Airways Boeing 777 that was preparing for take-off. As the ground crew backed away and the enormous aircraft dragged itself round in an arc towards the runway, he ran under the wings and hauled himself into the cavernous opening above the wheels.

At take-off, a number of passengers noticed that the man in black had not emerged from under the plane. Local Bahrain news reports claimed that by the time it was lumbering into the air, the captain had been told there might be a stowaway. But for some reason, perhaps because the sighting was unconfirmed, or because schedules were tight, or because runway security was not his responsibility, he did not turn back. This was put to BA and its response was that a captain would never take off if he believed security had been breached. Tim Goodyear, a spokesman for the International Air Transport Association in Geneva, describes the apparent decision to proceed with the flight as 'somewhat unusual. On the other hand, one cannot say that any captain should have behaved in a certain way.' Hindsight, he says, is a terrible thing.

Ayaz's family have had little time to grieve. They have spent the past week in the fields harvesting this year's onion crop. The harvest is good: mountains of red onions are piled by the roadside, but market prices are bad again. They make barely one pence a kilo. Since Ayaz's death the family of five brothers and four sisters face a mountain of debt.

The small village of Dadahara sits in the broad, green valley of the Swat river in northern Pakistan, close to the Afghan border. The Queen visited in the sixties to see the beautiful, once-forested mountains. But there is little work now, little opportunity for education and only one telephone between 3,000 villagers.

Ayaz, a keen cricketer and footballer, left school at sixteen and went to work in the family's fields, farming wheat, barley, corn and onions. 'He always spoke about going to work in America or England. But they don't give visas to poor people like us,' says his brother, Gul Bihar, twenty-six.

Seven months ago, Ayaz finally decided to join the thousands of young Pakistanis who travel to the Gulf states every year to work in construction, hoping to save enough money to send home to their families. He found an agent who promised him work as a labourer in Dubai. It would cost 120,000 rupees (£1,300) to arrange the flight, the visa and, the heaviest cost, to meet the agent's exorbitant fees. The family borrowed heavily from their relatives, and Ayaz, who spoke little Arabic, flew out to Dubai with a promise of a salary of 400 dirhams (£77) a month. It was more than many earn in Pakistan but, even if he saved most of his salary, it would still take at least two years just to pay back his relatives.

It soon became clear it would take Ayaz a lot longer to earn back his money. His employer in Dubai kept his passport and paid him just 100 dirhams (£19) a month, barely enough to buy food. 'He was a very strong man, very brave and very good at working. He just wanted to earn money for the family so his brothers and sisters could be educated and have a better life,' says Gul Bihar. 'He phoned us a few weeks before he died. He was very upset. He said: "I've been here for six months but I haven't been able to send you any money because I haven't been paid. What should I do?"'

Days later, without telling his family, he crossed to Bahrain and climbed on board the flight to London. Getting into the wheel bay of a Boeing 777 is not easy. It involves climbing 14ft up one of the aircraft's twelve enormous wheels, then finding somewhere to crouch or cling as the plane makes its way to the end of the runway and starts its deafening engines. Ayaz had to contort himself around the huge pieces of articulated steel while the Tarmac slipped by only feet beneath, the engine accelerating to 180mph. But it was probably only when the wheels left the ground and began to retract into the bay that he realised how much trouble he was in. 'There certainly used to be a belief that there was a secret hatch from the wheel bay into the cargo bay, and then into the passenger cabin, as if it were a castle with a dungeon and a series of secret passageways,' says Goodyear.

In fact, the undercarriage compartment has no oxygen, no heating and no pressure, and there is certainly no way out. By about ten minutes into the ascent, the temperature in the wheel bay would have been freezing. At 18,000ft, minutes later, while passengers only a few feet away were being served gin and tonic and settling down to watch in-flight movies, Ayaz would have begun to hallucinate from lack of oxygen. At 30,000ft the temperature is -56 degrees. Even if the young man managed to escape being crushed by the retracting wheel mechanism, he was as good as dead from the moment his feet left the runway.

'He didn't have a chance,' says Paul Jackson, editor of the specialist magazine *Jane's All the World's Aircraft*. 'At that temperature you're a block of ice – there's no way you're going to get away with it, unless the plane is forced for some reason to fly at an unusually low altitude.'

By the time the plane reached British airspace, he was almost certainly long dead. Shortly after 6 a.m., somewhere between twelve and twenty miles from Heathrow, the plane locked on to its approach path and began to descend over Barnes in south-west London. Between 2,000 and 3,000ft, the captain opened the undercarriage and lowered the wheels. The young man was tipped out into the early morning sky.

The moment Ayaz's body struck the Tarmac in the car park at the Richmond branch of Homebase, he became the problem of Detective Chief Inspector Sue Hill. She had a distressed supermarket worker and the badly disfigured body of a 'suntanned man, of Mediterranean or Middle Eastern appearance', but not much else to go on. The man was carrying a book with a few phone numbers in it, which suggested he was Pakistani, but no identification. 'It was harrowing,' says Hill. 'I sat in the Homebase car park and thought: "This is someone's son. What a bloody awful way to go."'

What struck Hill and her team immediately was how lucky they had been. It is difficult, in fact, to imagine how a body slamming into the ground could have contrived to avoid the B353 only feet away, the railway line at the end of the car park beside which is a primary school, or the tightly packed red-brick houses of Manor Grove just across the road. The police have cause to worry. Across the road from Homebase, a few yards to the left, is an enormous Sainsbury's super-market, completed a year ago on the site of a derelict gasworks. It was here, in October 1996, that nineteen-year-old Vijay Saini's own journey ended. He had stowed away in a jet from Delhi in the same way as Ayaz did, and fell out at almost exactly the same spot. His body lay undiscovered for three days. In August 1998 a couple drinking in the nearby Marlborough pub saw another body tumble from a plane and land on what they thought was the building site of the new Sainsbury's. Despite a widespread police search, that body was never found, and police think it may have landed in a reservoir. There were reports of a fourth body being discovered while the Sainsbury's complex was being built.

'The undercarriage is always lowered at the same point, that is why they are falling at the same place,' says John Stewart, of the airport noise-pollution lobby group Hacan Clear Skies. 'But it's an almost uncanny coincidence – these people fly right across the world in this way from different places, and they all end up in a car park in Richmond. If there are any more bodies to fall, that's where they will fall.'

Only one man is known to have survived such a journey. Vijay Saini's brother, Pardeep, was found at Heathrow in a disorientated state shortly after a flight from Delhi landed – he was thought to have entered a state of suspended ani-mation in the freezing temperatures.

It took Interpol, Pakistani community workers in the UK and a number of for-tuitous coincidences to track down Ayaz's parents. A committee member from the Pakistan Centre, a community organisation in Newcastle, happened to be holidaying in the Swat area, and came across a small village, the talk of which was the young man's death. He went to Dadahara. 'All the conversations that I had with his father, he was trying to plead for the body to be sent back,' says Shabbir Ahmed Kataria, who works at the centre. Kataria organised a collection to send the body home, with anything left over to go to the family.

On 5 July, three weeks after Ayaz died, his body began the final leg of his jour-ney. The coffin was taken to Heathrow and loaded into the hold of another British Airways plane, this time bound for Islamabad. Ayaz's father, Gul Diar, is a deeply religious man who has struggled to rationalise the death of his son. His wife suffered a minor heart attack after hearing the news and is in hospital recovering.

'Allah gives and Allah takes away. He was meant to die at this time,' said the old man, wearing a cotton prayer cap and stroking his long white beard. He greets guests and then walks out to the graveyard at the edge of his land. His son was buried here two weeks ago under a large mound of brown earth ringed by stones and covered in a dirty plastic sheet. Two large, plain slabs of slate stand up out of the top of the unmarked grave. 'My son was as strong as four men but he died in search of bread,' his father says.

Extreme measures. A farmer sets about burning foot and mouth-infected cattle in Lockerbie, March. (Murdo MacLeod)

All-consuming fire. Another bovine funeral pyre, this time in Longtown, near Carlisle. (Murdo MacLeod)

Streets of rage... Italian riot police shot dead a protester during the demonstrations against the G8 summit in Genoa in July. The carabinieri were later criticised for their heavy-handed methods. (Reuters/Dylan Martinez)

Running the gauntlet. Police and parents escort terrified children to Holy Cross primary school in north Belfast in September. The route to the Catholic school took them through a largely Protestant area. (Photopress Belfast/Alan Lewis)

SMALL WORLD

Austin, 1 May 2001

SARAH BOSELEY

At the mercy of drug giants

Refilwe is a spectral figure, so thin that the light from the huge hospital window at her back seems to pass through her. She sits as straight as a knife, all bone, white robe, and huge eyes gazing at nothing, breathing shallowly through an open mouth. She is thirty and has a son of seven. She has tuberculosis and her mouth is covered with the telltale white spots of a common infection she cannot fight off, because HIV is destroying her body's resistance.

Ask her how she is and she slowly turns her entire body towards you. 'I'm feeling better,' she whispers. It is a fiction maintained by the plump and jolly nurses at the Natalspruit hospital outside Johannesburg, who have dozens more like her on drips in wards 13 and 16, where anybody with any strength resists going because if you have HIV, you have no future.

Refilwe, impossibly, gets to her feet and makes her way with pitiful steps and the arm of a nurse to the door, a walking wraith. She is going to the TB clinic. They will sort out the TB but then they will send her home to die. She is fatally weakened and there are no antiretroviral drugs to take on HIV here.

Nokuthula, twenty-three, is also under a death sentence, for all that she appears robust with health. So is her eighteen-month-old son Sipho, whose name means a gift. The young mother has put herself and her child in the care of the traditional healer in the township outside Natalspruit hospital who gives them herb and bark infusions to make them strong. But traditional medicine could not save Nokuthula's husband, who died of Aids last September.

At an age when women in the west are embarking on families and careers, Refilwe and Nokuthula have begun the business of dying. They live in the East Rand suburbs of Johannesburg, South Africa, where one in five is estimated to be harbouring the virus that will kill them.

Across Africa and the developing world millions more will die of diseases that are treatable in the west, such as diarrhoea, meningitis, malaria, TB and Aids. The hospitals do what they can, but their best efforts are a sticking plaster on a haemorrhage. The western drugs they need are unaffordable. Life is priced too high.

Thirty-five miles away in Pretoria, a legal battle critical to the fate of many more women like Refilwe and Nokuthula, their men and their children, is about to begin. Case number 4183/98 in the South African high court is an action brought by forty-two pharmaceutical companies, including the British giant GlaxoSmithKline, against the South African government.

The case is an attempt to block South Africa from importing cheap medicines. The drug companies have spent three years and millions of pounds preparing the case.

They have retained virtually every patent lawyer in South Africa. On 5 March their barristers will try to stop the South African government from buying the medicines its people so badly need from countries where the prices are lowest, on the grounds that it is infringing world trade agreements.

The rest of Africa will be closely watching the outcome of the trial. So will developing countries on other continents. With the death toll from infectious diseases inexorably rising, especially in Africa, a tide of outrage is swelling among local activists and international aid organisations who see medicines denied to the sick in the name of commerce.

More than two and a half million people die every year from Aids-related illnesses. More than thirteen million children have lost one or both parents to the condition. There are more than thirty-two million men, women and children infected by HIV in developing countries. AZT and 3TC, the basic antiretroviral drugs in the West, would keep them alive and well, but the price tag is $10,000–15,000 (£7,000–10,500) per patient a year. The majority of employed people in South Africa, with whole families to support, earn less than $3,000 a year, and by comparison with most of the rest of the continent, they are rich.

But there are now alternatives – cheap copies of life-saving medicines called generics, made mainly in Brazil, India and Thailand whose national laws allow them to ignore drug patents in cases of dire human need. Thailand believes it could reduce the cost to $200 a year per patient. It is a price the South African government might be able to pay for the life of Refilwe and Nokuthula, but the drug companies, in Case 4183/98, afraid of the potential worldwide consequences if their prices start to be undercut, say no.

Today in Cape Town, at least 5,000 supporters of the successful grassroots Treatment Action Campaign will march on parliament to demand the medicines. At the same time in London, Oxfam is launching an international campaign demanding help for developing countries who want to use legitimate measures to buy or make their own cheap drugs, but who are bullied into submission by the lawyers working for drug companies and by the western governments who support them.

The pharmaceutical companies argue that they need twenty years of patent protection to recoup the vast sum it costs to research and develop drugs. They say it takes $1bn and at least twelve years to get a new medicine to market.

But, their accusers say, 90 per cent of those new medicines are designed for 10 per cent of the world's population in rich countries who can pay for them. The companies argue they already sell to developing countries at prices lower than in the West and that, with the approval of UNAids, the joint UN programme on HIV/Aids, five major companies have offered 85 per cent discounts on drugs that are badly needed.

That could bring antiretrovirals down to $1,500 per patient, low enough for poor countries to hand them out to a chosen few but, say critics, millions would still have to die.

The Pharmaceutical Manufacturers Association of South Africa, which is bringing the case with the international companies, says it supports any country's right to buy supplies of drugs that are cheaper abroad 'in exceptional circumstances'. But it argues that section 15c of the Medicines Act, passed by the South African government in 1997 to allow it to import cheap copies of western medicines, would give the health minister 'unfettered discretion to override patent rights for medicines in this country'. And it was appalled when the South African delegation told a World Health Organisation meeting in January 1999 that the new legislation was a model that the rest of Africa should follow.

It is not just Africa that worries the big pharmaceuticals. On behalf of the industry the US government is taking the offensive to Brazil, which has had dramatic success in manufacturing its own cheap copies of patented drugs and now exports generics. Its price for an AZT equivalent is down from $15,000 a year to $4,000. There are now 60,000 people with HIV in Brazil who get free treatment.

At the heart of the growing legal battles directed against South Africa, Brazil and several other developing countries lies a little-known international agreement called Trips – trade related intellectual property rights. It was agreed within the World Trade Organisation (WTO) in order to ensure patent rights were respected around the world. The poorest countries have until 2006 to comply with Trips by passing their own patent laws. Under Trips, signatory states can pass clauses, as South Africa has tried to do, to bypass patents and make or buy cheaper drugs in cases of 'dire emergency', and few could argue Aids is less than that.

But the West's sharp legal minds, backed by vast drug company wealth, are willing and able to mount expensive challenges in the courts to uphold their patent rights – and thus the price of their drugs – as is about to happen in Pretoria.

For the first time, there is also about to be a challenge in the WTO itself. Last month the new US administration, which accepted substantial election funding from the pharmaceutical industry, asked for a WTO disputes hearing where it will claim Brazil is in breach of Trips. Oxfam and others fear the offensive against Brazil and South Africa marks a new determination by the drugs companies to resist the flouting of their patents by poor countries.

GlaxoSmithKline has recently threatened legal action against the Indian generics company Cipla, blocking its plans to bring a cheap version of Combivir – AZT and 3TC in one pill – into Uganda and Ghana. 'The implementation of WTO patent rules is taking place against the backdrop of a sustained campaign led by the pharmaceutical industry that may well erode the public health protection provided by safeguard provisions,' says an Oxfam report published today.

In Khayelitsha, a shanty town that sprawls over a vast plain near Cape Town's airport, the Nobel prize-winning volunteer doctors are raising the stakes. They pioneered the use of nevirapine, a drug that stops pregnant women transmitting HIV to their babies. Now the government is rolling out the programme to the entire country.

After the period of apostasy, when President Thabo Mbeki upset the medical world by doubting that HIV caused Aids, the government seems willing to seek out and use cheap drugs if it is allowed to.

Last year it opened an infectious diseases clinic – code for HIV – where people are offered counselling and treatment for the 'opportunistic infections' that can kill. They use fluconazole, a strong antibiotic most hospitals lack because of its price, to treat cryptococcal meningitis and thrush.

   In May, they will take the most radical step of all and start 150 adults and thirty children who are at death's door on antiretrovirals – the very medication that keeps people in the West with HIV alive. Dr Eric Goemaere, head of the South African mission of Medecins sans Frontières (MSF), sees it as a marker for the future. 'We are here on the frontline to show that it is possible and it will change attitudes totally,' he says.

   South Africa could by now be in the relatively advantageous position of Brazil, he believes, making its own cheap drugs and importing others. Perhaps Nokuthula's husband need not have died and Refilwe might be strong. There was a political willingness to use generics in 1997, but Case 4183/98 put a stop to all that. 'I have no hesitation in saying that I'm totally convinced that's exactly where it is,' Dr Goemaere said. 'The pharmaceutical companies blocked South Africa becoming like Brazil.'

   South Africa's director general of health, Ayunda Ntsaluba, says something similar: 'Three years down the road, access to medicines would have been completely different. We would be providing certainly for opportunistic infections, although it would be disingenuous to say we would have been providing triple therapy.'

   It is hard to be a doctor in Africa. Herman Reuter, a young South African of German extraction who works for MSF in Khayelitsha, has more medicines at his disposal than most, but he is clearly under strain. Doctors go into the profession to cure the sick, not temporarily staunch their wounds before they die.

   'We have our worse days and our better days,' he says. 'I saw one woman last Friday with a CD4 count of two [very low resistance to infection]. I said we hope to give antiretrovirals by May. She said: "Yes, but doctor, what happens until May?" I see many people die.'

   A very sick woman of about forty-one had been brought to his clinic that morning by her eighteen-year-old daughter. She had cryptococcal meningitis. A week earlier, she had been to a government hospital and was turned away. There was nothing they could do for her, they said. They did not have the right medicine. But they mentioned the MSF clinic.

   Dr Reuter was able to give her fluconazole, which costs around $4 for a 200mg capsule that will, for the moment, save her life. His last resort is to send the very sick to Somerset hospital in Cape Town, where pharmaceutical companies are running trials of drug combinations for HIV.

   There is a bitter irony in it. The trials cannot be run in Britain or the US where the drugs will be sold because everyone who needs antiretrovirals is on them. Refilwe and Nokuthula have no hope of a trial. Their best chance is to eat well, if they can afford to, to build up their strength and hang on.

   Refilwe, like the rest of the patients in wards 13 and 16, refuses to accept she has HIV. What is the point when there is no treatment? 'I don't know why I'm sick,' she says, barely audibly.

   Nokuthula places all her hope in the traditional healer, David Ngalana, even though he acknowledges he can give her only limited help. A large poster on the wall declares: 'Traditional medicine can cure almost all sicknesses but currently we cannot cure HIV/Aids.'

   Nokuthula knows nothing about Aids drugs. There are no antiretrovirals for the people of her township, so they may as well not exist. She will drink her tree-bark infusions and convince herself they failed to save her husband only because he did not take them properly. In that way, maybe, hope can triumph for a while over despair.

17 April 2001

JULIAN BORGER AND TERRY MACALISTER

The capital of capitalism

The home of global capitalism can be found just outside Dallas. Set in the midst of a sprawling industrial park, it is a huge, squat, pink stone edifice, with a sloping black roof like a rustic villa, but a villa made for giants.

It is the headquarters of Exxon Mobil, and it houses a plush management suite that is known across the energy industry as the 'God Pod', with the reverence befitting a corporation which last month emerged as the most profitable in the history of human endeavour.

It is no exaggeration to say the decisions made here in Irving, in this high temple of private enterprise, will shape the future of the planet.

Exxon Mobil, which trades in Britain as Esso, does not believe in the certainty of global warming – it casts doubt on evidence that industrial emissions of greenhouse gases are raising temperatures. And not only is it sceptical, it has conducted an aggressive and expensive public relations operation to challenge scientific orthodoxy on the subject, as part of its battle to halt international efforts to put an expensive cap on the smokestacks.

Now a new Republican government, elected with the help of $1.2m from Exxon Mobil, has abandoned the centrepiece of those international efforts, the Kyoto treaty on global warming. The Bush administration, staffed from the president down by former oil executives, has also ruled out plans to limit US emissions of carbon dioxide in the foreseeable future.

The exact link between campaign contributions and the subsequent acts of an administration can only be guessed at. But Exxon's critics argue that the behemoth's assertive embrace of any scientific evidence against global warming – however anecdotal or dubious in origin – has lent it a credibility it does not deserve. It has also given President George Bush 'cover' for his rejection of Kyoto.

The mood in Irving in the new Bush era is confident, even jovial. But it is equally clear that its executives have been put on their guard against complacency. Exxon Mobil (born of a mega-merger in 1999) has, to say the least, an image problem.

In Australia, the first ever conference of the world's green parties yesterday agreed to launch a boycott against Exxon and other US oil companies. They want to 'send a message' to the companies on the role they allegedly played in getting Mr Bush elected.

'We know we have a giant target painted on our chests,' said Ken Cohen,

Exxon Mobil's head of government relations and public affairs. Consequently, the company has decided to emerge from its customary insularity and mount something resembling a charm offensive.

And that is presumably why the outer gates of the God Pod were opened last week, and two of the corporation's vice-presidents were deployed to explain why Exxon Mobil remains dubious about global warming and how it is nevertheless cleaning up its act the free-market way.

Mr Cohen and Frank Sprow, in charge of safety and environmental health, both insist that Exxon Mobil's position has been misunderstood. Rather than denying the existence of global warming outright, they argue, Exxon Mobil is simply pointing out the room for error in such an ever-changing and unpredictable phenomenon as climate, and urging caution.

'You really can't bring human influence out of the noise of natural variability at this point,' Mr Sprow said. 'Science is a process of enquiry...I'd like the answer tomorrow afternoon but it may be a decade before the science really gets crisp, because there's so much fundamental information that has to be worked on.'

Even though the science may not be rock hard, Mr Sprow said, Exxon is working on alternative energy sources, such as low emission fuel cells for cars, and cutting down emissions in its refineries. It spends $12m a year researching means of reducing carbon dioxide emissions, and has so far managed to reduce its own output by 3 per cent.

These arguments have not convinced the corporation's enemies in the green camp. It is big enough and controversial enough to have galvanised an entire environmental movement, Campaign Exxon Mobil, devoted to keeping it under surveillance.

The campaign's spokesman, Peter Altman, argues that the vaunted $12m in carbon dioxide research is a fairly paltry share of the $17bn net income Exxon Mobil earned last year. Furthermore, he said, whatever beneficial effect that money might have is more than outweighed by the corporation's role in undermining the accepted wisdom that global warming is a real threat.

Other oil companies, such as BP and Shell, have crossed the barricades. At its annual general meeting on Thursday, BP will come under pressure from green activists who have laid down formal motions calling on the company to switch more resources to the development of renewable energy sources.

However, Exxon Mobil has kept up the fight on climate change, going out of its way to support maverick sceptics whose conclusions agree with its own.

'The big difference with Exxon is that it spends a lot of time and money in getting that message across,' Mr Altman said.

In particular, the Exxon chairman, Lee Raymond, has referred approvingly to a 1998 petition apparently signed by 17,000 scientists questioning the evidence for global warming. However, it later emerged that the petition had been circulated by a certain Oregon Institute for Science and Medicine, an obscure body of eccentric views whose headquarters turned out to be a large tin shed.

The petition had been disguised as the work of the National Academy of Sciences and it had been 'signed' by such authorities as Ginger Spice and the fictional doctors from the sit-com *M.A.S.H.*

The controversy, Mr Sprow said, had arisen from unfortunate misunderstandings. Mr Raymond had not sought to claim the Oregon petition as definitive, but only to raise provocative questions about the nature of climate change science.

Mr Sprow is urbane and sophisticated. He insisted repeatedly that Exxon is not 'in a state of denial' over global warming. However, on two vital issues it is clear that Exxon's position remains unchanged.

It does not have faith in the dire warnings issued this year by the UN-appointed International Panel on Climate Control (IPCC) and it is vigorously opposed to the Kyoto treaty.

In its latest assessment of the threat, the IPCC found 'new and stronger evidence that most of the warming observed over the last fifty years is attributable to human activities'. The panel, which consulted about 2,000 scientists from 100 countries, predicted that the earth would heat up between 1.4°C and 5.8°C over the next century, with potentially catastrophic results.

The report was presented as a scientific consensus, but Exxon challenges that claim. It points to the role of political appointees on the IPCC in selecting and summarising scientific evidence. The same sort of people were promoting a bureaucratic solution to the problem embodied in Kyoto.

Mr Sprow argued that there is little likelihood of Kyoto being implemented by the majority of industrialised countries, and that it would hardly make a significant difference to long-run greenhouse gas emissions even if they did.

For Exxon, these are both reasons to dump the treaty. For Kyoto's supporters, however, they are all reasons to put the treaty (which would require a 7 per cent drop in US emissions between 1990 and 2012) into effect quickly and then move beyond it.

By poking spanners into the works, the environmental lobby believes, Exxon is helping delay concerted action to stave off global warming and the chaos it may wreak with the climate.

'Exxon is grasping at straws,' said Kert Davies, the director of Greenpeace's US global warming campaign. 'They're looking for everything they can do to reposition the existing knowledge on global warming from fact to theory.'

Even before its current public relations drive, Exxon has had remarkable success in making its influence felt.

But perhaps more importantly, Exxon's executives appear to hold sway over a man who once dreamed of rivalling their success but failed as an oil-man and had to settle this year for becoming president of the United States.

21 July 2001

JOHN VIDAL

Death in Genoa

In front of me a young man lies dead under a white sheet. His body is surrounded by eighty police officers in gas masks, with riot shields, truncheons and guns. Not one looks more than twenty years old – the age of the dead man, Carlo Giuliani, from Rome. They shift nervously. No one knows exactly what happened. A doctor says the man has two head wounds. One looks like the wound from a stone, she says. The other, in his cheek, could be that of a bullet.

One demonstrator says he heard a gunshot. Another says he saw the body driven over by a police van, at the height of one of the worst riots that Europe has known in decades.

The youth lies dead and Genoa is burning, a city in which Tony Blair and his fellow leaders of the G8 group of the richest countries are meeting behind 13ft steel barricades, protected by 18,000 police officers. Questions are already being asked about whether city-based summits like this can be held again.

There is a temporary silence as an ambulance comes to take away the body, and both sides contemplate what has happened. But just 200 yards away, on a side street, eight officers have cornered another young man fleeing from them. They pile in and he takes twenty blows to his head and body. Amazingly, he gets up, bloodied, staggering and disoriented, then collapses. The volunteer medics rush to him.

The helicopters buzz 75ft overhead, and back in the square the shocked crowd is furious. They chant 'assassins, assassins' at the police.

This was one of most beautiful cities in Europe. Now stones and rubbish litter the streets. Shops, banks, supermarkets, post offices, garages and other businesses are destroyed. All around is desolation, fury and destruction.

Fires still burn round Brignole rail station. Police vans, armoured personnel carriers, water cannon and protesters rush through the town. Tear-gas is fired in one direction as the stones fly in another. Nobody knows quite what has happened or where trouble will flare. The only certain thing is that ninety-three have been injured, by the official tally. Behind me a park of twenty cars has been torched. The air is thick with smoke, tear-gas and anger.

Accusations of overzealous policing and violent demonstrators fly. But this is a complex situation. Not all protesters or all police are intent on wreaking havoc.

Up to 2,000 anarchists pulled the trigger for the violence. They are mainly German, with some Italians, French and other Europeans. Some are British members of the Animal Liberation Front, scrawling 'ALF' on the walls.

Of the 35,000–40,000 demonstrators here, all but that small minority of anarchists have signed up to the principle of peaceful protest. But the activists say the way the police reacted to the anarchists and ambushed peaceful marchers has inflamed thousands.

The Genoa Social Forum, with its 700 groups from across the world committed to non-violence, negotiated with the police and is devastated. 'This is unacceptable,' says a spokesman. 'We have been provoked by a level of state and anarchist violence that was unimaginable. The G8 and the government must be blamed, but we must accept our share of responsibility.'

In Via Tolemead, confrontation becomes inevitable the moment the police rush forward to grab the plastic barricades of one of the marchers. The crowd behind surges forward and three people fall. The police beat a man. The protesters surge forward and gain twenty yards. Suddenly the police are in retreat.

A spokesman for the protesters comes forward to negotiate: 'We had agreed this route,' he says. The police retreat again.

But now some of the anarchists have started stoning the police from a side-street. A van of carabinieri stalls and the anarchists launch themselves on it, as if on a wounded animal. In minutes they have broken all its windows. The five policemen inside open the doors and run for it. The van is torched, to cheers.

All day there has been mayhem. Sticks, stones, teargas, fireworks, flares, bottles and truncheons have been thrown back and forth. Barricades of wood and metal have been set alight under a bridge. It is now 7.30 p.m. In the distance protesters and the police are beating their drums under a pall of smoke. The battle for the city has lasted eight hours and may go on sporadically all night.

Hours after Carlo Giuliani's death, protesters have created a makeshift shrine, heaping red flowering plants they uprooted from a nearby public garden. A piece of notebook paper, weighed down with a tear-gas canister, is scrawled with the words: 'Made in G8'.

In one square, the anarchists still rule. A dozen have broken into a small supermarket, ransacked shelves and are handing out ice-cream and wine. They are dangerously drunk.

One, a German, snatches my notebook, spits in my face, raises his stick. He looks no more than twenty. His comrades strut around behind black flags and drums, smashing and burning everything, turning on anyone in their path.

STATE OF THE ART

Austin, 4 September 2001

6 February 2001

MATT WELLS

Forget rock chic, the result is just pop kid

Breaking all the rules of plastic pop, the latest manufactured band to be launched to a jaded record-buying public got it all wrong yesterday. They sang in tune.

The five young hopefuls propelled into celebrity by ITV's *Popstars* series revealed their secret weapon at a press conference in London's Heathrow airport, after jetting in from a recording session in Norway.

Instead of the standard 'Wait for the single' answer, the five responded to questions about their talent by bursting into a well-rehearsed a cappella version of the Simon and Garfunkel classic, 'Bridge Over Troubled Water'.

But the hair-tingling harmonies clashed somewhat with the yet to be named band's chosen image – scuffed denim and punky hair. The aim might have been rock chic, but the result was just pop kid. If they want to be taken seriously as pop stars, they are going to have to start misbehaving a bit more. The five, it seemed, had been carefully schooled.

Had any of them taken drugs? All five shook their heads solemnly, and Kym Marsh, twenty-four, said: 'We do not do drugs and we do not think it is cool for anyone else to do drugs.'

But what about those pictures of a scantily clad Myleene Klass, twenty-two, in a fly-on-the-wall documentary? 'It was a video diary that got blown out of all proportion. When I found out some of the things that were happening I just left,' said Ms Klass.

They must have blown their advances already? 'I am going to treat my nan and grandad...maybe a holiday somewhere where they can go and chill out,' said Danny Foster, twenty-one.

Even twenty-year-old Noel Sullivan, despite emerging as the band's leader, failed in his attempts to shake off his image as a mummy's boy when he revealed he had been on the phone to her constantly. And the greatest crime perpetrated by Suzanne Shaw, nineteen, was to have spoiled her pop-bob hairdo with some ill-advised extensions.

Still, there is plenty of time for bad behaviour. *Popstars*, the docu-soap that has followed the formation of a pop band from the cattle-call auditions of 3,000 largely tuneless hopefuls to the selection of the next big thing, is only halfway through its run. Things are looking up: this Saturday we learn of the pro-gramme-makers' horror at the discovery of Kym's big secret – her two children.

And while the pop kids may have been smiling in front of the cameras yesterday, the TV executives were guffawing behind them. The latest instalment of the series garnered almost twelve million viewers on Saturday night, making it one of the biggest entertainment hits of the year.

The group's first single, understood to be a version of 'Pure and Simple', already recorded by another manufactured band, Girl Thing, will be released on 12 March. 'Bridge Over Troubled Water' will almost certainly feature as the double-A side.

While strict cross-promotion rules prevent Granada from sharing in the single's profits, it stands to make a tidy sum out of merchandising and the inevitable album. Yet the band said they did not feel exploited, as alleged by Spice Girl Melanie C, who knows a thing or two about such matters.

Kym Marsh said: 'We are not silly and stupid. We are not dummies.' And so she landed her first punch: 'Everyone is entitled to their own opinion but this is where she started.' Ouch. That's a bit more like it.

6 February 2001

GILES FODEN

Eminem is a brilliant poet

The man is in town this week, and on the Nokia message board they're asking: 'Does anyone know how to get Stan as a ringer tone?' Which is all very postmodern and interesting, since the hit song overtly references the brave new world of telecommunications: 'Dear Slim, I wrote you but you still ain't callin'/I left my cell, my pager, and my home phone at the bottom...'

The variety of possible ways in which the singer can get in touch with his doomed fan are appropriately overspecified, considering Slim (Eminem's persona) at first doesn't reply to his fan's obsessive letter. Eventually he does get round to writing back: 'Dear Stan, I meant to write you sooner, but I've just been busy...' He continues: 'I'm sorry I didn't see you at the show, I must have missed you./Don't think I did that shit intentionally just to diss you.'

The irony in these lines is delicious, but just how good are Eminem's lyrics? Is all the fuss about him justified, or is it a case of hype over substance? In fact, a brief examination of Stan reveals it to have all the depth and texture of the greatest examples of English verse. To use the singer's own language, it's as 'phat' as Robert Browning – and it is with the Victorian master of sly irony that Eminem's true 'underground' work is done, just as much as with Scam, the band noticed in the song.

Of course, it's nothing new to make great claims for song lyrics. The work listed in *The Poetry of Rock'n'Roll*, a seventies anthology, might seem banal (Donovan?), but it has long been the habit of the more flamboyant Cambridge English dons to put popular music under the full glare of hermeneutic inquiry. It was Christopher Ricks who started it off, writing about Dylan from the seventies onwards. This Sunday, Ricks gives a talk on the subject on Radio 3. In 'Bob Dylan Among the Poets', he attacks the tired Keats v Dylan argument that his original pieces gave rise to. It was David Hare who set up the opposition, one that Ricks (quoting the recent Dylan song 'Not Dark Yet' alongside Keats's 'Ode to a Nightingale') says is actually a unity.

Other dons have followed suit: Eric Griffiths juxtaposing Talking Heads with

William Empson in Cambridge lectures during the late eighties. But it is rare for a singer to combine public outrage and textual richness in quite the way Eminem does.

But who is he, really? Like the Portuguese poet Fernando Pessoa, with his quiverful of pseudonyms, like the coy Eliot of 'Prufrock', or Walt Whitman's 'Song of Myself' – 'Do I contradict myself? Very well then I contradict myself, (I am large, I contain multitudes)', Eminem is a multiple, elusive experience, one that folds about itself like his near-palindromic name (from Marshall Mathers: M'n' M).

Who the 'real Slim Shady' is, in other words, is hard to say. As T. S. Eliot put it: 'The Naming of Cats is a difficult matter,/It isn't just one of your holiday games/You may think I'm as mad as a hatter/When I tell you a cat must have THREE DIFFERENT NAMES.'

Like Macavity, Eminem always has an alibi, and one or two to spare. It is as if there were always someone else walking beside him. The mistake his critics make is to see the songs as direct statements by the singer rather than discrete aesthetic objects. Is it inconceivable that the man who wrote Stan should also want to stab you in the head 'if you're a fag or a les'? Not necessarily, but Eminem 's critics should 'relax a little' as he advises Stan – should consider that this might be an artist toying with the place where celebrity and palatability meet, by passing deliberately inflammatory statements and by parodying less thoughtful rappers.

The 'I' voice has long been subject to modulation in English and American poetry. Browning's great dramatic monologues, such as 'My Last Duchess' or 'Porphyria's Lover', are the classic examples of this. Other poets, including Tennyson, Hardy, Kipling, Frost, Pound and Eliot himself, also mastered the form.

According to the *Handbook to Literature*, a dramatic monologue is a poem 'that reveals a "soul in action" through the speech of one character in a dramatic situation. The character is speaking to an identifiable but silent listener at a dramatic moment in the speaker's life. The circumstances surrounding the conversation, one side of which we "hear"...are made clear by implication, and an insight into the character of the speaker may result.'

In 'My Last Duchess', the speaker is an Italian duke who has had his flirtatious wife murdered, and is showing her portrait to (probably) an envoy from his next father-in-law. A 'picture on the wall', as in the chorus to Stan, furnishes the occasion for the poem.

Where Stan differs, and is in some respects more sophisticated – although it is a sophistication only possible in a mass-media, celebrity-driven world – is that both addressee and addresser speak in it. There is a further sophistication in so far as all listeners are in some sense co-opted into the Stan role.

By ironically dramatising two sets of letters, Stan also fits snugly into the tradition of the verse epistle out of which the dramatic monologue developed. It shares, too, some qualities of unreliable narration with 'Porphyria's Lover', in which another murderer speaks. As with Stan ('the morning rain clouds up my window and I can't see at all'), the weather fits the lunatic's mood: 'The rain set in early tonight,/The sullen wind was soon awake,/It tore the elm-tops down for spite.'

The speaker in 'Porphyria's Lover' goes on to reveal how much Porphyria loved him – so much that to enable them to be together 'her hair/In one long yellow string I wound/Three times her little throat around,/And strangled her. No pain felt she…'

If we don't accuse Browning of misogyny and incitement to violence here, we should extend Eminem the same courtesy. We shouldn't fall into the trap of Stan himself, who tells Slim: 'See, everything you say is real, and I respect you 'cause you tell it.'

It's clever that 'see' – as if you might hear, behind the layers of impersonation, an authentic voice saying 'Can't you see? This is a story, stupid'. It also has a touch of the bardic 'lo!': the poet saying – 'hey, look what I have made'.

Yet neither that voice nor even the one telling Stan that he's 'got some issues' (you bet) and that he needs counselling and that he and his girlfriend need each other can be said to be 'the true voice of Marshall Mathers' any more than the incitements to sexual violence can. The younger fans who buy Eminem 's albums probably understand this instinctively. Just as today's cinema-goers are more adept with movie conventions than their parents, so Eminem 's youthful fans can see between the lines, and the publicity stunts, that the tabloids lap up so eagerly. The joke is on the editors, in fact.

But what about those kids who do take it for real? As Mathers himself put it in an interview (sounding more like Paul Johnson than Public Enemy): 'There are kids out there who, believe it or not, want to be the have-nots.' The question of how much sympathy or disdain Mathers has for them, for the Stans of the world, adds another dimension to the song.

As does the question of how much he can be said to encourage them. To what extent, actually, can artists be held responsible for their works? This is a question poets have asked themselves for centuries, especially when dealing with tragic material. 'Go litel bok, go, litel myn tragedye', said Chaucer, sending *Troilus and Criseyde* out into the world like a paper boat. He knew it wasn't as simple as that – though it isn't just a question of words being akin to deeds either. 'Did that play of mine send out/Certain men the English shot?', Yeats asks, looking back on the Easter Rising in 'The Man and the Echo' (*Last Poems: 1936–39*). Eminem 's talent lies in his turning of these issues into the material of both his work and his personae. 'You could have rescued me from drowning,' Stan writes. 'Why are you so mad?' Slim replies. 'Try to understand…'

Try indeed. Stan, and much else in Eminem 's oeuvre, explores humanity's most profound experience: not just madness, but also terror, melancholy and (not least) laughter. In this view Eminem is neither the 'authentic voice of disaffected working class youth' (*Independent on Sunday*), nor 'a nasty little yob'(ditto), but a rapper whose genius is, principally, poetic.

You can hear that genius in the disposition of poetic stress in that opening verse of Stan – 'my cell, my pager and my home phone'. The pick-up of metre and sense between 'cell' and 'phone' puts a lot of weight on 'cell' – making us think, perhaps, of the other type of cell might be in order for Stan.

And of the phone tones themselves of course. Oh, and while we're on the subject, for the Nokia 3210 you can get the Stan ringer tone at www.dialaring.com.

7 February 2001

LETTER

Browning still beats Eminem

I assume the *Guardian* will be advertising for a new deputy literary editor once the men in white coats have taken poor Giles Foden into secure accommodation. Comparing the ravings of Eminem with those of poets like Browning and Eliot is preposterous.

> Patrick Burke
>   Ramsgate, Kent

2 March 2001

NANCY BANKS-SMITH

A shot in the dark

In the words of the great Frankie Howerd, 'I blame Dot.' And why not Dot? While the devout Mrs Cotton is not the obvious suspect for the shooting of Phil Mitchell in *EastEnders* (BBC 1), perhaps she heard voices. As we all did. There was enough said at Mel's wedding to inflame a saint. The groom was murderous, the bride tearful and the bridesmaid suicidal. Their footsteps rang hollow in the register office like a bad comic going off stage.

However, Mrs Owen, the groom's estranged mother (Sheila Hancock), carrying a load of roses on her head like the muffin man who lives in Drury Lane, and Phil Mitchell, the bride's ex-lover (Steve McFadden), carrying a load of booze, arrived uninvited and got on together like a pub on fire. Of the whole doom-laden wedding party, they seemed to be having much the best time. 'She's long been an inspiration to me,' said Mrs Owen, gazing mistily at a portrait of the Queen in her blue garter. 'The Mother of the Nation,' said Phil, who was just asking for a good slap. 'What a very nice boy you are', said the groom's mother, much moved.

Their happy association continued unabated at the reception. 'What a gentleman you are! One recognises a gentleman by his capacity to distinguish between a great Chablis and a cheap plonk,' she said, darting a basilisk eye at the bride and stubbing out her fag end in the wedding cake.

The odd thing is that quite recently she would have been right. The Mitchell brothers were loosely based on the Krays. Grant created charismatic mayhem and Phil swept up after him like a small, industrious dustcart. If not precisely nice, at least nicer. But ever since Grant left, Phil has morphed into the man who makes the mess. As Mel said this week: 'When exactly did you turn into your brother?'

For the benefit of those of you who are looking vacant, Phil enjoyed a

Christmas tryst with Mel and ever since has been looking at her longingly, like a bull terrier spotting a tree in Bow. As he is short and fat and she is tall and willowy, their confrontations have to be carefully staged to avoid a tasteless note of comedy. Mel chose, as they will, to marry Steve, who is tall and willowy too. At her wedding Phil took spectacularly to the bottle and put the boot in with some brio. It was now that one felt the lack of a swimming pool. In Dallas, where weddings were conducted on the patio, malcontents were cooled off by being thrown into the bijou pool. I tell you frankly that a flood in the gents, requiring a swift evacuation of the wedding party to the Queen Vic, is not the same thing at all.

Phil was running the Queen Vic. So the legendary Curse of the Queen Vic, which puts Tutankhamun firmly in his place, has struck again. Landlords of the Vic are routinely murdered. There was 'Dirty' Den Watts, shot with a bunch of daffodils as he strolled beside the canal, Eddie Royle, stabbed in Albert Square by, it is widely believed, Nick Cotton, and Grant Mitchell, driven into the Thames by his brother.

Phil's last words just before he was shot were tantalisingly: 'I know who you are!' No relation of Bing Crosby being in sight, that leaves us with the usual suspects: Ian, the bride's ex-husband; Steve, the current incumbent; Lisa, Phil's ex-girlfriend; Mark, who loves her hopelessly; and Dan, who appeared from nowhere to make up the numbers. Or you could ask Christopher Reason, who wrote the script.

What a shock for Phil's dinky Mum (Barbara Windsor) on her return from Lanzarote! Let us hope the Queen will, as ever, be an inspiration and comfort to her.

Ballykissangel (BBC 1) is back in fine form with Father 'Call me Vincent' Sheahan (real name, implausibly enough, Robert Taylor), a craggy new Australian priest, who looks as if roughly hewn from a coolabah tree, and a changed but charming cast, not one of whom could walk from a to b in a straight line. And that, even before Fitzgerald's opens. The outer habiliments of the late Brian Quigley, the rogue with the brogue, are found folded tidily on the shore, topped by his trilby like a cherry. It's the consensus at Fitzgerald's that he's done a bunk and the arrival of a number of large cheques drawn on the aptly named Banco Sinistre de Rio confirms it. Tony Doyle, who played Quigley, is, in fact, dead but we don't have to believe it if we don't want to.

28 April 2001

JONATHAN GLANCEY

The house that we built

King George VI declared the Royal Festival Hall open on 3 May 1951. Sadly, a number of VIPs attending the event – including Gerald Barry, director general of the Festival of Britain, and the Lord Mayor of London – missed His Majesty's declaration: they were stuck in a lift inside Britain's first major postwar public building. Embarrassing that, yet in the fifty years since, the Royal Festival Hall – the 'people's palace' – has been one of the most trouble-free and best-liked modern buildings in Britain.

Intellectually rigorous, elegant, impeccably built and open to all comers, the hall was and remains a triumph of democratic public design. It introduced the British public to a form of modern architecture that had been brewing since soon after the first world war, in Germany, France and the Soviet Union, but arrived here late and generally unappreciated. Although in many ways original, the RFH owed its pedigree to the radical architecture of early Soviet architects as much as it did to the less strident Scandinavian modernism that must have seemed so attractive to the hall's young British architects.

Those architects included Robert Matthew, Leslie Martin, Peter Moro and Edwin Williams. When the new concert hall was commissioned from the London County Council architects' department in September 1948, most of the design team, led by Matthew, were under forty. They produced what Wagner would have called a *Gesamkunstwerk* – a complete artwork. Although not quite completed when opened as the heart of the Festival of Britain, the building brought together the very best talents the nation had to offer.

Its foyers were light and generous, reflections of the Thames rippling from its whiter-than-white ceilings on sunny days. (It rained and rained throughout the Festival of Britain.) The 3,165-seat auditorium was raised on stilts inside the generous volume of the stone-clad structure, so that it sat, as Martin said, like an 'egg in a box'. This was a stroke of genius – and it still surprises. Because you can see from one side of the RFH to the other, through big windows, the auditorium appears to have done a runner. In fact, it's up above you, a surprise of warm wood, swallow-nest boxes and plush seats. It has a magnificent organ designed by Ralph Downes...all 10,000 tons of it. Lined in double concrete walls to keep the noise of trains crossing Hungerford Bridge at bay, it is as 'rich and as sensual', according to its architects, 'as 1951 would allow an interior'.

The reason for placing the auditorium above the foyers was not to show how clever the architects were but to solve a very basic problem: although situated on a magnificent bend on the river Thames, the site itself was tight, hemmed in on one side by Hungerford railway bridge and on the other by what was scheduled to become the Royal National Theatre. The solution? Build upwards so as to maximise public circulation space in the building.

'We have taken a cube of space roughly 200ft square and 80ft high', wrote Martin at the time. 'Within this space we have modelled and sculpted out the shape of the component parts and, as you move through the foyers and promenades, if you are aware of the excitement of its vistas and its continual unfolding of space, we shall not have failed.' They haven't.

For all its cool, rational logic, the RFH weaves a quiet magic on the three million people who pass through its unpretentious portals each year (the numbers increased dramatically from 1983, when the foyer doors were thrown open all day).

The real wonder, though, is that it was built at all. In 1948, with Britain worn out by war, the only buildings approved for capital expenditure were homes, schools and factories. The RFH went ahead, however, with a budget of £2m (it came in less than 1 per cent over budget), with Herbert Morrison, Lord President of Council and former leader of the London County Council acting as its guardian angel. In the event, the RFH took just twenty months to build, a remarkably short time given the constraints of the time and the radical nature of its design.

The RFH meant a great deal to the music world and to concert-goers who had been denied a major, purpose-built concert hall since 1941, when the Queen's Hall was burned out by a German incendiary bomb. The Royal Albert Hall, with its then decidedly dodgy acoustics, had always been a multi-purpose venue, for boxing as well as Beethoven.

Sir Malcolm Sargent was the musical advisor to the RFH and every attempt was made to create what might be described as a democratic acoustic. The aim was a sound that was equal and consistent when heard from any seat in the auditorium. This meant, in theory, that every seat could be sold at the same price – although in practice this has never been the case.

The stage was designed to optimise orchestral acoustics, so percussion and brass sections were sited on a concrete floor and the rest of the orchestra on timber. The reverberation time was intended to be 2.2 seconds (slightly warm) but ended up a rather cold 1.5. (A medieval cathedral, with its rich, echoing sound, is normally about eleven seconds.)

Yet, musically as well as architecturally, the RFH was judged a critical and popular success. The acoustic was praised by conductors and orchestras at the time for its 'modern' crispness. Today, a warmer sound is appreciated and the auditorium is to be subtly tuned as far as this is possible. Every last detail was intended to be the newest and the best.

Aside from the care that went into its musical properties, the RFH was a showcase of modern design – furniture by Robin Day, a distinctive bat-and-ball carpet by Peter Moro, who had worked on the De La Warr Pavilion, Bexhill-on-Sea, which was, in its much smaller way, a prototype for the RFH. The British public would have seen little to match it in modern intent, except, of course, for the stations, rolling stock and buses of Frank Pick's London Underground, much admired by Matthew, Martin, Moro and co, and made possible with the earlier political machinations of Herbert Morrison.

But...the RFH was never quite complete. Its backstage facilities were derisory and the face it presented to the Thames was a little grim, and temporary. In June 1964, the building was closed for eight months for a facelift. The big smile of its Thames-side elevation dates from this time.

Ever since, the RFH has been cluttered up inside, then stripped back a bit, then messed up again. Only recently has a considered, long-term plan been put into practice, with the architects Allies and Morrison commissioned to work through the building to both renovate and improve. Two of the practice's architects working on the RFH, Graham Morrison and Di Haig, were trained by Martin when he was professor of architecture at Cambridge. The new works, quiet and respectful, and due for completion in 2003–4, include a new recital room, the opening up of the garden roof terraces for the first time in many years, new bars and cafes extending on to terraces, new backstage areas and a general architectural wash- and brush-up. A slim new office will rise alongside Hungerford Bridge to house RFH and other South Bank Centre staff.

Meanwhile, the whole of the South Bank is being replanned under the direction of Rick Mather. A landscape architect is to be appointed in May after the RFH's fiftieth birthday celebrations and one of either Rafael Vignoly or FOA (Foreign Office Architects – just a name, and nothing to do with government wallahs) will be offered the commission to design a new arts building on the Jubilee Gardens site on the other side of Hungerford Bridge from the RFH. This was where the principal buildings of the 1951 Festival of Britain stood, including Powell & Moya's Skylon and Ralph Tubbs's Dome of Discovery.

Fifty years young, the RFH remains an evolving showcase of open, accessible, democratic architecture. It is as popular as it is a work of *sotto voce* triumph over austerity art.

2 May 2001

BRIAN LOGAN

Chicago, Adelphi Theatre, London

The casting of TV presenter and tabloid favourite Denise Van Outen in *Chicago* is more interesting than it appears. To the show's producers, the calculation must have been simple: people will pay to see *The Big Breakfast*'s brassy ex-hostess, especially if she wears a leotard and fishnets. It's a happy coincidence that her participation sheds new light on Kander and Ebb's musical.

Chicago 's tale of a floozy whose murderous career leads to showbiz celebrity was intended as a broad satire. But Van Outen's West End appearance – hot on the stilettos of Kelly Brook, Dannii Minogue and Jerry Hall – brings the show's argument, that we value notoriety over merit, troublingly close to home.

So is the starlet aware of how Chicago resonates with her own career? 'You're a phoney celebrity, kid,' says her character's lawyer, Billy Flynn, 'and in a coupla weeks no one will know who you are.' Certainly, Van Outen's biog in the programme inflates her slim credentials, coyly failing to mention that her last stage role, in *Stop the World, I Want to Get Off*, came when she was fourteen years old.

But even if there's evidence that she's rusty after the twelve-year sabbatical, Van Outen doesn't disgrace herself. OK, she can't hold a candle to the effortless charisma of musical veterans Clarke Peters as Billy and Susannah Fellows as Mama Morton. Both generate more heat with the arch of an eyebrow than their new colleague does when shimmying from head to toe. There's something sanitised, too, about the sassiness that Van Outen seeks to inject into her jailbird alter ego. She cuts a scrawny figure next to the toned bodies of the dancers and struggles to make the leap from her trademark 'Carry On' naughtiness to the killer sex appeal Roxy Hart ought to exude.

But she has a passable Monroe-ish purr and a likeable eagerness to please, while the flaws in her performance can be ascribed to Walter Bobbie's production as a whole. 'Let's go to hell in a fast car!' says one character, and I wished the show would. The jazz is fantastic, the staging crisp and funny, the story juicily cynical – but it has all got to be louder and sleazier, less slick and more human. There's nothing you couldn't invite your granny to see, if she hasn't already booked her tickets to see that nice young lady off the telly.

1 June 2001

PETER BRADSHAW

Torture! Torture! Torture!

What can you say about Jerry Bruckheimer and Michael Bay's big, loud, dumb, boring mega-movie – apart from Oof and Ouch and Aaargh and Zzzzzzzzzz? What response is there, apart from a yelp of incredulous dismay every five minutes? What historical insights can it offer – apart from the blinding revelation that maybe Steven Spielberg's *1941* wasn't quite that bad after all?

Fundamentally, the movie offers a vision of what *Titanic* might have looked like if the iceberg was a warlike Jap. It's a tremulous love story about a triangle of pretty young people in historical costumes – two best buddies and the cute nurse they both love – set against the mighty backdrop of war, planes, shooting, guns and ammo: a chick flick and a guy flick.

Ben Affleck is Rafe, the square-jawed, cubic-headed US army pilot who is temporarily away in England, winning the Battle of Britain single-handedly. If you thought that the war in the Pacific would be one second world war story that didn't need time out to patronise the Brits, you were wrong. The RAF squadron leader, soaking his stiff upper lip in a pint of limey warm brown beer, is overcome with gratitude for Ben: 'If there are any more like you, God help anyone who goes to war with America!'

Meanwhile, back in sleepy, peaceful Pearl Harbor, his comrade Danny (Josh Hartnett) is making time with Rafe's girl Evelyn (Kate Beckinsale). And so the emotional balloon goes up just as the sneaky Jap bombers arrive at 7.55 a.m., 7 December 1941.

Affleck, Hartnett and Beckinsale give performances of such somnambulist awfulness that the three of them achieve an almost Zen-like state of woodenness. This is bad acting above and beyond the call of duty, this is Purple Heart bad acting. And Cuba Gooding Jr, playing the African-American fighting man forced through prejudice to be a cook, is so camp he could be in the Village People.

Never at any time does director Michael Bay give any hint of the real human cost of war. At least *Saving Private Ryan* made an honourable attempt to show the ugliness of violence: the sweat, the pain – and the fear and hatred of the enemy. But all Bay requires of Ben, Josh and Kate is to look cute or, as it might be, overjoyed, or troubled.

The effects are indeed impressive, no question about it, and for the recreation of the attack itself there are some breathtaking scenes of what a warship looks like from the point of view of the bomb that's about to sink it. But the whole thing is an effect: the drama, the people, the emotions, everything. When Affleck and Hartnett take to the skies in their fighter planes in a feisty but doomed attempt to repulse the enemy, they looked like no one so much as Will Smith seeing off the aliens in *Independence Day*. It had about as much relationship to the reality of wartime combat as a Gap ad for khakis.

As for the Japanese themselves, the film smoothes away both America's 'yellow peril' racist invective and the realities of Japanese nationalist aggression: a kind of bogus two-way political correctness, somehow as insidiously offensive as anything else. The Japanese themselves are carefully drawn as a kind of modernised, New Labour Jap enemy, tough on the causes of foreign devils: they are thoughtful, almost regretful about launching the attack. On being congratulated on his brilliant strategy, the Admiral says sadly: 'A brilliant man would find a way not to fight the war.' There's even a shot of one Japanese pilot desperately signalling to baseball-playing kids to take cover before his duty to the Emperor compels him to reduce them all to ashes.

And it is the thought of being reduced to ashes that brings me to the most curious part of this film. After Pearl Harbor, the movie's final act is to show Hartnett and Affleck spearheading the retaliatory raid on Tokyo on 18 April 1942, commanded by Lt Col. Jimmy Doolittle (improbably and plumply played by Alec Baldwin) – a desperately dangerous mission. I won't give away what happens, but suffice it to say that Kate's final voiceover gestures towards the end of the war, informing us that this was the decisive turning point. 'America suffered, and grew stronger,' she says. 'Through the trial we overcame.'

Uh, yeah...? Is that how America overcame? Through the 'trial'? The one moment which really excited me in Pearl Harbor was when President Roosevelt (Jon Voight) rises miraculously from his wheelchair to show what can be achieved if we really try. Aha, I thought, is this a brilliant ironic reference to Peter Sellers' mad Nazi scientist in *Dr Strangelove*, who rises from his wheelchair and shrieks: 'I can WALK!' just as the nuclear anti-miracle is unfolding? Is producer Jerry Bruckheimer going to hint at a big historical truth: that Pearl Harbor led to Hiroshima and Nagasaki? Nope – no mention of it. As far as multiplex audiences are concerned, America's key response was that gallant, symbolic little raid on Tokyo, and naturally suffering and growing stronger – not the vaporisation of civilian populations.

What can be done about this film? I would suggest some sort of campaign of civil disobedience. But maybe we should just take cover as best we can as the bombs of stupidity and dullness and silliness detonate above our heads – $75m at the US box office in the first weekend? For you, Tommy, the war is over.

9 June 2001

SALMAN RUSHDIE

Reality TV: a dearth of talent and the death of morality

I've managed to miss out on reality TV until now. In spite of all the talk in Britain about nasty Nick and flighty Mel, and in America about the fat, naked bastard Richard manipulating his way to desert-island victory, I have somehow preserved my purity. I wouldn't recognise Nick or Mel if I passed them in the street, or Richard if he was standing in front of me unclothed.

Ask me where the Big Brother house is, or how to reach Temptation Island, and I have no answer. I do remember the American Survivor contestant who managed to fry his own hand so that the skin peeled away until his fingers looked like burst sausages, but that's because he got on to the main evening news. Otherwise, search me. Who won? Who lost? Who cares?

The subject of reality TV shows, however, has been impossible to avoid. Their success is the media story of the (new) century, along with the ratings triumph of the big-money game shows such as *Who Wants to Be a Millionaire?* Success on this scale insists on being examined, because it tells us things about ourselves, or ought to.

And what tawdry narcissism is here revealed! The television set, once so idealistically thought of as our window on the world, has become a dime-store mirror instead. Who needs images of the world's rich otherness, when you can watch these half-familiar avatars of yourself – these half-attractive half-persons – enacting ordinary life under weird conditions? Who needs talent, when the unashamed self-display of the talentless is constantly on offer?

I've been watching *Big Brother 2*, which has achieved the improbable feat of taking over the tabloid front pages in the final stages of a general election campaign. This, according to the conventional wisdom, is because the show is more interesting than the election. The 'reality' may be even stranger. It may be that *Big Brother* is so popular because it's even more boring than the election. Because it is the most boring, and therefore most 'normal', way of becoming famous, and, if you're lucky or smart, of getting rich as well.

'Famous' and 'rich' are now the two most important concepts in western society, and ethical questions are simply obliterated by the potency of their appeal. In order to be famous and rich, it's OK – it's actually 'good' – to be devious. It's 'good' to be exhibitionistic. It's 'good' to be bad. And what dulls the moral edge is boredom. It's impossible to maintain a sense of outrage about people being so trivially self-serving for so long.

Oh, the dullness! Here are people becoming famous for being asleep, for keeping a fire alight, for letting a fire go out, for videotaping their clichéd thoughts, for flashing their breasts, for lounging around, for quarrelling, for bitching, for being unpopular, and (this is too interesting to happen often) for kissing! Here, in short, are people becoming famous for doing nothing much at all, but doing it where everyone can see them.

Add the contestants' exhibitionism to the viewers' voyeurism and you get a picture of a society sickly in thrall to what Saul Bellow called 'event glamour'. Such is the glamour of these banal but brilliantly spotlit events that anything resembling a real value – modesty, decency, intelligence, humour, selflessness you can write your own list – is rendered redundant. In this inverted ethical universe, worse is better. The show presents 'reality' as a prize fight, and suggests that in life, as on TV, anything goes, and the more deliciously contemptible it is, the more we'll like it. Winning isn't everything, as Charlie Brown once said, but losing isn't anything.

The problem with this kind of engineered realism is that, like all fads, it's likely to have a short shelf-life, unless it finds ways of renewing itself. The probability is that our voyeurism will become more demanding. It won't be enough to watch somebody being catty, or weeping when evicted from the house of hell, or 'revealing everything' on subsequent talk shows, as if they had anything left to reveal.

What is gradually being reinvented is the gladiatorial combat. The TV set is the Colosseum and the contestants are both gladiators and lions. Their job is to eat one another until only one remains alive. But how long, in our jaded culture, before 'real' lions, actual dangers, are introduced to these various forms of fantasy island, to feed our hunger for more action, more pain, more vicarious thrills?

Here's a thought, prompted by the news that the redoubtable Gore Vidal has agreed to witness the execution by lethal injection of the Oklahoma bomber Timothy McVeigh. The witnesses at an execution watch the macabre proceedings through a glass window: a screen. This, too, is a kind of reality TV, and – to make a modest proposal – it may represent the future of such programmes. If we are willing to watch people stab one another in the back, might we not also be willing to actually watch them die?

In the world outside TV, our numbed senses already require increasing doses of titillation. One murder is barely enough: only the mass murderers make the front pages. You have to blow up a building full of people or machine-gun a whole royal family to get our attention. Soon, perhaps, you'll have to kill off a whole species of wildlife or unleash a virus that wipes out people by the thousand, or else you'll be small potatoes. You'll be on an inside page.

And as in reality, so on 'reality TV'. How long until the first TV death? How long until the second? By the end of Orwell's great novel *Nineteen Eighty-Four*, Winston Smith has been brainwashed. 'He loved Big Brother.' As, now, do we. We are the Winstons now.

21 June 2001

ADRIAN SEARLE

Only here for Vermeer

Closing my eyes and thinking of Johannes Vermeer, a mass of sights and sounds fills my head: feet walking on the tiles of a chequer-board floor, mild Dutch light, a plucked string, the clatter of a glass put down on a tray, muffled conversation, milk being poured from a glazed jug. Little spots of light like pearls, and pearls themselves, light delivered in little patted brushstrokes, light on top of light, on grains on a loaf, on buttons, brocade, a fretboard, the milk threading into the bowl.

I can almost taste Vermeer's colour: the lemony-yellow material of a woman's bodice, the crumpled whites of cloth, the transparent skin-pinks with the ghost of blue under the paleness, the intense vibrating blues of a dress, the glazed motifs on Delft plaques and tiles, the painted sky of a painting within a painting. Reddened cheeks and red lips, the flaring, impossible reds of *The Girl with the Red Hat*, and the vermilion that melts against grey in the rug in the foreground of *The Procuress*. Then the indeterminate ivory tone of a wall, exact but unnameable, like a word you reach for but can't quite find.

The people in the rooms appear aware of more than what is visible, though the tenor of their thoughts might be guessed at. The painter at his easel, looking at the girl. The girl holding herself still for him. A girl with a glass of wine to her lips, self-conscious because she knows the man is looking. The women alone at the window, and the whore smiling as she holds out her hand and the man fumbles at her breast. There have been doubts whether *The Procuress* is by Vermeer at all, but that doesn't stop you looking and wanting to look some more.

There is always something beyond in these paintings, something out of sight. Whatever is going on is mysterious, and speaks of a psychology that is only partly a matter of the more overt allegories and symbols that Vermeer, a Catholic, was at pains to set before us. In his *Allegory of the Faith*, the writhing snake retching blood on the tiles, the woman with her foot on the globe, her eyes on the clear glass sphere dangling from the ceiling, the tapestry of the crucifixion behind her, are all somehow less compelling than the way the light catches on the drapery, a kind of optical interference perhaps caused by the camera obscura the artist may have used to plot his naturalistic effects.

Thinking about, looking at and even dreaming Vermeer is one thing: Vermeer exhibitions are something else. I hear the ring of tills, credit cards chattering through the machine. I remember the 1996 show at the Mauritshuis in The Hague: the calm the paintings radiated, their invitations to a stilled world, and the ill- tempered jostling, the impossibility to connect. Not for nothing is the Mauritshuis called the Royal Cabinet of Paintings. It was like seeing Vermeer in a crowded lift.

The lift has descended to the basement of the National Gallery for the exhibition 'Vermeer and the Delft School', which opened yesterday. With little more than half of the exhibits that were at New York's Metropolitan Museum of Art, from where the show has travelled, the London exhibition has eleven paintings by Vermeer, two of them from the National Gallery itself and one from Edinburgh. Vermeer towers over the other twenty-four artists. The Delft School (which includes Rembrandt's brilliant pupil Carel Fabritius, Pieter de Hooch, Emanuel de Witte and Gerard Houckgeest) is a mixed bunch of artists who were working in the city in the middle of the seventeenth century, mainly painting for conservative local patrons.

I cannot really care about Jacob van Geel's gnarly woodland scenes, or Anthonie Palamedesz's merry bar-room topers. Egbert van der Poel is only really of interest for his renderings of the ruined city after the explosion that ripped it apart in 1654. His nocturnal fire and moonlit scenes are just, well, minor art. And no farm animals, please, even if Paulus Potter was the 'Raphael of the cows', as a nineteenth-century critic had him. There is much here that is terribly dull.

The engines of art history have been hard at work moving over the flat lands. It is good to see things in the context of their time and place. But a few Delft plaques and dishes in a cabinet at the National Gallery don't exactly round out our view. Historians cannot even agree whether the Delft School existed, or what defined it, although some of the better artists seemed obsessed with the naturalistic rendering of daylight, an interest in optics and the careful application of the laws of perspective.

Fabritius's two self-portraits, his views of the city and his sleeping sentry stand out as belonging to a quite different aesthetic from the artists actually native to Delft. He's so much rougher, more overtly painterly, than anyone else in the show. And, even in his little painting of a goldfinch on a perch, his work is worthy to be set against Vermeer's, however distant in attitude the two artists might have been. Yet to see them as anything more than geographic neighbours seems absurd.

Delft was prosperous, conservative, pious. It was also an unlucky town. In the sixteenth century it was visited by plague and famine and by Protestant riots. In the seventeenth century the city managed to blow itself up (Fabritius died in the explosion). Yet it appears it was an attractive, comfortable place, just an hour or so by foot, or on the half-hourly boat from the Hague. Samuel Pepys liked it. The streets and courtyard corners of Delft, with their red brick, the churches towering over the walls, children blowing bubbles in the gardens, families posing smugly for their portraits and snacking in the courtyards are visions of a world whose temper was as even as its tempo. The interesting stuff, mostly, went on inside, in Vermeer's quiet rooms.

The masterly perspectival renderings of the interiors of Delft's churches (the Nieuwe Kerk and Oude Kerk) by de Witte, Hendrick, Cornelisz, van Vliet and Gerard Houckgeest are as sober and as measured as the churches themselves. It is difficult to warm to these paintings. Warmth is not the point: endurance is, and being put in our place by God's laws and human perspective. The light may be cold here, but it is the same light that falls through Vermeer 's windows.

It always seems to me more profitable to look at artists such as Vermeer in less crowded circumstances. Most seventeenth-century Dutch painting was never destined for mass consumption, and certainly not for the blockbuster show. It is likely that more people will see this exhibition in a fortnight than lived in Delft in the 1660s, even if you could include those who walked from the Hague for the afternoon, or took the half-hourly boat.

16 July 2001

STEVEN POOLE

Picnic with Pavarotti: Hyde Park, London

Sixty thousand people are gathered in Hyde Park on Saturday afternoon to celebrate Safeway's range of Italian food. Ersatz, ivy-wreathed columns flank a giant scaffolding stage: cold pizza, of course, tastes better to the strains of a little light opera. The first act, likeable young British singer Russell 'The Voice' Watson, delivers a pleasantly surreal moment when he duets with Midge Ure on that much-loved La Scala classic, Vienna.

Then storm clouds gather overhead to presage the appearance of the terrifying Charlotte Church, with her teased blonde mane and meaningless décolletage, waving her arms and giggling like an android programmed by an evil scientist to act bubbly. She proceeds to demonstrate the full horror of her coarse, wobbly voice. During 'Tonight' from West Side Story, she recalls the falsetto of Dame Edna Everage. She murders Gershwin's 'Summertime' with a lugubrious nymphet nastiness and ear-poppingly bad intonation. The leader of the orchestra is several times caught on the large screens wincing up at Church in painful disbelief.

'You've been a wicked, wicked audience,' the devil-child finally announces. So there was a reason for the punishment after all. I move to make some more notes, but only scratch the page. Charlotte Church has sucked all the lead out of my pencil.

A biro is found in time to witness the next act, Vanessa-Mae. Regardless of the wet T-shirt image, she is an excellent violinist, with quicksilver technique and the flawless intonation of a good folk fiddler. She plays a rousing set of techno-rock hybrids, switching between electric violin for woozy fuzz solos and acoustic for more ethnic moments, and at one point generously bends over to allow a burly roadie to adjust the transmitters that are dragging down the back of her hipster trousers.

At last, it is time for Luciano himself, and who better to introduce him than Angela Rippon? The hirsute man-mountain strides gingerly to the front and spreads his arms, beaming infectiously, before launching into a number from *Tosca*. This two-hour set of tuneful arias and 'popular Neapolitan songs' is split between the tenor and soprano Annalisa Raspagliosi, a vision in cantilevered crimson, who – especially in her thrilling delivery of 'Tacea la notte placida' from *Il Trovatore* – has all the musical dynamics and tonal beauty that Satan forgot to give Charlotte Church in return for her soul.

The orchestra, conducted by Leona Magiera, has thankfully lost the top-heavy, metallic, amplified sound it was suffering from earlier. Yet Pavarotti himself appears to be glossing over the vocal demands with splendid face-acting: his thick, angular, black eyebrows are burly, jousting caterpillars; his eyes crinkle for pathos; he bares his teeth savagely for tragedy.

After a fifteen-minute interval, Pavarotti comes back refreshed, presumably having eaten a horse, and rises to the occasion with a magnificent 'Vesti la giubba' from *I Pagliacci*. He is now soaring powerfully and precisely, with a delightful rhythmic playfulness. Joined by Raspagliosi, he encores with 'O Sole Mio' and the drinking song from *La Traviata*, during which he manages to convey a genuine thirst. The crowds are still shouting bemusedly for 'Nessun Dorma' as the great man leaves the stage to quaff a well-deserved crate of Chianti.

8 September 2001

MARK LAWSON

What's the point of ballet?

The keys to our psychology usually lie in childhood, and it is true that, at the age of seven, there was an incident involving tights. My primary school in Leeds was preparing a Christmas performance of *A Windmill in Old Amsterdam*. There would be a chorus of mice. Mrs White asked for volunteers. The hands raised were all female. But, wanting coeducational rodents, the teacher conscripted me and my friend Sean O'Gorman.

At the dress rehearsal, the costumes were revealed. The mice would wear tights with a cotton-wool bobtail glued to the rear seam. It's relatively unlikely that anyone who knows about football is reading a piece about ballet but it's vital to understand that we were supporters of Leeds United, whose key players at this time were Billy Bremner and Norman Hunter, two of the most masculine tacklers in football history. The latter even possessed the game's most intimidating nickname: Norman 'Bites Yer Legs' Hunter.

If Bremner and Hunter had anything to do with tights, it was perhaps to buy their wife a pair for Christmas. 'We can't wear these,' whispered Sean O'Gorman. On the day of the full performance, his mother phoned in to report that he had chickenpox, an illness I now regard as diplomatic. And so, on a Friday afternoon in Yorkshire, in the land of Norman Hunter, in a line of dancing mice in tights, I was the only boy. Professional criticism has produced many tough reviewers – Tom Paulin, Victor Lewis-Smith, A. A. Gill – but their style would appear gently constructive beside what was said on the playground over the next few days.

I begin with this confession because it's commonly assumed that men who dislike ballet consider *Swan Lake* an affront to their masculinity. They regard dance as feminine or effeminate. And certainly this prejudice is something most men must overcome: ballet lessons are what your sisters did when you were at football practice.

There is a popular homophobia against the art form. When Ronald Reagan ran for president, his Republican handlers were genuinely concerned about the reaction of right-wing voters to the 'negative' that his son was a ballet-dancer. There was a popular joke in the 1980s that when President Reagan shouted 'Nancy' in the White House, both his wife and his son came into the room.

Such conditioning is hard for a man to defeat. But, by adulthood, I really believe that I had. When ballet came my way as a television critic – as, on the

BBC2 of the eighties, it was surprisingly likely to – I tried to resist any vestigial impulse to write about *Match of the Day* instead. But now I discovered problems with the form that were not psychological but artistic.

The first of these was that dance seemed to demand an off-putting level of technical knowledge from the viewer. Unless the performer actually fell over, it was hard to know whether they were dancing moderately or spectacularly. The same is true of classical music and art – where only an expert can really detect a wrong note or incompetent brush stroke – but with those forms the spectator has the compensations of emotion, colour, story.

Except, admittedly, in the case of atonal music and art of the blank or nearly blank canvas variety. And it seemed to me that dance, whether classical or contemporary, shared with minimalist symphonies and abstract painting a problem of narrative. While great art can contain no story and bad art can consist of nothing but plots, our natural instinct when faced with entertainment is to try to extract a tale or meaning. Watching ballet, I was never sure whether to think 'He's angry with her' or 'She's trying to stab him' or 'He's asking the gods for help' and so on.

The problem is that we are most comfortable with art that achieves its effects verbally. It's no coincidence that the mass art forms are literature, cinema, pop, television and theatre. Even with a Beethoven or Mozart symphony, it's comforting to have a programme or sleeve note revealing what the piece is 'about'.

With dance I always felt as if the audience had to provide mental subtitles for a silent movie. Some choreographers compensate with the use of mime, but this further repelled me, mime being the only art form lower on my list than ballet.

There was one more obstacle: snobbery. Even more so than opera, ballet – and especially the Royal Ballet – seemed to belong to an ageing, braying elite more concerned with the availability of champagne at the interval and whether the men in the audience were all wearing black tie than with what was happening on stage.

And so dance became the hole in my entertainment portfolio. But this never seriously mattered until I began to present radio and television arts programmes. These shows were expected to cover the waterfront culturally and there would have to be dance items. Fortunately (as I then felt) these would be few because ballet is the artistic discipline that scores the least viewer and listener interest. On the arts broadcasting waterfront, dance is just a little patch of cobbles by the quay.

There was the further protection that my radio co-presenter would willingly do the ballet reviews and indeed at one point delivered links while taking part in a masterclass with Twyla Tharp. Unfortunately, a presentational *pas de deux* that suited both of us stumbled when she took the summer off. Her replacement was an Arsenal supporter who probably thought that Ninette de Valois was a second-division French football team. And so I had to bite the ballet.

I was put under the tutelage of two balletomane BBC producers. They stood on point even in the queue at the coffee bar and would talk affectionately of 'Madame', as I came to understand that Dame Ninette was known to those who know. Eventually, one evening 30 years after my last serious exposure to live dance in that Leeds production of *A Windmill in Old Amsterdam*, I was taken to the restored Royal Opera House for an evening of modern dance.

In Philip Roth's novel *The Human Stain*, there's a scene in which, in present-day America, Vietnam veterans are taken under supervision to Chinese and Korean restaurants in an attempt to help them lose their hatred of Asian people and culture. Specially trained supervisors sit at the table in case the old soldiers suddenly attack or abuse a waiter who reminds them of the Vietcong.

When I read Roth's book, it reminded me of my own chaperoned visits to the Royal Ballet. In the same way, this was a deliberately controlled introduction. Modern ballet – in an evening on contemporary and erotic themes – was thought to be a safe beginning. If forced to submit first time out to *The Nutcracker*, there was the risk I might go psycho and start shouting about mice in tights.

That first evening at the Royal Ballet, called 'A Celebration of International Choreography', included Ashley Page's *Hidden Variables* (to music by Colin Matthews) and John Neumeier's *Lento*, a duet danced to the second movement of Shostakovich's *First Piano Concerto* by Darcey Bussell and Otto Bubenicek.

During my pre-match I was advised to react to dance as you might to a Howard Hodgkin painting, the point being that the artist's work, though abstract, has figurative titles (*Afterwards*, *The Last Time I Saw Paris* and so on). The viewer looks for patterns, shapes, textures and colours in the paint, guided by the hints in the painting's name. Applied to choreography, this technique picks out patterns and formations on stage, prompted by music and title.

This approach slowly opened to me the secret of ballet, which is, like so many secrets, sexual. To my astonishment, large parts of modern dance involved women or men opening their legs and then men or women putting their heads between them. Simulated sodomy had resulted in the prosecution of the National Theatre but, on that one night at the Royal Ballet, I watched what seemed to be simulated fellatio and cunnilingus, followed by a piece for three male dancers set in a San Francisco bathhouse that involved sodomy. And it brought not lawsuits but enthusiastic applause from people in tuxedos and furs.

I'm not being facetious about this. Far from its popular reputation as an effete and pretentious art form, this modern dance was the most physical and sensual theatre I'd ever seen. This was the point of ballet: that it utilised the body in a way no other entertainment could match, except perhaps athletics at Olympic level. The Ballet Preljocaj production of *Romeo and Juliet* at Sadler's Wells was more rawly sexual than the film *Intimacy*.

Subsequent evenings proved that this had not been a complete cure. I admired the sight and sound of William Tuckett's piece based on Arthur Miller's *The Crucible*, but the work exemplified ballet's problem with narrative: to someone who knew the play, did those movements of the feet equate to a particular speech? A performance by the Kirov Ballet – my first exposure to classical ballet – restored my prejudices: all that pretty tripping and exaggerated mimed emotion on the faces.

Where dance worked for me was when it most resembled an animated Hodgkin picture. Indeed, a particular favourite – Ashley Page's *This House Will Burn* – was based on modern paintings (by Stephen Chambers), to a jazzy score by Orlando Gough. Gesture and props, including a huge bed with a red duvet at the centre of the stage, told an impressionistic story of unrest within a family.

As a convert, what surprised me was how ballet had failed to publicise the physicality and eroticism at its heart. Perhaps the prejudice and snobbery enveloping the art form in Britain simply kept this information suppressed.

The Royal Ballet, though, now has a chance to spread its secret. A new director, Ross Stretton, has just been appointed. He's an Australian from the Sydney Opera House, and the presence of the erotic and the absence of the snobbish are almost definitions of Australian culture.

When I went to see him, Stretton had been at his desk only a few days, still pink-eyed from a 24-hour flight. He said straight away that he had been appointed, in part, to bring in a new audience: people who thought dance wasn't for them.

But don't many people stay away because they think you have to know the steps? 'That's right. I see my job as taking the pressure off the audience. There's a long tradition in classical ballet of technical perfection and the need to appreciate that. It is intimidating. But, in modern dance, just respond to the movement, the music.'

The revelation for me, I said, was how sexual ballet was. 'Absolutely. Well, I'd say sensual. And I want the costumes to emphasise the bodies. For me, dance is about joy in the body.'

Did he appreciate the extent to which ballet in Britain is seen as the province of a rich elite? 'Yes. Actually, even at the Sydney Opera House we had red carpets and so on. But we did eventually get a new audience in.' How? 'Through younger, fresher programmes and advertising that says this place is for you as well. That's what I want to do here. I need to change the concept of what ballet is. My line is that the Royal Ballet can please everyone but not necessarily on the same evening. It's not replacing black tie with denim, we need to get both in.'

Stretton confided that he did not intend to wear black tie to premieres. He would also have to look at ticket prices. On his laptop was a memo to the marketing department. They had asked what message he wanted to get across. He had typed: 'Excitement – ecstasy – movement – sensation of the body.'

I wish him well. Ross Stretton sounds like my kind of ballet man.

6 October 2001

JAMES WOOD

Tell me how does it feel?

A few days after the events of September 11, this newspaper published a response by Jay McInerney, supposedly the creator of 'the definitive modern New York novel'. He told us that on that very Tuesday, still shaken and shocked, he took lunch at Time Cafe, 'a once fashionable dining spot'. And who should immediately enter but 'the actress Jennifer Beals... a camera around her neck, looking slightly dazed'.

Later, McInerney repairs to the apartment of another New York novelist, Bret

Easton Ellis. On Bret's kitchen counter he sees an invitation to a literary party, and blurts out: 'I'm glad I don't have a book coming out this month' – a statement he knows to be 'a selfish and trivial response to the disaster, but one I thought he would understand.' Bret replies that he was just thinking the same thing. Then Jay says to Bret: 'I don't know how I'm going to be able to go back to this novel I'm writing.' He adds, to the reader: 'The novel is set in New York, of course. The very New York which has just been altered for ever.'

Is McInerney right? Will the horrid alteration of America's greatest city also alter the American novel? One is naturally suspicious of all the eschatological talk about how the time for trivia has ended and how only seriousness is now on people's minds – not least because the people saying it are usually themselves trivial and, as in McInerney's piece, are thus unwitting arguments against their own new-found seriousness. Doubtless, trivia and mediocrity will find their own level again, in novel-writing as in everything else. And besides, the 'New York novel' – as opposed to the novel set in New York – is a genre of no importance at all. If I live the rest of my life without having to come across another book like Bret Easton Ellis's New York novel, *Glamorama*, I will have very happily been what Psalm 81 calls 'delivered from the pots'.

There has, of course, been great fiction set or partly set in New York: Melville's story 'Bartleby', which is set in a Wall Street office; Stephen Crane's *Maggie*; *The Great Gatsby*; the last section of Theodore Dreiser's novel, *Sister Carrie*, which rails splendidly against the capitalist inequities of what Dreiser calls 'the Walled City'; a chapter of Celine's *Journey to the End of the Night*; Henry Roth's great novel of immigrant life, *Call It Sleep*; Bellow's *Seize the Day* and *Mr Sammler's Planet*. Yet as soon as one recalls these novels, it becomes difficult to imagine the precise ways in which they would have been different had they had to accommodate a mutilation of the kind visited upon the city on September 11. And that is partly because they are already dark books, in which the city looms jaggedly. It is only the McInerneys, for whom Manhattan is a tinkle of restaurants, who are suddenly surrounded by the broken glass of their foolish optimism. The pessimist is already ruined, and knows it.

What also unites these dark works of fiction is that their foci are human and metaphysical before they are social and documentary. They are stories, above all, about individual consciousness, not about the consciousness of Manhattan. Here, terrorism may well have an impact. For after all, the dream of the Great American Novel has for many years really been the dream of the Great American Social Novel – certainly since John Dos Passos and Sinclair Lewis.

The Great American Social Novel, which strives to capture the times, to document American history, has been revivified by Don DeLillo's *Underworld*, a novel of epic social power. Lately, any young American writer of any ambition has been imitating DeLillo – imitating his tentacular ambition, the effort to pin down an entire writhing culture, to be a great analyst of systems, crowds, paranoia, politics. In short, to work on the biggest level possible.

The DeLilloan idea of the novelist as a kind of Frankfurt School entertainer – a cultural theorist, fighting the culture with dialectical devilry – has been woefully influential, and will take some time to die. Nowadays anyone in possession of a laptop is thought to be brilliance on the move, filling his or her novel with essaylets and great displays of knowledge. Indeed, 'knowing about things' has become one of the qualifications of the contemporary novelist. Time and again novelists are praised for their wealth of obscure and far-flung social knowledge. (Richard Powers is the best example, but Tom Wolfe also gets an easy ride simply for 'knowing things'.) The reviewer, mistaking bright lights for evidence of habitation, praises the novelist who knows about, say, the sonics of volcanoes. Who also knows how to make a fish curry in Fiji! Who also knows about terrorist cults in Kilburn! And about the New Physics! And so on. The result – in America at least – is novels of immense self-consciousness with no selves in them at all, curiously arrested and very 'brilliant' books that know a thousand things but do not know a single human being.

Zadie Smith is merely of her time when she says, in an interview, that it is not the writer's job 'to tell us how somebody felt about something, it's to tell us how the world works'. She has praised the American writers David Foster Wallace and Dave Eggers as 'guys who know a great deal about the world. They understand macro-microeconomics, the way the internet works, maths, philosophy, but... they're still people who know something about the street, about family, love, sex, whatever.'

But this idea – that the novelist's task is to go on to the street and figure out social reality – may well have been altered by the events of September 11, merely through the reminder that whatever the novel gets up to, the 'culture' can always get up to something bigger. Ashes defeat garlands. If topicality, relevance, reportage, social comment, preachy presentism and sidewalk-smarts – in short, the contemporary American novel in its current, triumphalist form – are novelists' chosen sport, then they will sooner or later be outrun by their own streaking material. Fiction may well be, as Stendhal wrote, a mirror carried down the middle of a road but the Stendhalian mirror would explode with reflections were it now being walked around Manhattan.

For who would dare to be knowledgeable about politics and society now? Is it possible to imagine Don DeLillo today writing his novel *Mao II* – a novel that proposed the foolish notion that the terrorist now does what the novelist used to do, that is, 'alter the inner life of the culture'? Surely, for a while, novelists will be leery of setting themselves up as analysts of society, while society bucks and charges so helplessly. Surely they will tread carefully over their generalisations. It is now very easy to look very dated very fast.

For example, Jonathan Franzen's distinguished new novel, *The Corrections* has just appeared in America. It is a big social novel trying hard not to be one – softened DeLilloism. Franzen has announced a desire to take the DeLillo model and warmly people it with characters. It's an admirable project. But there is a passage near the end of *The Corrections* about the end of the American twentieth century that is pure social novel, and which now seems laughably archival: 'It seemed to Enid that current events in general were more muted or insipid nowadays than they'd been in her youth. She had memories of the 1930s, she'd seen firsthand what could happen to a country when the world economy took its gloves off... But disasters of this magnitude no longer seemed to befall the United States. Safety features had been put in place, like the squares of rubber that every modern playground was paved with, to soften impacts.' As McInerney might say,

'I'm glad I don't have a novel coming out this month.'

The other casualty of recent events may well be – it is to be hoped – what I have called 'hysterical realism'. Hysterical realism is not exactly magical realism, but magical realism's next stop. It is characterised by a fear of silence. This kind of realism is a perpetual motion machine that appears to have been embarrassed into velocity. Stories and sub-stories sprout on every page. There is a pursuit of vitality at all costs. Recent novels by Rushdie, Pynchon, DeLillo, Foster Wallace, Zadie Smith and others have featured a great rock musician who played air guitar in his crib (Rushdie), a talking dog, a mechanical duck and a giant octagonal cheese (Pynchon), a nun obsessed with germs who may be a reincarnation of J. Edgar Hoover (DeLillo), a terrorist group devoted to the liberation of Quebec who move around in wheelchairs (Foster Wallace) and a terrorist Islamic group based in North London with the silly acronym Kevin (Smith).

Rushdie was at it again in his most recent book, *Fury*, a lamentable novel that combined hysterical realism – dolls, puppets, allegories, a coup on a Fiji-like island, rampant and tiresome caricature, and noisy, clumsy prose – with the more traditional social novel. Alas, the social-novel part of the book was set in Manhattan, and offered a kind of diary of last year's Manhattan events. We encountered Rudy and Hillary, Jo-Lo, the Puerto Rican parade, Bush versus Gore, the film *Gladiator* and so on. Of course, the book was already obsolete when it appeared in early September, just before the terrorist attack. Its trivia-tattoo had already faded. But now it seems grotesque, a time-stamped scrap of paper.

It ought to be harder, now, either to bounce around in the false zaniness of hysterical realism or to trudge along in the easy fidelity of social realism. Both genres look a little busted. That may allow a space for the aesthetic, for the contemplative, for novels that tell us not 'how the world works' but 'how somebody felt about something' – indeed, how a lot of different people felt about a lot of different things (these are commonly called novels about human beings). A space may now open, one hopes, for the kind of novel that shows us that human consciousness is the truest Stendhalian mirror, reflecting helplessly the newly dark lights of the age.

13 October 2001

ZADIE SMITH

This is how it feels to me

The critic James Wood appeared in this paper last Saturday aiming a hefty, well-timed kick at what he called 'hysterical realism'. It is a painfully accurate term for the sort of overblown, manic prose to be found in novels like my own *White Teeth* and a few others he was sweet enough to mention. These are hysterical times and any novel that aims at hysteria will now be effortlessly outstripped – this was Wood's point and I'm with him on it. In fact, I have agreed with him several times before, in public and in private, but I appreciate that he feared I needed extra warning that I might be sitting in my Kilburn bunker planning some 700-page generational saga set on an incorporated McDonald's island north of Tonga. Actually, I am sitting here in my pants, looking at a blank screen, finding nothing funny, scared out of my mind like everybody else, smoking a family-sized pouch of Golden Virginia.

But to my surprise I find I do want to say a few quick things about that article, and about book stuff in general. The first is this: any collective term for a supposed literary movement is always too large a net, catching significant dolphins among so much cannable tuna. You cannot place first-time novelists with literary giants, New York hipsters with Kilburn losers, and some of the writers who got caught up with me are undeserving of the criticism. In particular, David Foster Wallace's mammoth beast *Infinite Jest* was heaved in as an exemplum, but it is five years old, and is a world away from his delicate, entirely 'human' short stories and essays of the past two years, which shy away from the kind of totalising theoretical and thematic arcs that Wood was gunning for. If anyone has recently learned a lesson about the particularities of human existence and their separation from social systems, it is Wallace.

But even if this were not true, frankly, literature is – or should be – a broad church. Whatever the weaknesses of the various writers Wood mentioned, I don't believe he would wish for a literary landscape missing a book such as Rushdie's *Midnight's Children* or DeLillo's *White Noise* – the very books, in fact, that have cast such a tremendous shadow over two generations of American and English fiction. Yes, Jonathan Franzen's soon-to-turn-up *The Corrections* is a blatant attempt to redress that imbalance and return the intimate voice to a DeLilloesque structure, but I wonder if even that isn't an artificial project. I read Flaubert and Nabokov for the varicoloured intimacies of life, I read Zora Neale Hurston to hear the songs of love and earth, and I read *White Noise* to experience, yes, a Frankfurt school comedy, in which every boy, girl, man, woman, black, white, lesbian, Jew and Muslim speaks in exactly the same way: like DeLillo. When you pick up DeLillo, you know that's what's coming, just as when you pick up Carver you give up the hope of finding talking dogs or octagonal cheeses. So it goes. (For flippancy and short sentences, Vonnegut's your man.)

We cannot be all the writers all the time. We can only be who we are. Which leads me to my second point: writers do not write what they want, they write what they can. When I was 21 I wanted to write like Kafka. But, unfortunately for me, I wrote like a script editor for *The Simpsons* who'd briefly joined a religious cult and then discovered Foucault. Such is life. And now, when I finish a long day of CNN-related fear and loathing mixed with eyeballing my own resolutely white screen, I do not crawl into bed with 500-page comic novels about (God help me, but it's OK I'm going to call on the safety of quote marks) 'multicultural' London. I read Carver. Julio Cortazar. Amis's essays. Baldwin. Lorrie Moore. Capote. Saramago. Larkin. Wodehouse. Anything, anything at all, that doesn't sound like me.

Sick of sound of own voice. Sick of trying to make own voice appear on that white screen. Sick of trying to pretend, for sake of agent and family, that idea of putting words on blank page feels important. I think – I'm not sure, but I think – that I and the other 'comic' writers Wood mentioned in his article now have the most pointless jobs in the world. Even Posh Spice *et al* surely fall into the cheering-the-troops department. We are more like a useless irritation; the wrong words, the wrong time, the wrong medium. Obsessed with our knowledge when the last thing people want is the encyclopaedic. I cannot be the only writer who took to heart Pynchon's call to arms in *Gravity's Rainbow*, many years ago now: 'We have to look for power sources here, and distribution networks we were never taught, routes of power our teachers never imagined, or were encouraged to avoid... We have to find meters whose scales are unknown in the world. Draw our own schematics, getting feedback, making connections, reducing the error, trying to learn the real function... zeroing in on what incalculable plot?'

Except... er... it turns out that the plot is horrendously simple. It has to do with things like faith. Revenge. Poverty. God. Hatred. So what now? Does any-one want to know the networks behind those seeming simplicities, the paths that lead from September 11 back to Saudi Arabia and Palestine, and then back to Israel, back further to the Second World War and back once more to the First? Does anyone care what writers think about that? Does it help? Or shall we sing of love and drawing rooms and earth and children and all that is small and furry and wounded? Must we produce what you want, anyway? I have absolutely no idea.

But still I'm going to write. If only because Wood is right and there are still books that make me hopeful, because they function as human products in the greatest sense. Bellow's *Seize the Day*, Melville's 'Bartleby', Nabokov's *Pnin* – works that stubbornly speak and resonate, even in these image-led, speechless times. But it is a trick of the light that makes us suppose these books exist in soulful opposition to more recent examples of 'dialectical devilry'. These books are works of high artifice and there isn't a decent novel in this world that isn't. Their humanity derives from their reverence for language, their precision, their intellect and, more than anything, from their humour. It's all laughter in the dark – the title of a Nabokov novel and still the best term for the kind of writ-ing I aspire to: not a division of head and heart, but the useful employment of both. And I could mention dozens of novels (I haven't been writing, but boy, I've been reading) that create a light in my head in between the news bulletins. Tolstoy's *The Death of Ivan Ilyich* – a miniaturist tale of a bourgeois man dying a bourgeois death – every time I read it, I find my world put under an intense, unforgiving microscope. But how does it work? I want to dismantle it as if it were a clock, as if it had parts, mechanisms. I wonder if Wood will take that question, then, as a replacement for my earlier one. Not: how does this world work? But: how is this book made? How can I do this?

But he might see even that question as too intellectual in approach. I think Wood is hinting at an older idea that runs from Plato to the boys booming a car stereo outside my freaking window: soul is soul. It cannot be manufactured or schematised. It cannot be dragged kicking and screaming through improbable plots. It cannot be summoned by a fact or dismissed by a cliché. These are the famous claims made for 'soul' and they lead with specious directness to an ancient wrestling match, invoked by Wood: the inviolability of 'soul' versus the evils of self-consciousness and wise-assery, otherwise known as sophism. Well, it's a familiar opposition, but it's not very helpful (it's also a belief Oprah shares, and you want to be careful which beliefs you share with Oprah). I wonder some-times whether critics shouldn't be more like teachers, giving a gold star or a black cross, but either way accompanied by some kind of useful advice. Be more human? I sit in front of my white screen and I'm not sure what to do with that one. Are jokes inhuman? Are footnotes? Long words? Technical terms? Intellectual allusions? If I put some kids in, will that help?

I want to defend the future possibility of some words appearing on pages that will be equal to these times and to what I feel and what you feel and what James Wood feels; that is, this fear that has got us all by the throat. He argues against silence and against intellectual obfuscation. He says: tell us how it feels. Well, we are trying. I am trying. But as DeLillo dramatised (again, in *White Noise*), it is difficult to discuss feelings when the TV speaks so loudly, cries so operatically, it seems always, in everything, one step ahead. Yet people continue to manage this awesome trick of wrestling sentiment away from TV's colonisation of all things soulful and human, and I would applaud all the youngish Americans – Franzen, Moody, Foster Wallace, Eggers, Moore – for their (supposedly) small but, to me, significant triumphs. They work to keep both sides of the equation – brain and heart – present in their fiction.

Even if you find them obtuse, they can rarely be accused of cliché, and that – as Amis has argued so well recently – is the place where everything dies. Cliché, generalisation, symbol (think 'west', think 'east') all put a tongue to the lie of how people experience their worlds. And particularity is the enemy of cliché. But clichés are made so very quickly these days (already the London of *White Teeth* – 'multicultural', 'trendy' – is a kind of genre) and these writers will need their wits about them (yeah, and their hearts) if they are to outpace them. I truly hope they are not cowed by these renewed assaults on 'clever writing', calls for the 'death of irony', the 'return of heart'. There was always a great deal of 'heart', of humanity, in these writers. If I could choose one story to be printed alongside this article as demonstration, it would be Foster Wallace's 'Forever Overhead', a ten-page effort that has come to obsess me quite as much as the miserable death of poor, terminally middle-class Ivan. In this story nothing much happens. Just a boy on his thirteenth birthday. A swimming pool. A hot day. But it has every moment of my childhood in it, probably every moment of yours. And in lines reminiscent of Larkin ('it is a machine that moves only forward') he makes the queue to a diving board the story of every human being's progress to self-con-sciousness, the blessing of it and the curse.

Sometimes it seems purely an American trick, this ability to draw the uni-verse, as Carver and Fitzgerald did, into a circumscribed artificial, yet human, space. Sometimes I get depressed about that. Then I remember that in a slightly quieter way (in so far as no one goes for them in Saturday papers), we have our own intelligent, young 'human' writers this side of the water – Toby Litt, Lawrence Norfolk, Diran Adebayo, Tibor Fischer – but whatever, whatever. Let's not descend into lists, which are always partial and tempered by friendships and past sexual favours. Let's just be careful with terms like 'human' and 'civilised'. Let's be careful of equating either of those immediately with 'soul' or 'heart'. This is not the time for easy slippage between nouns and adjectives.

Finally, I want to explain how I feel about that mocking white screen. September

11 has, as Wood suggested, made this problem more urgent and intractable. Most mornings I think: death of the novel? Yeah, sure, why not? The novel is not an immutable fact of human artistic life, after all, just a historically specific phenomenon that came and will go unless there are writers who have the heart, the brain and, crucially, the *cojones* to keep it alive. Personally, I find myself more and more struck by controlled little gasps of prose, as opposed to the baggy novel. I admire the high reverence for the blank page shown by Kafka, Borges and Cortazar. Cortazar (recommended to me, actually, by Foster Wallace) writes as if every extra word is a sort of sacrilege. The instinct is almost religious, as if to say: and if it is to be stained, proceed slowly and with the utmost care. Which seems the exact opposite of the American/English instinct: I must cover the world in my shit immediately.

Is it this reverence, this care, this suppression of ego that Wood wants to see from us? It is what I want to see from myself, but whether I will manage it is another matter. It will take sympathy – a natural instinct, a sentimental reflex – but it will also take empathy, which I still contend is largely a matter for the intellect. Your brain must be up for it, for making that necessary leap. At the moment, my brain feels like cat food. So I may never prove to be much of a writer – a real writer, the kind I like to read – but then again, maybe I will. I'm not sure how much it matters any more. But we shall see.

SPORTING LIFE

Steve Bell, 1 November 2000

DAVID DAVIES

Wondrous Woods rips up records and rivals

Tiger Woods finally did what no other golfer has ever done and what no golfer may ever do again: he won his fourth consecutive major championship, a simply fantastic feat. In winning the US Masters on Sunday for the second time he took his championship-winning streak to five of the last six, demonstrating that in modern golf there is no one remotely as good.

On Sunday afternoon Woods, the world No. 1, was paired with the world No. 2, Phil Mickelson, and two groups in front was a man who has very recently occupied both those positions, David Duval. And yet, when the bell rang and Tiger stood up, both men sat on their stools, mesmerised by the awesome ability of this phenomenal golfer.

On Sunday evening, wearing the green jacket and facing the world's press, Tiger at last smiled. He had broken down and cried when the last putt was holed and in the heat of battle had played as if hypnotised, so fierce was his focus.

Now, though, he could be happy and, despite promptings from some eager for controversy, the words 'grand slam' did not cross his lips. 'Now that you've won it,' he was asked, 'what do you want to call it?' Woods said: 'I'll let you guys decide – you guys are very creative.'

Then it was put to him outright. 'Is it a grand slam in your eyes?' Woods looked the man in the eye and said: 'I've won four.'

He was wise not to continue with an earlier assertion that all four majors at the same time somehow must be a grand slam, not only because the weight of opinion is that it must be done in a calendar year but also because he must suspect he is capable of the real grand slam.

So for now it is the simultaneous slam, or the straight slam, maybe even the Tiger slam while the grand slam still awaits the attention of this extraordinarily gifted player.

The magnitude of his achievement surpasses anything done previously by the game's greats. Ben Hogan won three in one year in 1953, the Masters, the US Open and the Open at Carnoustie, but was unable to play in the US PGA because it clashed with the Open. In any case, the concept of the slam had not been reinvented, as it was by Arnold Palmer in 1960, and Hogan played in only six events in his glorious year, winning five.

Jack Nicklaus had a chance to hold all four majors at the same time, albeit not consecutively, when he arrived at Muirfield with three under his belt – the US PGA, which was played in February of 1971 and then moved to August for 1972, and the Masters and US Open of 1972.

He played the first three rounds so conservatively that he did not even carry a driver in his bag. He arrived at the final round with Lee Trevino and Tony Jacklin ahead of him, cast caution aside, smashed his driver miles, got round in

66 and failed by one shot.

Since then no one has won more than two on the trot, let alone by some of the margins Woods has put together. He took the US Open by the humiliating margin of fifteen shots, the Open at St Andrews – where he completed a career grand slam – by eight shots and the only close-run thing was the US PGA, where he was taken to an unlikely play-off by Bob May.

Sunday's win was not in any of those categories. Woods said he 'grinded it out' and, given that his 68, rather than the official 72, is actually par for him, that is true. But what it amounted to was a slow strangulation as he choked the life from his competitors. On several occasions Woods made mistakes but, just as Nicklaus before him, he is the greatest putter in the game.

The despair he wrought in Duval and Mickelson, who had to stand there and witness as he holed putt after important putt, was sufficient to destroy them. There was a spell, beginning on the 7th, when he single-putted five consecutive greens, each vital psychologically, giving his competitors no hope whatsoever.

Mickelson had good reason to hope that the seven-footer at the 7th would be missed, given it was a nasty slider on the slippiest of greens, but it went in dead centre. At the 8th Woods again birdied after a second shot that finished 40yds wide of the green. A chip to 10ft did the trick.

Then it seemed Woods must surely bogey the 9th, his second shot spinning back off the green, trickling down a bank and leaving him with a 30yd chip. He hit it to seven feet and again it went in. But, if such putts are sickeners, they were as nothing to the one he holed at the 10th.

Woods misjudged his second, which ran to the back fringe, elected to putt down the frighteningly fast green and somehow succeeded in leaving it 10ft short and 10ft wide. It was an awful effort but of course he holed it and afterwards unhesitatingly picked it out as the most crucial of the round. 'By far the biggest putt,' he said. 'Making that was big.'

Just how big became clear on the next tee. Mickelson must have been close to desperation and, in going for a big drive through trees leading to the fairway, caught one of them and dropped down 100yds from the tee. That is an automatic bogey and Tiger closed for the kill.

From 149yds he almost holed his second shot, the ball running over the edge of the hole and stopping 18in away. As soon as the ball stopped, his caddie, Steve Williams, proffered the putter and Woods snatched it eagerly. He could hardly wait to get there and ensure the inevitable two-shot advantage.

There were further challenges to come, of course, but it seemed Woods knew his destiny. At the 13th he hit a drive he had been practising since January but had not used to that point, a shot he called 'a big slinger' that curled round the left-handed dog-leg as if on rails. Mickelson had hit his best drive there Woods was 25yds past him, another devastating psychological blow.

The final chances went to Duval, who at least had been spared from actually witnessing what Woods was doing. Over the closing two holes he hit some great shots but, when it came to the cold-blooded bit, the putting, he could not summon the courage. There was the 10-footer on the 17th, the easiest putt on that green, which was not hit hard enough and then, cruelly, a four-footer on the 18th.

That too was underhit and like its predecessor trickled away on the low, or amateur, side. Both were failures of will, hit by a man who had bowed his knee. 'It is not easy for me to talk about this,' said Duval afterwards.

The perfect scenario would have been for Duval to hole that putt and for Woods to do as he did: march majestically up the 18th fairway, hit two shots to 18ft and then hole the birdie putt.

It would have made for more drama but with no added significance. That lies in the achievement, the like of which we may never see again.

18 May 2001

RICHARD WILLIAMS

The triumph of Houllier's true Reds

A football club made for high emotion reached a new peak on Wednesday night in Dortmund when Liverpool claimed their third cup of the season and their first European trophy in seventeen years, allowing 20,000 supporters in the stadium and many more at home to experience an eruption of joy and relief.

If their victory over Alaves was not, strictly speaking, the most exalted achievement in Liverpool's history, at least when considered next to the defeats of Borussia Monchengladbach, Club Bruges, Real Madrid and Roma in the continent's senior club tournament, then the result contained something of perhaps equal value: the knowledge that it gave an official stamp of certification to the amazing renaissance of a team who, barely two years ago, had become a bit of a laughing stock.

The Liverpool supporters in the Westfalenstadion were certainly aware of the deeper significance of this Uefa Cup final. These were the people who had lived through the years of decline and decay, when the philosophy of unsparing and unselfish endeavour inculcated by Bill Shankly and maintained by Bob Paisley became distorted beyond recognition by the forces of money and ego. It is the measure of Gerard Houllier 's achievement that the era of Neil Ruddock and Stan Collymore already seems like ancient history.

As the players, wearing their medals, lined up to face the banks of fans, they shared a chorus of 'You'll Never Walk Alone'. At that very moment the Basque supporters were applauding their own players from the field. The two sets of noise – unrestrained euphoria on the one side, dignified resignation on the other – created an antiphony that was almost as electrifying as anything that had happened in the match.

Tempting though it may have been to reach for the superlatives, this was not the greatest European final ever played. That would be the 7-3 match between Real Madrid and Eintracht Frankfurt in 1960, with Milan's 4-0 demolition of Barcelona in 1994 a runner-up in pure footballing terms. There was no Di Stefano, Puskas, Savicevic or Maldini on the pitch in Dortmund on Wednesday. But there was human drama of the most uplifting kind, which is something you don't get every week of the season.

'The good thing about the team,' Houllier said afterwards, 'is that you never feel there is a split or a lack of togetherness when something goes wrong. That is a major improvement.' It is also, without question, the characteristic that has taken them successfully through three cup finals this season, each of which presented its own test of the team's moral strength.

On Wednesday it was impossible not to be reminded of something Houllier said only a few months after he took sole charge of the club, when I asked him if he would ever consider emulating Gianluca Vialli's willingness to send out a Chelsea team containing no English players. 'I think there would be a kind of Liverpool heart that would prevent me from doing that,' he replied. 'I'm too keen and too happy to have four or five lads who are Liverpool-born.'

It would be unduly simplistic to suggest that the locally produced players in Wednesday's team – Robbie Fowler, Michael Owen, Jamie Carragher and Steven Gerrard – are the core of the line-up. Such a claim would devalue the contributions of Sami Hyypia, Markus Babbel and Gary McAllister. Nevertheless, the awareness of the importance of sending out a side containing 'a Liverpool heart' has surely been central to the reforging of the link between the team and the supporters. The Owens and Gerrards may not be as accessible to the fans as the stars of the past, but something in their demeanour and their wholehearted attitude sustains that precious bond.

The match was deep into sudden-death overtime when the moment arrived that would sum it all up. Jordi Cruyff, who could be proud of his display, was chasing a ball deep in his own half, close to the touch-line. Gerrard, giving Cruyff five yards' start, stretched his legs in a withering sprint. The two players arrived at the same time but, although they are both young and solidly built, there was never much doubt which of them was going to leave with the ball. The great Tommy Smith himself could not have won possession with greater physical finality.

When Houllier brought in seven foreign players in the summer of 1999, he remarked that six of them chose to come to Liverpool when, by staying with their existing clubs, they could have played in Europe. 'I'm proud to say that they decided to come to us,' he said. 'I'm not daft to the point of thinking that it's for my blue eyes – which are not blue – but I think it's because to them Liverpool is a name and it's a good challenge to bring back the tradition of success to this club.' And they were offered competitive salaries, naturally. Anyway, some of them got their reward on Wednesday, and it is hard to imagine that the supporters of any other club could have saluted their achievement with such an outpouring of gratitude.

Not that this team represents the finished article. In goal, Sander Westerveld makes outstanding saves but is too fallible when judgment rather than reflex is required. The sooner Houllier acquires another left-back to allow Carragher to move into the central defence, alongside Hyypia, the better. McAllister's dead-ball kicks were crucial to Wednesday's victory but in the run of play he is operating on borrowed time and a new creative influence will be required to partner Gerrard in midfield.

And, despite his beautifully timed and executed goal in Dortmund, Fowler's future remains uncertain, although it would be sad to see the embodiment of the background and spirit of so many of the club's fans plying his trade elsewhere. Given what appears to lie ahead for Liverpool, he might be best advised to stay put.

7 July 2001

RICHARD WILLIAMS

The real success of Tim, nice and not at all dim

The question to be asked about Tim Henman is not why he has not done better before but how he has managed to do so well at all. When the only other tennis player in the country within spitting distance of his talent was born and raised in Canada, the magnitude of his achievement can hardly be overestimated.

While he was battling to turn the fortunes of yesterday's semi-final, winning the third set in less than a quarter of an hour for the loss of a mere four points before the rain arrived, observers could only wonder where, coming from a world of cucumber sandwiches and sensible shoes, he had acquired such competitive fury.

The frequent journeys taken by newspaper and television reporters back to Reed's School in Surrey this week exposed a background of genteel privilege which could hardly be mistaken as a forging house for champions. To emerge from the rhododendron bushes and fight his way to the top echelon of international tennis players unquestionably represents a triumph of willpower over conditioning.

He is the face of middle-class home counties England: polite and reasonable, devoid of pretension or presumption.

In terms of international sport at the beginning of the twenty-first century, this represents an almost insurmountable handicap. He has not battered his way through the US college system, where introverts are trampled underfoot, or fought to escape from some East European hellhole, acquiring a full range of survival techniques en route. He grew up in a world where niceness and decency are the most desirable of personal virtues, and where a sense of struggle and a hunger for victory have to come from within.

Which is why the fist-pumping looks more than a little bogus and why it is also absolutely necessary if he is not to settle for life as a respectable also-ran. Like Boris Becker, but to a much greater degree, Henman needs to summon up a stroppy alter-ego who can provide the extra dimension of aggression that will turn his classically proportioned game, its all-round competence topped off with a marvellous gift at the net, into a winning proposition at the very highest level.

In that respect he is curiously reminiscent of Damon Hill, another product of middle-class affluence, who was also unprepared for the harsh and unforgiving ego-clashes of top-level professional sport, and for the peculiar magnifying effect of the mass media. Many people were surprised when Hill won the BBC's sports personality of the year award before he even became world champion. He seemed so patently ordinary, so bland, that the question was – what personality?

Henman is not even as outgoing as Hill, or as prone to sticking his foot in his mouth when attempting to employ humour to enliven dull press conferences, or to endow himself with a profile the media could use. But he does display the symptoms of a similar discomfort in the spotlight.

Neither personality incorporates the sort of salient characteristics that please tabloid newspapers. Hill, whose father was world-famous, worked hard in childhood at being anonymous. What he did not want, above all, was for his life to be illuminated only by his father's reflected glow. Henman comes from an environment in which modesty and reticence are prized – just look at the controlled behaviour of his parents in the players' box during his matches.

The significant difference between Hill and Henman is that whereas Hill, having missed two chances at the Formula One world championship, prepared for his year of success by making himself the centre of a team that included his manager, his wife, a couple of best friends and an image consultant, Henman has chosen to approach Wimbledon 2001 by stripping away his principal professional support mechanism.

After years of being told that his relationship with David Felgate, his coach, had trapped him in a comfort zone, Henman took action in April and severed a relationship that stretched back to his teenage years, before he turned professional. He says the criticisms had nothing to do with his decision, but the fact is that he and his critics had come to the same conclusion and his denials have probably been designed to protect Felgate, who is still a friend whose wife continues to manage Henman's business affairs.

Rather than hire another coach straight away – although he was deluged with offers – Henman opted to spend a year on his own, facing up to the problems he encounters on the court with only his own intellect and imagination to help him.

'It's something I enjoy,' he said of his new self-reliance, 'because I've worked out a few aspects for myself. I think it's been a good challenge for me mentally. But it's always been about me. It doesn't matter if you have a coach, a psychologist, a trainer, a masseur, a stringer, you know, it's all about what you do on court.

'I've always played for myself and that's evident now. But I've said all along that this game is tough enough without trying to do it all on your own and, after Wimbledon, I'll certainly be looking again to get a coach.'

Whatever the future holds, he may look upon the time he decided to take responsibility for his own successes and failures as the time he turned into the tennis player Britain always hoped he would be.

10 July 2001

STEPHEN BIERLEY

Ivanisevic fulfils his destiny

And so he did it. Goran Ivanisevic, one of the most unpredictable talents that tennis has produced, finally won the Wimbledon title at the fourth time of asking, defeating Australia's Pat Rafter 6-3, 3-6, 6-3, 2-6, 9-7 yesterday afternoon amid the sort of scenes of wild enthusiasm and rapturous joy that had never been witnessed on the centre court.

About 10,000 fans, some of whom had begun queuing on Sunday, paid £40 a ticket to transform the denouement of the 115th championships into the most vividly memorable of sporting occasions.

Only in Davis Cup matches, played between nations, does this sort of carnival atmosphere pervade tennis, for it is the rich and the sponsored who normally attend the major finals, more's the pity. Australians and Croatians combined with Britons to lift this match beyond mere rivalry.

The names of both players were bounced around the famous arena with the unparalleled intensity of a football crowd. Yet there was not a trace of ill-feeling. All was pure unfettered delight, ultimately tinged with a little sadness for Rafter. 'Someone had to lose, and I'm the loser again,' said the Australian, drawing a sustained and heartfelt 'Aah' from the crowd. They loved Rafter, they loved Ivanisevic.

It was the most glorious and improbable of finals. Nobody in his right mind could have believed at the beginning of the fortnight that the man from Croatia would achieve his dream. Entering Wimbledon he had won only nine matches this year. His left shoulder, which will be operated on in December, was painful and his confidence shot to pieces. Ranked No. 125 in the world, he was given a wild card on the strength of his previous performances, having lost the final to Andre Agassi in 1992 and Pete Sampras twice, in 1994 and 1998.

Not since Boris Becker won the title as a seventeen-year-old in 1985 has there been such an unlikely winner. But whereas the German exploded from nowhere, seizing the moment with the nerveless authority of youth, the 29-year-old Ivanisevic had all but slipped over the horizon. He was tagged 'the most talented player never to have won Wimbledon'. No longer.

Today he is due back in his native Split, where thousands more will gather. It has been a quite astonishing story, one to rival this year's restoration and rejuvenation of Jennifer Capriati, the Australian and French Open champion.

Because it was Ivanisevic, because he would walk on the backs of crocodiles to cross a river, the final was as unpredictable as the man. For six matches he had controlled his volatile temperament. But midway through the fourth set, when he was foot-faulted after pounding down a service winner and then saw a second- service ace called out, he went berserk, flailing his arms, kicking the net and appealing to the umpire, Jorge Diaz.

Rafter watched and waited, perhaps hoping that Ivanisevic 's split personalities would unravel. The Australian cricketers, including the Waugh twins, Glenn McGrath and Shane Warne, were mightily amused. No third umpire to sort this one out.

But Rafter, twenty-eight, knew Ivanisevic would regroup. 'It was too big an occasion for him to let that sort of thing worry him and get him down,' he said. In fact the Croat, having calmed himself, was more annoyed at losing his serve for a second time in that fourth set, thereby giving Rafter the advantage of serving first in the fifth.

Rafter, who was beaten in last year's final by Sampras, had surprisingly lost his opening service game, the quality of the Ivanisevic returns catching him on the hop. The second set was a mirror image, but this time it was the Croat who lost his serve in the second game.

The noise was immense, the tension electric. Occasionally, both players were interrupted by rogue shouts as they prepared to serve but generally the crowd, for all its exuberance, observed tennis's spirit of hushed competition.

After Ivanisevic 's fourth-set eruption the fifth could not have been more tense, with both players aware that one slip could be fatal. The strain was immense, tension clawing at Rafter at 4-4 when he went 0-30 down on his serve, and then gripping Ivanisevic.

With Rafter 7-6 ahead, Ivanisevic was two points from defeat, scrambling to safety courtesy of arguably grass court's most potent serve. It is a two-edged weapon, capable of cutting him off at the knees when it fails, but the Croat was serving beautifully now. A leaping backhand service return coupled with a powerful forehand return had Rafter reeling. Another forehand winner off a 96mph second serve saw the Australian struggling at 15-40.

'I decided to give him a really slow serve at this point,' said Rafter. 'I got it perfectly, just how I wanted it, because I thought he was very tight. He whacked it by me. "Bad move," I thought.'

Such is pressure. Ivanisevic crossed himself and aimed a kiss at the heavens. Nobody, but nobody, can squander two match points with double faults. He did. The third Rafter saved with a wonderful lob, the fourth saw his end – Ivanisevic forcing an error on a 109mph second serve.

The Croat's celebration was a joy to behold, and Rafter was generous in defeat. It was only later, when it was pointed out to him that he was again part of history, that the Australian snapped: 'I'm sick of making bloody history.' But even then the two-times US Open champion managed a smile. It was, after all, Ivanisevic's day. Destiny had deemed it so.

28 July 2001

RICHARD WILLIAMS

It's not about the drugs, if any, it's about the achievement

Lance Armstrong is looking fitter than ever. Lighter and stronger, with his body fat ratio surely as low as a healthy man's can go, he has spent the last three weeks outdoing his own already remarkable achievements and giving cycling fans memories that should live alongside the greatest moments from the long and vivid history of the Tour de France.

There is flame in Armstrong's eyes and an implacable desire in his soul. At the foot of l'Alpe d'Huez last week, having lulled the opposition by feigning exhaustion every time a motorcycle-borne TV cameraman came near, he turned and stared into the face of Jan Ullrich, his principal rival, before accelerating away to produce one of the most prodigious feats of solo climbing the race has seen.

Four days later, when Ullrich crashed on the descent from the Col de Peyresourde, Armstrong stopped and waited for him to recover. And as they crossed the finishing line at Luz-Ardiden the following day, Ullrich extended a hand to the American in a gesture filled with meaning and, if you are susceptible to such things, with beauty.

Yesterday afternoon Armstrong got off his bike here in St Amand-Montrond in the dead centre of France to be told that, at the end of a 61km (38-mile) time-trial, he had won his fourth stage of the Tour and increased his lead over Ullrich by more than a minute and a half. As he has done every day since he took over the yellow jersey a week ago, he mounted the podium to receive kisses, flowers and the acclaim of the spectators, many of them children, crowded behind the barriers at the finish of the day's stage. What he is not receiving, however, is the unanimous admiration of those who have followed the Tour for the past three weeks.

This story of the man who beat cancer to win the world's most gruelling sporting event, which only two years ago seemed to be a feat without parallel in sport, is now being widely seen in a different light. Armstrong is almost certain to win the Tour for the third year in a row in Paris tomorrow, making him only the fifth rider in history to achieve that feat. But he will do so at the centre of a gathering vortex of disbelief concerning his relationship with drugs.

Armstrong has consistently denied taking drugs and there is no direct evidence against him but there were those who, right from the start, refused to believe that he could have made his way back to the top without the help of illegal methods after he had undergone treatment in 1996 for testicular cancer so advanced that it had spread to his brain and his lungs. Two years and five months after his discharge, he did something which, in his pre-cancer years, he had failed to achieve: he won the Tour. Last year he did it again, and now he is on the verge of joining Louison Bobet, Jacques Anquetil, Eddy Merckx and Miguel Indurain in the record books. This could only have happened, according to his accusers, with the aid of a systematic and sophisticated doping programme.

Others, formerly ready to give him the benefit of any doubt, now look at recent circumstantial evidence and feel that Armstrong has abused their trust. A year after French police seized medical refuse, including hypodermic needles and bandages, discarded by Armstrong's US Postal team during the Tour, a judicial inquiry has yet to produce its findings. And three weeks ago, as the 2001 Tour set off from Dunkirk, the *Sunday Times* published information linking Armstrong to Dr Michele Ferrari, an Italian who has worked with many cyclists and who in September will be called into a court in Bologna to answer charges of treating riders with erythropoietin, or EPO, the illegal drug that enhances endurance by increasing the proportion of red corpuscles in the blood.

The evidence against Ferrari includes this month's revelation by an Italian rider, Filippo Simeoni, a member of the Cantina team between 1996 and 1998, that the doctor dispensed EPO and human growth hormone to the riders and advised them on how to mask the presence of these substances. Armstrong, hearing rumours that the *Sunday Times* knew the dates of his meetings with Ferrari at his clinic in Ferrara, going as far back as 1995, pre-empted the revelation by giving an interview to an Italian newspaper in which he admitted the existence of the relationship but denied that doping was a part of it.

This week he held a press conference at which he confronted his chief accuser and again declared his innocence. 'I've lived by the rules,' he said. 'Something like human growth hormone – you think someone with my health history would take something like that? There's no way.'

Of Ferrari, he said: 'I believe he's an honest man, a fair man, an innocent man. Let there be a trial. Let the man prove himself innocent.' He said he had not worked with the doctor during the present Tour, but would have no qualms about resuming the relationship if Ferrari were cleared by the court. 'With what I've seen with my two eyes and my experience, how can I prosecute a man who I've never seen do anything guilty?'

Armstrong talked briefly about his use of a hypobaric chamber, a sort of tent that replicates the effect of training at altitude. Unlike many of the great cyclists of the past, he has an acute awareness of what goes on in his own body. His autobiography, *It's Not About The Bike*, in which he described in detail the surgery and chemotherapy he endured at Indianapolis University's medical centre, made it clear that he is not one of those who lie down on the operating table, close their eyes and ask no questions.

A sharp mind such as his could not be fooled into taking something illegal without knowing it. Neither would he be unaware of the precise boundaries of legality. It would be unrealistic to believe that Armstrong went through his formative years as a junior triathlon and swimming champion in Texas without at least observing the existence of anabolic steroids. During his cancer treatment, EPO was administered. His medical knowledge, at least in a couple of specialised areas, must be well above average. And if it has enabled him to operate up to the very margin of the rules, as may be the case, then he cannot be criticised for that.

He is an extraordinary man in many ways. No one who saw him destroyed by the Alps in 1993 during his first Tour, lying in total distress in a bunk in his hostel in Serre-Chevalier three days after he had become the youngest rider ever to win a stage, could help but have a special admiration for the determination with which he came back to master the event and eventually to dominate it.

Brash and arrogant on his arrival in big-time European cycling, he learned his lessons fast. Although there are still those who find him difficult to like, there is no question the surly boy from a featureless Dallas suburb has adapted successfully to an alien culture. He now speaks French, Italian and Spanish well enough to conduct interviews in all three. His illness also gave him new perspectives on human existence. 'When I was sick,' he said, 'I saw more beauty and triumph and truth in a single day than I ever did in a bike race.'

No doubt a psychologist would trace his independence and his motivation back to a difficult childhood. His mother was only seventeen when he was born, and his father left before their son was two. 'I've never had a single conversation with my mother about him,' Armstrong wrote. 'Not once. In twenty-eight years she's never brought him up, and I've never brought him up.' Her single-handed success in building a life for them, and her devotion to his nascent career, must also have left a powerful impression.

But there is a bigger question here than merely one man's guilt or innocence. When it comes to doping, after all, sport is always in denial of one sort or another, whether it is the family of Tom Simpson refusing to accept the presence of amphetamines in his body and in the pocket of his racing shirt as he fell dead on Mont Ventoux in 1967, or Ben Johnson lying and lying and lying until he finally gave way and admitted that he had won the Olympic 100 metres gold medal in 1988 by cheating.

In terms of cycling, history multiplies the resonances. In the old days just about everyone doped and nobody worried about it. The first police raid on the Tour teams, at the end of a stage in Bordeaux in 1966, changed nothing. Nor, it seems, did the raids of 1998, which followed the arrest of the *Festina soigneur*, Willy Voet, in his drug-packed van, at least if the discoveries on this year's Giro d'Italia are anything to go by.

Guilty or not, Lance Armstrong exists in a climate modified by changed attitudes and values, not least those of the mass media. Will his achievements be allowed to stand alongside those of, say, Fausto Coppi and Jacques Anquetil, or is he to be judged by a different set of criteria? 'I cannot prove a negative,' he said this week, 'so it's always going to be a tricky situation. When they find a test for one thing, then somebody stands up and says: "Well, you must be doing the next thing." When they find a test for that, then they say: "Well, you must be using the next thing." It goes on and on.'

As well as the accusers and the recently disillusioned, there is a third group following Armstrong's progress to the podium on the Champs-Élysées. These are people predisposed to believe his expressions of innocence while reserving their right not to be surprised by anything the future may reveal. They are not advocates of cheating, but they acknowledge the fundamental impossibility of imposing a completely drug-free regime on bicycle racing. Their opinion of Armstrong was summed up yesterday by a friend of mine, a German journalist covering his nineteenth Tour. 'My admiration,' he said, 'is bigger than my suspicion.'

2 August 2001

GIDEON HAIGH

Catching the essence of a team's unity

Twenty-four years have elapsed but the sensation of arriving at Trent Bridge brings it all back. It was the third Test of that summer, too – the return of the prodigal Yorkshireman.

Boycott had eked out 20 in three hours, like a man batting in Braille. Then he jabbed anxiously to second slip, Rick McCosker, a straightforward chance to a competent catcher. The moment is frozen in a Patrick Eagar photograph: McCosker, arms flailing, deposits the ball gently on the ground.

It is one of cricket's liveliest 'what ifs', an inflexion point in the game's history, where chance seemed to interpose and life was never quite the same there-

There are all kinds of reasons why these historic moments should not take place on Saturday afternoon. One involves the crowd, an especially slobby section of which broke into 'Who ate all the pies?' when Warne was named man of the match. In the new Radcliffe Road stand there is a small nook described as 'the Sobers Waiting Area'. This is presumably to distinguish it from the rest of the ground: 'the Drunks' Waiting Area'.

Still the situation is not utterly hopeless. Fatuously optimistic to the end, I believe that England will not be whitewashed and, as has happened in the past four Ashes series, may well pick up a consolation win after the opposition has passed the post. This contention depends entirely on the return of Nasser Hussain, Graham Thorpe and Michael Vaughan and England getting back to something like the team that served them so well for the twelve months prior to Pakistan's win at Old Trafford. The England team in the form of last summer, with a settled batting order and credible back-up bowling, would not have been disgraced in this fashion.

It also depends on the selectors recovering their nerve. That certainly means ignoring all the press-talk piffle about dropping Mike Atherton and Alec Stewart simply because they might not go on tour. For any Test match you play the strongest available team that is doubly true in an Ashes series against this Australian team it is triply true.

They also have to escape from the negativity that has characterised their recent thinking. Atherton's return to the captaincy was the most obvious example. No one seriously imagined that someone so battered by a decade of Ashes disasters really had a chance of inspiring the team in the desperate situation it faced after Edgbaston. The choice was made solely to prevent Marcus Trescothick or Darren Gough being battered the same way.

Everyone must hope – Atherton above all – that we never again have to watch his apologetic captaincy or his celebrated post-match press conference impression of a man with a giant gobstopper stuck up his arse.

The reprise of this show was followed by the appearance of Duncan Fletcher who, by saying little and winning much, had built up a reputation as a Deep Thinker. He may have blown this on Saturday when he broke off from his stonewalling to defend the selection of Robert Croft as a man with a good record of bowling against Australia.

This is something that had passed me by, as well as the whole of Australia. It had evidently escaped Atherton's attention too. The captain had so much faith in Croft's bowling that he gave him three overs in the match, one more than he allowed Craig White. Far from fulfilling the selectors' apparent intention and playing five bowlers in this Test, England ended up playing three. Croft's inclusion, based on his batting, was again negative, bordering on defeatist.

When I got home, my nine-year-old asked: 'Dad, have England ever won the Ashes?' (Answer: 'Yes. But long before you were born.') before changing the subject and asking if he could watch a proper sporting competition on telly, ie the wrestling on Sky.

They say victory has a hundred fathers and defeat is an orphan. But for English cricket, victory would have thousands of sons while defeat is childless. A vicious circle has developed: every humiliation England endure against

Australia makes it less likely that my boy's generation will be enthused by cricket – and thus less likely that the wheel will ever turn.

6 August 2001

JIM WHITE

The commentator

At one point during his demolition of the England bowling attack on Friday, Adam Gilchrist leathered a ball delivered by Andrew Caddick with such venom you can only assume he had just caught it sleeping with his wife. Reporting on the shot, Sky's Paul Allott said: 'And he's cut that between point and gully...'

Meanwhile, on Channel 4, Richie Benaud was commenting on the same act of brutal assault. 'Ho ho,' he chortled, watching the ball flash across the outfield. 'My that was hit. He laid back his ears and whacked it.'

The sense of communicated pleasure, the absence of cliché, the entertaining imagery – just some of the reasons why the dozen stag party members filing into Trent Bridge last week wore matching T-shirts featuring Richie Benaud 's face and not the amiable Allott's.

And then there's the voice. As you make your way into a cricket ground these days, you sense Benaud all around you. Earlier this season, I was queuing for admission to the one-day international at the Oval when a man arrived at the turnstile and realised he had left his ticket in his car. As he forlornly walked back to retrieve it, another spectator turned to his friend and, in those familiar Australian tones, said: 'Bit of a schoolboy error that, I thought.'

Benaud has become the lingua franca of cricket. Everyone talks Benaud. It involves taking a word, working it slowly around in the little hollow formed between thrust-forward bottom lip and the front of the teeth, and simultaneously raising one eyebrow in knowing commentary. Thus, when he appears for this interview, immaculately dressed, white hair at a racy length just covering the ears, and says 'good morning' in that so familiar tone, it takes a monumental act of self-control not to reply in fluent Benaud.

So it seems only fair to establish the ground rules early on, and ask if he minds being so imitated. 'In the late eighties, a chap in Australia called Billy Birmingham started bringing out tapes imitating me,' Benaud says, establishing immediate eye contact with that same, slightly reptilian sideways glance he employs to camera. 'I have various problems with what Billy does – to do with sniggering at Asian names, we could do without that. And we could do without the swearing. Rory Bremner I have no problem with, he is a satirist and a very funny one too.'

So he enjoys the joke, then? 'Yes,' he says, doing his best to disguise a hint of weariness at the direction the questioning is taking. 'The only thing that really annoys me is when all of a sudden you hear yourself on the radio advertising Smith's tyre shop or Blenkinsop's jam. They simply can't do that. And in Australia, occasionally, I have to take action. It happens on local radio all the time; people tell me they've heard me endorsing this or that. It is straight-out dishonest; they are saying to potential customers that I am backing their product, and that's just crooked.'

You can understand why companies might try to pass off an endorsement as if from Benaud. According to his Channel 4 employers, his appeal is so enormous that more than 20,000 people have already downloaded a virtual Richie cartoon figure from their cricket website that utters a few pieces of prize Benaud as their screen-saver. Which is instructive, as the channel's remit when it took over the cricket contract last summer was to revolutionise the way the game was broadcast. And here it is, centring its coverage on a septuagenarian commentator who has been a fixture in the way the game has been reported since his debut on BBC radio in 1960.

'When BBC lost the rights, I assumed I would never broadcast on British television again,' he says of his switch of channels. Which was, presumably, an alarming thought.

'I never worry about things like that – it is the way life goes,' he says. 'At the time, Channel 4 issued a statement that it was going to change the whole face of televised cricket. It was not going to have any grey-haired fogeys in the commentary box. Well, while David Gower can look after himself, that concentrated my mind. My wife and I had been in business for thirty-eight years, we sat down and said: "OK, we'll have to do a few other things." Then suddenly an offer came in from Channel 4, and we asked them to talk to our literary agents, and when they came through with a figure we said: "Yes, that sounds very interesting." That was the key to it.'

The money?

'No, no, no,' he smiles. 'The concept sounded very interesting. It was sad leaving the BBC, not quite like being divorced, but you don't leave after a period stretching from 1960 to 1999 without feeling a certain number of pangs.'

Though he uses the term in a self-deprecating way, the reason why Channel 4 could add Benaud to their roster was that, despite his advanced age, no one could remotely describe him as a fogey. He captained Australia in the fifties and early sixties, yet so rarely does he mention his own playing past, there must be a substantial proportion of his fan base who do not realise he ever even played the game. As yet, for instance, we have not heard his thought on whether Steve Waugh's Ashes-winning tourists are the finest cricket team in history.

'I steer away from comparison,' he says. 'I think the modern-day players are absolutely brilliant. And a lot of traditional people say to me: "That's rubbish, these guys couldn't hold a candle to you – I remember seeing you bowl out England at Old Trafford in 1961." I say: "Yup, before tea time on the last day, can you remember what my bowling figures were? Well, I can tell you: I had none for 80 in the first innings and none for 40 up to tea in the second." The problem with relying on nostalgia for commentary is that people only remember the good things.'

Benaud puts much of his technique – his economy with words, the way he resists the temptation to call the Australians 'we' – down to his training. Not for him the route now favoured by commentators of using their playing careers as a shop window for a move into the media on retirement. He was a journalist by profession. In the days when cricket was no more than a paid hobby, he earned his corn working for the *Sydney Sun* as a police reporter.

'I did the midnight rounds for eight years,' he recalls. 'I worked under a fellow called Noel Bailey. He taught me something I could do now – if the phone went and someone said "we need 300 words immediately", I could dictate it. You get this inbuilt thing ticking in your head about the number of words you're doing. Same way as now I've got an inbuilt thing about what time is left and how many words are required to fill it. In your ear you're hearing "25 to go, 20 to go, 10, 9, 8..." At the same time you can hear people in the gallery shouting at each other..."3, 2..." and you say "good night" on one. And it's just practice, but it's got to work. Doesn't work, you go and do another job.'

Has he ever made a mistake?

'Of course. I remember at Lord's once, a West Indian spectator came on the field and did some acrobatics and I said something about it, and I got a voice in my ear – it was the director: "Lovely story, Richie, one of the best I've ever heard. It would have been awfully nice if I had a camera on it."'

In fact, Benaud says, he still has much to understand about the medium in which he works. 'The best thing I can do after a Test back home is walk up to the shops,' he says. 'Daph, my wife, leaves me to it and goes shopping, while I'm stopped by maybe fifty people who want to have a word. It's a rare day when I don't learn something about the production or my performance. And occasionally it is of tremendous use.'

All the same, there must have been a point at which he realised he was rather a good commentator? 'It's not possible to answer that except by saying I only achieve anything through hard work,' he says. 'But I don't want to say that because it sounds a bit pretentious. In 1956, television started in Aus, but I didn't utilise it until 1963. I watched and studied, kept looking and listening for seven years before I tried my hand at it.'

Ever since, he has lived a dual-hemisphere existence, five months in Australia, five months in England, and the rest of the year in Nice. Nearly forty years without being cold. '1962 was the last time I saw a winter,' he smiles.

Does he still, though, get as excited as he did back then? 'The honest answer is, I can't remember. I was very excited by the start of this series, as excited as I've been for a long time. And I'm disappointed England were not more competitive – I have never known a side so affected by injury.'

How long does he feel he can continue engaging with the game?

'I'm seventy now,' he says, before pausing, raising an eyebrow and pursing his lips. 'I'm very much hoping to make it to seventy-one.' Economical, understated: pure, fluent Benaud.

3 September 2001

DAVID LACEY

Now, at last, we can forget 1966

Now all of England is on fire. The pessimism of eleven months ago had already given way to guarded optimism but after the extraordinary events here on Saturday night English joy has, for the moment at least, good reason to be unconfined.

Beating the Germans at football always did lift the nation's hearts. Beating them 5-1 in Germany will have come close to blowing the nation's minds. This was ecstasy in spades.

For thirty-five years England have lived on the tale of the day a World Cup was won against West Germany at Wembley. Shortly before the countries met in the Olympiastadion here to contest automatic qualification for the 2002 tournament, Geoff Hurst was on German television recalling his hat trick.

From now on talk of hat tricks against Germany will revolve more around Michael Owen, each of whose goals on Saturday certainly crossed the line. Having wrought havoc in the Bayern Munich defence for Liverpool in the Super Cup in Monaco, Owen returned to Bayern's home ground to give Muncheners the full Monty. As gaps in Rudi Voller's awful defence yawned, he simply tore along the dotted lines.

'For me, Michael Owen has something very special,' enthused Sven-Goran Eriksson, whose stock as England's coach is now in the upper stratosphere. 'He's a good footballer and his technique is excellent but he also has two things which are difficult to find in a player. He's very cold when he gets a chance and he's very quick. When you have that combination it's a killer.'

David Beckham, groin strain forgotten, commanded an England performance as he had never done before. Equally crucial were the tactically adroit performances of Steven Gerrard and Paul Scholes, who denied Germany the mastery of the midfield that they had been so meekly allowed at Wembley last October, when Dietmar Hamann ran the match and scored its only goal.

That Germany victory, a swift revenge for England's 1-0 win in Charleroi that had bundled them out of the European Championship, begat Kevin Keegan's resignation and the glum scoreless draw in Finland under Howard Wilkinson, which finally persuaded the FA to look abroad for the next man to run the national squad.

Eriksson always did seem a sound choice by the FA. Now the appointment has taken on the touch of genius. England, three points behind with a game in hand, can finish only level with Germany in Group Nine if Germany win their last game against Finland, but crucially Eriksson's side are four in front on goal difference and will still go through automatically if first place has to be decided on the head-to-heads. Of course they still have to beat Albania in Newcastle on Wednesday and Greece at Old Trafford on 6 October. Even in the heady aftermath of Saturday's match Eriksson tried to keep a sense of proportion.

'After a victory like this there is always a danger of thinking that you can put out a shoe or a foot or a leg just to win a game,' he said. 'The game on Wednesday is not so glamorous, so tomorrow we must try to forget this victory and be focused on Albania. It would be a small disaster if we beat Germany away and then lose to Albania at home. Then this victory tonight would be worthless, more or less.'

Those are wise words, though it is hard to imagine his cool England team being carried away even by Saturday's historic win: the first time Germany have ever lost in Munich, only their second home defeat in World Cup qualifiers, their heaviest to England at full international level and the most dramatic turn-around in a return bout involving German opposition since Joe Louis battered Max Schmelling to a jelly.

On Saturday Germany's defence suffered a similarly nightmarish, if less phys-ically painful, experience. When in the sixth minute Carsten Jancker punished some ball-watching by the England defence, prodding the ball past David Seaman after Oliver Neuville's header had surprised Sol Campbell and Rio Ferdinand, some bad memories came floating back.

In the event, the sloppiness of falling behind merely made the manner of England's recovery even more impressive. Eriksson's plan was to exploit the nar-rowness of Voller's back three by getting Gary Neville and Ashley Cole into the spaces behind the German wing-backs Marko Rehmer and Jorg Bohme while Owen and Emile Heskey advanced through the inside-forward channels.

Chronically inept German defending played its part but so did England's character. 'I think the reason why we came back into the game was that our players believe we have a really good team and that we can do good things,' Eriksson reflected. 'If you don't believe that, it doesn't matter how good you are. These things must always start in the head.

'I told the players before they went out on the pitch that, if you play football as you can, we can beat anyone. If we want to play as we did against Holland (to whom England recently lost 2-0 in a friendly at White Hart Lane), we can lose against anyone. Either way it's very easy. But if we can go on like this in impor-tant games, we can lose a friendly now and then – it doesn't matter.'

Eriksson pointed to the shot rifled into the left-hand corner of the German net by Gerrard in first-half stoppage-time as the crucial moment in England's victory. 'To go in leading 2-1 instead of drawing 1-1 was a great difference both for us and for them.'

Owen's equaliser in the twelfth minute, a sharp volley after Gary Neville's for-ward header had caught the defence moving out too late and left Nick Barmby onside when he nodded the ball square to the Liverpool striker, might still have been dashed by offside against other England players, but the flag stayed down. On another night Sebastian Deisler might have scored a crucial goal at a crucial time for Germany instead of dragging the ball wide, and just before Gerrard's goal Seaman made his most important save, keeping out a low snap-shot from Bohme.

Although England needed only two minutes of the second half to increase their lead, Beckham's sharp centre enabling Emile Heskey to nod Owen through for his second goal, how different might things have been had Jancker not directed a free header the wrong way just before the hour.

Once Gerrard had neatly dispossessed Michael Ballack before setting up Owen's hat-trick, to be followed by Beckham and Scholes combining to send Heskey through a thoroughly dilapidated and depressed defence for England's fifth goal, the Olympiastadion was emptying in droves.

Long before the end, the German supporters did not think it was all over. They knew.

So now England and their Coles are bound for Newcastle, where a warmer welcome than usual awaits Owen at the court of St James.

NOT FORGETTING...

Steve Bell, 13 June 2001

15 November 2000

JAMES MEEK

Patenting life

One hot, dusty day in September 1893, at the sound of the starting guns, the rich prairie soil of the Cherokee Strip in Oklahoma was darkened by a flowing wave of humanity, horses and wagons. The US government was giving away 13,000 square miles of Indian territory to any settler able to race fast enough to stake a claim. One hundred thousand men, women and children stormed across the starting line to seize their piece of land.

More than a century after the Great Land Run became a symbol of the American frontier spirit, another rush for rights is under way. This time the claimants are in white lab coats and business suits, and the arena is the chemical sequence which makes us what we are: the set of genes each of us carries, in trillions of copies, in the cells of our bodies.

Research commissioned by the *Guardian* shows that pharmaceutical companies, biotech firms of all sizes, government institutes and universities have filed patents on a staggering 127,000 human genes or partial human gene sequences. They have patented genes which make our brains work, which build our bones, which make our livers grow, which keep our hearts beating, which can give increased chances of getting cancer and which may predict our likelihood of becoming addicted to drugs. They've patented genes even before they know what they do: they've taken out speculative patents on treatments based on genes even though no such treatments exist.

Our genes are nature's software – chemical codes honed by millions of years of evolution to fabricate the substances that make us what we are. Scientists' new knowledge of these codes, and their commonest flaws, promises to make the twenty-first century an era when some of the deadliest diseases are eradicated. By patenting gene sequences, the claimants argue, they are ensuring they will be able to recover the money they have spent to find them, and gain the financial incentive to work out how to use them to benefit humankind. Not so, argue the critics of gene patenting. For one thing, to claim exclusive rights to commercial exploitation of something everyone is born with is to abuse the patent system, which was set up to reward inventors, not discoverers.

Some genes are more valuable than others. Professor Simon Lovestone, of the Institute of Psychiatry in London, is one of a group of several dozen scientists around the world about to spark off a new gene hunt when they publish the results of research pinpointing a region of human DNA where a gene contributing to the onset of Alzheimer's disease is to be found. One 'Alzheimer's' gene, known as ApoE, has already been identified, but by itself it is a poor indicator of how likely someone is to get the disease. Patent control over a second Alzheimer's gene would make reliable advanced diagnosis more likely, and could contribute towards developing a cure. One estimate of the annual market for Alzheimer's therapy is £100bn. An Alzheimer's gene patent, even without a cure, would do wonders for a firm's share price in the cut-throat world of biotech competition.

Had Professor Lovestone and his collaborators been working for a private firm, they would have held off publishing details of their discovery until they had found the exact location of the gene, recorded its chemical sequence, and filed a patent application. This is what the Icelandic firm DeCode did with its recent announcement that it had found a 'schizophrenia gene'. By publishing early, Professor Lovestone's team throw the hunt open to everyone. A big private firm is quite likely to find the gene first, and patent it. If Lovestone et al find it, they may patent it too – a 'defensive' patent, to keep the gene in the public domain. 'Our academic group will publish as soon as it can, in order that other groups may work on it,' said Professor Lovestone. 'Of course it would cause me anguish if another group found the gene and patented it. We want to be the ones to find it because of normal academic competitiveness. If somebody else finds it and then clamps some kind of restriction on it which prevents others working on it, that would make me very unhappy.'

He could see the biotech companies' point of view: 'There is the argument that being able to patent genes encourages firms to spend large amounts of money on developing tests and therapies based on those genes. I don't know what's right and what's wrong, I really don't. I think it's genuinely difficult. I find the patenting of genes anathema, but equally I think it's absolutely essential that big pharmaceutical companies are involved in this kind of research. It's probably no longer possible for governments to sponsor this sort of work.'

The patenting of human genes tends to be seen as largely a US-driven phenomenon, fuelled by idiosyncratic American patent laws, but just as the Cherokee Land Run fades into insignificance compared to European appropriation of colonies, so European firms have become some of the most enthusiastic stakers of claims on human DNA. Patent applications on no fewer than 36,083 genes and DNA sequences – 28.5 per cent of the total claimed so far – have been filed by a single French firm, Genset. Andre Pernet, Genset's chief executive officer, said: 'It's going to be a race. The whole genome will have been patented two years from now, if it hasn't been done already.' He said Genset did not claim patents on genetic data without 'adding to its usefulness', although neither the company nor its partners have so far produced any treatments based on their patented sequences.

Genset is working on drugs linked to two patented genes – one associated with prostate cancer, another with obesity. 'If I invest $45m per year finding useful drug targets using isolation genetics and genomics, then I can demonstrate usefulness, and I think these are valid patents,' said Pernet.

So far, gene patent holders have trodden cautiously in enforcing their monopolies. They like to maintain, publicly, that they have not actually patented genes – only a specific use for them. But in gene patents, the written sequence of the gene's chemical code, and the description of its function, are usually the only novel things there.

The Utah-based company Myriad Genetics, for instance, has patented two human genes, mutations that make women more susceptible to breast cancer. It has patented these in the context of a test for susceptibility to the disease – but the technology to carry out the tests is patented by other companies. What Myriad brings to the table in terms of 'novelty' is the gene sequence and nothing more. One patent lawyer likened it to a lock and a key: all the locks are similar, but the key is unique.

Patents aside, Myriad is trying to introduce something novel to the world of genetic testing – a monopoly. It has stopped US labs screening for mutations on a non-profit basis by demanding they pay a licence fee. In Britain, its local agent has taken a more cautious approach so far. The company claims it must recoup the $10m it spent tracking down the genes. But much of the work involved was actually carried out by others, including non-commercial scientists in Britain who dispute Myriad's rights to ownership of one of the genes.

In this complex and important area, one thing is clear: the British government is not going to rock the boat. Tony Blair's reported anxiety to keep genetic sequence information from the Human Genome Project in the public domain does not extend to keeping genes out of the patent arena. Judging by a parliamentary reply he gave in February when asked about Myriad's approach, he neither knows, nor cares about, the difference between a genetic test and a drug, between a gene patent and the patent on a traditional medicine.

'We have no interest in the particular issue to which the honourable gentleman refers, other than to ensure that people get the best treatment possible,' he said. 'We have no more interest in one specific drug than another.'

5 December 2000

JEANETTE WINTERSON

A porn reader

When was the last time you looked at a girlie magazine? We see them subliminally every time we walk into a newsagent and we think we know enough to talk about them even when we never open one. My own view was fairly relaxed until I spent the weekend in the company of *The Best of Big and Black*, *Only 18*, *40 Plus*, *X-treme*, *Nude Readers' Wives*, *Forum* and *The Very Best of 50 Plus*.

Feminism seems to have had no effect on pornography. There is much more of it than in the sixties and seventies, and it has become both mainstream and acceptable. I travel a lot, here and abroad, and at airports and railway stations, I have noticed the old top shelf is often double the size and halfway down. What does this signify? That more men buy porn than ever before? That men are shorter than they used to be? That women want it in their face? That pornography is just a lifestyle magazine?

Reading the message is not easy. In the white corner are the likes of Andrea Dworkin and Catharine MacKinnon, who have argued, with varying degrees of success, in the American courts and media, that all pornography is violence

The last word... V. S. Naipaul, winner of this year's Nobel prize for literature, pictured at the Edinburgh International book festival in August. (Murdo MacLeod)

An ordinary genius: actor Timothy Spall. 'Most people walking about aren't heroes, and the bottom line is that someone's got to play them,' he told the *Guardian*. (Eamonn McCabe)

Pulling power. Candace Bushnell, author of *Sex and the City*, the book that led to the successful TV series starring Sarah Jessica Parker. (Eamonn McCabe)

Richie Benaud. '1962 was the last time I saw a winter,' says the spin bowler turned cricket commentator. (Tom Jenkins)

against women. In the red corner are the good-time guys, such as Hugh Hefner, Paul Raymond, Richard Desmond, who claim it's just business as usual and the girls enjoy it. Desmond has recently bought the *Express*, further blurring the line between business and exploitation. When a porn baron takes over a national newspaper, how do we read the signs?

Desmond would argue, as they all do, that there is no exploitation. The sex industry fulfils a need and pays a wage. We won't go into the differential between how much most of the women are paid and how much most of the men make, as photographers or agents or publishers. Even if the women took their real share of the money, the industry is still an exploitative one. Why? Because it exploits every woman on the planet. The majority of women do not want to pose for sleazy magazines, nor do they want to be thought of in those terms. I know men claim they can think of their wife in one way and a sex model in quite a different way, but the message is uniform. This is what women are for. Take their clothes off and they're all the same. They want sex all the time. They want it from strangers. They want it from you.

I know two men who use pornography regularly. One travels home on the same train as I do and sometimes I have to sit next to him. I am often the only woman in the small first-class carriage and the camaraderie of pinstripe and gin and tonic is stifling enough, without having *Hustler* by my elbow. The man is discreet, he is polite, but it makes me uncomfortable. I told him so on one occasion and he said, kindly: 'It's not about you.'

The second man I know through his girlfriend. She feels undermined by the magazines by the bed, but can't say anything because she'll lose him. He tells her she's not liberated and doesn't have a sense of humour. What's interesting is that her despair and my discomfort are dismissed by both men as our problem. Pornography is not the problem. We are.

This is the message of the magazines. Far from being sex that dare not speak its name, and hiding in a brown wrapper, soft porn is as ordinary as a page three girl. The success of the pornographers has been to use their nursery vocabulary – 'romp', 'giggle', 'tease', 'tug', 'playful', 'girls', 'bounce', 'cuddly', 'toy', 'spank', 'naughty' – as a defence as well as a turn-on. There's nothing threatening here. It's just a 'frolic'.

Mixed in with the nursery is the adolescent graffiti of toilet walls – 'horny', 'wank', 'pussy', 'cum', 'spunk', 'tit', 'suck', 'hole'. It's as easy to read as a tabloid headline and about as intelligent. Before I'm told I shouldn't be taking my brain to bed, let me say that none of the women in the magazines I've read this weekend has any brains – or maybe their brains are removed for the photographs and put back afterwards. I couldn't care less about naked women all over the place – a woman's body is never offensive – I care that these women are made to look stupid, sound stupid and act stupid. That's what's degrading – not waving your arse in the air, but being turned into a stupid cunt.

Sorry for the language but how often do you hear it on the streets? Now you know why.

Let's look at the pictures. There's not a lot of variety. How can there be? Once you've shot it every way up, a body is just a body. To disguise this sameness, and to justify the growing quantity of porn, the titles become the most inventive thing in the magazine. What's the difference between *40 Plus* and *50 and Over*? There isn't one. What does *Nude Readers' Wives* have that *X-treme* doesn't? Nothing.

Weirdly, porn-lingo is always ahead of porn-pics in selling the stuff. It's rather like the way kids love to repeat the first handful of words they learn. The vocabulary of shelf- porn is dick-shrinkingly tiny, but it's a multiple orgasm to pornographers and their readers. Take away the titles and suggestive coverlines, and I would defy anyone to tell which magazine they are looking at.

For me, the most disturbing element in all the drying sameness is the shaved pubic hair. How many women actually shave their pubic hair? According to the sex mags, all of us. In real life, the only females without pubic hair are little girls. Do you remember the story of Ruskin's impotence? The only naked women he had seen before his marriage were Greek statues and they, of course, are hairless. When he got married, he recoiled in horror from his wife's bush and never went near her again. Are our private parts so scary that we either have to turn them into pre-pubescent fantasies or preparation for the operating theatre?

The lesbians are no different. That is, the tease-lesbians who take up an astonishing amount of bed-space in men's porn. Men are threatened by lesbians – they get on in the world and they might get off with your wife. In porn-land, lesbians are safe sex-toys, who blither about how much better it is with a boy on hand (or somewhere) and act about as aroused as a castrated guinea pig. They always have lots of floppy blonde hair. They have long fingernails, too, which tells me they never put themselves where a man has right of way.

Right of way is what porn-land is all about. It may be that men's insecurity in a changing world, where their role and power has been reduced, prompts the need for a fantasy world that offers itself as reality. A world where men are on top. A world where sex-barter is the only exchange between men and women. It's a comforting, closed world where women are at once everywhere and excluded. It's a conservative world, where for all the panting poses, there is neither freedom nor change.

Week after week, it's the same old stuff, and I don't mean the women – I mean the way they are represented. Women change. Pornography stays the same. At least heterosexual porn does. The battle to get gay porn in the high street is not about morals, it's about what upsets existing fantasies. It's fine to see women playing at being lesbians, but what if they really fancy each other? Anyone who has looked at gay men's porn will realise what's radical about it is the self-conscious theatre. Nobody pretends it's real life. Queers don't need to prop up assumptions of male and female, so when it comes to sex, we know how to have fun. If you're a porn-reading straight male, that's even worse than having to deal with a real woman.

It looks like those mad old feminists were right after all. That top shelf isn't about sex, it's about power.

16 February 2001

DAVID MCKIE

The monkey puzzler

Quite a few people know that orchestra is an anagram of carthorse. Rather fewer have yet discovered that Manchester City is an anagram of synthetic cream. But it takes a crossword compiler of genius to discover that The Old Vicarage, Grantchester, yields the anagram: chaste Lord Archer vegetating.

Or to be more precise, it takes John Graham, eighty today, who for forty-two years has delighted, enthralled and sometimes exasperated *Guardian* readers with the cryptic crosswords which appear nowadays under the pseudonym Araucaria. The word means monkey puzzle, as in the tree of that name. He chose it when, in December 1970, the crossword editor, John Perkin, removed the cloak of anonymity from the *Guardian's* team of compilers and invited them to pick sobriquets of their own. Monkey came from the influence in those days of Desmond Morris's book, *The Naked Ape*, and also from a standard endearment in the Graham household. The puzzle speaks for itself.

Graham was a priest in the Church of England when his first *Manchester Guardian* crossword was published in the paper in July 1958. He was a reader of the old liberal *News Chronicle*, rather than of the MG, though his politics were to the left of either's. He was further left than you might think, says an old friend: very interested in the Levellers, for instance. He came out of academic Oxford, where his father was the dean of Oriel College, to read classics at King's College, Cambridge, till the war intervened. He joined the RAF and flew in some thirty operations as an observer, having failed to become a pilot. In a sequence of events he relates with brisk modesty, he had to bale out in Italy and go into hiding, was rescued by the Americans and got mentioned in dispatches – an honour you always got, he insists, if you baled out and the enemy did not catch you.

Then it was back to King's, this time to read theology, and on through a succession of curacies, chaplaincies (as at Reading University for ten years from 1962) and higher incumbencies. Some were not what you might have expected for someone essentially shy and hardly cut out for the social whirl: it is hard to imagine Graham as the priest in charge of St Peter's in London's Eaton Square. The living that followed in Huntingdonshire (Houghton and Wyton) seems more in keeping. By this time, having won an *Observer* competition for crossword setters two years running, he had been headhunted by the *Guardian* and engaged to set its crosswords once a week or thereabouts.

It was a sideline to start with, but became a necessity at the end of the seventies when Graham and his first wife divorced. Under the rules of those days, that disqualified him from continuing in the ministry. Setting crosswords pays pretty abysmally even now; back then it was hardly a basis for prosperous living. But the *Guardian* bumped up his crossword quota and his practice grew. Now he is setting six Araucarias monthly, as well as one in three of the quick crosswords, contributing cryptic puzzles to the *Financial Times* and setting a monthly puzzle for *Homes and Antiques*. They are all put together at an upstairs desk in the cottage in Somersham, a village between Huntingdon and Cambridge, where he has lived alone since the death of his second wife, Margaret, seven years ago.

The Archer anagram, which appeared six weeks ago, dispersing in one crisp sally any suggestion that his powers might be failing as he neared eighty, was, like most of his work, a blend of diligence and inspiration. And, perhaps, just a bit of luck with the language. I assumed he had hit on 'chaste Lord Archer' and found himself, to his delight, left with the letters to form the viable word 'vegetating'. But no, vegetating came first, and the letters remaining made 'chaste'. One reader was entranced enough to write to the paper declaring that this made Graham 'the Tiger Woods of crossword compiling'.

There are several conspicuous virtues that took Tiger Graham to the top of his trade. He is unfailingly fair. With Araucaria you don't look up the solution the next day to see why he defeated you and conclude that he never gave you a chance. And that is no accident. Every puzzle he sets is sent to a checker (unpaid: the rewards of crossword compiling are not lavish enough for it to be otherwise).

The Araucaria puzzles are checked by a woman in Wiltshire who will sometimes say of a clue: that's too hard or, even, that is impossible. Or beyond the likely comprehension of solvers who may be fifty years or more younger than John. 'Her job,' says the sage of Somersham, 'is to be as critical as possible.' Some of the clues she questions are kept rather more are amended. The result is the ideal challenge – a puzzle where at some stage or other you think: 'Curses, Araucaria has foxed me this time.' But you persist, and an hour or so later, he hasn't.

He is the most ingenious of setters, both in his crossword designs and in his clues. His specialities are theme puzzles (which he didn't invent, but developed) where a central figure or concept informs much of the puzzle. Some commemorate heroes. One of the most famous was built around the heroes of South African resistance to apartheid. Another was a tribute to Leonard Bernstein, known to be a fan of *Guardian* crosswords.

Few of this kind can have been more inventive than the one he devised for the *Guardian* last Christmas, in the year that marked the 250th anniversary of Johann Sebastian Bach's death, which was all about the composer. The answer to 1 across was Bach's name. Elsewhere the answers included St Matthew Passion, B minor Mass, Art of Fugue, Goldberg (as in variations), Brandenburg Concerto, Well-Tempered Clavier, oratorio, the names of three cantatas, and Handel. One contemplated the completed grid and thought: 'That just isn't possible.'

Sometimes on Saturdays he uses a form which he did invent: the alphabetical jigsaw – twenty-six slots, starting with every letter from A to Z, with clues in rhyming couplets, where you have to work out not just the answers but the right place to put them. But the clues themselves are hardly less remarkable. Just catch sight of them on the page, and you're irresistibly tempted to start on them straight away. Here are some from the first signed puzzles. Lean man with bad feet he's the greatest (7,4). It's painful on the seventh and first Sunday after Easter (7). Correcting sets in the North? O don't! I can't bear it (11).*

As for the anagrams, even the Old Vicarage at Grantchester isn't, in Araucaria's view, his best of all time. That honour is reserved for a Christmas puzzle where the clue involved the seasonal sentence: 'O hark the herald angels sing the boy's descent which lifted up the world' which, being disentangled, yielded: 'While shepherds watched their flocks by night, all seated on the ground.'

Not all compilers, it has to be said, approve of these methods. He used to be seen by some as a dangerous heretic. There are those, even now, who think he is undesirably liberal. A great *Observer* setter who used the pseudonym Ximenes set down a list of rules which should not be broken. Araucaria quite often breaks them, in the interests of free expression and fun. In this he is followed by some, though not all, of his *Guardian* colleagues. To me, the most obvious Araucarians are two of the younger setters, Paul and Enigmatist, both of whom as teenagers sent puzzles to Graham asking for his opinion. He would not call himself their mentor, but that is what he is.

Restored to his priestly duties after the death of his first wife, Graham is still in demand for occasional sermons, funerals and periods filling in when one local priest departs and the next one is yet to arrive. Just as he is in demand for that mighty army of *Guardian* readers for whom Saturday is never quite Saturday unless there's an Araucaria waiting at the end of the day. I leave him about to start work on a puzzle for *Homes and Antiques*, where, unlike the *Guardian*'s crossword editors, they choose his themes for him. This time it is chairs. 'I don't know very much about chairs,' he says, just a little plaintively. But just wait till you see what he'll do with them when he does.

* Cassius Clay (Cassius in Julius Caesar clay feet); Whitlow (Whit Sunday, the seventh after Easter, and Low Sunday, the first); Orthodontic (concealed in the clue).

19 February 2001

SIMON HATTENSTONE

Toff at the top

As you may expect, it's hard to ignore Lady Victoria Hervey 's knickers. Walk through the front door of her London boutique and they stare you in the face. Naughty, naughty, logo knickers. 'Yes please,' says one pair across the crotch. 'I'm bad,' says another. Fabulous! Meanwhile, Lady V is in a tizzy. Posh Spice is due here any hour and the new stock has not yet arrived. Maybe Posh will fancy the knickers as a little prezzie for David, I suggest, trying to be helpful. What about 'Open sesame'? Or perhaps 'Lip service'? Lady V, the new It girl, is not convinced.

She arrived on the scene when her nipple tastefully popped out at a charity bash for fighting breast cancer. A few weeks ago 'toff totty Vicky' was crowned Queen It when she made it on to page three of the Sun. Hervey (as in Harvey Smith, rather than scurvy) most recently grabbed the headlines when she announced that she was too old to marry Prince William. Not that he'd asked.

Lady V says they have an amazing range of customers for their designer labels.

'From Japanese tourists to pop star wives. We get quite a lot of foreigners,' she says. 'But then we do get Meg Mathews, Patsy Kensit. Martine McCutcheon is one of our best customers...'

She suggests we retreat to a 'nasty little caff' for a chat. Lady V is 6ft tall with a perfect little nose and perfect skin, and a tight little mouth. Her face is long and thin like a racing car. She says goodbye to darling Zulu, her Norfolk terrier. He is tied to a table leg and continues to run in confused circles. We are in the heart of Knightsbridge and I've just spent a pound on the loo at Harrods. 'That's quite funny,' she says. 'I'm just going to spend a pound. Huhhuhu.' She laughs ever so delicately. As if she's clearing her throat.

Her lime-green mobile phone rings. She's just received it in the post, and she loves it: 'I'm not sure if Ericsson sent it me.' It's her assistant. Lady V turns my tape-recorder off and tells her to make sure she locks the shop door when she goes downstairs. Why? 'She's alone in the shop. There's this gang of black women that work around here. They robbed Jimmy Choo next door, they rob loads of places. They put a security guard from Harrods in hospital a couple of weeks ago.' And they've never been nicked? 'No. Nobody's managed to bust them.'

Akademi, the boutique, opened last year. Akademi is Turkish for academy, explains Lady V, who has three As and a B at A-level. 'Can you belieeeeve, although it's such a crap thing, only three of us got an A at general studies in our whole year. Apparently it's common sense. I'm not your typical It girl.'

What is an It girl? 'It girls used to be girls that sort of run around London just going to parties. But that's not what I do. I do have a day job, which It girls don't normally have. They wake up for their night life. I've got my shop and I've got my modelling and all of that.'

She doesn't want to say it, she's far too discreet, but if we're being perfectly frank, It girls in the past have tended to be a little bit thick, a little bit stuck-up. They drink too much champagne, snort too much cocaine and say some very silly things indeed. Lady V doesn't even go to that many parties. Sometimes no more than three a week.

For so long, Lady V, whose brother is the Marquess of Bristol, was merely a background It, a baby It, shadowing Tara Palmer-Tomkinson and Tamara Beckwith. A year ago, she and her boyfriend, millionaire restaurateur Mogens Tholstrup, split up and everything fell into place. 'Since I've been single, it's all got a bit mad. My career always goes much better when I haven't got a man...You've got to have all these men like drooling over you, huhuhu.'

But there is more to Itness than desirability and availability. There's karma. 'I guess if you're happy – you know, I'm just happy the whole time now – you give out positive energy.' And she wasn't happy when she was going out with Tholstrup? 'I don't want to talk about it. Boring.'

Although she will come into her inheritance when she marries, she stresses that it is important for her to be financially self-sufficient. 'Since I set up my own business I'm more confident. I'm not stupid. I'm not a dumb model.'

In the past, she says, she felt put down. In what way? 'Girls are bitchy. Most of my good friends are men.' But even with men there are problems when you're the It girl. 'There is always the question of, you know, them hoping for something else.' As she talks, I try to make out the writing on her cashmere top, but it's obscured by a denim jacket

It can't be easy being an It girl. We draw up a list of the pros and cons. Lady V heads straight for the cons. People, for starters. She tells me of an unbelievable incident the other night. She was in a club with friends and suddenly this girl from nowhere parks herself at their table, on their sofa. What did she say to her? 'Well I was quite rude actually. This girl was just sitting there smiling. So then I went up to her and I said: "Can you move? This is our table." Sitting on our bit of sofa!'

She says that so often she'll be at a party and some girl will just walk up to her, acting all friendly in the vain hope that some of Victoria's Itness will rub off on her. 'You suddenly get these girls who try to be your best friends and I can see right through them.' Total strangers? 'Yeh, you get some really su-per-fic-ial people. They think: "If I hang out with Victoria I'll get invited to these parties, and there'll be this person and that person." They'd just love to be in a stupid magazine.'

Then there are those awful girls who can't stand Lady V simply because she's done well for herself. Envy's a terrible thing, she says. 'People like to rip each other apart.' She doesn't think much of human nature? 'No, it's horrible.'

And then there's the press, the paparazzi, the hyenas. She says it's disgusting that the press can get away with so much in this country. It wouldn't happen in France, where she spent much of her childhood. 'England is far too liberal with the press. The way they hound people.' She tells me of the time she came out of a restaurant and was, literally, quite literally, chased down the street by the paparazzi. 'I suddenly thought, I'm just Victoria Hervey. Imagine what Princess Diana went through. Horrible.'

I'm beginning to feel confused. Surely, the point about being an It girl is that you get your picture in the paper all the time. She strokes her hair thoughtfully. 'That's the problem. You've got to accept that side of it. Which I don't really like...'

I'm beginning to feel more confused. Lady V writes a column for the *Sunday Times*, which documents all the wonderful people she's met over the week – the very column that ex-It Tara used to write. Now, when she goes to parties, she has to take a camera with her 'to do my little bit of photography'. Victoria takes out an envelope of newly developed photos. There's lovely Patrick Cox, who's a super partygoer, Simon Le Bon looking a little the worse for wear, Elton's boyfriend David, Minnie Driver's sister Kate. She has met so many useful people at parties. 'I looked in my address book the other night and thought, most of these people I've met, I have met them at parties.' Only last Wednesday she met Donatella Versace, who was lovely. Partying is a philosophy, a mantra. 'You've got to go out to meet people. If you sit at home all night, you're not going to achieve anything.'

She takes out a picture of herself hugging Mick Jagger. He looks as though he's in a state of shock. Lady V explains why. She sidled up to him, danced next to him, then flung her arms around him. Meanwhile, her friend Jodie snapped the pic. Bingo! But there was a problem. 'When he saw the camera, he freaked. I suddenly thought: "Well God, I would have freaked out."'

So Lady V has turned into her own worst enemy: the paparazzi, the hyenas.

Celebrities must be terrified of her. 'I don't want to make enemies. If I put a picture in, I always ask first.' The picture of Jagger is for her personal photo album.

She says the difference between her and the paparazzi is that celebrities trust her, embrace her as one of their own. So they all find comfort in each other? 'If I was Elton John or whatever, you're not going to trust people. I don't even trust people I meet, so at least if you're with people whose careers are the same level or whatever, you feel safe – you know they're not going to screw you over and go to the press about something.'

If she feels exploited by the press, why did she do a topless picture for the *Sun*? She looks appalled. 'Look that was *GQ*. They put it in the *Sun*.' Was she happy that the magazine sold the pictures on to the Sun? 'No. I didn't know till I saw it. Sales went up 250,000, 300,000. David Yelland [the editor] told me. Apparently it sold out everywhere, and what did I get from it?' What's the difference between taking her clothes off for *GQ* and taking them off for the *Sun*? 'It's just different isn't it? It is different.'

Hervey has lived with the media all her life. Her very Itness has been enhanced by a dramatic and traumatic family history. Her late father, the Marquess of Bristol, was jailed for three years after a botched burglary. Within the past two years both her half-brothers have died: John was a drug addict who blew the £17m family fortune over ten years; Nicholas hanged himself in 1998. Was she close to them? 'Nooooah, we had a court case with John for fourteen years. He tried to kidnap my brother, he vandalised our cars.' So it was good riddance? 'Yah, he was evil...but it's sad, you know, that we didn't get on.'

What was Nicholas like? 'Schizophrenic.' She giggles. She claims that John's addiction turned her against drugs. 'What happened to him was just awful. When you see someone lose everything, it puts you off. I mean he blew everything.' She whispers. For a moment, she looks truly grief-stricken.

My balance sheet of positives and negatives is lopsided. Can she think of any more positives? She grins. 'Yes, the freebies.' She flashes the lime-green phone at me. These days she has drinks paid for her, clothes paid for her, taxis, chauffeured cars. She says it's not simply the It factor. 'Remember I am a girl, so I'm quite lucky in that respect.' Recently, she had a blinding revelation. 'The real irony of this is that the poor get poorer and the rich get richer. Because the better known you are, the more freebies you get given. It's really unfair.'

Does that bother her? 'It doesn't bother me, but I sometimes think about it and think I'm now doing well and I'm getting sent free stuff the whole time and some people have to really save up for it.'

I ask her whether there are any issues that enrage her, that she'd storm the streets for. 'Tax,' she answers instantly. 'What annoys me is when these families have got like twelve children and we're paying for these kids.' Because they're claiming benefit? 'Yeah. And because they work out that they make more money being on the dole than having a job, they just laze around.'

We wander back to the shop and talk about what happens to an It girl when she grows up. Lady V hopes to marry in a few years, but not before she's proved herself a self-made woman of substance and made enough money to get the hell out of England and live somewhere hot.

On my way out, I remember I've forgotten to ask the most important question. What is she wearing? She looks delighted. Positive publicity. A pair of Bruce jeans tottering in at £180, a big bull-buckled belt (£170 to you, madam), Chanel diamante shades (around £130), priceless snakeskin boots and a Toby Pimlico cashmere top (£255). At last I can make out the words on the top. 'High maintenance,' it says.

2 April 2001

EMMA BROCKES

Hungry reporter is now fulfilled

When David McKie was growing up in Leeds, what mattered in life was reported in the *Yorkshire Post*. The *Guardian*, then Manchester based, existed for him as a right-thinking paper on the wrong side of the Pennines. 'The *Post* had lots about Yorkshire cricket in it,' he says, 'which I knew to be the most important subject in the world.'

It wasn't until he was studying at Oxford in 1957 that his priorities changed. It was the time of the Suez crisis and McKie and his fellow students turned to the *Guardian* to articulate their unease. 'It told us that we were quite right in thinking that this was an immense wickedness and a huge piece of incompetence. From then, I always wanted to work for the *Guardian*.'

David McKie retires this week after working for the paper for thirty-five years and occupying every position from junior reporter to assistant news editor to Peter Preston's deputy during some of the paper's toughest times. He is known presently to readers as a political columnist and the author of the devilish weekly dispatch, Smallweed.

'He is amazingly knowledgeable on a huge range of subjects,' says Alan Rusbridger, the editor. 'He is painstakingly fair to people. He is fantastically punctilious about details and accuracy and he writes like a dream. There is no job in journalism he can't do better than anyone else. He has never won a prize, but he is one of the great journalists of our time.'

McKie's first day in the newsroom was on 4 October 1965. The paper was sixteen pages thick, cost five old pence and if you found a photograph, you had reason to celebrate. McKie, whose first news editor was John Cole, later political editor of the BBC, was given an underwhelming salary of £1,750 a year.

'They rather took the view, that if you worked for the *Guardian*, it was a terrific privilege and did you really expect to be paid as well? So they paid starvation rates. But if you wanted to work for a paper that was left of centre and cherished writing, then there was nowhere else you wanted to go.'

His ambition was to become a political reporter and he eventually achieved it after serving time on the news and features desks. To McKie, politics comprised the exact mix of the serious and the wacky that made his own writing so powerful.

'Having employed the term "bog standard" last week,' he wrote recently, in a needle-sharp column, 'I am now assailed with requests to explain what it means.

I shall answer this in one brusque and immaculate sentence: I haven't the slightest idea.'

To staff, he represents everything that justifies the peculiar loyalty that the *Guardian* inspires. While political reporter, McKie was mindful not to grow too fond of his subjects, although he inevitably developed friendships with politicians on both sides of the House. 'My two closest friends in the Labour party were Neil Kinnock and Roy Hattersley. That caused difficulties, particularly when Neil became leader, because I was writing leaders condemning him. One of the politicians I most revere is John Biffen, a really good, honest, decent man. Some of the anti-Thatcher Tories became good mates. When people condemn politicians, I say, wait a minute, what about Jack Ashley, a man with no ambitions to rise up the tree, but only to serve his constituents and do the best he can for the party.'

In retirement, McKie will continue to do what he has loved but not always found time for, to write for the paper. What he will miss most, he says, are those chance encounters with colleagues and readers that excite his ever-renewing interests. 'It is those conversations,' he says, 'when you talk about something not particularly relevant to anything and suddenly you think, that's jolly interesting. That will be a terrible loss.'

The biggest challenge of his career, says McKie, came in the early eighties with the formation of the SDP and the subsequent split, in the *Guardian* office, between those in support of it and those loyal to the ailing Labour party.

'David Owen came up to me at a party conference and denounced the *Guardian*. "Say what you like about the *Daily Mail*," he said, "at least it knows what side it's on." And I said: "We know what side we're on, we're on our side. We're not here to be on the Labour party's side, we're not here to be on the SDP's side, we're here to define our own terms, approve those parties that come close and disapprove the rest."'

He is the standard to which we all aspire.

14 April 2001

JULIE BURCHILL

Britain: a lot better than you think

I like most things about young, working-class women – even the stuff that other people, theoretically workerists, sneer at under cover of 'good taste'. I like white bread more than brown. Instant coffee more than that stinking, bitter, overpriced slop. I like the names Sharon and Tracey – say them to yourself without prejudice, just listening to the sounds they make, and you'll see how much more attractive they are than lumpy old handles such as Emily and Elizabeth. And how much more honest and human are those young mothers who, pushed beyond endurance at the supermarket check-out, finally give their grizzling brat a light slap and crow triumphantly, 'There! Now you've got something to cry about!'

And before all you Horrifieds of Hampstead write in and accuse me of sanctioning child abuse, save your energy and your manky recycled notepaper if you really believe that a spontaneous slap in a public place inevitably leads to methodical torture and murder by a tattooed stepfather, you're only revealing your own anti-prole prejudices. Anyway, better a swift smack in a supermarket any day than, say, the creepy, middle-class hot-housing that forces so many over-examed teenagers to top themselves, or the enforced beatings and buggery 'enjoyed' at any of our major public schools.

I can't help but think of this earthy mother's cry whenever I pick up a newspaper these days. Ever since this country lost the Empire, it has been beating itself up in some way, shape or form. Oooh, we can't do sex like the French! (Despite the fact that recently surveyed Frenchwomen claimed that two out of three of them would rather shop than shtup.) Oooh, our food's the worst in Europe! (Ever tried eating in Germany?) Oooh, our education system stinks! (Excuse me, we're not the country that's made a deity out of Jerry Lewis.) And the ultimate obscenity: who really won the war? (Said with wry, knowing smirk.) This was particularly rich coming from the sort of soft, self-adoring cosmopolitan type who invariably finds a way to weasel out of any conflict more taxing than beating up his wife, but who would very probably have been the first to feel the difference if the other side had won. Then there were the milksops posing as sophisticates who would bang on about how our continental cousins were so good at enjoying themselves with sex, wine and food – and then start tut-tutting whenever those surveys came out with us Brits topping the polls for drink, drugs and divorce! Just because we cut straight to the chase and don't piss around with finger-bowls and foreplay! If joie de frigging vivre is what you're looking for, Johnny Englishman's your man!

Can anyone beat themselves up as good as the English can? Start the day with an apology to the colonies, take a grovelling lunch of humble pie with a visiting dignitary, and we'll still have time to get that hair shirt on before a supper of bread and gruel. No wonder they call masochism *le vice Anglais*. For example, it's a stone fact that the economies of Germany and Japan have been in a hell of a state for a good half-decade, yet I know many otherwise intelligent people who refer to the German and Japanese economic miracles as if they're still present and correct, just so as not to spoil the perfect line of their own self-loathing.

Even Cool Britannia, though it might have seemed like we were showing off, was just part of our bipolar condition – the manic babble to the usual depressive whinge. By banging on about how good we were at fashion, food and pop music –kids' stuff – we were actually damning ourselves with faint praise. We still aren't the meat of the matter, our subtext went, just the silly little cherry on top of the Fondant Fancy.

And now we really do have something to cry about. Cattle with foot and mouth, royals with foot-in-mouth, floods, a third-world rail system, crime up and, despite copious state handouts to our film industry, you've got more chance of seeing a good Iranian flick these days than an English one. Worse, something has happened that surely indicates that British morale is at an all-time low – we've started to think that the French are actually really, really good at pop music!

It may well be that things are not as nice as they could be, but the idea of Britain being the most beleaguered cesspool on the planet only stands up in a vacuum. Everything is relative, and when you compare us to other countries, suddenly things aren't quite so grim. (As the refugees from countries far and near who have made this country the Number One destination on their various itineraries will vouchsafe.) Where else, exactly, is there? The third world? No cheers! America? I'd rather live in a toilet than in the evil empire. Russia? Used to be good, but since the end of communism, the life expectancy has dropped by ten years, productivity has been cut in half and they pay you in dog food. 'Newly free eastern Europe' ? Yeah, it's so great there that they're all coming over here. Corrupt France, racist Germany, boring Belgium? Keep'em!

A bit of perspective never goes amiss, and in the midst of all this doom and gloom it's worth remembering what we've got that others haven't. A sense of humour. A love of the underdog. The idea that a corrupt politician is still worth getting upset about. That inbuilt bullshit detector that makes mincemeat of philosophers, politicians and Martin Amis. 'They' used to talk about the people of England who had not spoken yet but that might be because 'their' heirs, the chatterers, haven't shut up long enough to give them a chance. And everything they say is such a downer. I can't help but think that the disgusting behaviour of young Brits abroad might just have something to do with the non-stop disapproval of their 'betters'.

It's strange the liberal establishment can see that it might be counter-productive to tell people they're bad all the time, individually – look at the coochy-coo treatment given to the murderers of James Bulger – but it doesn't seem to occur to them that if you tell a people how crap they are constantly, they might think, well, may as well be hung for a sheep as a lamb.

More and more, when it appears to me that this country is rather overcrowded, I long to deport not the mild immigrants but the bellicose natives who have a good word to say for every country but their own. Oi, Mortimer, eff off back to Tuscany. Nigella, Provence for you, luv. And as for Louis de Bernières, with his ignorant comments about the 'anti-education, anti-culture attitude of the white working class' (yeah, and the black working class are queueing up for the opera), it's off to Cephalonia he goes, and let the communists deal with him. With that lot gone, who knows, dear old Blighty might well enjoy a reversal of fortune.

10 July 2001

JAMES MEEK

Which one's Naomi?

I'm sitting in a seedy cafe in the sixth *arrondissement* opposite a *charcuterie* which boasts that it is 'champion in France for head cheese'. I'm seething because Christian Dior hasn't invited me to his fashion show. What have I ever done to Christian Dior? Is it because I know nothing about *haute couture*, and have spent the past year writing about genes and clones?

A few minutes away, at the École National Superieur des Beaux Arts, elongated models are loping along the catwalk in Dior dresses which, if they can be worn at all without a team of seamstresses, stylists, nurses and metalworkers in close attendance, will sell in low double figures. Opposite my cafe, meanwhile, Parisians stride over a pedestrian crossing almost slowly enough for my pen to capture their sense of style, if only the precise lexicon of the fashion writer was at my disposal.

In my notebook I scribble a practice verbal sketch: 'Late-forties, striped woollen top, blue-white, tapering big stripes down blue jeans, tapered leg, gold bracelet, short hennaed hair, black sandals, beige shoulder bag.' I feel something is missing. What blue? What black? How do I know it's wool? I make a better fist of a group of two women who look fetching from the back. 'Dove-grey ankle-length dresses, belted at the waist, black sandals, matching wimples.' Ah, those would be nuns.

I ask my neighbour in the cafe, a young mother called Isabelle, what *haute couture* is. She is, after all, French – she might know. 'It's very difficult to explain. It's something you can't wear in the street or to work,' she says. 'It's not casual. It's for very rich people. It's not for me.'

The Versace gig that evening is held in the lower portion of a monumental building opposite the Eiffel Tower, the Theatre National de Chaillot, which looks like a cross between a dictator's mausoleum and the Red Army Theatre in Moscow. There's a plaque on the wall saying: 'Here, on 10 December 1948, the Third General Assembly of the United Nations proclaimed the Universal Declaration of Human Rights.' But now it's available for functions.

Shoals of black Mercedes glide around the entrance. Black is the default colour of the fashionist regime controlling entrance and the fashionist sympathisers trying to get in, limned with shades of mauve and purple beyond the imagination of all but the most creative industrial chemist. Seeing my invitation, the door-minders are forced to let me in, not without a certain reluctance. Or was it pity? We pass through a grubby lobby, flanked by wall-to-ceiling time-lapse back projections of unfurling roses, and into a maelstrom of camera crews, photographers and implausibly glamorous bouncers. There are rich middle-aged men with taut terracotta skin managing to look at once sated and ravenous, and rich middle-aged women whose delicious clothes and diamond bracelets do not prevent them looking stricken with anxiety. The fashion writers greet each other with the knowing warmth of mercenaries who renew acquaintance with each new war. I could say they were a set of bitching, backbiting harridans, but they aren't. They seem the most together, human people there, and the ones who are making nice clothes work for them. Watching couturier after couturier, season after season, has its rewards.

I am stopped again, before I can reach the inner sanctum, by an elegant goon. Perhaps it is because I am wearing clothes with a collective value of less than a thousand. Pounds, dollars or euros, though not quite francs. Perhaps it is the £5 haircut. The bouncer yields to the invitation card. The show itself takes place in a modestly sized hall, lined with two rows of gold and purple chairs on steeply raked stands facing each other. The catwalk runs down the middle, adjacent squares of transparent glass with red, pink and purple roses underneath. Christina Ricci and escort are sitting in the front row. She has committed the celebrity sin of punctuality. With a flapping of shutters the photographers settle on their prey. Puff Daddy arrives with a woman of supernatural beauty. Kevin Spacey strolls in, tugging Naomi Campbell by the hand. 'She's pissed off 'cause nobody's noticed her,' murmurs a neighbour. 'That's her pissed-off face.'

With the seats filled, the hall takes on the appearance of a celebrity House of Commons. Kevin is the prime minister, Christina and Puff are the foreign and home secretaries, Naomi is supermodel without portfolio. The music changes from ambient to hard pounding and the show begins. A model strides out in a tight-fitting green dress with black poppy-like motifs printed on the fabric. My neighbour draws my attention to the fact that this is the supermodel Amber Valetta. I make a note. Amber withdraws only to reappear again instantly, in a different dress. But it isn't Amber. It's uncanny how a stylist can take a couple of dozen women of roughly the same body type – tall, thin, long-legged, high cheekbones – and make them look indistinguishable save hair colour and the odd tattoo. They all have the same gigantic eighties hair, piled up and swept back like a hyena's mane, and they all have the same panda eyes and wet lips, like Daryl Hannah as an android in *Blade Runner*.

I ask a helpful fashionista about the odd locomotion of the models. Apparently, backstage the couturier will paste thematic guidelines in Eurenglish for models to follow on the catwalk. 'Think the warrior', for instance. I don't know what Donatella Versace was after but it could have been 'Think pest control'. In five-inch stiletto heels, the models stomped down on the glass as if they were skewering a particularly unloved form of vermin – mice, perhaps, or paparazzi – with every step.

The clothes have a collective hallucinogenic effect. To put it another way, each new dress imprints on the image of the previous one, till what I retain in my memory is an expressionist mosaic of glittering thigh-high boots, skin-tight fabrics splashed with beads of jet, jags of sequins drawn across shoulders like rake marks in a Zen garden, trimmings of fur and feathers, breasts barely veiled in sheerest net, and dresses that are only the rumour of a garment floating over the upper half of the body. This is the autumn-winter collection, but Versace must have high hopes indeed of global warming if anyone is to wear them outside at that time of year.

When the sheerest of the sheer stopped in front of Kevin Spacey and posed her pose, hip to the right, hip to the left, I noticed the actor's mouth was hanging open. It stayed that way for a while and then he leaned back and laughed and spent the rest of the show leading the applause while Naomi Campbell tried without much success to engage him in conversation.

Next day I went to Dominique Sirop's show, at the Theatre des Champs-Élysées. It came after Jean-Paul Gaultier, and before Givenchy. Sirop was the Paraguay-South Korea game you went to if you didn't get tickets for England-Germany. I asked one of Sirop's aides, Jean-Philippe, one of the hardest questions I've ever tried to ask, harder even than: 'Aren't somatic cells more genetically stable for cloning than embryonic ones?' I asked: 'Who is Dominique Sirop?'

'Who is he? He's an artist.' Jean-Philippe seemed surprised by the question, and gazed up at the Maurice Denis frescoes in the upper gallery for inspiration. 'I think he's a visionary. He like women very feminine, sophisticated, glamour. He like the body of a woman to express something very sensitive, and he want to serve the body of the woman, to...magnifier.'

I thanked him and went to talk to someone else. Gradually I found out a little about Dominique Sirop. He's forty-five, he's had his own couture house for five years, he used to work for Yves Saint Laurent, and then for Givenchy. What isn't clear is exactly where he stands in the opaque hierarchy of *haute couture*. But the champagne flows at the Sirop show. The models are spindly enough to make the casual bystander lose sight of them when they pass in front of a light gantry, and provoke fears that their legs might snap under the weight of a trouser suit. The clothes look suitably fantastic and unwearable by the normally proportioned, with lots of mauve, thigh boots, satin, leather, fur and feathers. But there is little in the way of an international media presence, no supermodels, no Hollywood stars.

After the show, I approach Sirop. He is slim, with short, wiry hair, and an impression of weariness and impatience in his face. He wears a sky-blue satin shirt and black trousers. He is sitting on a prop from the show, a gold throne draped in mauve satin. I ask him a question. He glances at me, assesses face, jacket, shirt, trousers, shoes and haircut in a microsecond, and moves away in the opposite direction without a word.

With the help of a passing transvestite cable TV presenter, Vincent MacDoo, dressed in a superb Givenchy ensemble, and a friendly ex-model, Margot, I manage to hold Sirop still for a time. Some of his clothes are cut by laser, but he is proud to wield the scissors himself. 'I look at the fabric, I sculpt the fabric with my hand, on the body. Every time I try to take a piece of fabric and find the most simple cut.' He points to dress number eleven in his collection, *errance de luxe*, an evening gown in tobacco silk. 'That was made with only two cuts of the scissors. After that you play with the fabric around the body.'

I asked how you get to be a big name. 'I have some stars but the difference between me and the big houses like Dior, I never say who wears my dresses. I don't need to make *publicité* with the stars. If you want to be well known, you need to have somebody like Arnault. If you have big talents, you have to have a lot of millions to push your talents. You can't make it on your talents alone because you need a lot of millions to have promotions, to push your name. I know one day I need to find somebody like Arnault.'

There's an advert on the streets of Paris for a new restaurant. 'Finally,' it says, 'a restaurant which isn't fashionable.' Somebody is trying to start a fashion for the unfashionable. Fashion is always chasing its tail, and it is impossible to find its source, certainly not at the couture shows, which are ever more the apexes of invisible marketing empires exploiting an almost scientific law: everybody wants to wear something that everybody wants to be wearing.

After Sirop, I repair to the archives to confirm my growing suspicion that Christian Dior could not have invited me to his show, even if he had wanted to, because he is dead. I find that, indeed, he died in 1957. He has been deified as a brand, with John Galliano his current avatar. A couple of years before he died

Dior wrote: 'Elegance is within reach of every woman without spending extravagant sums for her wardrobe, if she adopts essential rules of fashion and sticks to choosing clothes which suit her personality. Simplicity, good taste and care are the basic rules of elegance and these three principles are priceless.' All the rest is head cheese.

31 August 2001

OLIVER BURKEMAN

How I got a table at the Ivy

Among the most cherished secrets of the rarefied upper stratosphere of British celebrity life are the secret telephone lines operated by the finest restaurants for the purposes of last-minute reservations. Knowledge of the number is a basic criterion for admission to the ranks of *über*-celebrityhood, and few such numbers are as cherished as that belonging to the Ivy, the impossibly exclusive celebrity haunt in the heart of London's theatreland, which was this week voted the capital's most popular restaurant by the dining guide *Zagat* for the fourth year running. For the lucky non-celebrity who manages to blag a reservation – usually done by ringing a year in advance – it is, the guide's contributors reported, so star-studded that it is 'like eating in front of the telly' except, presumably, that you might find yourself eating a £125 portion of Beluga caviar, which didn't form part of Tesco's range of microwaveable meals-for-one last time I looked.

So when Andrew Lloyd Webber inexplicably decided to commission Rolling Stone Ronnie Wood to paint a group portrait of the pinnacle of the British entertainment world, he chose the Ivy's internal list of its most loyal patrons as a guide. Elton John, David Furnish, Kate Moss, Naomi Campbell, Mick Jagger, Simon Callow, Joan Collins, John Birt and Janet Street Porter all made the cut. They are the initiates: they know the number.

And the number, I can exclusively reveal, is '192'. You ring it, and a Scottish woman answers. The conversation involves a coded ritual, in which you have to ask for 'the Ivy restaurant in London' and a computerised voice reveals another number. You call this, and ask for a table for two, for lunch, today, for half an hour's time. The person on the other end suppresses a snigger (another special code) and politely informs you that this will not be possible – all clearly part of the restaurant's attempt to deter non-celebrities. We arrive, as planned, at 1.30 p.m.

The American sociologist Erving Goffman, who is not on the Ivy's guest list, partly because he is dead, has elaborately described how social behaviour in all sorts of public spaces – restaurants, offices, shops – can be decoded by applying the metaphor of a theatre. Planned, public performances happen on stage; the backstage stuff is visible only to the privileged and trusted. And the most immediately obvious fact about the Ivy is that they've got the stage management all wrong.

The restaurant occupies an anonymous corner of two roads in Covent

Garden, its stained-glass windows rendering celebrity-viewing impossible from the street outside. But inside it's another story: even to enquire about reservations, you get to walk right into the centre of the restaurant, the heart of the celebrity action. Here, in the informal, lowish-ceilinged, cream-painted, wooden-floored dining area, the privileged access is open to everyone, for nothing.

The only problem is that, while enquiring about the possibility of an immediate reservation, you have to hold your neck in place in order to avoid appearing to be there just to gawp at famous people, which causes muscle pains. You can study the bookings schedule at close quarters, too. (There is somebody called Cruise on it, but it's not Tom.)

And how weird is this: there actually is a table, available in a mere hour. (I'm careful not to mention the purpose of my quest, since the Ivy, according to rumour, shuns press attention, being above such things.) Would I like to have a drink in the bar while I waited? The prospect of drinking alone for an hour, nakedly exposing myself as a celebrity-watcher, does not appeal. I mumble something about having to step outside to phone my dining companion. The call takes one minute. Self-congratulatory thoughts about how easy it had proved to pierce the self-reinforcing myth of celebrity exclusiveness amply fill the remaining fifty-nine.

We take our seats at 2.30 p.m. The first thing you notice is the attitude of the serving staff, which is utterly bereft of all posh-restaurant snootiness, exuding the trademark understatedness that marks out an establishment as truly upscale. The second thing you notice is the restaurant critic and acclaimed comic novelist A. A. Gill, dining with two other men. (Gill is so closely identified with the Ivy that he even features on the menu as author of a book on the restaurant and its feted owners, Jeremy King and Chris Corbin.)

We eat, respectively, salmon fishcake and navarin of lamb, both spectacular, and both accompanied with the waiter's recommendation of pommes allumettes, which turn out to be the Ivy's only concession to pretension, because they're french fries, although, admittedly, superior ones. The lamb costs £13.75 the fishcake £11.75 – which would be sensationally good value even if Zoe Ball wasn't seated half a metre away. Zoe is, sadly, our only celebrity sighting, although somebody who leaves just as we are entering may have been Charlotte Church's former manager, Jonathan Shalit.

But, as we move on to Scandinavian iced berries in hot white-chocolate sauce and hazelnut ice cream, the truth begins to dawn: starting your meal at the Ivy at 2.30 p.m. is nothing to be proud of whatsoever. You can tell it in the sympathetic expressions of the waiters: dining at 2.30 p.m. marks you out as a celebrity-spotter rather than a celebrity. It means you haven't got to hurry along to your next high-powered assignment. It means you can't afford the £425 bottle of wine that is the crowning glory of the wine list, and wouldn't be able to figure out why it was better than the cheaper red you bought by the glass even if you could. It means, in short, that you are nobody. The celebrity bubble, it turns out, is rather harder to pierce. It is a flawlessly self-reinforcing system: the non-famous people come to look at the famous people. The famous people come because they need to be looked at by non-famous people, to feel secure in their sense of themselves as famous people. And the secret number stays a secret.

Lunch for two, excluding wine and service, but including a panoramic view of the restaurant critic and comic novelist A. A. Gill, £54.50.

4 October 2001

JESS CARTNER-MORLEY

Let them eat cake

I am eating Jennifer Lopez's wedding cake. It has soft layers of sponge between wedges of nutty chocolate that taste like melted Baci (an Italian sweetmeat). On a velvet sofa a few yards away, Jennifer and whatsisname are soppily feeding morsels to each other like the newlyweds they are. My slice has the loop of a 'J' on the pink and white icing. I am considering keeping it as a souvenir.

I am not, I should point out, in the habit of gatecrashing celebrity weddings. My presence here is entirely above board. The embossed invitation in my jacket pocket reads: 'Donatella Versace has the pleasure of inviting Jess Cartner-Morley to a dinner celebrating the wedding of Jennifer Lopez and Chris Judd. Tuesday 2 October, 9.30 p.m., Villa Fontanelle, Lake Como.'

The telephone call had come two days before. Donatella is having a small dinner for her honeymooning friends, at home in Como. Am I free? Funnily enough, I think I might just have a window for that. Donatella's parties, after all, are legendary. And a celebrity wedding dinner: well, it's like *Hello!* come to life.

Word spreads quickly. Like musical chairs, there are never quite enough of Donatella's invites to go round. Wardrobe crises loom, and are disregarded (with Jennifer Lopez in the room, no one is going to be looking at anyone else). And there are etiquette issues to be negotiated. What is the form when invited to the wedding party of someone you don't actually know? Does one buy them a toaster?

The big question, though, is why we're invited at all. Much as I enjoy my own company, I find it hard to believe the Lo-Judds personally requested spending part of their honeymoon with me. There must be another explanation. Rumours fly: Donatella is lending them the villa for their honeymoon (true, I think) and they are giving her some glitzy publicity in return; Donatella will use the occasion to announce that she is producing the J-Lo clothing line (not true, thankfully.)

Thirty minutes out of Milan, suburbia gives way to beautiful mountain landscape. The driver Donatella has kindly lent me asks how many times I've stayed at Villa Fontanelle before. He is disappointed that I've never been there. He has heard it's very beautiful.

He's right, of course. At the end of cobbled lanes thick with the scent of citronella candles, Villa Fontanelle is a lakeside palazzo of dreamy elegance. The entrance is flanked by violinists on plinths and waiters with trays of pink champagne: in a typically Donatella touch, they all wear black masks, lending an air of *Eyes Wide Shut* hedonism.

The hostess and guests of honour are still upstairs, leaving us mere mortals to gawp in peace. Those looking for Versace rhinestones to sneer at are disappointed: all is in impeccable taste, with thousands of tiny scented candles and blush-tinted orchids. The view from the sitting-room balcony is Disney-beautiful: candle-edged lily pond giving way to fireflies buzzing across the clear lake, full moon above the smoky mountains beyond, lights twinkling in distant hills.

It is now 10 p.m. This continental late dinner time is all very sophisticated, but I'm starving. Fortified with canapés (caviar on melba toast, obviously), I stake out the territory with fellow gawpers: in the absence of a seating plan, it is vital to work out where the important people are likely to sit and position ourselves at the next table. From this vantage point, we take a celebrity count. Frankly, it's a bit mediocre. There is Patsy Kensit, who looks as if she is about to burst into tears, but might just be overdoing the pout; Jamie Theakston, looking tall and gawky surrounded by diminutive, gelled Italians; a very pretty girl in a red dress who someone said was Michael Caine's daughter; and, oddly, the former *EastEnders* actor Paul Nicholls. There are no pastel suits or big hats. Disappointingly instead, it's a sea of this season's black Versace.

The gleam of candyfloss hair in the candlelight signals the arrival of Donatella, in a clinging, floor-length leopard-print dress with silver sparkly bits, closely followed by Jennifer and Chris. La Lopez is in ponytail, hoop earrings and a tight jade-green satin all-in-one jump suit. I'm disappointed that we don't get to see the £50,000 Valentino dress, but I guess that would have been rude, given who her hostess is and there's no denying that she looks incredible.

Everyone applauds the new couple, who, irritatingly, upset our plans by taking a table in the marquee, which we had written off as B-list. After gnocchi with porcini, we relocate to the centre of the action, hovering nonchalantly on sofas, so I can't tell you what the main course was.

Now, I know that the cool thing would be to say it was all very dull, and I would have had more fun in the pub. True, lots of glamorous parties are utterly tedious. When the crowd are fashion people, the atmosphere wilts from lack of sexual crackle and pop: most of the men are gay, and the few that aren't are so intimidated by being outnumbered 20:1 by beautiful women that they skulk in corners drinking. But it would have required serious pretensions to miserygutdom to be arch about this do. A wedding party gives everyone an excuse to drop the veneer of seen-it-all-before boredom and be excited. Everyone claps and grins along to the slightly embarrassing salsa troupe when the newlyweds dance, commoners and B-list celebrities alike stand and coo. And for whatever reason, they don't seem to mind grinning strangers eating their cake. Ain't love grand?

PASSING THROUGH

Austin, 20 January 2001

IAN MCEWAN

Malcolm Bradbury

Like Howard Kirk, the academic Machiavelli of *The History Man*, Malcolm liked a good party. Just as that novel is structured round social gatherings, so were the literary conferences over which Malcolm brilliantly presided. A Cambridge college, a German monastery set in a desert of potato fields, a disintegrating Polish palace, were some of the settings for the best intellectual revels of the eighties and nineties.

Music, dancing and sex were not conspicuous ingredients. The business was talking and drinking – complementary human pleasures in which Malcolm took serious delight. After the last conference session of the afternoon, people would begin to gather in the bar and the circles formed. Limitless wine, writers far from home with nowhere else to go, nothing else to do: a delicious freedom was in the air, and the anticipation of a long journey into the night across unknown territory.

Naturally, for such a social creature, the seminar was Malcolm's element. I remember the first I attended, in October 1970. I had arrived at the University of East Anglia to do the MA in literature. The other outsider was Jon Cook from Cambridge, who is now dean of studies at UEA. Malcolm was in his late thirties then, and with his piled-up hair, narrow knitted tie and lopsided grin there was something of the miscreant teddy boy about him. In his hesitant, lilting voice – so hard to place, that accent – he set out for us the course of study ahead – nineteenth-century comparative literature, the modern American novel, literary theory – and then led us into a general discussion about the novel.

It was a brilliant session. Within minutes, it seemed, he had communicated a sense of adventure – the vitality of the novel as a form, its deep seriousness, its variety, the pleasures as well as the instruction in life it conveyed, its rich past and unguessable future. The general discussion began – a more formal version of the partying years ahead of us.

Malcolm was always a good listener. He emboldened his students to feel clever. He could make the most reticent of them feel like Oscar Wilde. It was part of Malcolm's automatic generosity to laugh easily at other people's jokes. Who can forget that delighted, whinnying giggle?

I would have denied it at the time, but I was keen to impress him. I think we were all intellectual show-offs that day. I remember parading my reading of Ortega y Gasset. Jon Cook appeared to be the world expert on Hegel. How tolerant Malcolm must have been. But he knew what he was about. We came away exhilarated, and determined to start on the huge reading list he had given us.

There was no dedicated creative writing course at UEA in 1970. However, along with the academic work, one was permitted to submit fiction at the end of the year in place of a long essay. This was a startling innovation in those days.

Three weeks after our first seminar, I gave Malcolm an essay on the American novelist, John Barth, and a carbon copy of my first short story, 'Conversation With a Cupboardman'. We met in a pub to discuss the story. He was mostly interested in getting me to describe what I was trying to do. I didn't really know. The story seemed to have written itself.

'I like it,' he said at last, unemphatically. 'It's publishable. But let's not think about that now. What are you going to write next?'

'Another short story. It's about a boy anxious to lose his virginity who makes love to his younger sister.'

'Can I have it by the end of the month?'

I handed in essays to Malcolm on Borges, Mailer, and on theories of representation, and I continued to give him stories, some of which were collected up later into my first book. It was not his style to interfere in the style, structure or content of what I did. But he knew how to motivate.

Fiction, as I was seeing it through his eyes, was the highest calling. I continued to fulfil the academic requirements, but I only cared about the stories. Malcolm was my reading public. I wrote in the certainty that I would receive a close reading – and this was an extraordinary privilege.

His reading list alone was changing my life. It was the Americans, above all, that he wanted us to read. The ambition, the social range, the expressive freedom of American writing made English fiction seem poky and grey. To find bold and violent colours became my imperative. Echoes of Roth and Burroughs crept into my stories. The struggle with influence, Malcolm told me once in the pub, is part of the pleasure of finding your own way.

In the years that followed we met from time to time in whatever monastery or palace the British Council had rented for conferences. There, Malcolm's tentative, judicious style granted a licence to younger writers. He was fair, so we could be savage in our judgments. As a critic, he lacked cruelty almost to a fault. He was an instinctive celebrator, rather than destroyer, of reputations. However late it got, Malcolm would be one of the last to get to bed. What he relished was a conversation with a direction, a beat. Gossip was fine too.

Another bottle is opened. A certain writer, someone says, no longer does interviews. Only press conferences. Publicity hunger versus reclusiveness bring us to Pynchon, until the fatwa in 1989, the world's most hunted writer. Inflated, whimsical, a world view stifled by paranoia, someone says. Malcolm hears this out, then defends inflated, only to a certain cast of English mind – to some novelists paranoia is not a disabling mental condition, but the motor of ingenious plot making.

By way of Melville, through Kafka, we arrive at an eminent novelist. The consensus around the table is that her sentences are no good – cliché-heavy, unrhythmic, no surprises. Therefore, she is no bloody good at all. Malcolm champions her: it's true up to a point about the sentences, but there's a certain kind of writing that gives pleasure through its design, its architecture. In the geometry of these moral schemes there's a beauty that no individual sentence can yield.

Can a good novel be written badly? We've been around this a number of times before. And who are today's best sentence makers? Malcolm makes the case for

Martin Amis, together with some exquisite examples he has by heart. Two weeks before, Martin has given Malcolm a finely executed pistol-whipping in the *Observer* for his novel, Rates of Exchange. The critic remains scrupulously detached from the workaday resentments of the novelist.

Since his death, there is one encounter with Malcolm that haunts me. In the dazed hour immediately after winning the Booker Prize in 1998, I was surrounded by excited voices, and pulled from press conference to interviews, and from crowded rooms to answer questions in television trucks and radio cars. At some point I lost the Booker publicity people, or they lost me, and I stepped through a door by mistake into an empty hall. I went through another door, and found myself in a long, straight, ill-lit corridor.

Coming towards me, from some distance away, were Malcolm and his wife Elizabeth. We approached each other as in dream, and I remember thinking, half seriously, that this was what it might be like to be dead. In the warmth of his embrace was concentrated all the generosity of this gifted teacher and writer. His artful reticence and his passion for literature transformed my life.

3 January 2001

STEPHEN MOSS

George Carman

When George Carman, who has died aged seventy-one, announced last August that he was retiring from the bar because of ill health, his home in Wimbledon was immediately besieged by the press. Carman, visibly sick and walking with difficulty, granted all an audience. He claimed to dislike the limelight, but he knew he was a star, and he enjoyed the fame that a string of sensational cases in the last twenty years of his career gave him.

Carman's case list was matchless: Jeremy Thorpe, the spy Geoffrey Prime, the Sun against Gillian Taylforth, Elton John, Tom Cruise and Nicole Kidman, Ken Dodd on charges of tax evasion, Imran Khan against Ian Botham, the *Guardian* against Jonathan Aitken, Mohamed Al Fayed against Neil Hamilton. He said that other QCs, in tax and shipping for example, were equally adept, but the difference was that his cases were the stuff of life, each one an unmissable piece of theatre.

He knew that was where his interest and his talent lay. 'I would not like to practise in areas of the law remote from the human condition and the human problem,' he once said. His view of cases was psychologically based: he sought to persuade his clients to 'remove their mental veils', and a key tactic was to observe each member of the jury and pick out individuals to whom he could appeal.

Carman was frequently criticised for character assassination in court – one victim, Jani Allan, whose sex life was held up to universal derision – told him that 'whatever award is given for libel, being cross-examined by you would not make it enough money'. But he had no regrets about the way lives withered in the face of his attacks. 'That's a matter of judgment for people who decide to involve themselves in the luxury of litigation,' he said brusquely.

There were also dark suggestions of skulduggery concerning the way in which last-minute pieces of evidence would suddenly appear. Carman put it down to good fortune. 'A lot of things turned up by chance. The Jani Allan diary [detailing her sex life] turned up in the course of the case it wasn't as if I kept it back. If we'd had it, we would have had to disclose it. Equally, with the Gillian Taylforth video ["I give good head," she declaimed to her fellow partygoers suggestively brandishing a sausage and wielding a bottle], two people arrived at a newspaper in the middle of the case.'

In the Taylforth case, in 1994, Carman successfully defended the *Sun*'s allegation that the *EastEnders* actress had had oral sex with her fiancé Geoff Knights in a Range Rover on a slipway off the A1. The case had everything: soap opera, sex and the plaintiff's delightful explanation that her fiancé had had to loosen his trousers because of an acute attack of pancreatitis. It made Carman a household name and the barrister who everyone wanted on their side in a libel action.

In 1996, the Pakistani cricketer Imran Khan hired Carman to defend him in a libel case brought by England cricket stars Ian Botham and Allan Lamb. The two England players sued Khan after he said that illegal ball-tampering was common among fast bowlers, and over a newspaper article in which he allegedly accused them of racism. Again, Carman won the day.

The following year, he represented the *Guardian* against Jonathan Aitken, who had sued the paper over allegations of improper contacts with middle eastern arms dealers. Aitken's case collapsed following another of Carman's trademark eleventh-hour revelations. 'The records of his wife and daughter's air trip to Switzerland emerged in the course of the case. We didn't have them at the start. We didn't know it was coming. More importantly, neither did he.'

His last major case was at the end of 1998, when another former Tory minister, Neil Hamilton, failed in his libel battle with Mohamed Al Fayed. By then, however, Carman was already fighting prostate cancer, and showed less sparkle in court than in the cases on which his reputation rests.

Carman became the best-known QC in the country, but he was hardly the barrister that central casting would have chosen. He once said that in a biopic of his life, he would like the foursquare John Thaw to play him. He was 5ft 3in, paunchy, and had a plummy voice that he had manufactured at Oxford, where he studied law after doing national service.

The northern accent of which he divested himself came from his native Blackpool. Both his parents worked in retailing, his father in furniture and his mother selling women's clothes. His mother was ambitious, both for herself and her son, and pushed the young Carman hard. He was educated at Upholland College in Lancashire, a Roman Catholic seminary, and briefly considered becoming a priest, though he later said it was only because he was attracted by the idea of delivering sermons. In any case, he discovered girls.

When he went up to Balliol College, Oxford, the accent had to go. 'I made a conscious effort to divest myself of a regional accent as soon as I realised I wanted to go into public life,' he later admitted. He also lost his Christian faith at Oxford, and found it difficult to cope with the death of his mother when he was in his twenties.

He practised on the northern circuit and found the early years a struggle. 'After five years, I was earning as much as a Manchester bus driver without over-time. I almost left the bar three times,' he recalled. But he resented suggestions that his twenty-five years in the north were merely a preparation for his fame in London. 'I wasn't some little country boy who came here,' he said. 'I'd studied law at Oxford, done my pupillage in London, and built up a successful practice on a great circuit that had produced many great advocates.' He became a QC in 1971.

Nevertheless, he accepted that the Jeremy Thorpe case, in which he success-fully defended the former Liberal leader against charges of conspiracy to murder the model Norman Scott, was the watershed in his career. It brought him south and put him on the front pages for the first time.

Carman remembered the career-changing moment precisely. 'I had met David Napley [Thorpe's solicitor] in the early seventies and worked for him intermit-tently,' he recalled. 'He rang me in 1978 to say that Thorpe was probably going to be committed for trial on charges of conspiracy to murder and that he was going to retain me. Thorpe was committed for trial – I heard it on the one o'clock news in Cornwall – and I realised that it would be the greatest profes-sional challenge I had faced, and that it might affect my career. It did. Thorpe was tried in May 1979 and it was a sensation. The case had everything, includ-ing the dog Rinka.'

Success in the Thorpe case projected Carman into the super-league and, now based in London, a string of headline-grabbing cases cemented his reputation. He defended Geoffrey Prime, the GCHQ spy, a scion of the Vestey family who had beheaded his wife and put her head in the freezer (Carman secured a ver-dict of 'diminished responsibility'), Maria Aitken – the sister of Jonathan – against charges of smuggling cocaine and Ken Dodd against charges of tax eva-sion. His reputation as a coiner of *bons mots* is exaggerated, but here he did pro-duce a memorable line when he declared that 'some accountants are comedians, but comedians are never accountants'. His brother-in-law was an accountant, so he knew what he was talking about.

Carman was proud of winning Dodd's acquittal, and even prouder of secur-ing the freedom of Dr Leonard Arthur, the paediatrician charged with attempted murder after prescribing 'nursing care only' for a Down's syndrome baby. Carman's summing-up was a masterpiece. 'He [Arthur] could, like Pontius Pilate, have washed his hands of the matter,' Carman told the jury. 'He did not, because good doctors do not turn away. Are we to condemn him as a criminal because he helped two people at the time of their greatest need? Are we to con-demn a doctor because he cared?'

He prepared his closing speeches carefully, but did not, as critics suggested, practise them in front of a mirror. He had the first three or four sentences and the all-important peroration written down, and delivered them verbatim, but for the middle section he would work from notes to allow for some degree of spontaneity.

Carman is likely to be remembered primarily as a libel barrister, but his remarkable run of successes in criminal cases in the eighties should be given due weight. He described libel as the 'last chapter' in his career, and did not make his first serious incursion into the field until the Sonia Sutcliffe case in 1990. Before that, he had done civil cases, personal injury and contract, as well as criminal cases. He was invited to become a judge in Hong Kong in the eighties, but declined. His excuse then was that his wife was unwell, but he later said that he would have found it hard to keep quiet on the bench, and preferred the 'blood and sand of the arena'.

Carman married three times, though only listed two of his marriages in Who's Who. When pursued on this point by the *Daily Mail*, which was attempting to 'carmanise' Carman, he said that he had suppressed the details of his first marriage to protect his wife, whom he had married very young, and that the general public did not have to submit to the same rules as litigants. Each of his marriages ended in divorce. He is survived by his son Dominic, and four grandchildren.

13 January 2001

JON COOK

Lorna Sage

Lorna Sage, who has died in Norwich two days before her fifty-eighth birthday, was one of the most brilliant literary critics of her generation. The success of her memoir, *Bad Blood*, brought her a new readership at the end of her life. But before the book's publication she had established an international reputation as a critic, scholar and writer who made reviewing into her own distinctive art form.

She was a charismatic teacher at the University of East Anglia, where she worked from 1965 until her death. Her passion for literature and her learning inspired generations of students who worked with her. She was not a person who needed to be reminded that good teaching is central to the profession of an academic.

Sage was born in Hanmer, a village on the English–Welsh border. Her memoir gives a vivid account of her childhood. She learnt early on about the strangeness of families and the value of reading. Initially, she was brought up in the village rectory with her grandparents and her mother. Her grandfather, who lived a life of sexual scandal and frustrated ambition, introduced her to books. Her grandmother introduced her to the secret lives of women.

Reading provided an alternative world, a way of living apart in the midst of family turbulence. When her father returned from the second world war, the family moved from the old rectory to a newly built council house. But the new possibilities presented by postwar reconstruction were shrouded by older patterns of English provincial custom and prejudice. In her own description, Sage was an 'apprentice misfit'. This sense of self fuelled her determination to make her own way on her own terms.

In 1953, she moved across the border into England as a pupil at Whitchurch high school for girls. Here, she discovered a love of Latin to add to her love of reading. She learnt, too, the importance of being top of the class: intellectual success was a means of keeping moral disapproval at bay. Outside the proprieties of an English girls' grammar school, there were other fascinations: boys and the discovery of the power of her own beauty. Sage grew up with the sounds of rock 'n' roll and a sense that the old ways were no longer any good.

At fifteen, she met Vic Sage, the man shortly to become her first husband. At sixteen, she was married and pregnant. At seventeen, she gave birth to her first and only child, Sharon. Undaunted, Sage continued to pursue her intellectual ambitions. She applied to Durham University to read English, and was awarded a scholarship. Her brilliance found a way through circumstances that might well have overwhelmed other women of her age and class.

St Aidan's College altered its rules to allow access to women students who were also wives and mothers. Vic had also been awarded a place to read English at Durham. In 1961, a unique student family took up residence in a traditional English university.

Even though their marriage was to end in divorce, the intellectual and emotional partnership Sage established with Vic was to last throughout her life. Their careers ran in parallel: both graduated with first-class degrees in 1964; both moved on to Birmingham University, where Sage studied at the Shakespeare Institute. In 1965, she became an assistant lecturer in English at the recently established University of East Anglia. In 1967, Vic took up a similar post at the same university.

The institution that she joined was small, intense and experimental. Malcolm Bradbury and Angus Wilson were colleagues. The Shakespearian critic and scholar, Nicholas Brooke, who had taught Sage at Durham University, was also there, as was the writer, Jonathan Raban. Both became close and lasting friends and discerning readers of her work.

In the late sixties, another significant friendship began with the historian and politician Patricia Hollis (now a government minister). Young women academics in a predominantly masculine environment, Sage and Hollis developed their friendship through their teaching.

Well before the invention of 'new historicism' they taught what was, at the time, a unique course on the urban landscapes of the 1830s and 1840s. Questioning a simple-minded distinction between fact and fiction, they analysed the rhetoric of nineteenth-century fiction, philosophy and government reports, finding in the forms of language a guide to the mentality of a culture.

This kind of teaching appealed to Sage, precisely because it made teaching a form of research. She believed university teaching should open up fields of inquiry rather than deliver settled doctrines. Her teaching grew out of the latest discoveries in her reading. Her seminars were intellectual events, where some new line of critical thought would unfold.

If Sage was a charismatic teacher, throughout the late sixties and the seventies she developed her identity as a critic. Early publications on Milton grew out of her work as a graduate student. These reflected her growing interest in neo-Platonism, an interest that was to take her to Italy and the archives and galleries of Florence.

Neo-Platonism was a source of endless fascination. It played a crucial role in the English poetic tradition, something that could be traced in the work of Milton, Shelley and, in a transatlantic version, the poetry of Wallace Stevens. More than a set of philosophical doctrines, it offered a way of both imagining and managing the world, it was possible to be both this worldly and other-worldly at the same time.

Sage's major study of neo-Platonism and English poetry was uncompleted at the time of her death. Instead, there was an abundance of other published work. During the seventies, she established her reputation as an authoritative reviewer of contemporary fiction. She worked with a number of distinguished literary editors, including Terence Kilmartin at the *Observer*, and Ian Hamilton at *New Review*.

For Sage, reviewing was serious criticism. Her habit was to read all the available published work of any author she was reviewing. She was deeply engaged by the idea of writing about literature before it became canonical. Her reviewing was an opportunity to forge a style that could be both intelligent and accessible.

Literary London became part of her actual and imaginative topography. It provided an alternative to academic life, but also a complement to it. Moving back and forth between what Sage described as 'Grub Street and academe', she could combine the intellectual authority of the university with the stylistic energy of the great literary journalist. It also enabled her to satisfy that temperamental need to be inside and outside whatever world she was in.

By the end of the seventies, her first marriage had ended and her second marriage to Rupert Hodson had begun. This relationship was intimately connected to another doubling of her world: her research had taken her to Italy, where they met. She decided that she wanted to live in Italy and England, and developed a regular pattern of teaching at UEA during term time and writing in Italy during vacations.

New and important friendships developed with Gore Vidal and Angela Carter. The friendship with Carter was deeply important to Sage, and coincided with another development in her work. From the late seventies onwards, she published widely on women writers and woman's writing. In 1983, her study of Doris Lessing appeared. In 1991, she published *Women in The House of Fiction*, a brilliant study of women's fiction in the twentieth century. In 1994, a short book on Angela Carter came out, and in the same year she edited a collection of essays on Carter, *The Flesh and The Mirror*.

But her concern was not simply to write about women, rather to make their work more widely and intelligently known. She wrote introductions to fiction by Katherine Mansfield, Christina Stead and Virginia Woolf. In 1994, she was appointed editor- in-chief of *The Cambridge Guide to Women's Writing in English*.

As with so much of her work, Sage's engagement with women's writing combined passion with intelligence. She was attracted to women who wrote in order to survive and to overcome the cultural circumstances they had to endure. She was a feminist, but not one who wanted to live out her life as a public martyrdom. She was contemptuous of the way that men intrigued against women, but wanted to make her way in the world as she found it. She played a central role in the academic life of UEA. She was twice dean of the school of English and

American studies and, in 1994, was appointed to a chair in English literature.

The last five years of her life were increasingly dominated by the illness that eventually caused her death. Sage did not suffer fools gladly, and often the world seemed increasingly full of them. Although physically diminished by illness, she continued to write and teach with undiminished energy. Her *Cambridge Guide* was published in 1990, but what preoccupied her most was the completion of the memoir that provides such a compelling portrait of her as a young woman.

Life grew very hard for her. Her second marriage was under strain, but she was heroically supported by Sharon and a small circle of friends. At the time of her death, she had many projects in train and more to give to a literary culture she had done so much to shape. She is survived by Rupert Hodson, Vic Sage, Sharon and her granddaughter, Olivia.

19 January 2001

POLLY TOYNBEE

Auberon Waugh

De mortuis nil nisi bonum is a good enough maxim if it means you should not stamp on the libel-free grave of someone you never dared rubbish face to face in life. But I did. And he retaliated – often. Auberon Waugh's death has been eulogised at phenomenal length, not least in two pages in this organ (five pieces in the *Telegraph*). He was a 'genius' who 'will surely be seen as the Dean Swift of our day', writes his old friend A. N. Wilson. Someone else cites Dr Johnson, forsooth. 'The greatest journalist of my generation', writes Lord Gowrie cringingly of the man who hounded him mercilessly for years. 'All prigs and puritans will sleep easier in their beds tonight', opines the *Telegraph* leader.

In the *Guardian* obituary Geoffrey Wheatcroft says Waugh's foes were 'baffled by the boyish camaraderie of old Fleet Street, not to say its tradition of ecumenical friendship'. And baffled we remain. I remember it well – the old world of El Vino's wine bar in Fleet Street, where left-wing lambs and right-wing lions downed their differences in bottles of champagne – (no women allowed at the bar). It was all just a game, old boy, at the end of the day, once the copy had been filed. What did it matter what you wrote or who you wrote it for so long as it was witty, clever and preferably wicked? Everyone in Grub Street had their saleable trade mark, right or left, but was anything really serious?

The world of Auberon Waugh is a coterie of reactionary fogeys centred on the *Spectator* and the *Telegraph* who affect an imaginary style of thirties gent – Evelyn was the icon. Battered brown trilby, chalk-stripes, sit-up-and-beg bike with a basket full of books from the London Library are the accoutrements. The mindset is all Evelyn Waugh too – the smells and bells of aristocracy and old Catholicism (recusant priest-holers only – God forbid any happy-clappy stuff). Effete, drunken, snobbish, sneering, racist and sexist, they spit poison at anyone vulgar enough to want to improve anything at all. Liberalism is the archenemy – Shirley Williams was Waugh's *bête noire*. While do-nothing conservatism is their mode, they enjoy extremism of any complexion and excoriate the dreary toil of incremental improvement – bor-ring, sin-cere and social workerish. The worst thing is 'doing good'. Their snobbery is of a vulgarity beyond belief – yahoos capering in genteel suits.

Their language is as self-consciously class identifying as their voices – Waugh sounded like something out of the BBC sound archives. Their words cling to the prep school and nursery of the forties and fifties – hence that bizarre conservative epithet 'nanny' or 'nanny state' applied to the Labour women they especially loathe, as if every voter had a starched Norland nurse lurking in their mental attic. Many of the obits refer to Waugh's boast that he was 'a practitioner of the vituperative arts', but the limited vocabulary of this little tribe of scribes is reduced to those blasé upper-class generalities – ghastly, boring, silly, disgusting, odious, repulsive, bogus, hideous or goody-goody – house style *passim* in most of the *Spectator* and *Telegraph*, lazy in-words of an exclusive clique.

We might let Auberon Waugh rest in peace were it not for the mighty damage his clan has done to British political life, journalism and discourse in the postwar years. They have perpetuated the myth of the superior cultured English gent as an archetype. Although Waugh's loathing of American culture made him uniquely amongst this bunch a pro-European, (he loved to be a 'maverick'), this coterie has led the spirit of anti-Europeanism that pervades the Tory party and country. Christopher Booker, Richard Ingrams and the rest posit a brave little England of crusty, country-living, upper-class eccentrics versus the dread (another of their words) bureaucracy of Brussels. It's the old world charm of Whisky Galore mischief-making and John Buchan plucky patriots against the humourless foreign swine. They have contributed to a nation afraid of change or modernity, peddling false, sentimental tradition and an upper class yesterday unavailable to virtually everyone else. While pretending to debunk cant, they demolish every attempt at reform. 'Political correctness' is the tired, lazy little label attached to all change for the better. Oh, how naughty of Waugh to compare a wine to 'a bunch of dead chrysanthemums on the grave of a still-born West Indian baby'. Swiftian? Knickers.

As a style of journalism, theirs is empty and destructive. All that matters is a joke or two. Swift was serious, used humour as a deadly weapon of conviction and risked jail for his opinions. Knee-jerk abuse of any politician was Waugh's stock-in-trade when he was a political commentator. It was not, as he pretended, a badge of some kind of honesty but quite the contrary, an idle unwillingness to engage with any politician's attempt to make life better for anyone else – least of all 'the workers' he used to mock in order to shock. The pens of these lofty jeerers drip with universal indiscriminate malice over good and bad people alike, with as much interest in the difference as Jonathan Aitken's 'sword of truth'.

Don't imagine that the breed is dying out. Boris Johnson, editor of the *Spectator*, is only thirty-six, a writer of just this humorous stamp, with mannerisms to match. The fact that the obits proclaim Waugh 'the most courteous and loveable of friends', or that Boris Johnson is also a charming and affable fellow is neither here nor there: by their printed words we shall judge them (and be judged). Johnson and I are currently arguing weekly on television. After our first encounter he pressed me to write a piece for the *Spectator* about why the right is so nasty and why liberals are on the whole nicer – his idea and something he disarmingly thought true: good medicine for his complacent readership, he said. I doubt he wanted them converted, just aroused.

It was tempting but I refused. He grew indignant. Why not? I explained it concerned exactly that 'ecumenical tradition' in old Fleet Street that Wheatcroft so extolled yesterday. Why would I want to write in a right-wing magazine graced by Bruce Anderson as political commentator, the unspeakable Taki and a fusillade of writers of the ilk described above? Politics in the *Spectator*, I said, is just an Eton Wall Game between left/right tribes. Joining in the mud-slinging fun only adds to the general idea that the *Spectator* is right – it's all a jolly jape and none of it really matters. Consider William Hague – tax cuts for the rich, public service cuts for the rest, pulling out of Europe, stuffing yet more into prison, installing Bush's missile system. Where's the joke? I never understood why Michael Foot and A. J. P. Taylor wrote for Beaverbrook as his trophy lefties, satisfying the right's perennial wish to think that in the end there is no real difference between civilised Oxbridge-educated people sitting cosily around the same dinner table.

27 February 2001

MATTHEW ENGEL

Donald Bradman

Sir Donald Bradman, who has died aged ninety-two, was the greatest cricketer of the twentieth century and the greatest batsman who ever lived. He was also arguably the most famous of all Australians – and among the most influential. Sport played a major role in giving the young nation of Australia global standing, self-belief and a sense of identity. The tragic boxer Les Darcy and the racehorse Phar Lap played a part in this process, but nothing could match the phenomenon of Bradman.

His batting statistics are indelible and incredible, incomparably ahead of everyone else who has played the game. Seventy-two other players – including some indifferent ones – have scored more runs in first-class cricket, and his totals of Test runs and centuries have been surpassed. But, in Bradman's time, a first-class match in Australia, let alone a Test match, was an event, and then the war intervened.

He thus went to the crease in major cricket only 338 times, but in 117 of those innings returned with a century – a strike-rate above one in three, better than twice the ratios achieved by such greats as Jack Hobbs, Len Hutton, Walter Hammond or Denis Compton. His first-class average was 95.14; his nearest rival is on 71.

Most famously of all, he went out at the Oval in his last Test innings needing only four to finish with an average of 100, and was bowled second ball by Eric Hollies, of Warwickshire, for a duck. It was as though the gods of cricket had reclaimed the invulnerability they had loaned him – though his final average,

99.94, remains so resonant that the Australian Broadcasting Commission uses it as its post-office box number.

In life, as in cricket, he came closer to immortality, outliving his contemporaries, rivals and enemies. There were always plenty of those – despite the near-perfection of his cricket, he was a complex, often troubled, man. Though he achieved everyone else's fantasies, he never seemed to find true fulfilment.

Yet he embodied the Australian dream. He was a country boy, born in Cootamundra, in rural New South Wales. His father was a farmer and carpenter – not rich, not poor. None of his schoolfriends lived near him, so, in solitary moments, he invented a game that involved throwing a golf ball at the base of the family water-tank. He then had to whack it with a cricket stump. Though the ball fizzed off the tank at high speed and unpredictable angles, by the time he was ten, Bradman could whack it with the stump more often than not.

When he was twelve, he made a 100 for Bowral high school against Mittagong. For a while, he played more tennis than cricket and seemed to be settling for a career in estate agency. However, when he was seventeen, Bradman played for Bowral against Wingello, who had the ace leg-spin bowler Bill O'Reilly. Bradman was dropped twice early on off O'Reilly, who got him out first ball when the game resumed the following week. In between, he scored 234.

Next match, he scored 300. In October 1926, he was invited to Sydney to practise for the state squad. A year later, aged nineteen, he was in the New South Wales team, scoring a century on debut. The following year, he scored 1,690 runs, a new Australian record. By November 1928, he was in the Test team, and seared by a match that England won by 678 runs. Bradman made 18 and one, and was dropped from the next game to be replaced by one Dr O. E. Nothling. He was soon back, and no one ever thought of dropping him again.

England, at this stage, were in one of their rare intervals of superiority over Australia, and had the world's leading batsman in Walter Hammond. Bradman scored two centuries in the series, one in defeat, one in a consolation victory. No one had the faintest idea that England would not win the Ashes again by fair means for another twenty-four years, and that one man would be primarily responsible for this.

They got an inkling in the first week of 1930, when Bradman scored 452 not out for New South Wales against Queensland. But he was still rated behind another youngster, the more stylish Archie Jackson. Bradman's unclassical back-lift would, it was thought, find him out on soft English wickets. In the event, Jackson failed in England (he died of TB three years later) and Bradman's tour was a triumphal procession.

It might be easy to imagine Bradman from this distance as a dull and mechanical batsman, something of a Geoffrey Boycott. In fact, he scored his runs at a phenomenal rate – the 452 came in 415 minutes, barely imaginable today. When he got to England, the style became more firmly established. It was almost metronomic, starting with the push for one first ball.

He was the master of timing. His eye was so extraordinary that he could make up his mind what shot to play a microsecond later than anyone else and his judgment was so impeccable that the decision was almost always right. He eliminated the risk that comes from lofting the ball, and hardly ever hit a six in consequence.

His batting was both intuitive and intellectual. As Neville Cardus said, he was that rare and devastating combination, 'a genius with an eye for business'. A Bradman innings was not as beautiful as one by Trumper or Woolley or Jackson, but it was awesome, and he drew unprecedented crowds from people just anxious to say they saw one.

In England in 1930, he became a colossus. He began by inaugurating his tradition of an opening double-century at Worcester, and hit 1,000 runs before the end of May. In the five-match Ashes series, he scored 974, 69 more than the record set by Hammond eighteen months earlier: 254 at Lord's, 338 at Leeds, 232 at the Oval. At Leeds, he made 309 in a day: a modern Test batsman does well to score a century in that time. Cardus insisted that essentially this was a triumph for cricketing orthodoxy: 'He is a purist in a hurry: he administers the orthodox in loud and apostolic knocks.'

Hammond was displaced completely as the world's batting champion, and there are those who argue that he never recovered as a cricketer or as a man. There have been moments when other cricketers – Denis Compton in 1947, Brian Lara in 1995 – have been almost as dominating, and perhaps even more exciting. But for Bradman, this was just the beginning.

He returned to Australia a hero, and progressed east from Fremantle by train to be greeted rapturously at every railway halt along the Nullarbor Plain. His team-mates, meanwhile, were making the transcontinental journey by sea, and growing ever more jealous. Though Bradman was assiduous at giving credit where it was due, the classic cricket team dichotomy between the individual hero and the collective was now in place. Inevitably also, skirmishing began with the Australian cricketing authorities, who fined him £50 for writing a book about the tour.

These battle lines remained in place throughout the thirties, and, in 1931, he came close to accepting an offer to play Lancashire League cricket for Accrington. There was insufficient money in cricket to provide the income his celebrity demanded, and a hasty sponsorship deal had to be cobbled together. The wicket was made slightly higher and wider in 1930–31 still Bradman scored prodigiously with further double centuries against the West Indies and South Africa. Some in England thought they had spotted a weakness in him against top-class wrist-spin. But as England came to Australia in 1932–3, their new captain, Douglas Jardine, had other plans.

Thus began the most notorious Test series of all time, in which England regained the Ashes by unleashing their fast bowlers to bowl bouncers at the Australians, with a field (now illegal) concentrated behind the stumps on the leg-side. This meant the batsmen had no alternative but to fend the ball to the fieldsmen, or get hurt. Imperialist arrogance, and poor reporting of the tour, ensured that the English establishment and public were slow to realise the sheer degeneracy of this strategy. The initial reaction was that the Australians were whinging, and that a way had been found to beat them again and blunt Bradman at last. Even in these circumstances, he averaged nearly fifty-seven.

When bodyline was repudiated, and normality restored, Bradman resumed his untroubled progress. He was a fraction less domineering in the remaining three Ashes series of the decade, but only a fraction. In 1934, he scored another triple-century in the Leeds Test. In 1936-7, he led Australia back from 2-0 down with triumphant performances in the last three matches. In 1938, as captain, he again scored 1,000 runs in May, and averaged more than 100 throughout. It should have been the happiest, as well as the most triumphant, decade any sports- man has ever had. It was never quite like that.

After the 1934 tour, Bradman was taken ill with acute appendicitis and peritonitis. He missed the 1934-5 season while recuperating. He moved from New South Wales to South Australia to accept an offer from a cricket-loving stockbroker (later jailed for fraud), which left some ill-feeling. Even the travelling got to him: he was seasick and later airsick.

And the tensions within the Australian team worsened. Bradman, a pernickety, near-teetotal Protestant (religion mattered in thirties Australia) with a Calvinist work ethic, was not a natural soulmate of the witty, happy-go-lucky, left-leaning Roman Catholics like O'Reilly and Fingleton, both of them later journalists with a waspish turn of phrase, often used against Bradman. 'Fingleton,' Bradman complained later, 'conducted a vendetta against me all his life.'

Moreover, though his marriage to Jessie was a triumph – and was to remain so for sixty-five years until her death in 1997 – the Bradmans ' eldest son was to live for only a few hours. Their daughter, Shirley, developed cerebral palsy and their surviving son, John, had polio as a child. He pulled through, but was often estranged from his father later. Son and daughter survive their father.

The whispering increased after 1939, when cricket became less relevant. While other Australians had daredevil wars, Bradman – bizarrely enough – was declared to have defective eyesight, and spent the time in Adelaide. He was apparently often unwell, and there was some doubt that he would ever return to play for Australia in the hastily arranged series of 1946-7.

He did appear, though, and carried on where he left off, striding to 187 in the first postwar Test, more than England made in either innings, but only after refusing to walk for what England were certain was a perfectly fair slip catch by Jack Ikin when he had 28. In the next game, he scored 234. And so on. In 1948, pushing forty, he came back to England for his farewell tour.

By now, he seemed a mellower figure, willing to return the adulation of the crowds. His enemies in the dressing room had retired, the newer generation were less inclined to question his deification and, when cricketing mortality finally seized him at the Oval, it was possible to see it in very human terms.

John Arlott was commentating. 'I wonder if you see a ball very clearly on your last Test in England, on a ground where you've played out some of the biggest cricket of your life, and when the opposing team has just stood round you and given you three cheers, and the crowd had clapped you at the wicket...I wonder if you really see the ball at all.' But, came the cynical riposte: if Bradman had a tear in his eye, it was for the first time.

He was knighted in 1949, then slipped easily into the role of cricketing elder statesman. He gave up stockbroking and became a selector and administrator, dealing firmly with the throwing crisis that convulsed the game at the end of the fifties. He played golf, off scratch (of course), remaining rooted all the time to his marriage and suburban home in Adelaide.

With elaborate courtesy, Bradman replied personally to all his correspondents into his nineties. But the answer was nearly always 'No', if it was a request for an interview. He spoke about bodyline in 1983, the fiftieth anniversary. After that came near-total silence. Eventually, he stopped going to the Adelaide Oval, and became reclusive, indeed a bit of a curmudgeon, boycotting the celebrations laid on for his own ninetieth birthday.

However, when a Wisden panel in 2000 voted him the cricketer of the century, with 100 votes out of 100, he issued a statement of delight. His reputation as a cricketer has never been questioned. As a man, he remains enigmatic. Though his fame extended only to the cricketing countries, within its limits it far exceeded the transient public obsessiveness with a Gascoigne or a Beckham and, in his own buttoned-up way, Bradman found it desperately hard to cope.

'You can't tell youngsters today of the attraction of the fellow,' said one of his opponents, the England bowler Bill Bowes in 1983. 'I mean, business used to stop in the town when Bradman was playing and likely to go in – all the offices closed, the shops closed everybody went up to see him play.' 'Our Don Bradman' was a song of the thirties. But he was always his Don Bradman.

3 March 2001

JAY RAYNER

John Diamond

The journalist, writer and broadcaster John Diamond, who has died aged forty-seven, did not battle his illness bravely. Nor was he courageous in the face of death. He developed cancer and, despite treatment, it killed him.

As he wrote in his bestselling book, *C: Because Cowards Get Cancer Too*, first published in 1998: 'I despise the set of warlike metaphors that so many apply to cancer. My antipathy has nothing to do with pacifism, and everything to do with a hatred for the sort of morality which says that only those who fight hard against their cancer survive it, or deserve to survive it – the corollary being that those who lose the fight deserved to do so.'

It was the kind of clear-eyed opinion, acutely expressed, which John's enormous circle of friends and colleagues had come to expect of him.

It was a horrible irony that the illness that eventually ended his life was also, professionally, the making of him. He was successful before, of course: he was well known around media London as the master of the quickly delivered opinion piece, first person or otherwise, to a tight deadline. His career as a radio and television presenter was burgeoning, and he had earned enough money to indulge his fetish for electronic gadgetry, fine tailoring or overpowered motorbikes, on which he rarely went further than the corner shop.

But the column he published in his regular slot in *The Times*, in April 1997, in which he announced that a lump on his neck had been diagnosed as a cancerous tumour, changed everything.

As he continued to chart the course of his illness, through treatment to terminal diagnosis and beyond, there was a growing realisation among both readers and editors that his immense facility for language, previously expended for the most part on the smallest of domestic issues, had disguised a writer of immense talent and skill. His column won him a prestigious What the Papers Say award, and his book was received with glowing reviews, both of which events gave him huge pleasure.

John Diamond was born in Stoke Newington, north London, the son of a biochemist and a fashion designer, and one of three brothers. He remained close to his family, and was particularly proud of his secular Jewish upbringing, which informed almost all of his opinions. Though he travelled far from his childhood in east London – a serious shlep by taxi to Hammersmith – he liked people to know that he had started a long way outside the media world of which he became such a part.

Though he would eventually receive an honorary doctorate from Middlesex University, he was not good at exams. A scholarship to the City of London school was withdrawn after he failed his O-levels, and he left at sixteen to work as a solicitor's clerk. He managed, after passing a few exams in his spare time, to gain a place at teacher training college, and for four years taught drama and English at a girl's school in Hackney.

After leaving teaching he broke into journalism by joining a company that published newsletters about the property business. His boss wrote a column about property for the *Sunday Times*, and, during a three-week holiday, asked John to take it over in his absence. There, displaying the kind of chutzpah for which he became rightly famous among his friends, he went about the paper announcing himself as the deputy property editor and offering pieces on almost anything other than property. Within a few weeks he was working regularly on the *Sunday Times* magazine.

John's tastes were essentially as eclectic as those of the editors who commissioned him. A member of the Labour party from the age of sixteen, he did write a column on politics for the *Daily Mirror*, under the short-lived editorship of his friend Roy Greenslade, but, for the most part, his work was on the softer side. He wrote about everything and anything – from travel, cigars and cars, to the role of the fax machine in modern life and the importance of a good whisky in a man's life.

He had the true hack's hunger for the byline, and he would no doubt have found it galling that his death would give a number of his friends and rivals the opportunity for one the day after.

Until his illness literally stole his tongue, he was also a regular presenter on BBC radio, his talent for which was recognised by the judges in the Sony Radio Awards. A feverish interest in technology led to his presenting a series of *Tomorrow's World*, columns in computer magazines – for which he won awards – and, in the days before the rest of Fleet Street had properly mastered the machinery, a way of winning extra time if ever he was running close to a deadline.

If the circumstances called for it, he would file a first paragraph by modem – and then just hit a few random keys on the keyboards. The frantic editor would call John on his mobile to be told that something must have gone wrong with the modem, that he was away from home but would be able to refile on his return, thus winning him the extra time he needed.

If his copy sometimes arrived a little close to deadline, it was always worth waiting for. The decision to start writing about his cancer was, he later said, not a particularly calculated one. His brief at *The Times* had been to write about the minutiae of domestic life. He simply felt that it would have been dishonest if, in the week of his diagnosis, he had written about anything else.

It came at a curious time in British journalism, when every paper seemed to have a columnist writing about their disease or personal trauma. In the *Observer*, Ruth Picardie was recording the progress of the breast cancer that would eventually kill her, and some critics argued that there was now an almost ghoulish appetite among editors for dispatches from the very edges of mortality. John's answer was the sheer quality of his prose.

In recent years, he had begun to write an always witty column for the *Jewish Chronicle* and, after his diagnosis, had even joined a synagogue – though this, he told friends, was not because he had discovered God. He remained an atheist to the end but, he said, he wanted his children, Cosima and Bruno, to know something of the Judaism into which they had been born.

Until surgery on his tongue forced him to contribute to conversations through swiftly scribbled notes, John was regarded by many inside the worlds of journalism, politics and the arts in which he moved, as a fabulous wit and raconteur. It was no accident that the summer parties he threw with his second wife, the journalist and cookery writer Nigella Lawson, were attended, in turn, by the famous whom he so enjoyed collecting around him, and who, in return, so loved him.

In the summer of 1999, there was another John and Nigella party, this time thrown for them by the architect Lord Rogers, and his wife, Ruthie. It was, we were told, to mark ten years of their relationship, though, as John had only recently been informed that his condition was terminal, it was clear we were celebrating an extraordinary life as well as a marvellous marriage.

A crowd of more than 200 people, including a number of New Labour cabinet ministers and half the authors on the Waterstone's bestseller lists, stood in the great vault of Lord Rogers' minimalist home as John, now essentially mute, made an extraordinary speech of thanks to everybody for their support by writing on to an overhead projector beamed up on to the wall.

I saw him last just before Christmas. He had complained in print that friends who had been asked to write his obituaries were refusing to show them to him, as though they were some gift not to be opened until the big day. He had seen this one, written some time ago, but had made no comment at all. I asked him now what he thought of it, and he scribbled me a message on his pad. 'I just hope they're not paying you for it on publication,' he wrote, with delicious optimism. I was able to reassure him that they weren't.

We should, I suppose, be thankful that the gap between the commissioning of this article and its publication was so much longer than any of us had dared hope on the warm summer's night he gave his speech at Richard and Ruthie Rogers' house.

14 May 2001

RICHARD DAWKINS

Douglas Adams

This is not an obituary – there'll be time enough for them. It is not a tribute, not a considered assessment of a brilliant life, not a eulogy. It is a keening lament, written too soon to be balanced, too soon to be carefully thought through. Douglas, you cannot be dead.

A sunny Saturday morning in May, ten past seven, shuffle out of bed, log in to email as usual. The usual blue bold headings drop into place, mostly junk, some expected, and my gaze absently follows them down the page. The name Douglas Adams catches my eye and I smile. That one, at least, will be good for a laugh. Then I do the classic double take, back up the screen.

What did that heading actually say? Douglas Adams died of a heart attack a few hours ago. Then that other cliché: the words swelling before my eyes.

It must be part of the joke. It must be some other Douglas Adams. This is too ridiculous to be true. I must still be asleep. I open the message, from a well-known German software designer. It is no joke, I am fully awake. And it is the right – or rather the wrong – Douglas Adams. A sudden heart attack, in the gym in Santa Barbara. 'Man, man, man, man oh man,' the message concludes. Man indeed, what a man. A giant of a man, surely nearer seven foot than six, broad-shouldered, and he did not stoop like some very tall men who feel uncomfortable with their height. But nor did he swagger with the macho assertiveness that can be intimidating in a big man. He neither apologised for his height, nor flaunted it. It was part of the joke against himself.

One of the great wits of our age, his sophisticated humour was founded in a deep, amalgamated knowledge of literature and science, two of my great loves. And he introduced me to my wife – at his fortieth birthday party.

He was exactly her age; they had worked together on *Dr Who*. Should I tell her now, or let her sleep a bit longer before shattering her day? He initiated our togetherness and was a recurrently important part of it. I must tell her now.

Douglas and I met because I sent him an unsolicited fan letter – I think it is the only time I have ever written one. I had adored *The Hitchhiker's Guide to the Galaxy*. Then I read *Dirk Gently's Holistic Detective Agency*.

As soon as I finished it, I turned back to page one and read it straight through again – the only time I have ever done that, and I wrote to tell him so. He replied that he was a fan of my books, and he invited me to his house in London. I have seldom met a more congenial spirit. Obviously I knew he would be funny. What I didn't know was how deeply read he was in science. I should have guessed, for you can't understand many of the jokes in *Hitchhiker* if you don't know a lot of advanced science. And in modern electronic technology, he was a real expert. We talked science a lot, in private, and even in public at literary festivals and on the wireless or television. And he became my guru on all technical problems. Rather than struggle with some ill-written and incomprehensible manual in Pacific Rim English, I would fire off an email to Douglas.

He would reply, often within minutes, whether in London or Santa Barbara, or some hotel room anywhere in the world. Unlike most staff of professional helplines, Douglas understood exactly my problem, knew exactly why it was troubling me, and always had the solution ready, lucidly and amusingly explained. Our frequent email exchanges brimmed with literary and scientific jokes and affectionately sardonic little asides. His technophilia shone through, but so did his rich sense of the absurd. The whole world was one big *Monty Python* sketch, and the follies of humanity are as comic in the world's silicon valleys as anywhere else.

He laughed at himself with equal good humour. At, for example, his epic bouts of writer's block ('I love deadlines. I love the whooshing noise they make as they go by') when, according to legend, his publisher and book agent would lock him in a hotel room, with no telephone and nothing to do but write, releasing him only for supervised walks. If his enthusiasm ran away with him and he advanced a biological theory too eccentric for my professional scepticism to let pass, his mien at my dismissal of it would always be more humorously self-mocking than genuinely crestfallen. And he would have another go.

He laughed at his own jokes, which good comedians are supposed not to, but he did it with such charm that the jokes became even funnier. He was gently able to poke fun without wounding, and it would be aimed not at individuals but at their absurd ideas. To illustrate the vain conceit that the universe must be somehow preordained for us, because we are so well suited to live in it, he mimed a wonderfully funny imitation of a puddle of water, fitting itself snugly into a depression in the ground, the depression uncannily being exactly the same shape as the puddle. Or there's this parable, which he told with huge enjoyment, whose moral leaps out with no further explanation. A man didn't understand how televisions work, and was convinced that there must be lots of little men inside the box, manipulating images at high speed. An engineer explained about high-frequency modulations of the electromagnetic spectrum, transmitters and receivers, amplifiers and cathode ray tubes, scan lines moving across and down a phosphorescent screen. The man listened to the engineer with careful attention, nodding his head at every step of the argument. At the end he pronounced himself satisfied. He really did now understand how televisions work. 'But I expect there are just a few little men in there, aren't there?'

Science has lost a friend, literature has lost a luminary, the mountain gorilla and the black rhino have lost a gallant defender (he once climbed Kilimanjaro in a rhino suit to raise money to fight the cretinous trade in rhino horn), and Apple Computers has lost its most eloquent apologist. And I have lost an irreplaceable intellectual companion and one of the kindest and funniest men I ever met. The day Douglas died, I officially received a happy piece of news, which would have delighted him. I wasn't allowed to tell anyone during the weeks I have secretly known about it, and now that I am allowed to, it is too late.

The sun is shining, life must go on, seize the day and all those clichés.

We shall plant a tree this very day: a Douglas Fir, tall, upright, evergreen. It is the wrong time of year, but we'll give it our best shot.

Off to the arboretum.

4 August 2001

PETER STANFORD

Lord Longford

Though conducted simultaneously, the two crusades that made Frank Longford, who has died aged ninety-five, a household name in Britain were an odd combination. The first, launched in the early seventies, aimed to outlaw pornography and presented him as a prurient reactionary and a shameless hypocrite touring the sex clubs that he wanted to close down. The second, which continued for the last three decades of his life, attempted to win parole for the moors murderess, Myra Hindley. Here Longford was at his most liberal, Christian and naïve, building on a lifetime of interest in prison reform, to argue that Hindley, and indeed all offenders, could be rehabilitated if society was prepared to forgive.

Of the two, it was his lonely battle to help Hindley that revealed the true man. The pornography escapade was an aberration, embarked upon against the advice of old friends and under the influence of Mary Whitehouse and anti-libertarians. From the day his report came out, Longford rarely returned to the subject.

It was in the area of penal reform that he made his most lasting contribution. A Labour politician, who spent a record twenty-two years on the Lords frontbench, held junior office under Clement Attlee in the forties and later sat in Harold Wilson's cabinets, Longford could, when he resigned in 1968, have rested on his laurels. But he was not a conventional politician, and retirement gave him the freedom to take up the unpopular cause that was closest to his heart without fear of damaging his party.

It was not only his appearance – noble cranium and mad scientist's tonsure – that set Longford apart from his government colleagues. Though a committed Labour party member, and a regular attender of PLP meetings and annual conferences well into his nineties, he saw politics less as a career and more as part of a moral crusade. Conscience came before party loyalty, heart before the head.

Such a stance belonged more to the nineteenth-century philanthropic tradition than to twentieth-century Westminster. And, in many senses, Longford was a nineteenth-century figure, struggling, often with humour, to deal with the problem of being born too late. Like William Wilberforce and Lord Shaftesbury, his was a privileged upbringing. Like them, he was a devout Christian determined to translate faith into action. Like them, he was an unpredictable combination of political savvy and childlike clear-sightedness.

The essential difference between the three was that while Wilberforce reformed the slave trade and Shaftesbury the factories, Longford only aspired to alter the penal system. His failure could not be put down only to the changed climate of the twentieth century. His own character played a part. Never one to manage a concerted campaign, to push and cajole friends to a cause that many cabinet colleagues regarded indulgently as 'Frank's hobby', he was too much the individualist, too fond of argument for argument's sake – an effect of his thirties time as an Oxford politics don – and, ultimately, too lightweight in Whitehall to carry the day.

With his knack for making people laugh, and his tireless enjoyment of social-ising as well as socialism, it was too easy to ignore the fact that Longford was way ahead of his time in questioning the direction of prison policy. Though his prophecy of the failure of the punishment-oriented system of mainly Conservative postwar governments was repeatedly borne out, he never managed to translate his vision into workable reform.

That is not to say he was without substantial achievements: it was just that the goals he set himself remained outside his grasp. He dreamed of being a reforming home secretary, an ambition that prompted his old friend Evelyn Waugh to remark: 'and then we would all be murdered in our beds'.

A prison visitor since the thirties, Longford was still going, two and three times a week, to visit the abandoned and despised in jail until close to the end of his life. Though the tabloids portrayed him as a man who got a kick out of contact with infamous killers – a throwback to the 'Lord Porn' caricature – such 'names' made up only one per cent of those Longford journeyed to see.

An example: in the late eighties, he was contacted by the solicitor for a young Dutchman, convicted of a drugs offence, sent to Albany prison on the Isle of Wight, suffering from Aids and cut off by his family. Longford was the only per-son to visit this dying man, a gesture repeated in countless episodes that never made headlines but which brought succour and relief.

He also initiated practical measures to ease offenders' reintegration into soci-ety. He founded the New Bridge in 1955, the first organisation dedicated to ex-prisoners' welfare. In 1970, he established, in New Horizon, the first drop-in centre for homeless teenagers. Until the end, he spent time at New Horizon's offices, oblivious to its users' sometimes rough teasing, anxious to understand what had alienated them from the mainstream.

He also contributed a series of learned reports on penal reform during Labour's period out of office between Attlee and Wilson. He chaired the com-mittee that, in 1963, recommended the setting-up of the parole system, still the bedrock of the current system.

Attlee admired Longford's passion for society's outcasts and tried, often against his colleagues' advice, to harness it. In the 1945 Labour landslide, Longford – then Frank Pakenham – stood for Oxford, but was defeated by Quentin Hogg, later Lord Hailsham. Attlee was persuaded to elevate him to the peerage, and bring to Labour's sparsely populated Lords benches a youthful thinker who had been Sir William Beveridge's right-hand man on his landmark welfare state report.

Longford was tempted to decline the offer and await a suitable by-election, but feared that, since his childless elder brother was in poor health, it was inevitable that he would soon become the Earl of Longford. But acceptance effectively relegated him to the role of also-ran in Labour politics. Without a Commons seat, he remained an enigma to his colleagues, outside the main-stream and, for some, a figure not to be trusted.

Initially, however, he won rapid promotion. In 1947, Attlee made him, as Chancellor of the Duchy of Lancaster, responsible for the British zone of occupied Germany. It was Longford's finest hour as a minister. For a year, he worked tirelessly to stop the Germans starving to death. He reopened schools and hospitals, and worked with American and French counterparts on the currency reform that would bring stability to West Germany.

He fought the foreign secretary, Ernest Bevin, for a reappraisal of the industrial dismantling of the occupied zone under the reparations policy, but Bevin refused. On the ground, Longford saw – sooner than his superior – that cooperation with the Soviets was impossible, and that partition was inevitable. Konrad Adenauer, the father of West Germany, came to regard him as his people's one true friend in London.

This tribute was prompted perhaps by Longford's optimistic avowal to the Germans that the British had forgiven them the wartime excesses. His remarks caused a storm of outrage in a country still suffering rationing. Attlee was persuaded to move him to the Ministry of Civil Aviation, where he proved a successful minister, save for the mishandling of the report from a crash enquiry that almost cost him his job. Attlee stuck by him, and later raised him to First Lord of the Admiralty, just outside the cabinet.

In opposition after 1951, Hugh Gaitskell, who had shared rooms with Longford at Oxford and referred to him as his 'oldest friend', kept him at the centre of Labour affairs, even when he became chairman of a City clearing bank. The appointment caused some raised eyebrows in the square mile, where Longford was blackballed from at least one financiers' club.

After Gaitskell's death in 1963, however, Harold Wilson had no time for such an unpredictable figure. Though included in the 1964 cabinet as leader of the Lords, Longford knew he was only there as a sop to the Gaitskellites. Wilson treated him with personal kindness but professional contempt, remarking that Longford – who had got a double first at Oxford – had a mental age of twelve.

By his own admission he was 'ineffective' in the treacherous atmosphere of Wilson's cabinets. Even as colonial secretary in 1966, he was so dispirited that he failed to master his brief and was quickly removed.

He had talked with Gaitskell in the early sixties of taking up Tony Benn's Disclaimer Act and renouncing his peerages – both the inherited title, which finally came his way in 1961, and the barony awarded by Attlee. Then he would be free to seek a Commons seat at the 1964 general election and, if successful, a cabinet post as head of a major department. Gaitskell had given qualified support. Wilson, however, pooh-poohed the idea. It was a deeply frustrating period. In terms of prestige, Longford had reached the pinnacle of his career but, in practice, he was impotent, and often resorted to playing up to his image as the cabinet jester.

Wilson talked often of sacking Longford, so when he resigned from government in January 1968 over the abandonment of a commitment to raising the school-leaving age, it was a matter of jumping before being pushed. If Benn, Richard Crossman and Barbara Castle all recorded their relief at his departure in their diaries, the Queen continued to hold him in high esteem. In 1972, she made him a knight of the garter.

After 1968, Longford devoted himself to his campaigns and to publishing. He had already produced several volumes of autobiography and one book – *Peace*

By Ordeal, on the background to the 1921 Anglo–Irish treaty – that was regarded as a classic. But his later efforts, while tackling ambitious subjects like humility and forgiveness, were politely, though unenthusiastically, received.

From the floor of the House of Lords, as well as continually pushing the government on prisons policy, he spoke often on Ireland, a country he regarded as his home. It was a claim – dubious since he spent the vast majority of his life on this side of the Irish Sea – that occasionally got him into trouble. While still in Wilson's cabinet, he attended the fiftieth anniversary celebrations of the Easter Rising, and was photographed next to his old friend, President de Valera.

Though he remained sentimentally attached to Ireland, Longford broke every tradition of his Anglo-Irish ascendancy family. He was born into a military, Protestant, Conservative and Unionist clan, and educated at Eton and New College, Oxford. As an adult, he embraced the Roman Catholic church and Irish nationalism. His failure to follow his soldier father, who was killed at Gallipoli when Longford was nine, remained an open wound.

In 1940, he was invalided out of the forces after a nervous breakdown. He regarded the episode as the ultimate humiliation, but came to believe that it gave him some insight into the degradation of those sent to prison and shunned by society.

In Elizabeth Harman, whom he married in 1931, Longford found the emotional warmth and love denied him as a child by a difficult, and often cruel, mother. Made painfully aware of his insignificance in her eyes next to his elder brother, he only recovered a sense of self-esteem while at Oxford. At a summer ball, he was asleep on a couch when spotted by Elizabeth, one of the most beautiful and sought- after undergraduates of her generation.

'The face was monumental beauty,' she later wrote, 'as if some Graeco-Roman statue...had been dressed in modern clothes.' Two years later, when they were both lecturing for the Workers Educational Association in Stoke, at the height of the thirties depression, love blossomed.

It was Elizabeth, a great-niece of Joseph Chamberlain, who convinced Longford to join the Labour party. In return, having been converted to Catholicism while at Oxford by the Jesuit Father Martin D'Arcy, he persuaded her to join him in the Church of Rome. He found great strength in the moral certainties of Catholicism.

The Longfords enjoyed an extraordinarily happy marriage, touched by tragedy with the death, in 1969, of their daughter Catherine in a car crash. They remained active in their various political, literary and campaigning activities well into their nineties, relaxing only to enjoy their countless grandchildren and great-grandchildren at their cherished Sussex home, Bernhurst. Longford gave the family seat, Tullynally Castle in Co. Westmeath, to his son and heir in 1961 upon inheriting it.

With friends and family, his razor-sharp wit could flourish, while in public he felt he had to restrain it in the interests of being a better Christian. All the best stories about his eccentricity – and there were many – were first told, and no doubt embellished, by Longford himself.

Myra Hindley became part of his extended family – the large group of writers, politicians and activists who satisfied his continuing need to be in touch with what was going on in the world. Such consultations would usually take place over lunch at the House of Lords. His conviction that Hindley would one day be his guest there went unfulfilled.

She was, in many ways, an unworthy recipient of his concern. He ransomed his good name for her, but, once convinced he was no longer the key to her release, she moved on to other advisers. He saw what was happening, but saw it as natural and inevitable, and continued to strive for her freedom.

Longford's memory will live on, if not for the scale of his achievements, then certainly because of his courage, tenacity and nobility in trying. He was a man of great intelligence and moral strength. He is survived by his wife, four sons and three daughters.